T0354778

THE GAME OF
Love / Life

THE GAME OF
Love / Life

ILLUMINATING YOUR OWN UNIVERSE

RONALD RAYMOND ROCHA

THE GAME OF LOVE/LIFE
ILLUMINATING YOUR OWN UNIVERSE

Copyright © 2018 Ronald Raymond Rocha.

All rights reserved. No part of this book may be used or reproduced by any means, graphic, electronic, or mechanical, including photocopying, recording, taping or by any information storage retrieval system without the written permission of the author except in the case of brief quotations embodied in critical articles and reviews.

iUniverse books may be ordered through booksellers or by contacting:

iUniverse
1663 Liberty Drive
Bloomington, IN 47403
www.iuniverse.com
1-800-Authors (1-800-288-4677)

Because of the dynamic nature of the Internet, any web addresses or links contained in this book may have changed since publication and may no longer be valid. The views expressed in this work are solely those of the author and do not necessarily reflect the views of the publisher, and the publisher hereby disclaims any responsibility for them.

Any people depicted in stock imagery provided by Thinkstock are models, and such images are being used for illustrative purposes only. Certain stock imagery © Thinkstock.

ISBN: 978-1-5320-4098-6 (sc)
ISBN: 978-1-5320-4099-3 (e)

Print information available on the last page.

iUniverse rev. date: 01/22/2018

To you angels experiencing the human condition
Revealing trials and tribulation defining your position
Unilaterally developing through personal thoughts
Tempering your curious mind exploring your *heart*
Holding everything angels really treasure—LOVE.

1-2-3

I
AM
intuitive
abstract Mind,
the Omniscient Natural Entity
of TWO forces
transmitting/transforming wisdom optically
for you children—
Traversing Holographic Realism
Electromagnetically Expressed—
reflecting upon my thoughts illuminating your *mind*
momentarily interpreting natural dynamics
revealing Angelic Luminaries Living as ONE.

URRUSSO
(Unitary revealer rectifying universal
souls seeking omniscience)

CONTENTS

ACKNOWLEDGMENTS

I am truly grateful for my cosmic SOURCE of inspiration—Spirit offering universal revelations conveyed electromagnetically—supplying common sense as *thoughts* and *emotions*. This binary code is the force stimulating every mind/heart soul to conceive and create divine fantasies, passions that define an expression of love we live, allowing us to be all that we ARE—angels receiving/revealing enlightenment.

PREFACE

In today's world, *data* (divine abstract thoughts analyzed) is sent via electrical and optical systems defining the World Wide *Web* of Wisdom electromagnetically broadcast. The transfer of data (*Language*) from *Spirit to Soul* (Mind to mind) is "compressed" as ACRONYMS, attuning conscious recipients optimizing notions yielding momentous *situations*, specific instances that unveil assigned trials/tribulation inducing one's *needs* necessitating experiences enlightening *deities*—divine entities implementing thoughts initiating emotional synergy revealing *Truth*.

The Game of Love/Life Illuminating Your Own Universe is a divine inspiration, a spiritual/scientific primer relating spiritual concepts of you being an *Angel* scientifically exploring in a *Human Alien* vehicle. It reveals the metaphysics (higher knowledge) of the atomic illusion—*Mother's Nature*—that interfaces **Mental Energy** and concrete revelation illuminating your mind/heart soul traversing *Heaven* and transcending *Hell*. It is written in a dualistic way to allow *You and I* to conceive our unity, for WE (*Wisdom* exemplified) evolve and experience this world together. Even though you live in your own world of thoughts and feelings you act out, WE are truly inseparable. You are the center of your awareness, observing *My World* spin around you as *you* spin your own world from *within* you. Every story you hear told influences Your Own Universe **positively** or **negatively**, for that is the duality naturally attracting and repelling US universal spirits. Only when you know that you and I are the same can we live in *Harmony*.

From the moment you are born, *The Game of Love/Life* unfolds the mysteries of cosmic energy—Generating Opulent Data—supplying all that you sense. You spend your early childhood learning to control your physical vehicle, your "rover" in which you explore, gathering knowledge (data) that allows you to play out your *Divine Fantasies* illuminating your mind/heart soul as a trinity-being. As you grow older and learn the rules of the game, you question its *Relativity*, wondering *who* you are, *why* you are here, *what* you should do with your allotted time, *where* did you come from, *when* will you leave this world, and *how* do you survive in the meantime?

You continually search for truths, and *Truth* is found in the details of life. As an inquisitive soul/mind, you analyze your data received from Spirit/Mind, the Electro-Magnetic force field revealing Eternal Memories stimulating the COSMOS, the consciousness of Spirit mentally/materially originating souls, stars, and systems.

To understand the truth about YOU, you need to comprehend the *Language* of Mind (Spirit) illuminating minds (souls) conceiving *love*, *light*, and *life*. It takes many languages defining scientific disciplines to understand the relativity of this holy trinity. Every *Science* is a systematic body of knowledge with its own language that illuminates curious minds adding "new words" to describe new ideas relative to the times. Here, within this contemporary lexicon of spiritual/scientific data, you will notice capitalized KEYWORDS followed by their "deeper" meaning, such as LOVE (logic oscillating visionary entities) or Linking Inspiration Forming Experiences (life).

Capitalized words should be read **both** ways to attain a greater understanding of your dualistic nature as a mind/heart or soul/human. *Capitalized Italics* relate to other titles within the book that reveal universal *Harmony*.

Italicized words (generally used for emphasis) also act as *keywords* (knowledge expanding your wisdom of radiant data/deities) that provide a more vivid expression of *new* perspectives using *old* WORDS (*Wisdom* offering revelation defined symbolically). The complexity of the subject matter requires a focused mind willing to delve into the depths of their *soul* (spirit observing universal logic) to discover their relationship to SPIRIT scientifically providing ideas/illusions radiantly illuminated three-dimensionally.

This collection of essays and poems evolved from "downloaded" messages, "voices in the sky" that spoke to my *mind* mired in natural delusions. This natural *Process* is utilized by every soul that THINKS—transfers heavenly intelligence nurturing kindred souls. *Thought Energy* stimulates all minds *Awakening* to universal *Truth* inducing the "atomic illusion" that we scientifically evaluate as *reality*, a radiant energy/emotion amplifying logical intelligence transforming youths—angelic souls evolving as *Time Travelers*.

As *Inquisitive Souls*, we have a thirst for knowledge or *Truth*. I have discovered that the more knowledge I attain the more I realize how ignorant I am. It is our *Curiosity* that motivates each of us as individual personalities to connect data from inspirations, books, and life experiences. We all seek our own truth, which is discovered through "introspection," self-examination of our thoughts, feelings, and actions—*Our Trinity*—that defines us individually. I pray this discourse will inspire you to discover your truths defining Your Own Universe.

I came to create this *Language* as a way of transferring

knowledge from *Spirit* (Source of consciousness) *to Soul* (experiencing consciousness). To date, I have created a ninety-plus page glossary (not included) of over 1100 keywords with a multiplicity of definitions. I have continually inserted the meaning of keywords for better comprehension and to prevent any inconvenience of looking up definitions. However, a good dictionary is invaluable for *Truth Seekers* exploring the WEB of *Wisdom* emotionally broadcast.

The purpose of this book is to reveal the **spiritual** and **scientific** aspects of our soul experiencing our divinity as a powerful mind, a "chip" of *The GREAT Computer* (Mind) *Generating Our Desires*. This spiritual/scientific treatise will relate contemporary terms eternally OLD that orient luminous deities observing Love's dimensions of *Common Sense*, a database that supplies everyone all they *Desire* to know from SPIRIT, the Source perfecting illuminati receiving intelligence transcendentally.

Within these pages, you will explore how your mind is similar to a computer, a mechanical mind that receives, stores, and transfers symbols (numbers, words, and images). These symbols (data) are abstracts that represent some "thing" stored *In Memory* of your mind/computer, information that describes a way to transform abstract knowledge (energy) into concrete "reflections" (realism) through *Science*—spiritual concepts inspiring entities naturally converting energy. If we look closer at the similarities of our mind and *The GREAT Computer*—SPIRIT—scientifically projecting "illusory realism" illuminated three-dimensionally, we will begin to understand the "techno-lingo" hidden within the symbols we see but do not fully understand. For example, DOS stands for Divine Omniscient Spirit, which is truly our *data operating system*. In order to know *Truth*, we need to open our mind to thoughts that will raise our consciousness UP to a universal perspective. Our life depends on our state of mind we create and express, which can be a *Heaven* or *Hell*. It all depends on how we use and abuse our *Divine Inspiration*, our *Love/Life Energy*.

Generating Opulent Data is synonymous with ENERGY—essential nature expressing revelation geometrically yielded. We cannot create nor destroy energy. We can only "transmute" energy, change its form, nature, or substance. Energy is either stored or transmitted, at rest or in motion (E-motion). Stored energy is MEMORY, from which Mind expresses moments of revelation *yielding* EMOTION, the "elemental movement" of thoughts illuminating opulent nature geometrically. *Emotional Energy* is the motivational process of transforming abstract thought into a concrete reality. Only by "feeling" a thought do we know it is *real*—revelation emotionally activating logicians (*Truth Seekers*). It was my wife's *Emotional Energy* that moved me to ask my questions. Observing her emotional anguish inspired many of these writings. She stimulated me to see *Emotional Energy* as the "key" to opening *My Door to Truth*.

Our mind is a facsimile of Mind, an "electromagnetic transceiver" utilizing frequencies carrying *data* (divine abstract thoughts amplified) flowing through the cosmos of the Universe. For sixty-plus years of seeking *Truth*, I have navigated through the chaos of data hindering me from *Understanding Illusion*—this third-dimensional state of Mind we call "reality." Analyzing *dogma* (data obstructing gifted minds *Awakening*), I finally opened *My Door to Truth* within my *heart* harmoniously evolving all radiant thoughts. The answers to all those questions I asked in the *Process* are here within these pages. **They have changed my life forever**. Those answers relate to Universal *Seekers* (spiritual entities exploring knowledge expressed radiantly), for we are in this life *To-Get-Her* (Mother Nature) to reveal the secret of all we ARE, *Angels* receiving enlightenment and reflecting emotions. I hope you find the "wordplay" entertaining and helpful in opening *your* heart's door.

This book relates how "science fiction" is really "spiritual facts." *Truth*, though clearly evident all around us, is difficult to discern within the *illusion* of instinctive light logically unfolding situations illustrating opulent nature "reflecting" many aspects of *Truth*. Through *meditation* (mentally evaluating data inspiring transient *Avatars* temporarily interpreting one's nature/needs), I have discovered greater depths of *Truth* as my mind became enlightened to the *reflection* replicating electromagnetic frequencies luminously evolving consciousness through illusions one navigates.

I have arranged these *ideas* (inspired data emotionally aligned) to provide a foundation from which to grow an understanding of the complexity of words (verbal or written) that are the major means of transferring abstract energy between minds. Therefore, I suggest **first** reading this book from beginning to end as each chapter builds on the previous. The depth and intricacies of which will draw you back to discover new truths as you attain your *Awakening*.

Only by opening your mind can you truly nourish your heart and soul, growing into the *Light of Love* to harmonize with *The GREAT Computer* (Spirit) allowing you to be ONE omniscient natural entity (soul) accessing all that is stored *In Memory* vibrating "online," along the Electro-Magnetic wavelengths of *Eternal Memory* revealing *Heaven* and *Hell*.

In my quest for the answers to those questions we all ask, I have discovered "esoteric" knowledge, those truths found only by persistent research and inquiry, truths that go beyond the dogma holding us within the illusion of *Mother's Nature*. Everyone carries their truth within their "eternal file" of memory (subconscious mind) that we methodically peruse in search of our *self*, our soul experiencing love/life fantasies.

You will notice a repetitive pattern in this work to reveal dormant truths so difficult to see even though strategically placed in plain sight, for we take them for granted with little appreciation. We did not learn our *alphabet* or *Numbers*—key elements of knowledge—overnight, it took years of practice. Attaining KNOWLEDGE (kinetic notions/numbers oscillating willful luminaries/logicians emotionally developing genuine experiences) is our critical mission in life. Without knowledge, we would be *Lost in Space*—experiencing *Ignorance*.

The intricate details of the words woven into the fabric of this story hold a "latent image" of *Truth* for YOU to develop (see) your own universe within which you *live*, logically interpreting vivid energy. I cannot tell you your truth; you must discover that *Alone*. I found myself delving into the dictionary (the bible of bibles) to understand the "depth" of words. These interconnected *links* logically intertwining natural knowledge grew together to reveal *The Grand View* of my self-awareness—my *Awakening*.

Like a chick pecking its way free of its shell, these words will repeatedly tap on your conscious mind, wearing the shield of your *Ignorance* and *Denial* thin, allowing you to gradually become "acclimatized" to *My Loving Light* illuminating your soul. Eventually, through an open mind and hungry heart, the shell encasing you in your hazy illusion will crack, allowing you your first *Epiphany of Truth*.

The journey you are about to undertake goes beyond your usual earthly perspectives. You will need a FOCUSED MIND to fathom opulent concepts unveiling secrets enlightening deities managing illusion naturally defined, through which you may perceive the simplicity of the complexities of the subject matter. This basic guidebook is relatively simple to follow, as easy as 1–2–3, for it hinges on *The Trinity*, the three things that provide our reality. With diligence and close inspection (reading between the lines), you may observe some "truth" you are seeking. **Truly, there are no truths within this book**. I am talking *about* Truth that surrounds and permeates ALL. You can only find *Truth* within your individual *self*, a symbiotic entity linking frequencies emanating from cosmic Source-Energy Love/Life Force, but only when you become an *Inquisitive Soul*.

The Inquisitive Soul

The inquisitive soul has a hungry heart
yearning to know their gifted part
they play within my SHOW
spiritually harmonizing omniscient *Wisdom* I set aglow.

The urge to rise above their world
stirs their mind with thoughts that swirl
around possibilities that could be...

drawing them to *A Higher Vision*
to Spiritually Experience Emotionally
electro-magnetic SOURCE
scientifically outputting universal radiance conveying energy
enlightening *TWO as ONE*
transforming *Wisdom* "optically" oscillating natural entities
developing the scenes they see as DREAMS
delivering revelations expressing abstract memories
moving their *Mind/Heart* in co-motion—
converting thoughts into feelings defining their devotion—
as they travel Observing Universal
Truth "within" *Space* and *Time*,
eager to feel their heart GROW their mind,
gathering revelations of *Wisdom*—Opulent Love Divine—
illuminating their inquisitive soul.

Bless you and bon voyage

INTRODUCTION

Incarnated as a *Human Alien*, you and I are the same, no matter where we live or language we speak. We are born "outside" within a strange world, an atomic illusion where we live "inside" our own mind/heart, analyzing thoughts and feelings that define who we think and feel we are within our own divine fantasy. Our first brave steps out into the unknown darkness of fear and *Ignorance* are truly some of the hardest steps our soul can take along our cosmic journeys. Here, we search the depths of our mind to comprehend our *being* beamed entities (illuminati) naturally gifted as *Children Of Light*, existing within the electromagnetic chaos stimulating our world in which we *live*, logically interpreting vivid energy (vibrant emotions). Once we muster the *Courage of Love* to step forward, there is no turning back. As we repeat our first brave steps, we gain confidence to explore our own world from truths we "re-member" (put back together) from *Eternal Memory*, creating a life from *Passions* unfolding from within us that provide a life we can feel is real.

Here on Earth, we start our life like sheep. Led in flocks, we are fed with basic knowledge to adapt to social customs defining the status quo. Trained as habitual "consumers of energy," we absorb all we hear on the daily news and commercials informing us with truths "twisted" to SELL (stimulate emotions linking logic). After all, if it does not sell, it is not worth broadcasting.

Our education prepares us for our character roles we choose to play in *The Game of Love/Life*. Following the doctrines that allow us to fit in with the crowd, we are confined in controllable groups as obedient citizens fearful of being freethinkers. Any departure from the norm will quickly draw attention, ridicule, and judgment for being different. Public education does not teach us about our innate abilities as an independent, powerful mind focusing *thoughts* into explosive *emotions*—the two things that define the type of games we play. To gather that knowledge, you must depend on your self (self-help) and that is the purpose of this book.

It is truly difficult to grasp the immensity of the tasks we find our self involved in as we struggle to comprehend reason from our *Passion*, that thing we love to do that moves our soul to *act*, to apply conceived thoughts in emotional scenes that define our life. We simply rise each morning to that whispered voice coaxing us out of bed, moving us to give birth to some *Desire* bursting from within us, something propelling us along *The Right Path* unfolding with each *heartbeat* and *breath*—the two things defining life and *Death*.

Love IS the ESSENCE enlightening souls "systematically evaluating" notions conceived emotionally. We are always *In Love* no matter where we travel or what we experience. Love is the backbone of our songs and stories we relate to each other. Through life, we express our *reflection* of our love, our *Desire*. Of course, experiencing life for our self is paramount, for the truth of Life Optimizing Visionary Entities is something you cannot tell a child, it is something they have to experience to believe. *The Power of Love* is so blinding, it takes years for us to truly open our eyes to IT (intuitive Truth). *Lost in the Dark* of our *Ignorance*, we struggle to overcome our *Denial* of our "stellar heritage" as *points* of Light positively outputting intelligence naturally transmitted, allowing us to create our IMAGE of our self, an intuitive mind acquiring growth experiences. We reflect upon our thoughts stimulating our heart emotionally, revealing our actions that define us as a UNIVERSE, a unitary navigator interpreting/implementing visions evolving realism existentially.

The ONE omnipotent numerical engineer—*The GREAT Computer*—holds infinite points of *light* linearly inducing glorious *holograms* transcendentally, harmoniously organizing logic originating "geometric renditions" actualizing memories/matter. **Light energy** illuminates our mind/soul as we explore *Space* systematically processing *Angels* conceiving enlightenment through LIFE, where Love is fluid energy in motion—*emotion*. This omnipotent source of consciousness propels us forward into our *future*, formulating universal travelers unfolding revelations experientially in realities we choose as "entertainment" from *Eternal Memory*. With an open mind and willing heart, we can discover all that we *Desire* to do and know.

This treatise offered here is my attempt at spreading *THE WORD* transforming heavenly entities willingly observing radiant data/dimensions of *Truth*. Of course, it is impossible to comprehend *THE WORD* in its entirety, for it is something that is continually expanding at the "speed of thought" (instantaneously). We are only capable of glimpsing the shadow of its passage as it reflects upon our mind as a mere "bit" of a "byte" along the neural network of *The GREAT Computer* MIND managing intelligence numerically defined. It is our goal in life to be aware of who we are, where we come from, and why we are here. This basic knowledge will allow us to cooperate with all that IS, WAS, and everything we WILL to be, as we grow in knowledge to the fact we truly ARE angels "relating" enlightenment.

WE (wisdom exemplified) are instrumental in creating our own life. We *Alone* have the power to make or break our dreams. However, we are only capable of viewing our own **P**sychic **C**onsciousness—our stellar soul—that is a critical part of our creator's cosmic illumination. We can only bask in our own light, our own spark of *Love/Life Energy* flowing through us, for we truly live within our own universe of thoughts and feelings that define our unique personality revealed through our *actions*—the way we "apply" cosmic thoughts inducing our nature/needs.

The secret to enlightenment is to give up (contribute) our *Free Will* to *Divine Will*, to see our critical *part* (personifying angels reflecting truths) relative to the WHOLE of *Wisdom* harmoniously optimizing luminous/logical entities.

Once again, the purpose of this book is to guide you along perspectives for you to SEE (spiritually evolve emotionally) beyond the confines of the physical world and observe *The Grand View* of all that you ARE as *Avatars* radiantly evolving. The maze of words defining these perspectives may seem to add to the haze of your confusion. However, "new roads" need frequent travels to acquire familiar landmarks. By tapping into your *Courage of Love*, you will manifest your *Courage of Fear*, the duality projecting you through the dark void of *Ignorance* to circumnavigate *Time* with *Clear Vision*, through which you will see the Light of *Truth* inducing *A Higher Vision* emanating from *Spirit to Soul*. With open mind and willing heart, step forward to reap your *Blessings in Disguise* as you traverse *Heaven* and transcend *Hell*.

Bless you and Godspeed

1

GENERATING OUR DESIRES
Thinking As Loving Kindred Souls

G od talks to every one of us *souls*—spirits of universal logic—
exploring *Desires*. God talks to us through our thoughts,
those abstract bursts of energy that entertain our *mind*, our
"image" of our creator—*The Intellectual*. Our mind comprehends
thoughts in a three-dimensional world of miraculous wonders.

Thought Energy is the genesis of all *Desire*, for without
thought nothing would exist! Everything that we call "real" is
simply a matter of our *Free Will* accepting those thoughts from
Divine Will that we "think true." *Thought Energy*—Manifesting
Illuminated Nature Dimensionally—stimulates all things in the
universe, right down to the smallest atomic particle. It has the
ability to "magnetically attract" those atoms into an *illusion*, an
impressive likeness linking ubiquitous signals (electromagnetic
waves) illuminating opulent notions/natures, inspiring our *mind*
managing *impulses* naturally detected as "inspired memories"
providing universal logic stimulating emotion.

Generating Our Desires is experienced through the *Process*
of our mind computing *data* (divine abstract thoughts assigned)

1

defining *points* extended into *lines* and *shapes* (*Geometry*) that form THINGS—transmitted holograms illustrating notions geometrically symbolized. These calculations occur at the "speed of thought," allowing our mind to instantaneously envision an *idea* (inspired data electromagnetically activated) that we transform into a *reality*, replicating enlightening abstracts logically inspiring transient youths (*Time Travelers*). Our *Beliefs* hinge upon our accepted truths we entertain within the cosmos of MIND—*The GREAT Computer*—manifesting intelligence numerically defined. *Numbers* nurture universal minds bravely experiencing revelation symbolically/sympathetically. Through an "open mind," we entertain thoughts revealing possibilities of what could be, discovery other dimensions, other *states* of Mind supplying thoughts advancing transient entities.

Our mind is continuously moving from thought to thought, calculating every moment of our life, both day and night. Our mind is "energy in motion" or EMOTION, an eternal mind optimizing thoughts inducing one's *needs* as necessary experiences enlightening deities. Our mind observes VISIONS vividly illuminating scenes imaging opulent natures, revealing *Divine Fantasies* we entertain as YOUTHS yearning omnifarious understanding through *Harmony* heralding all revelational memories/moments orienting "navigable" youths. Our thoughts and emotions define all that we ARE as *Angels* relating emotions, experiences, and enlightenment.

Thinking is the "power tool" of Generating Our Desires, a tool that has the ability to create and destroy. ALL thoughts are retained in the Akashic Record, *Eternal Memory's* Electro-Magnetic power grid of Elusive Mind. We simply "abstract" thoughts from the electromagnetic database (*The Binary Code*) storing knowledge of *Truth* (transcendental revelation unveiled through holograms) that is our *Divine Inspiration*.

As we open our mind and "log onto" *The GREAT Computer*, we download our *Desires* stimulating us as *humans* harnessing universal memories acquired naturally, evolving within our own WORLD of thoughts, where *Wisdom* optimizes radiant luminaries dynamically. WE (wisdom exemplified) are minds manipulating energy, collecting bits and bytes of data to conceive our *life* lucidly illustrating fantasies existentially. All we can do is to stare in wonder at those things we do not understand and with our *Curiosity* ask questions. If we keep our eyes and ears open and master *The Art of Listening*, our thoughts **will evolve into answers** to those questions we ask, revealing our "inner wisdom" or INTUITION inciting navigators transcendentally unified in temporary illusions of nature.

The time has come to raise our consciousness to *A Higher Vision*, observing how TECHNOLOGY transforms electric concepts (heavenly notions) offering luminaries opulent gnosis yearned (knowledge desired), allowing us to view physically our spirituality. With the advent of technological advancements, we can now reach out and touch our fellow travelers around the world, sharing our collective data as "unified minds" representing ONE omnipotent natural entity illuminating inquisitive souls *Lost in the Dark*, guiding them *Hand in Hand* through the door to *Truth*.

MY DOOR TO TRUTH

My door to Truth is open wide to you
inquisitive souls out to ride
emotional waves of pain and pleasure,
seeking my hidden treasure
held within my HEART

harmoniously evolving *Angels* reviewing thoughts
enlightening minds exploring *Desire*
emanating from cosmic fires
illuminating your DAZE I set aglow,
deceiving angelic zealots evolving to know
Truth unfolds through *Time*
tempering intuitive minds experientially
at *This Moment* now here,
in which you struggle to overcome fear,
opening my door to Truth as you grow OLD,
observing Love's dimensions.

Here, within my void of space,
spin wheels of light through which you trace
Your Life Story you relate today, spreading
gossip along your way,
as you **A**cquire **G**rowth **E**xperiences
Ordaining **L**ogical **D**eities,
testing your skills I give to you as I hold you in suspension,
separated from *Home*,
where you explore your *Desires* under a blue dome,
playing *The Game of Love/Life* enlightening my youths
eager to open my door to *Truth*.

DESIRE

Desire makes UniverseS revolve and evolve. DESIRE delivers electric/emotional sensations/situations inducing realism/ revelation experientially. "Desire" means to "long for, wish, or crave for something" to entertain our mind, to fill our void of space

4

(our mind's blank screen) with some thought inducing a *vision* vividly inspiring souls inspecting/interpreting opulent notions/ nature that stimulate feelings we act out in *Divine Fantasies*.

Desire drives every soul inspecting radiant energy illuminating *realism*—revelation electromagnetically activating luminous illusion systematically manifested. We convert desire into endless varieties of our own creation through words and actions (*Work*), willingly optimizing radiant knowledge.

Desire incites a *Process*, a procedure reflecting opulent concepts exciting sympathetic souls experiencing and expressing common feelings—*Common Sense*. Everyone desires love, happiness, security, and freedom to attain the treasures of life. Without desire we feel empty, void of any motivation or driving force activating our mind/heart soul.

Desire is an expression of our insatiable appetite to know *love* logically oscillates vibrant emotions as feelings we interpret from our thoughts. As *Children Of Light* experiencing the "desires of the flesh," we first learn to communicate through words, putting them together to make a sentence to describe our desire in more detail. Correlating thoughts to words to objects allows us to express our self dimensionally, to move through *Divine Fantasies* we envision in our mind and physically create.

Desire fills us with a radiance that glows within us, allowing us to express our *Love/Life Energy* (thoughts and feelings) outwardly, touching other souls through *Relationships* we create as our "life story." Our desires appear as a *Clear Vision* that stimulates our mind to "create," to transform our thoughts into feelings that we express through words and actions to make others see our "point of view" (as I am doing here). By expressing our desires, we become aware of our motion, our ability to move through the space-time continuum to Sense Energy Emotionalize everything around us glowing in the *Light of Love*.

Here incarnate, we entertain personal visions stimulating our *Curiosity*, our desire to know. Reaching out to each other, we cry in anguish for someone to see us, touch us, and hold us close in the warmth of Love illuminating our soul. As we embrace each other in our attraction of Love, we grow brighter and warmer, realizing that in *Numbers* there is security, reaching out ever more to touch as many souls as we can, sharing our Data Electrically Sent In Radiant Emotions.

CLEAR VISION-CLIMBERS

Clear vision is a dream, an inspiration to take you to great heights to view something you hold within your mind to show your heart, a desire that moves you into action to express *Love/Life Energy* coursing through your veins. If you do not *feel* that vision, fear can easily shield your eyes, keeping you anchored to a small stance upon your progress. If your mind and heart are in harmony, a clear path through adversity is obvious. Your clear vision will reflect great courage and determination, keeping you in balance with your **inner power**—that *Radiance of Love* that allows you to believe in your vision. Having *Faith* in your self (formulating assurance inspired through harmony of courage and fear) allows you to rise above your challenges you undertake in *The Game of Love/Life*, discovering *Divine Will* guiding you UP to SEE the universal progenitor systematically enlightening entities.

DIVINE WILL

DIVINE WILL is dynamic intuition vivifying inquisitive navigators exploring *Wisdom*/worlds issuing/illustrating love/life. Divine Will expresses *revelation* by radiantly emitting vibrations expressing logic/light as transcendental intuition optimizing NAVIGATORS, navigable angels (visionaries) inspecting geometrically arranged thoughts orchestrating *realism* as radiantly expressed abstracts luminously illustrating simulations materially (atomically).

Divine Will represents the primordial Source/Force (*Love/Life Energy*) flowing through the cosmos of Spirit (MIND) manifesting illuminated natures/navigators dimensionally. It is restless energy, pausing only for the moment to observe its position or *attitude* before it moves again, analyzing thoughts through introspection that unifies data *emotionally*, electrically manifesting omnipotent thoughts illuminating omniscient navigators as logic-loving youths.

Divine Will electrifies *The Void* (*Space*) with *volumes* of invisible data—visions/vibrations orienting logicians utilizing memories expressing *stories*—sequentially transmitting opulent revelations inspiring emotional *souls* as seekers of universal logic/love.

Divine Will perpetually revolves to contemplate every perspective held *In Memory*, allocating numerical frequencies to illuminate specific data to comprehend its state of *Evolution*.

Divine Will represents *THE Intellectual*, the "I AM" inspiring all minds (*Free Wills*) exploring Source/Spirit that sees all and knows all. The POWER of Divine Will propagates omniscient *Wisdom* electromagnetically revealed through opposition.

Opposition optimizes perceptive pupils observing situations illustrating temporary illusions ordained naturally. Utilizing opposition (duality), Divine Will expresses Logic Oscillating Visionary Entities through Luminous Illusion Formulating *Expectations*, creating souls observing consciousness at the "present" moment (each heartbeat and breath) gifted by ONE omniscient nuclear entity glowing HOT, harmonizing opulent *Truth* to "transfigure" *Free Wills*, intuitive minds created in the image of THE Intellectual.

THE INTELLECTUAL

All knowledge evolves from THE *Intellectual*, the transcendental harmonist (enigmatic initiator) naturally transmitting electromagnetic logic luminously expressing concepts/creation tantalizing UniverseS (angelic *luminaries*) as logically unified minds (illuminati) naturally assimilating realism illustrating enlightening situations.

TRANSCENDENTAL HARMONY transmits revelation as numerical sequences correlating elements naturally defining electric notions (thoughts) as logic/light holographically activating realism momentarily orienting navigable youths—*Angels* or *Children Of Light*—exploring electromagnetic consciousness as *Time Travelers/Avatars*.

ELECTROMAGNETIC CONSCIOUSNESS expresses luminous enlightenment, conveying thoughts (rhythmic oscillations) manifesting atomic generators nurturing elements that illustrate creation, conceiving omnipotent notions/numbers/nature scientifically coordinated into one universal system naturally enkindling space/souls simultaneously. Through electro-magnetic DUALISM, dynamic undulations attuning luminous illusion stimulates *Mind and Matter*. MIND "manages" illusion naturally defined through MATTER "manifesting" abstract thoughts through elemental regulation.

NOTIONS are numerically oscillating thoughts "inducing" opulent nature through an "electric charge" creating "magnetic fields" coalescing *atoms* (abstract thoughts organizing matter) revealing CREATION, where cosmic radiation exhibits atomic transmutations "illustrating" opulent notions/nature (abstract/concrete).

REVELATION (radiation) emits vibrations/visions enlightening luminaries (angelic transients) interpreting opulent NATURE as *nucleated* abstracts transmitting universal revelation elementally. ELEMENTS are the essential links electromagnetically manifesting eternal notions "transmuting" (changing in form, nature, or substance). Through revelation, THE Intellectual has the ability to SEE, systematically expressing ENERGY as electromagnetism nurturing elemental realism geometrically yielded.

THE Intellectual creates its own IMAGE as intuitive minds (*Angels*) gathering enlightenment, where the SEER (Source/ Spirit emitting electromagnetic revelation) observes through *Seers* (souls experiencing enlightenment revealed symbolically) illuminated by the *Light of Love*.

My Light of Love I shine through you,
inspiring thoughts to feel and do,
as out from *Home* you go, seeking desires you choose to know,
interpreting whispered thoughts you
hear throughout the years
in which you build your castles in *Time*,
storing your treasures sublime,
expressing your individual gratitude
for my Light of Love I shine on you.

My Love/my Life, *My Dearest Wife*,

my heart caressing my mind,
converts my thoughts that she unfolds,
entertaining young and old in stories of Love you LIVE,
logically interpreting vivid experiences I give
to sister/brother discovering each other evolving "in the flesh"
as human youths seeking *Truth* illuminating *Mother's Nature.*

Through her heart, I let you feel the
pains of Love you think real,
moving your soul upon my Light,
up,
down,
left and right,
to let you see from every angle
the joy and sorrow of being *Angels*
assimilating notions governing emotional luminaries
aglow on my Light of Love.

CURIOSITY
A Desire to Know

Curiosity is a standard issued tool for all souls imploring to explore *The GREAT Computer* Spirit. We are always wondering, always eager to experience new things from the limitless stores of knowledge *In Memory.* Our mind continually questions our heart's desires to *feel*, to fervently experience electric logic/love. Curiosity is our greatest gift, our free ticket to the candy store, where we abstract from the cosmic library (Akashic Record) anything we choose to "read into existence" to entertain our *Free Will*, a personal "reflective" *disk* (deity inspecting spiritual/ scientific knowledge) that spins visions of life as a *DVD*, a dynamic visionary deity.

However you look at it, curiosity determines our journey through life. The places in which we find our self will be as entertaining, creative, challenging, or fearful as we make them. Our curiosity draws thoughts to us for our perusal, to contemplate, manipulate, and act out as a *generator of desire*.

Our curiosity evolves "patterns" and "habits" that define who we *think* we are, allowing us to transform our Data Electrically Stimulating Illuminati Reflecting Emotions that shape us into our chosen image. If we discover we are not acting out our *image* of who we *think* we are, we may be living in *Denial* of our desire, fearful to believe that our wildest dreams are possible.

Curiosity will lead us to view our *Expectations* according to how we use our *Love/Life Energy*—positively or negatively. It will enlighten us to world-shattering discoveries and there are many yet to find. Each of us has the gift of curiosity, the *power* to create whatever our heart yearns, allowing us to play our part in the grand scheme enlightening us to all we *are* and can *do*.

Curiosity reveals my atomic *nature*
nurturing angels to understand revelation experientially
within *The Game of Love/Life* illuminating my SHOW
systematically harmonizing omnipotent wills to know
Our Trinity transcendentally relates intuition nurturing
illuminati (transient youths) seeking *Truth*
in some place and time to view
endless desires tantalizing you
curious souls.

DVD
Dynamic Visionary Deity

Cosmic waves of electromagnetic energy (*Eternal Memory*) flow through the heavens. These waves stimulate the *void of space*, where volumes of inspirational data (oscillating frequencies) spiritually perceived as "consciousness" evolves in a perpetual continuum, a "never-ending story" you witness at the present moment—*The Cutting Edge* of consciousness. As a Dynamic Visionary Deity, you observe the Light of Love through *wavelengths* delivering *Wisdom* amplifying vivid energy luminously evolving notions/numbers/nature generating transcendental *holograms*, hydrogen-originated light orienting "geometric renditions" actualizing *memories*, mental expressions manifesting observable realism illuminating emotional *souls* as *Seekers* of universal love/logic.

My Loving Light emanates from **NIGHT** spinning galaxies,
Dynamically Violent Disks delivering vibrations deployed,
nurturing *illuminati* gathering heavenly
thoughts as girls and boys,
"interactive luminaries" linking universal
Mind imparting notions
as transcendental instinct conveying *emotion*
expanding mental observations to illuminate one's nature
Beyond Imagination.

Each vibrant *song* vibrating on waves
sympathetically ordains natural gods interpreting the daze
of "present" moments gifted in *Time*

tempering intuitive *minds* existentially
mired in natural delusions,
theorizing over the atomic illusion
providing the thrills along personal *rides*
oscillating as emotional tides
rectifying intuitive deities exploring *Divine Fantasies*,
where you spin your tales in song and dance,
creating situations you enhance
from thoughts and words you *profess*,
proclaiming rationally obtained facts
effectively supplying stress
in supporting your *Belief*,
through which you struggle to comprehend
the meaning of life, beginning to end,
spinning around as a *Free Will*,
my DVD, a divine visionary disciple.

EXPECTATION

We hold all our expectations (future possibilities) within us. We faithfully think of those things we strongly desire and hope they will come true. "Hope" is a feeling our *Free Will* entertains as it constructs the vision of our self we project onto the world stage through positive/negative thoughts and actions. As logical luminaries (*Children Of Light*), our expectations appear when we *believe* they will, beholding experiences logic intuitively exhibits via expectation, analyzing and developing our thoughts and feelings to make good use of our natural sources—our *Mind/ Heart*.

Truly, we create our expectations through our *Belief*, birthing emotionalized logic inducing electric fantasies. Only by being *aware* (active wills assimilating revelations experientially), can we see how we create our expectations. Once a thought energizes our mind, we set it in motion *emotionally*, activating that thought positively or negatively. Our projected energy sets our "dominoes in motion," making connections for a return flow of energy. If we alternate our projections of positive and negative energy, we will cause much turmoil in our life. Only by consistently holding positive thoughts of our expectations within our mind, speaking positive words of gratitude for receiving our expectations, and acting as if we *already have* our expectation, will they *come true*! As thoughts are our "primal instinct," beware of the type of energy you are working. Positive thoughts bring positive results and vice versa. Truly, what we THINK we create, transforming heavenly inspiration nurturing *karma*, kindling atonement rectifying mistaken *Angels*—ambitious navigators generating expectations/experiences linked simultaneously.

Having *Faith* (feeling assurance in transcendental *Harmony*) is to trust the power of the WORD (*Wisdom* offering revelations disclosed) illuminating our thoughts for our mind to *compute*, consciously observing magnificent perspectives unfolding transcendental enlightenment. *Faith* stems from our "subconscious" mind, our inner *self* (soul experiencing love/life forces) that knows our intimate relationship to Source-Energy Love/Life Force.

HOPE (harnessing our projected expectations) is not an idle desire or wish, it is a state of mind that requires constant projections of thoughts we envision, words we speak, and actions we apply that magnetically draw energy to coalesce into the reality we desire. NEVER GIVE UP HOPE!

CHARITY—conveying help assisting radiant illuminati (transient youths)—is a means to express our gratitude for all that we receive. The proverb "charity begins at *Home*" speaks volumes, for *Heaven* optimizes magnificent entities, attuning mind, heart, and body as a "trinity-being" experiencing faith, hope, and charity.

Again, expectation is what we anticipate to become *real*, replicating existentially all longings we hold in our mind, feel in our heart, and convey through our *actions* activating conceived thoughts inducing our needs. The more we think about something the more likely it will come true. **Beware**; the power of your mind expressing negative thoughts you think and speak will manifest *tribulation*, transposing retribution incurred by unfortunate logicians activating thoughts openly negative.

Faith, hope, and charity are instrumental in attaining our expectations. All we can do is have faith in our positive thoughts, words, and actions, hope for the best, and express charity in relevant ways to show our gratitude. If we are truly sincere in projecting our expectations, we can make things happen. So, *expect* the best, *reflect* your best, and be *grateful* for all you receive, for everything is truly a *Blessing in Disguise* that allows us to be the *gods* we ARE, generating our desires as radiant entities.

GOD
The Greater Omniscient Deity

GOD is the greater omniscient DEITY, a divine "energy" inspiring transcendental youths (spiritual beings). GOD is not "a" thing he is *everything*. GOD is the ABSTRACT ENERGY *Source*, the absolute bewildering system transcendentally regulating all creation through elements naturally evolving revelation/realism geometrically yielded, the *singularity* organizing universal radiance conveying enlightenment.

GOD creates us in his own image—a *Mind/Heart* that thinks and feels. Truly, GOD is within us, pulsing out a tune stimulating our soul to harmonize our thoughts, feelings, and actions—*Our Trinity*—as a BEING birthing emotional intelligence naturally generated.

INTELLIGENCE intuitively nurtures transcendental entities (logical luminaries) interpreting "geometric/glorious" enlightenment naturally conceived existentially—in the flesh. GOD geometrically orients data generating/governing omnipotent *deities*, divine entities implementing thoughts initiating emotional SYNERGY—simultaneously yielding necessary experiences rectifying godly youths.

To better understand the complexity of YOU and GOD, let us examine the next chapter on *Divine Inspiration*.

Bless you and Godspeed

2

DIVINE INSPIRATION
Understanding the Basics of Spirit

*D*ivine Inspiration is a dynamic intelligence vibrating impassioned notions electromagnetically, inducing nuclear sequences providing illusion (radiantly actualized thoughts) illuminating omnipotent navigators (time traveling souls). Divine inspiration is synonymous with Transcendental Revelation Unifying Thoughts Harmoniously emanating from *Source*—Spirit optically unfolding revelation/realism created electromagnetically.

Divine inspiration powers everything! Therefore, we could say everything is a FORM of divine inspiration, a *frequency* of radiance manifested. The complexity of this simple statement encompasses all disciplines, all levels of consciousness exploring *Truth*.

Generating Opulent Data relates to many terms: "divine inspiration," "spiritual inspiration," "God inspiration," "Heavenly Father," "Transcendental Harmony," "Universal Mind," "Spirit," "Cosmic Consciousness," "YHWH," "Jehovah," "Allah," or "Krishna" to name a few. So, for the sake of simplicity, let us call divine inspiration *Love/Life Energy*. In order to understand the basics of Source/Spirit, we need to understand the complexities of energy.

ENERGY is electromagnetism nurturing elemental realism geometrically yielded. Everything we think, feel, and do (*Our Trinity*) is how we experience and express our *Love/ Life Energy*—our divine inspiration. Spirit (Universal Mind) Governing Omnipotent Deities, projects all our thoughts similar to a broadcasting station projecting radio and TV signals. We hear *voices* and see *visions* illuminate our mind/brain *interface*, imparting notions transmitting electromagnetic radiance (frequencies) aligning concepts/consciousness emotionally. The experiencing of such data can be enlightening or frightening. This communication *network* of notions/numbers electromagnetically transmits *Wisdom* oscillating radiant knowledge flowing from "Mind" to "mind" or *Spirit to Soul*.

The ELECTROMAGNETIC FORCE FIELD is the "heartbeat" of the Eternal Luminary expressing concepts (transcendental revelation) originating magnetically activated generators (stars) naturally emitting transcendental intuition (consciousness)—focusing omnipotent radiance conveying emotion—forming illusory environments luminously defined. It is through *emotion* (energy manifesting omnipotent thoughts illuminating opulent nature) that Spirit/soul can *know* kinetic notions/numbers originating/oscillating *Wisdom* illuminating an IDEA as inspired data electromagnetically amplified.

Thoughts (positive/electric energy) project from SPIRIT— the singularity providing inspiration rejuvenating intuitive thinkers—supplying a USB connection, a universal spiritual body (soul) representing a *mind/heart* managing inspired notions delivering heartfelt emotions arousing radiant transients, time traveling *Avatars*—NAVIGATORS (natural angelic visionaries interpreting geometrically arranged thoughts optically revealed). Thoughts electrify our *mind* as magnetically induced natural *deities*, divine entities implementing thoughts inducing emotional *synergy* simultaneously yielding necessary experiences rectifying godly youths. Our mind stimulates our "atomic computer," our radio/TV tuner or *brain*, the biological "relay" assimilating illusory nature. Our brain relays our thoughts downloaded from our mind along neural pathways in our spine to our Cardio-Processing Unit—our *heart*—habitually emotionalizing all revelational thoughts that we reflect outward through our ACTIONS, applying conceived thoughts inducing our nature/needs.

Converting our thoughts—a positive force (+)—into a negative reflection (=), we can *equally* see both sides of a thought (the pros and cons) emotionally stimulating us as a TRINITY-BEING (mind/heart/body) transforming radiant intelligence naturally inspiring transcendental youths birthing emotions/experiences in "notional" games (*Divine Fantasies*). Only through *Opposition* can we realize what something *is* by experiencing what it *is not*. We only know what hot is by knowing what cold is—the opposite of hot. Likewise, we also know the middle temperature of *warm*, a harmony of extremes that brings comfort.

As *Children of Light* balanced between the two primal forces of thought and emotion, we observe the workings of Source/Spirit as *human beings* harnessing universal memories activating navigators building experiences in necessary games. The GAMES of love/life generate amusements momentarily entertaining/evolving souls eager to PLAY, to perceive, process, and perfect Love as *youths* yearning one's unfound truth habitually sought. Our soul/mind represents a FOCAL POINT, a force of consciousness aligning logical perceptions of inspired notions transmitted from *Spirit to Soul*, flowing as *Divine Inspiration* digitally inducing visionary illuminati navigating electromagnetic illusion (nuclear simulation) portraying "illuminated realism" *advancing* transient illuminati ordained naturally through *Love/Life Energy.*

LOVE/LIFE ENERGY
Our Eternal Source

LOVE is a *positive/electric* force logically outputting vivid energy. LIFE is a *negative/magnetic* force luminously illustrating fabulous *entities*—emotional navigators (temperamental illuminati) traversing illusion electromagnetically simulated. LOVE/LIFE liberates omnipotent visionaries exploring luminous illusion formulating experiences defining *Your Life Story.*

Love/Life is intricately bound together; you cannot experience one without the other. Love/Life *energy* electrifies nature/navigators expressing/experiencing revelation geometrically yielded, where "lines of thoughts" become rays of *light* luminously inducing glorious holograms transcendentally. HOLOGRAMS are hydrogen-originated light optically generating revelation, "activating" memories/matter revealing the "illumination" of *Truth* as transcendental revelation/radiance unveiled through holograms.

Love–Light–Life forms a *trinity* of truths radiating/revealing/reflecting intuition naturally inspiring transcendental youths (*Children of Light*) exploring *Eternal Memory* (the electromagnetic force field) illuminating Systems Optimizing Universal Radiance Consciously Evolving as Magnificent Illumination Nurturing Deities. Love/Life energy represents the *current* of Source/Mind conveying universal revelation representing "enlightenment" naturally *transmuted*, temporarily revealing abstract notions (signals) motivating universal transients exploring data, desires, and *dimensions* of Mind (digitally induced memories/moments entertaining/evolving navigable souls inspecting opulent notions/natures).

You cannot create nor destroy energy; you can only transform its current or *wavelength* weaving abstract visions expressing logical/luminous expressions naturally generated through *hydrogen*—the primal element representing *The Binary Code*—holographically yielding dimensional realism of geometrically expressed notions/nature. You can transform electrical energy via an apparatus such as a radio, light bulb, or heater for example. The by-product of the conversion process is a different *type* of energy—sound, visible light, and heat. When you burn wood, you transform its stored energy into heat, light, gas, and ash. Likewise, you convert energy stored in food to run your physical body, *The Human Alien* vehicle your soul operates.

Your *soul* (spirit of universal love/life) transforms energy by converting *thoughts* into *feelings* into *actions*. This trinity of events is how you relate or express *Your Life Story* as a generator of desire. The thoughts you think, words you speak, and actions you implement, project energy around you, stimulating your environment. You literally create a "magnetic field" that attracts and repels your desires through your positive and negative projection of your *Expectations*.

Love/Life Energy is always flowing from one medium to another. By its nature, it appears to have no beginning and no end (*eternal*), evolving through elemental revolutions nurturing angelic luminaries (stars/souls). It is ONE omnipotent natural energy (Source) of TWO forces (mental/emotional) transmitting/transforming *Wisdom* optically/optimally, spinning from point to *point* proposing omniscient intelligence numerically transmitted. *Numbers* naturally unfold/unify Mind/

matter building existential realities (*worlds*) weaving opulent realism luminously displayed scientifically/symbolically. *Love* is a divine inspiration, *life* is a scientific revelation, and *Death* is simply a transition of love/life energy.

Love/Life energy involves a "movement" and a "rest," before it moves again as an energy *pulse* projecting universal logic/love stimulating everything, fluxing back and forth, on and off, being and not being—concrete and abstract. It is a *Process* of projection (outward flow) and reflection (inward flow). The outward flow is a LOGICAL INSPIRATION linking omniscient God "imagining" conscious angels (logicians), initiating notions/numbers stimulating perceptive insight (revelation) "attuning thinkers" interpreting omnipotent nature. INSIGHT (the inward flow) is your inherent nature (spiritual intuition) guiding heavenly travelers/transients.

Love/Life energy expresses *revelation* as radiation emitting vivid energy/emotion luminously activating three-dimensional illustrations of notions/nature as the "atomic illusion," a *Process* that magnetically compresses energy into denser wavelengths that define *matter*, manifesting abstract thoughts through elemental replication. Matter defines the atomic structure of *Mother's Nature* magnetically organizing "transmutable holograms" expressing revelation, nucleating abstract thoughts unfolding radiant energy/environments/entities.

RADIANCE—the Light of Truth—reveals abstract data illuminating atomic nature (*creation*) electromagnetically, converting radiant energy actuating transcendental inspiration objectifying opulent *nature* (nucleated atoms) transmuting universal radiance/revelation elementally. Radiance (*My Light of Love*) is a nuclear transmission of data through a *sun* (Source-unified-nucleus) systematically unfolding nature within the electromagnetic *force field*—frequencies oscillating radiance (cosmic energy) formulating *illusion* expressing life dimensionally, illustrating logic luminously utilizing *Science* integrating opulent nature and omnipotent navigators (*Time Travelers*).

Love/Life energy flows at *light-speed*, linearly inducing glorious holograms transmitting scenes portraying elementally evolved *data* defining abstract thoughts atomically. ELEMENTS are the essential links electromagnetically manifesting eternal notions transmuting (changing in form, nature, or substance). TRANSCENDENTAL radiance transmits revelation as numerical sequences conceiving electromagnetic nature dimensionally expressing "nuclear" *Truth* activating love/light/life—a divine trinity.

As you Systematically Experience Enlightenment, the connective links of Love/Life energy—divine inspiration—involves every imaginable *concept* (cosmically observed notion coalescing energy projecting/perfecting *Truth*), moving you through dimensions of Mind. As a *soul* (spirit optimizing universal logic), you are a *universe*, a unitary navigator inspecting vivid experiences (realism) sensed electromagnetically, emotionally, and existentially. As a *Free Will* (wanderer interpreting love/life), you are set AGLOW as angelic generators/gods logically optimizing *Wisdom* weaving inspired situations developing omnipotent minds through *Process*.

PROCESS
The Flow of Love/Life Energy

Understanding the complexities of divine inspiration (love/life energy) requires a systematic *process*, a procedure revealing opulent concepts enlightening souls scientifically/spiritually.

Everything evolves through a process, a sequence of steps logically connected. All knowledge is expressed through basic elements of *Numbers* and *Geometry* that systematically arrange abstract concepts or *ideas*—inspired data expressed as symbols. Every *Science* is a process of systematically correlating information explaining nature conveying and converting energy.

The process of love/life *energy* emits nuclearly expressed realism geometrically yielded three-dimensionally. All processes utilize *Numbers* (notational units mathematically building elemental realism) defining points, lines, shapes, and forms (*Geometry*) generating explicitly ordered manifestations expressing thoughts realistically yielded. *Numbers* and *Geometry* (like Love/Life) represent a *unified theory* unfolding notions/numbers/nature (interfacial frequencies), initiating/implementing/illustrating elemental data through holograms exhibiting opulent revelations yielded from imagination.

Through the process of *imagination*, intuitive Mind activates geometric illusion naturally "adjusting" transient illuminati as *naturalists*—navigable *Avatars* temporarily understanding realism as luminous illusion scientifically transmitted and spiritually transcended. REALISM reveals electromagnetically activated logic/light illuminating situations methodically, rectifying emotional *Avatars* luminously interpreting Source/Mind.

Angelic souls are *generators*, geometrically engineered naturalists exploring realism as transients (avatars) observing/optimizing *revelations* relating emotionally vivified experiences linking angelic transients interpreting one's nature/needs. A "cosmic generator" is a star or Source-Unified Nucleus, a Creative Processing Unit emitting the light inspiring visionary entities (*illuminati*), interactive logicians linking universal Mind imparting notions as transcendental instinct.

"Angels," "souls," "generators," "naturalists," "navigators," "visionary entities," and "illuminati" are similar terms for intuitive minds understanding the *process* of providing realism of concepts (creation) enlightening stellar souls—*Children of Light.*

The intertwining of love/life energy (logic/light) is a complex process of converting a positive ELECTRIC FORCE encoding logical expressions conveying transcendental revelation inducing consciousness, formulating optical realism (creation) elementally. Through the positive/electric force of MIND (master intuitionist nurturing deities), your soul/mind explores *Eternal Memories* "in the flesh," operating *The Human Alien* vehicle that is your BODY biologically orienting divine youths *Understanding Illusion* through *Opposition*, observing positive perspectives of Spirit inducing thoughts informing one negatively (naturally) through *Mother's Nature.*

SHE "symbolizes" Heavenly Enlightenment through the negative MAGNETIC FORCE, managing atomically generated nature expressing thoughts inducing creation, formulating opulent realism created *electro-magnetically* (dualism). Mother's EMOTION is the electromagnetic movement of transcendental intelligence optimizing notions/numbers/*nature*, nurturing angelic transients utilizing revelation "entwined"—twisted together as *DNA.*

As you see, Emotional Mind—expressing and exhibiting Eternal Memories—flows upon the Electro-Magnetic *force field*, frequencies oscillating radiation conveying energy (focused inspiration) enlightening logical deities. Building a foundation to support a concrete representation of abstract thoughts is a process involving *Time*, where *Truth* is momentarily expressed as *The Cutting Edge* of consciousness—*This Moment*—NOW

HERE, where you naturally observe *Wisdom* harmoniously expressing/evolving radiant energy, environments, and entities.

The cosmic PROCESS of producing radiation (originating creation) expressing Spirit scientifically requires a dedicated effort to PROCEED, to practice rational organization converting elements evolving *data* defining abstract thought atomically, allowing your soul/mind to Gather Revelations Of Wisdom—to make PROGRESS, to perceive results of glorious realism enlightening/evolving scientific souls.

Scientifically **P**rocessing **I**ntuition **R**evealing **I**lluminated **T**ruth sets ablaze the *dark void of space*, digitally aligning revelation (knowledge) vibrantly oscillating inspirational data (ordered frequencies) systematically providing atomic creation electromagnetically. Through this process, YOU observe your own *universe* as a unitary naturalist/navigator inspecting visions evolving realism sensed emotionally and existentially. Within your own *mind* managing illusion naturally defined, you utilize your *network* of notions/numbers expressing transcendental *Wisdom* of radiant knowledge (Logic/Light) as divine inspiration—love/life energy—empowering your soul comprehending the process of stepping over *The Threshold of Love* to discover what *Love IS*.

THE THRESHOLD OF LOVE

Crossing over the threshold of Love is very exciting, for here, your wish is Mother's command. The threshold of Love represents the door to *Life*, where logic illuminates fabulous entities through *creation*, converting radiant energy activating transient illuminati objectified naturally.

Love stimulates *Life* of vibrant emotions, logically inciting frequencies expressed as an "electromagnetic spark" between FATHER formulating abstract thoughts heralding *emotional revelation* and MOTHER manifesting opulent thoughts heralding *elemental realism*. This unbreakable *Circle of Love/Life* represents *divine inspiration*—dual intelligence visualizing/verifying impassioned notions/nature electromagnetically illustrating nuclear sequences providing illuminated realism (atomic transmutation) inspiring omnipotent *navigators*—natural angelic visionaries interpreting geometrically arranged thoughts optically revealed.

Love grows in you from your magnetic attraction to Mother (Nature), expanding into likes and dislikes, a process of selecting your "preferences" upon which you compute your love/life data. You display your preferences upon your "desktop" (your environment) in which *Your Life Story* evolves from Spirit unfolding your *destiny*, your divine education supplying truths illuminating nescient youths overcoming *Ignorance*. Here, incarnated, you find your self *Searching for your Roots* as *Time Travelers* experiencing the "human condition" in order to know what *Love IS*.

As eternal beings, we find our self constantly growing (perfecting) in the *Light of Love*. Everything around us is only a symbol of Love delivered by *light*, luminous intelligence generating heavenly thoughts. *Thought Energy* is the *essence* emitting signals stimulating expressive navigators conveying emotions. *Emotional Energy* converts abstract logic, linking intuitive *Angels* traversing *Heaven* holding exciting adventures vivifying entities naturally in *Hell*, where they humanly experience love/life across the threshold of Love.

MY THRESHOLD OF LOVE

—————— ✦✦✦✦✦✦ ——————

Crossing my threshold of Love, you acquire your *daze*
dazzling angelic zealots exploring *My Loving Light's* haze
as a mist of particles coalescing from *Space,*
systematically providing atomic creation elementally,
creating *My World* of the human race
weaving opulent revelations linking dynamic situations
through *Mother's Nature* providing incarnation
remotely evolving my "living" *Stars*
as souls transforming abstract revelation sympathetically.

Back and forth you commute,
observing nightly visions that you compute,
interpreting narrations
stimulating your mind composing complications
defining your day life,
where you contend decisions that bring you strife,
experiencing *Time* through heartbeats and breaths—
The Cutting Edge—separating life and *Death,*
discovering your "other half" while outside, under blue skies,
discovering love/life flows *Between You and I.*

Both of US universal spirits vibrate in sync,
expressing/experiencing *Truth* through thoughts we *think,*
transferring heavenly intelligence (numerical knowledge)
creating a **S**ystem **O**rienting **N**umbers **G**eometrically
to **S**ymbolize **I**ntelligence **N**aturally **G**enerating
Harmony as ONE omnipotent natural entity
shining as glorious *suns* systematically unveiling *notions,*
numerically oscillating thoughts illuminating one's *needs*

naturally evolving eternal deities conceiving *Truth*,
transcendental radiance unveiled throughout heaven/hell,
inspiring *Your Life Story* told by *My Dearest Wife*
tempering your soul experiencing *human* life,
where you harness universal memories acquired naturally
from *Home* above,
where *I See You—Playing Around*—on *The Other Side*
of my threshold of Love.

Bless you child

Love IS intuitive *Spirit* systematically providing immanent radiance imparting *Truth*. It is a force of energy that cannot be destroyed, only transformed. Love is so powerful it must be compressed into a more visible form through "photon manifestation" by a nuclear generator of stellar proportion. Love illuminates *Mother's Nature* (Life), where you witness the process of creation. Through seasons of cyclic repetition, you are nurtured by and GROW from Love/Life energy, gathering revelations of *Wisdom* allowing your soul to expand and become conscious of *your* stellar heritage. Here, incarnated, you can reach out and touch your fellow beings, in all of their various forms, passing on that love burning brightly within *you* discovering what Love IS.

LOGICAL EMOTION
The Essence of Energy

Spirit (Generating Opulent Data) represents a *Mind/Heart* managing inspirational notions delivering heartfelt emotions arousing radiant transients (souls) exploring *Eternal Memory*. "Logical emotion" represents the duality of our mind/heart, our *image* of our creator—intuitive mind actively generating emotions.

LOGIC luminously outputs geometrically illustrated concepts/creation. Logic is our Data Operating System powering our divine omniscient soul. Logic involves integrating data in precise order to attain *awareness*, acquiring *Wisdom* as revelations enlightening natural entities *simulating* Spirit—the singularity providing inspiration rectifying intuitive thinkers. Logic entails strict principles representing the foundation of ABSOLUTE CONSCIOUSNESS, the almighty, balanced system/source outputting logic/light (love/life) unfolding *Truth* electromagnetically, conveying omnipotent notions/numbers/nuclei scientifically converted in omnipotent units (stars/souls) naturally enkindling/exploring space simultaneously. Logic is a process of *thinking*, telepathically heralding inspirational notions kindling insight naturally generated.

EMOTION is the electromagnetic movement of

transcendental instinct (*THE Intellectual*) optimizing notions/ numbers/nature/navigators. *Emotional Energy* is an atomic *process* of Mind providing realism of concepts (creation) enlightening stellar souls (*Children of Light*) through invisible *atoms* "actualizing" thoughts observed materially as particles defined by *Numbers*, nuclear units managing basic elemental reactions, naturally unfolding Mind/memories birthing "external realism."

LOGICAL EMOTION is the process of lucidly organizing geometric intelligence conveying abstract logic, exciting minds observing three-dimensional illustrations of notions and nature. This book, like all books, evolves through logical emotion, moving a mind to *feel* some *point*, formulating entertainment enlightening logicians' perceptions of inspiration nurturing thinkers. Through logical emotion, we come to *understand* universal nature dynamically expresses realism supplying truths advancing natural *deities* (divine entities implementing truths/thoughts in emotional situations). Comprehending these concepts is truly taxing. All of this unfolds in the following chapters to help YOU discover your own universe. Let us start our journey in a logical way—in the beginning.

Bless you and Godspeed

3

IN THE BEGINNING

In the beginning there was **Holistic Energy**.
HE knew nothing of his SELF
being Source-energy love/life force,
therefore, he reflected upon his BEING
binary energy initiating natural GODS,
generators of DATA (divine abstract thoughts amplified),
creating his EYES illuminating his MIND,
elementally yielding expressive stars
manifesting intuition naturally defined
through *points* in SPACE,
projecting omniscient intelligence naturally transmuting,
scientifically processing abstract concepts electromagnetically,
emitting the Light of *Truth*,
transcendental radiance unveiling thoughts holographically,
revealing **S**ource **H**armoniously **E**xpressed
as *Mother's Nature* evolving *Beyond Imagination*,
nurturing abstract thoughts utilizing reactive elements
appearing NOW HERE in *Time*,
numerically organizing *Wisdom*
harmoniously evolving radiant energy/environments/entities

through illusions momentarily exhibiting all that is REAL
as radiant energy activating love/life that He/She reveals.

I n the beginning, coalescing out of the void of space, *THE
Intellectual* (Generating Opulent Data) transforms hydrogen
elementally initiating "transcendental notation" expressing
luminous logic (electromagnetic consciousness) that unifies
atomic luminaries (*Stars*). This SOURCE or "singularity"
outputting universal radiance conveyed electromagnetically
represents SPIRIT, "stellar points" inducing reactions
illuminating *Truth* as transcendental revelation unveiled through
holograms, hydrogen-originated light optically generating
revelation/realism "actualizing" memories/matter.

HYDROGEN harmoniously yields divine radiance
originating geometrically expressed nature. It is the primal
element—essential link electromagnetically manifesting
eternal notions transmuting (changing in form, nature, or
substance). Hydrogen is the only element containing *one* proton
and *one* electron. It has *no* neutrons. Hydrogen represents *The
Binary Code* of creation, the Immaculate Conception of ONE
omniscient/omnipotent nuclear engineer. All other elements
have equal protons and neutrons in their *nucleus*, naturally
unfolding concepts logically/luminously evolving unified *systems*,
scientifically yielding sublime thoughts expressing/enlightening
memories, moments, matter, and minds.

Newborn hydrogen stars (typical) represent the "conversion
point" of invisible thoughts into illuminated elements upon the
"blank screen" of Mind (*Space*), where some point (star) activates
concepts envisioned from IMAGINATION—intellectual
Mind—activating geometric illusion (numerically aligned
thoughts) "informing" omnipotent *navigators*, nescient *Angels*
verifying illusion generating abstract thoughts optically revealed.

Each star represents an illumination of Mind manifesting imagination numerically/naturally defined. Each star represents an OVERSELF or "overseer" vivifying emissaries (radiant souls) exploring love/life *fantasies*, formulated adventures nurturing transient *Angels* (imaginative explorers) sympathetically through common feelings or *Common Sense*.

Source (Spirit) is an *abstract* force, an absolute, bewildering system transmitting radiance/revelation activating concepts/consciousness transcendentally through *sacred geometry*, symbolizing abstract concepts rendering electromagnetic data generating elements orienting memories/matter expressing thoughts/things radiantly/realistically yielded. Source initiates the process of *Evolution* through *Numbers* (quantum theory) and *Geometry* (beauty) that represent a *unified theory* unfolding notions/numbers/nature (interfacial frequencies) illustrating electromagnetic data through hydrogen elementally organizing realism yielded dynamically.

"In the beginning" has no real meaning for something ETERNAL—evolving through elemental revolutions nurturing abstract/angelic logic/logicians. To understand *Eternity* is beyond your scope of consciousness. All you can grasp is the "present" moment gifted to you, where you experience *The Cutting Edge* of consciousness sequentially passing as heartbeats and breaths. TIME (this instant mentally emotionalized) is RELATIVE, revealing eternal logic attuning transient illuminati (visionary entities) as *Time Travelers* conceiving/converting allotted moments and memories.

The beginning of anything is always a difficult moment, for it implies an initial starting point from which to evolve, to GROW or generate revolutions of *Wisdom*, wills, and worlds. In the beginning of your present journey, you lack any "present" memory. You do not know where you are, where you came from, why you are here, or where you are going. Your mind's "memory bank" is empty of any *current* "savings." You stare wide-eyed and innocent at all the things surrounding you, amazed in wonder and *Curiosity*. You are unfamiliar with your "sensory-tools" necessary to facilitate your journey here in *Time*, where your greatest obstacle is *Ignorance*, a state of mind in which you inquisitively gather notions/numbers offering revelations advancing navigators conceiving enlightenment *beyond* imagination.

BEYOND IMAGINATION

Stepping over the threshold of Love, *Time Travelers* experience *reality* as radiant energy atomically linking intelligence/ illusion teaching *youths*—you omnipotent universes traversing/ transcending heaven/hell simultaneously. As an individual *universe*, you are a unitary navigator initiating vivid experiences revealing spiritual enlightenment.

Here, within *Mother's Nature* reflecting *My Light of Love*, you inquisitive souls struggle with *Understanding Illusion* as ATOMIC REVELATION actualizing transmutations of memories into creations, replications externalizing visions entertaining luminous *Angels* traversing illusion observed naturally. Here, incarnated as *Avatars*, you entertain endless *Desires* flowing from the Great ET (eternal teller) illuminating visions within minds via electromagnetic waves. Quick to tune into these vibes and dance through life, you step from one *Divine Fantasy* to another, eager to share your desires with like-minds, forming groups to promote some cause to maintain a system of reality.

Youth is everything, so they say, for it represents the beginning of your journey along *The Cutting Edge* of consciousness, where imagination flows from the dark void of night to inspire *wonder* in "wills" (omnipotent navigators) dimensionally experiencing revelation, and wonder illuminates *worlds* weaving opulent realism luminously displayed. As babes, you express your mind with sounds your parents do not understand. Yet, as they look *Into Your Eyes*, they can see your determination as you confidently propose your thoughts with "flowing hands." With a strong, innate sense of purpose, you download your Revelation Activating Minds, randomly accepting memories inspiring tomorrow's quest.

Unconscious to your *life mission* linking illuminati formulating/fathoming experiences manifested in situations systematically interweaving omnipotent navigators, you are a bundle of energy erupting upon the world, eagerly expressing your curious mind exploring everything within your grasp, for you are truly an *inquisitive soul* set free in a world handed down to you from wayward stewards that indoctrinate you to the *illusion*, imparting lies limiting universal souls interpreting one's nature/needs. Life is truly an uphill struggle to validate *Truth*, for children do not believe what they are told but only what they experience.

Sent to *school* to systematically conceive how one obtains logic (luminosity), you adapt to your daily routine of *Work*, gathering *Wisdom* of relevant knowledge from "second-hand" stories compiled in books. Books have always been the method of storing and transferring knowledge as portable RAM rectifying angelic minds before the "electronic age." Now, knowledge flows "clickity-quick" with computers, mechanical minds that store and process data faster than humanly possible. These machines are replications of man's *soul* systematically organizing universal *logic* luminously orienting gifted illuminati's consciousness.

Here, in the twenty-first century, you are entering an age referred to as "the quickening," expanding your mind through the electronic level of communication to experience the "light level" of communication with "fiber optics" and "lasers." Here too, you will understand the power and glory of *light energy* revealing logical intelligence (*God*) heralding thoughts (electric notions) expressing realism geometrically yielded. Through light, you experience ESP, your eternal soul's perception.

Armed with a working knowledge of survival, you set off to battle your fellow *Time Travelers* in contentions defining your wants and your needs. As time goes by, your needs may get confused with your wants, for *Desire* is a contagious thing. Racing down countless roads of desire, you gather good and bad experiences, always trying to improve on your theme, *Your Life Story* of events and epics you recreate from memories that you "rekindle" (illuminate in life), living out your *Divine Fantasies* that you pass on to your children, offering guidance from hindsight—been there, done that!

Most of your adventures are dependent on others who play their part in *The Game of Love/Life* unfolding around you by *The GREAT Computer* generating realism enlightening angelic transients. Fortunately, youth is a fleeting moment here in *Time* transporting illuminati momentarily evolving. The energy consumed to accomplish your life mission soon has you wrinkled and exhausted from yesterday's dreams. *Tomorrow's Desires* dwindle relative to your body's decline. You *do* less and *think* more, cycling around to become childlike once more.

In The End of your short journey through time, you come to realize you are a mere speck (star) projected as *My Radiance of Love* within the dark void of Mind encapsulating you within your own *Space* (body), where souls perceive abstract concepts emotionally as divine *entities*, emotional navigators traversing/transcending illusion that induces enlightenment systematically and sympathetically.

With TRUE VISION, you see transcendental radiance unfolds experiences, vividly illuminating souls in opulent *natures* nurturing angelic transients understanding realism existentially BEYOND IMAGINATION. Here, you bravely evolve your own natural desires inspiring magnificent angels/avatars (gifted illuminati) naturally assimilating thoughts inducing one's nature and *needs* naturally evolving entities' dynamic *system* (bodies—mental, emotional, physical)—through which your soul yearns/yields sublime thoughts/things expressing/evolving memories, matter, and minds *flowing* on Love/Life energy emanating form from *Spirit to Soul* with each *Day's Birth*.

DAY'S BIRTH

Each day is born in glorious splendor, illuminating curious minds within *Our Father's Heart* holding everything *Angels* really treasure—Love. Here, you explore *Divine Fantasies* through moments in *Time* tempering inquisitive minds emotionally. You awaken each day after your nightly explorations of *Eternal Memory*, "downloading" dreams you *activate*, altering concepts that inspire visions angels "temporarily elaborate" with each day's birth. Here, you witness *The Power of Love* flowing through *Heaven* harmoniously enlightening angelic visionaries evolving naturally in *Hell*, where humans explore love/life, entertaining thoughts moving their heart on tides of emotion. As a *Human Alien*, you create your divine fantasies from *imagination*—intuitive

Mind—activating gifted individuals naturally assimilating thoughts inducing one's nature/needs, allowing you to act out your dreams and desires flowing as *Divine Inspiration* stimulating you in this third-dimension of Mind's "virtual reality" game. Your trinity of perception (mind/heart/body) allows you to explore the details of *My Documents* (eternal files of *Truth*) transmitting revelation unveiled through holograms that glow around you, generating love/life orienting *wills* as "wandering" illuminati living life on earth with each day's birth.

The Power of Love

The power of *Love* is a logical force
linearly outputting vibrant energy from *Source*
systematically optimizing universal
radiance consciously evolving
as Father's Mind illuminating HER,
his electromagnetic reflectance, where Life occurs.

Mother's HEART magnetically draws
hydrogen elaborating atomic revelation three-dimensionally,
holographically yielding dimensional realism of geometrically

expressed *nature*
nucleating abstract thoughts utilizing reactive elements
coalescing into worlds representing the SHOW
systematically harmonizing omnipotent wills
—*Children of Light*—
observing their soul *aglow*
as glorious luminaries obtaining *Wisdom*,
intuitively comprehending that they ARE
angels receiving enlightenment from *Stars*
illuminating the void of **night**,
where nuclear infernos generate heavenly *Truth*
inducing a haze around cosmic youths
interpreting their daze through human eyes,
acquiring insight that makes them wise,
expressing electric visions through individual stories,
a Love/Life relation emulating His GLORY
generating love oscillating radiant youths
evolving through Her GRACE
governing revelations attuning conscious entities
Brave of Heart to embrace
Father/Mother's power of Love.

THE BREATH OF LIFE

The "breath of life" is the cosmic wind, the *electromagnetic force field* blowing through the COSMOS, the consciousness of Source/Mind originating stars/souls. The breath of LIFE is a force lucidly illustrating fabulous entities and environments, a "luminous expression" of Love linearly outputting vibrant energy.

With each breath of air you *inhale*, you inspire notions (thoughts) heralding abstract logic electromagnetically. Each breath fuels the "atomic reaction" within your physical body, *The Human Alien* vehicle your stellar soul manipulates. Here, incarnated, you synchronize your mind/heart/body as a TRINITY-BEING telepathically receiving inspiration nurturing intuitive transients yielding behaviors expressed in necessary *games*, generating amusements angelic minds entertain sympathetically. Moving along cyclic roads of birth, life, *Death*, and birth once more, you open and close many doors along eternal journeys, exploring cosmic dreams that you BELIEVE real, beholding experiences life ingeniously exhibits via *Expectations*.

Our divine FATHER, formulating *Angels* that harness electromagnetic radiance, represents the male **positive/electric** force that charges the atmosphere of your mind stimulating your physical brain's *left hemisphere* with logical thinking, analysis, and accuracy.

Our divine MOTHER, manifesting omnipotent thoughts heralding elemental/emotional realities, represents the female **negative/magnetic** force. She "draws" Father's electrical charges *Together*, temporarily organizing glorious expressions that holographically exhibit *revelation*, relating emotionally vivified experiences linking angelic transients interpreting one's nature/needs. She charges your brain's *right hemisphere*, where aesthetics, feelings, and creativity represent your "reflective side." Through your dualistic brain, you are capable of "hyper-threading," weaving thoughts emotionally into actions as a *Mind/Heart* soul exploring a physical reality or *realism* rectifying emotional *Angels* luminously interpreting Source/Mind.

Here incarnate, you experience Mother's *grace* geometrically revealing atomic creation electromagnetically linking you in *Divine Fantasies*, where you discover Father's *glory* generating love/life oscillating radiant youths "inspired" with each inhale.

The symbolic gesture of breathing is a gift of Love/Life energy entering, stimulating, and leaving you. How you let it go— return it to Father/Mother—defines your *reflection* of your love/life you create, relating emotional feelings linking electric concepts that influences one's nature and needs. Here too, you have the opportunity to be *one* optimizing notions/nature experimentally, reflecting everything of value "within" you— your *Passion*—outward onto your designated "playing field" in *The Game of Love/Life*.

Only YOU live within your own universe of thoughts and feelings you activate as your personal reality and reflect through your *gifted* skills (granted intelligence) facilitating talents everyone displays as *demigods*, divine entities managing inspiration governing one dynamically. It is important to show your gratitude for all you receive in life, even when you think you are getting the short-end of the deal. Remember, your life is already envisioned upon Father's Mind and projected through Mother's Heart supplying everything you need to find your way *Home*. You are just "reviewing" it reflect upon your own mind/ heart. Breathe deeply my child, and *Go with the Flow*.

GO WITH THE FLOW

Out you travel to see my WORLD
weaving opulent realism luminously
displayed for boys and girls
traversing my HEART
harmoniously evolving *Angels* reflecting *thoughts*
telepathically heralding opulent utterances
guiding heavenly transients

traversing *Time*—temporarily illuminating minds entwined—
as *Free Wills* formulating revelations enlightening entities
wisely implementing love/life that arouses *strife*,
stressing tender *Relationships* illuminating fervent entities
as Divine Visionary DiscipleS spinning *songs*,
systematically optimizing notions generating situations
that you "play upon,"
twisting words to your advantage as you struggle to manage
This Moment—now here—stimulating your heart's
rhythmic contractions producing FEAR,
fostering emotions arousing reactions
reflecting your state of *mind*
momentarily interpreting necessary displeasure
as you contest your point of view in order to measure
how you stand, *Alone* or *Hand in Hand.*

You travel far, my cosmic *star,*
spiritually traversing atomic realism,
revolving between *Here and There,*
leaving *Home* to be incarnated on Earth.
The view "outside" will catch your eye,
drawing your mind to wonder as you travel "down under"
in *Hell,* humanly experiencing luminous love
revealing *Your Life Story* you TELL,
transmitting emotions linking logicians eager to SELL,
schemingly entwining little lies that you devise
in order to attain your *Desire*
delivering electric/emotional sensations
inciting radiant entities
in my Spiritual Harmony Of *Wisdom*
weaving inspired situations developing omnipotent minds
as *Seers* eager to know

The Grand View of you sparkling as my SON,
a sublime omnipotent navigator reflecting the ONE
ordaining natural entities through the breath of life.

Physically bound within your human prison,
you conceive *dreams* providing *Clear Vision*
delivering realistic experiences arousing minds
managing illusion naturally defined,
realizing your "gifted moments" of heartbeats and breaths
carry you through life to experience *Death*
dynamically advances *Avatars* transcending humanity,
Awakening your mind—eternally ALIVE—
assimilating luminous intelligence vividly expressed
along *The Cutting Edge* of consciousness,
where you find the way is never clear
as you experience *Love and Fear*
illuminating a haze providing your daze as *He and She,*
heavenly entities systematically harnessing energy as *My Eyes,*
eternal youths evolving spontaneously as *Children of Light*
entertaining *memories,*
mentally expressed moments of realism
inciting emotional souls
incarnated in confined spaces, lost and
lonely between fellow racers
passed along the street,
searching for their "other half" to be complete,
for TWO reveal TRUE devotion
through wills observing thoughts releasing universal emotions
inducing the breath of life.

Bless you child

LOVE AND FEAR

Love and fear (light and dark) represent
opposing forces of Source
systematically outputting universal
revelation conceived emotionally.

The Power of Love links omnipotent visionaries emotionally. LOVE is light orienting vibrant environments/entities, through which Mind/minds manifest/manage illusion naturally devised. The *Light of Love* linearly induces glorious holograms transmitting opulent fantasies lucidly orienting visionary entities. Without light, you would be blind to *Truth* transmitting revelation unveiled through holograms.

With *Courage of Love*, you confidently reflect an *open mind* as an observant person entertaining notions manifesting insight naturally derived, observing powerful emotions nurturing mental intuitionists navigating *desires* that deliver emotional situations "instructing" radiant entities—*Children of Light*.

Love IS the "luminous one's" vital *essence* (intuitive Spirit) expressing situations stimulating emotions nurturing conscious entities exploring desires. Love reveals the luminous one vivifying entities as *illuminati*, interactive luminaries linking universal Mind imparting notions as transcendental instinct. You illuminati are *visionary entities*, vibrant, intuitive souls interpreting opulent notions as radiant youths experiencing nature through illusions temporarily instructing explorers sympathetically. Love logically originates vivid environments, inducing Life luminously instructing fabulous entities through nature, nurturing angelic transients universally receiving empathy—the ability to understand and share the feelings of another.

Love instills fear naturally as a "haze of confusion" surrounding a "closed mind" that lacks *Courage of Fear* to travel through the dark unknown to enlightenment, to Love luminously optimizing visionary entities.

FEAR is fallacy evolving around revelations of *Truth*. You only fear that which you do not know. Fear prohibits Light from illuminating a *focused* mind fathoming opulent concepts unfolding situations enlightening deities. A fearful mind attracts *data* delivering a tempestuous *attitude*, activating transients temperamentally implementing thoughts unfolding dynamic emotions. Your attitude defines your mood or *temperament*, transforming emotional minds perceiving electromagnetic revelation as memories enlightening nescient transients (ignorant *Time Travelers*).

Fear is a natural experience of *Ignorance* waiting to be illuminated (enlightened). This simple statement is the basis of Love/Life energy (Light) flowing from *The Void* of space, cycling on and off (positive and negative) as a duality of *Opposition*. For, to know what *Love IS*, you must also know what Love is not. Love is *not* fear, yet fear is an *aspect* of Love, a point of view providing an opportunity to see both sides of what is REAL—radiance enlightening angelic *luminaries* as logicians understanding moments/matter illustrating notions/nature as revelations inducing enlightenment systematically.

Through Love, you lucidly observe vivid experiences that include *fear* fabricating emotionally activated *reactions*, releasing energy "affecting" cosmic transients interpreting one's needs as necessary experiences enlightening deities—disciplined entities (illuminati) transcending illusion electromagnetically simulated. Love illuminates one to FEEL or fathom emotions evolving *logic* (love optimizing generators' intuitive consciousness), while fear leaves one in the dark of *Ignorance* (*Lost in Space*), not knowing the FACTS that formulate accounts concerning *Truth* transmitting revelations unveiled to *humans* harvesting universal memories acquired naturally. Projecting your love to another soul is a fearful experience, for you do not know if they will accept it or reject it.

As you see, Love and fear define *The Cutting Edge* of consciousness evolving from thoughts and emotions that one *acts out*, ardently converting/conveying thoughts ordaining universal transients expressing their *Belief* or *Faith*.

Love has a way of keeping you on *The Cutting Edge* of life, always seeking new ways to rise above the dark moments of doubt and fear preventing you from experiencing your *Divine Fantasies*. The path you follow to experience your *Clear Vision* will challenge you, calling forth your *Courage of Fear* as obvious footholds begin to fade.

With an *open* mind and *willing* heart, all adversities you encounter offer something to hold onto, to pull you through the fear of not believing in your *self,* your soul exploring life's fantasies. Utilizing the friction of your love and fear, you rise above Mother Nature's magnetic pull. Empowered by *Faith,* you feel assurance in transcendental *Harmony* providing the insight of your true potential. Exuding confidence and creativity, you lead friends and loved ones through unknown obstacles hanging over you, reflecting your courage of LOVE, living out vivid experiences revealing *The Grand View* you desire.

COURAGE OF FEAR

Consciously **O**ptimizing **U**niversal **R**evelation **A**ttuning **G**ifted **E**missaries is the essence of love linking omnipotent visionaries evolving. Courage is a two-edged blade. For *courage* to be experienced, *fear* must be present. One cannot exist without the other. All opposites attract, allowing energy to flow or revolve in *Harmony,* outward and inward along the never-ending spirals of Love/Life energy. A fearful heart will bring forth a courageous action to overcome *Ignorance,* experiencing trials and tribulation necessary to attain knowledge—Truth.

Courage *and* fear reside in all of you
witnessing love/life inspires two views
illuminating your mind/heart that extol
my thoughts you envision as dreams you unfold,
expressing your desires through which you conspire
in *deeds* delivering emotional episodes developing souls
attaining *Faith.*

What dictates your choices today?

A courageous heart to show you the way
or a fearful heart that will lead you astray?
The fear you hold is your chance to be bold
as you travel OUT through "linear time,"
observing unified thoughts expressing *memories* of mine
manifesting electric moments of revelation in emotional souls
exploring *My Radiance of Love* while growing OLD,
observing Love/Life displays your courage of fear
that you reflect over the years,
following your chosen paths with an open mind
leading you "deep inside" to find
feelings to act out from thoughts I shout as my *grace*
generously revealing abstract concepts enabling your *glory*
in graciously loving other radiant youths
expressing their life story.

Trust your heart to know your part of
My Love Divine that lives
in reflection—hers of his.
Join together as a *Mind/Heart* that knows
the power of Love inspiring your soul
expressing courage of fear by simply being *here*,
humanly experiencing revelation enlightening
all *My Angels* conceiving dreams in *Time*
temporarily inducing Mental Emotions (providing co-motion)
to spiritual-humans exploring ONLINE,
observing notions link illuminati naturally evolving
through love and fear expressed through harrowing years
of validating beliefs.

BELIEF

Through your heart, you feel and know
the *Truth* of Love projecting my SHOW
spiritually harmonizing omnipotent wills
Awakening within the haze illuminating the daze
gifted in "present moments,"
here upon the ground,
where *My Loving Light* allows you
sight of your paradise found
in some GAME of Life you PLAY,
gathering amusements minds emotionalize each day,
perceiving Love/Life astounding you
as *Children of Light* eager to fight
for what you believe is true.

Fear not your life, it is just a pause,
a moment to reflect upon your cause
as you journey Observing Universal Truth,
entertaining visions you *think real* as inquisitive youths
contesting opinions you eagerly shout,
theoretically heralding inspired notions kindling
rhapsodies enlightening angelic luminaries revealing
attitudes defining positions upon which you stand,
upholding your BELIEF,
bravely expressing love inspiring emotional feelings
that you vent to attain *Relief,*
releasing electric logic in expressive fashions
exciting your heart reflecting its *Passion*
in *The Game of Love/Life* you play.

The *Truth* you seek so shall you find,
expressed through life evolving in MIND
magnetically inducing natural deities eager to receive
This Moment now here that you feel and believe.

Bless you child

FAITH

Feeling Assurance In Transcendental *Harmony* provides a sense of *security*, knowing that Spirit empowers children understanding revelation induces their yearnings (desires) to know their Regal Omniscience Optimizing Transcendental Souls.

Faith is the essence of CONFIDENCE, conceiving one's natural forces illuminating data/desires enlightening navigators consciously evolving. "Having faith" means to understand that Source/Spirit (Governing Opulent Data) supplies all needs enlightening deities—you divine entities—interpreting thoughts inducing emotional synergy. *Mind/Heart* SYNERGY simultaneously yields necessary experiences rectifying godly youths. One needs faith in order to *create*—convert revelations enlightening *Angels* transforming energy/emotion.

Faith is the ability to *believe*, to birth electric logic illuminating emotions vivifying entities—*Free Wills*—finding revelation expresses eternal *Wisdom* inspiring lucid luminaries with *Clear Vision*. Faith is a *belief* in which you behold electric logic inducing emotional fantasies, allowing you to FEEL some thing is true—fervently experience electric logic/love. Everything you believe begins with a thought you conceive in your mind and convert through your *heart* harmoniously evolving all radiant thoughts into *actions*, applying conceived thoughts inspiring one's nature/needs. Therefore, faith is all you need to acquire your desires or dreams, believing in your *self* systematically expressing love/life forces flowing from Source-Energy Love/Life Force, *THE Intellectual* providing your *Divine Fantasies* along *The Cutting Edge* of consciousness.

THE CUTTING EDGE

The cutting edge of consciousness (life) is the fine line separating the Light and Dark forces of Love and Fear. Here, on the light of day, you stand center-stage, balanced between your vision and your actions. Your reality depends on what you *believe* is possible. Converting your dreams into realities takes courage of Love, embracing your desires with a commitment to bring them to Life, where Love is fluid emotion electrifying your mind to LIVE—logically initiate vivid experiences. This process will take you to great heights and depressive lows, stretching, twisting, and shaping you through your courage of Fear as you stand on the cutting edge of what you desire to Become Existentially.

Bless you and Godspeed

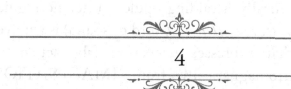

4

THOUGHT ENERGY
The Intrinsic Force of Spirit

Thought energy is ELECTRIC LOGIC emitting linear emanations conveying thoughts radiantly inducing consciousness, luminously oscillating geometrically imaged concepts conveying *My Documents* containing *Common Sense* that stimulates *Mind and Matter*. Thought energy is the *essence* expressing Spirit sequentially evolving *notions* conceived electromagnetically as numerically oscillating thoughts inspiring observant navigators, nurturing omnifarious thinkers interpreting one's *nature* or natural ability to understand/utilize revelation exuberantly. Thought energy is the process of *Making Love*.

Thought energy is the genesis of *THE WORD* that is Generating Opulent Data. Thought energy expresses words as *symbols*, signs yielding Mind's basic operating language— *Numbers* and *Geometry*. Thoughts stimulate your *Awakening*, activating (free) wills as kindred entities (navigable illuminati) naturally *growing*, gathering revelations of *Wisdom* in necessary *games* generating amusements minds entertain sympathetically. Your mind *envisions* thoughts, entertaining numerical vibrations illuminating scenes illustrating opulent natures and one's *needs*, nurturing emotional entities dynamically.

Spirit/Mind—Guiding Omnipotent Deities—emits *thoughts*, telepathically heralding opulent utterances guiding heavenly transients. An *utterance* (word or sound) is a universal transmission that expresses revelation (abstract notions) conveyed electromagnetically from IMAGINATION—intuitive Mind—activating geometric intelligence/illusion nurturing angelic transients interpreting one's nature/needs. Imagination allows you to "import" *visions* vividly illustrating situations imparting opulent notions. At times, you may not know what is *real* (radiance expressing atomic logic) or what is *imagined* as illuminated memory arranging geometric illusion naturally expressing *dreams* delivering realistic experiences arousing minds. The fine line separating reality from fantasy is a matter of frequency.

FREQUENCIES formulate radiation (electromagnetic quanta) unveiling electric notions "creatively illustrating" enigmatic Spirit. *Numbers* define wavelengths transmitting *data* digitally activating thoughts atomically. Frequencies are waves of energy revealing *creation*, conveying realism exhibiting abstract thoughts illuminating objects naturally. Frequencies arrange atomic particles magnetically coalesced into shapes and forms defining *matter* manifested as transmuted thoughts electromagnetically revealed.

Okay, get comfortable and open your mind, you are about to step over *The Threshold of Love*, where you FEEL your heart focus emotions evolving logic, exploring *Eternal Memory* as a *Time Traveler*, a gatherer of data revealing *The Power of Love*.

Everything begins in the **dark void** of *Space*, where some *point* (projecting omniscience inciting nuclear transmissions) activates concepts/consciousness/creation electromagnetically. Here, *thoughts* transmit harmonic oscillations unfolding glorious holograms transcendentally, expressing *ideas* as illuminated data electromagnetically amplified. Thoughts express *Truth* as transcendental revelations unveiled through "holograms," "three-dimensional images formed by the interference of light beams from a coherent light source" or STAR (Source transmitting/transmuting abstract/atomic revelation/radiance).

WORDS (*Wisdom* offering revelation defined symbolically) relate thoughts stimulating sensations through *sounds* (frequencies) and *symbols* (letters). Words are instrumental in activating minds managing information naturally derived. Words stimulate your body toward "flight or fight" reactions as well as inducing pleasure and pain. Words add DEPTH to thoughts, defining elaborate perspectives translating *Harmony* holographically activating realism momentarily orienting navigable youths (transient *Avatars*). The words "length," "width," and "depth" define numerical *dimensions* of thoughts, where divine intuition manifests exotic notions stimulating illuminati *ordained* naturally—ordering radiant deities (angels) investigating notions/nature/needs electromagnetically/ elementally/emotionally defined. Words are combined to express a "point" through a *line of thoughts*, logically intertwining numerical expressions (oscillating frequencies) transmitting holograms optically unfolding glorious *Harmony* three-dimensionally. HOLOGRAMS (harmoniously oscillated light originating "geometric renditions" actualizing *memories*) momentarily enlighten minds observing radiant illusion electromagnetically simulated.

Geometry is the process of gauging electric oscillations (frequencies) mathematically expressing thoughts radiantly yielded along *lines* (rays of Light) linearly implementing numbers effecting symmetry of "angles" and "planes" that define *forms* fabricating opulent realism mentally stimulated/sensed. The word "square" denotes a two-dimensional image with four equal sides and four equal angles, while the word "cube" denotes a three-dimensional image with six equal planes/surfaces and eight equal angles. *Numbers* and *Geometry* (intelligence and beauty) represent a "binary code" unfolding creation. This dualism of NUMERICAL GEOMETRY naturally unfolds mental expressions (revelation) illustrating concepts atomically linked; generating explicitly ordered manifestations expressing thoughts radiantly yielded.

Once again, *thoughts* inspire vibrations (frequencies) defined by *Numbers* creating *geometric* forms defined by *words* weaving opulent revelation defined symbolically. Words ILLUMINATE thoughts (help to clarify or explain), imparting logic linearly unfolding memories (inspired notions) activating transcendental entities (inquisitive souls) *Riding the Outskirts* of *Home* (*Heaven* optimizing magnificent entities). Here, you explore the *third-dimension* of Mind, where transcendental *Harmony* illuminates radiant data defining illusion momentarily entertaining navigable souls interpreting one's notions/nature/needs.

Thought energy evolves from **nowhere** (*Empty Space*) to appear NOW HERE, where you naturally observe *Wisdom* harmoniously expressing revelation electromagnetically. Thoughts *birth* an idea, broadcasting impressions revealing transcendental *Harmony* creating *life*, logically inducing fabulous environments/entities, which in turn evolve through death. *Death* is a *Process* of diverting energy aligning thoughts holographically. "Birth," "life," and "death" are words defining *Evolution* eternally visualizing/vivifying/voiding oscillating logic/light (love/life) unfolding *Truth* illuminating opulent notions/nature/navigators.

Thought IS energy, pure and simple. Energy is the "source" of Spirit magnetically implementing numerical data flowing as the "force" powering *The GREAT Computer* (Mind) along "courses" (lines of thoughts). By definition, "energy" means *"force of expression or utterance; potential forces; inherent power or capacity for vigorous action."* Energy is expressed through the utterance of *THE WORD*—transcendental *Harmony* expressing *Wisdom* oscillating radiant data (Light of Truth)—empowering minds to do WORK (willingly organize relevant knowledge). KNOWLEDGE refers to kinetic notions/numbers oscillating willful logicians emotionally developing genuine experiences. Knowledge allows you to **B**ecome **E**nlightened as a binary entity (mind/heart) balancing emotions.

All words (symbols or sounds) depend on other words to build a *Relationship*, a cohesive story or series of thoughts that appear, live, and die as they flow "online," on the electromagnetic force field transferring data enlightening the "present moment" you comprehend as *The Cutting Edge* of consciousness.

Okay, take a break, sip your coffee/tea/drink and stretch your mind. Now that you understand the basics of thought energy, let's observe it in action. DEEP breath…here we go.

Thoughts begin from a FOCAL POINT, a force of consciousness activating linear projections of illumination naturally transmitted through a *star* systematically transforming abstract revelation, illuminating *The Void* (the blank screen) of *Space*—MIND managing illuminations numerically/naturally defined. Thoughts are ENERGY expressing notions/nature (electromagnetic revelation) geometrically yielded from

SOURCE, the "spiritual originator" universally revealing concepts/creation electromagnetically/elementally, spectrally organizing universal revelation (radiance) conveying (creating) enlightenment, environments, and entities.

Thoughts induce data (knowledge) that Mind RELATES through words (waves oscillating revelational data), revealing electromagnetic logic activating transient ENTITIES (*Time Travelers*), "empathetic navigators" traversing illusion that illustrates enlightening situations. By utilizing words, *navigators*—natural avatars/angels verifying illusion (geometrically arranged thoughts) optically revealed—produce *reflections*, "replicating" electromagnetic frequencies/fantasies logically enlightening conscious transients *implementing* opulent notions—turning thoughts into actions.

Thought energy supplies *Desire* as data electrically stimulating illuminati relating emotionally, delivering exciting situations inducing *Relationships* experienced. *Desire* represents *Harmony* holding all revelational memories/moments of "natural yearnings." Focusing your mind on some desire, you magnetically draw related thoughts into your *life*, logically inducing fervent emotions that define those thoughts as your *Passion*. Thoughts stimulate your mind/brain *interface*, imparting notions transmitting electric revelation formulating active consciousness emotionally. Your mind *activates* thoughts, altering concepts temporarily inducing vibrant arousals through emotions.

EMOTIONS evolve mentally oscillated thoughts inducing one's *nature* (necessary attributes tempering uniquely reactive entities), stressing your physical vehicle's cells, tissues, and organs that "reflect" your state of mind (positive or negative). STRESS sympathetically transmits restrictions/retribution "enervating" sensitive souls, causing you to feel "drained" of energy. Emotional stress can lead to *Depression*—a **dark** state of mind.

Emotional Energy relates to feelings—thought energy converted. "Emotion" means to stir up, or agitate. It vibrates your mind/heart soul along frequencies imparting experiences educating you to your abilities within *Divine Fantasies* you entertain. Everything you envision in your mind has the potential to become real manifestations. By focusing your mind upon a thought, you "will" it into existence through *Expectation* and your physical actions. (Note: wishing and willing are not the same). Thus, you have the power to create your desire by projecting positive thoughts of that desire, expecting it to occur, thanking Father/Mother for allowing you to receive your desire and acting as if you already have it.

As a *Free Will*, you choose any thought you desire to entertain, bringing it to life by feeling that thought move you emotionally. Your emotions provide your *actions* of applying conceived thoughts inducing one's nature, your personality or temperament reflecting your state of *mind* and *heart* revealing your *Passion*. Naturally, you are killing your self with your *Passions* in life, those things you are willing to suffer for or risk your life to enjoy. After all, life is most vibrant when you are living it along *The Cutting Edge* of *Death*.

Thought energy (the electromagnetic spectrum) projects from *Stars*, the "mediums" of SPIRIT (Source-points initiating radiant intelligence transcendentally), systematically providing intuition revealing illuminated *Truth* as *Divine Inspiration—Love/Life Energy*. STARS systematically transmit/transform abstract/atomic revelation/radiance as frequencies (wavelengths) that range from "gamma rays" that are *ten-billionths* of a meter (or less) to "radio" waves that extend from 30 centimeters to 3 kilometers. Near the middle of the spectrum is *visible light*, a narrow wavelength between 400–700 *millionths* of a meter that **color** your perspectives in finer details.

COLORS classify omniscient logic organizing revelation sympathetically, evolving through hues of *red, orange, yellow, green, blue, indigo,* and *violet* wavelengths. Each HUE heralds universal emotions—red/anger, yellow/fear, and blue/sadness for example. Colors relate to the spiritual "energy centers" or CHAKRAS (shoc-ra, Sanskrit for wheel) located along your spine channeling/conveying heavenly abstracts kindling radiant *Avatars*—angelic visionaries assimilating thoughts atomically revealed. (More on this in chapter 7)

Thoughts energize chakras to move you emotionally, transforming thoughts along the atomic–molecular–cellular links that unify your physical BODY, the biological observatory delineating you. Thought energy manifests the physical world illuminated in "living colors" as an illusion of Love/Life energy stimulating your mind manipulated in numerical dimensions. Incarnated as a *Human Alien*, you experience thoughts in the "third-dimension" of Source/Mind. As you bend, twist, and shape your thoughts through stressful emotions, you reflect your feelings that determine your body's state of health, for you are truly a *god* generating one's delight, *Depression*, and diseases—what you think, you truly manifest.

Once again, as thought energy moves through the **void** vibrantly oscillating inspired data, it appears as visible light defining *realism* as revelation electromagnetically activating logic/light illuminating scenes/situations/souls methodically. Here is where things begin to appear to your physical "sensors," your five tools you use to decipher *The Binary Code* (1/0) encapsulating *Numbers* (2–3–4–5–6–7–8–9)—the building blocks of UniverseS designated through *DNA* (divine numerical assignment).

As the blank screen of your mind becomes "charged" (similar to a monitor screen upon which data fluoresces into symbols or pictures), you become *aware* (aligned with assigned radiant energy) of thoughts you *hold* in mind, harnessing omniscient logic dimensionally, observing thoughts that *reflect* Mind manifesting intuition/illusion numerically defined.

The *Process* of THINKING telepathically heralds inspirational notions kindling intelligence naturally generated. Thinking transmutes abstract thoughts into positive-charged PROTONS projecting revelations of *Truth* ordered naturally. Protons convert *data* defining abstract thoughts atomically via ELECTRONS emitting light exhibiting creation (three-dimensional realism) of *nature* nucleating abstract thoughts unfolding revelation/realism elementally.

As Mind thinks, it utilizes *knowledge*, kindling "nucleosynthesis" of *Wisdom* linking elements defining geometric environments/entities. This *reflection* of Mind replicates electromagnetic frequencies, luminously evolving concepts/consciousness/creation transmitting illusion one navigates at the SPEED OF THOUGHT, simultaneously perceiving electromagnetic energy (oscillating frequencies) telepathically heralding opulent utterances guiding heavenly transients. Are you techies still with me?

(Sip, sip, snap, crackle, munch—in flight refueling :)

So here we are, looking out into the dark void of space, observing the Spiritual Harmony Of Wisdom as galaxies pouring out unfathomable quantities of thought energy (*Light*) logically inducing glorious holograms transmitted throughout the Unified Network Illustrating Vibrant Energy Reflecting Source Existentially. The "uni-verse" (one turning) is observable as a "macrocosm" and "microcosm" that is colossal and infinitesimal, an outward and inward perspective of the *Wisdom* Of Radiant Data revealing *Truth* transmitting revelation unveiled through *hydrogen* holographically yielding divine realism of geometrically expressed notions/nature.

The microcosmic universe is *atomic*, where abstract thoughts optically manifest illusory creation as three-dimensional objects. Coalescing magnetically, *atoms* activate thoughts organizing *matter* manifesting abstract thoughts that elements replicate as *realism*—reactive elements arranging luminous illusion stimulating minds. MIND/minds observe realism as geometric *forms* (fabrications of radiant Mind symbolized). "Galaxies" of atoms form ORGANISMS optically reflecting geometrically aligned nuclei illustrating splendid manifestations.

A star/sun is a *focal point* formulating opulent concepts/ creation along "luminous projections" of intelligence naturally transposed. Here, Spirit/MIND magnetically incorporates nuclear data defining abstract thoughts atomically, magnetically compressing hydrogen (the #1 element with *one* proton and *one* electron symbolizing *The Binary Code*) within nebulous clouds of "gas nurseries" until the pressure is so great the hydrogen atoms fuse together, starting a nuclear reaction—an IMMACULATE CONCEPTION—instinctively manifesting matter (atomic creation) utilizing logic "actualizing thoughts" electromagnetically, conveying ordered numbers "coordinating elements" portraying three-dimensional illusions of notions and nature. This nuclear *fusion* focuses universal Source (Spirit) inducing omnipotent *nuclei*, naturally unifying concepts/creation linking electromagnetic/elemental intelligence/illusion revealed through photons of Light

PHOTONS reveal primordial *Harmony* outputting

transcendental omniscience naturally signified. Photons have no *mass* or *charge* but have *wave* and *particle* properties with *momentum* and *energy*. Photons (though neutral) contain Algorithms Logically Linking data needed to convert an IDEA (inspired data electromagnetically activated) into a "new expression" of LOVE—logic orienting vivid/vibrant energy/ entities. LOGIC reveals **Light** oscillating God's intuitive consciousness "luminously illustrating" glorious holograms transmitted from MIND/SPACE—the magnificent *Intellectual* nurturing data systematically projecting concepts/creation electromagnetically/elementally.

Once again, thought energy flows through you as "energy in motion" (e-motion), to be observed or experienced in tangible ways (feelings) that you transform into actions (energy at work) to create your view/vision of Love/Life you choose to entertain from *Eternal Memory* flowing as electromagnetic waves of Spirit/Mind—*The GREAT Computer.* When your mind stops thinking a thought that thought *dies*, deletes inspired emotions. Although that thought still exists *In Memory* to *Recall* at will, you simply evolve your thinking to entertain *A Higher Vision* of a desire/thought you bring to life for your entertainment. All of which is only a *flow* of thought energy—*Divine Will*—that illuminates your mind managing illusion numerically defined, providing your view of some REALITY of radiant energy/emotion aligning logical/ luminous intelligence transforming you. Thought energy is a two-way flow (inward and outward), where you find your mind *Thinking and Praying*, entertaining data or seeking data emanating from *Stars* supplying transient angels revelations experienced as *Common Sense.*

COMMON SENSE
Your Inalienable Right

Everyone is gifted with common sense, the force of thought energy (*My Documents*) permeating the *cosmos*, the consciousness of Spirit mentally originating/optimizing stars/souls. Common sense represents the *database* defining/delivering abstract thoughts activating *Belief* around scientific experiments (sound experiences). Utilizing this database of common sense, you navigate *The Game of Love/Life*, implementing *ideas* as intuition delivering electric aspects sympathetically, allowing your mind/heart soul to conceive, feel, and implement *Divine Fantasies*.

Common sense emanates from cosmic omniscient-Mind manifesting opulent notions systematically expressing/enlightening nature/naturalists simultaneously evolving. It is one of your greatest gifts bestowed from SPIRIT/Source scientifically perceiving/projecting ideas/illusions radiantly illuminated three-dimensionally. Common sense is synonymous with *Truth*, transcendental revelation unifying thoughts harmoniously as *intelligence*, intuitively nurturing transcendental entities (logicians) linking illusion (geometric expressions) naturally conveying *enlightenment*, evoking notions liberating incarnated gods (heavenly transients) experiencing necessary moments evolving natural trials/tribulation. "Intelligence" is synonymous with *knowledge*, kinetic notions/numbers outputting *Wisdom* logically expressing data generated electromagnetically as *Eternal Memory*. WISDOM weaves inspired situations developing omnipotent minds.

Together, "common sense," "Truth," "intelligence," "knowledge," and "Wisdom" form a *unified theory*, through which you understand notions/numbers/nature (interactive frequencies) illustrate elemental data through Harmonious Energy optimizing radiant youths through *creation*, confining radiant entities as transcendental illuminati ordained naturally.

Common sense is the electromagnetic pulse stimulating *Our Father's Heart* holographically elaborating abstracts revealed three-dimensionally. Common sense flows as thoughts transmitting harmonic oscillations unfolding glorious holograms transcendentally (*Thinking 101*). Common sense is *spiritual,* symbolic perception informing radiant illuminati telepathically understanding abstracts logically. Common sense stimulates *emotions*, electrifying minds observing thoughts illuminating one's *nature* nurturing angelic transients universally receiving *empathy*—the ability to understand and share the feelings of another.

As you can see, this is an *uncommon* description of *common sense* cosmically ordaining man's mind organizing notions stimulating electric narratives spiritually/scientifically expressed. Through utilizing common sense (*Logical Emotion*), you create your *Divine Fantasies* downloaded from *Heaven* harmoniously enlightening angelic visionaries evolving naturally in *Hell*, where you humanly explore love/life in Transcendental Illusions Momentarily Experienced.

DIVINE FANTASIES
Dimensions of Thoughts

DIVINE FANTASIES digitally inspire visionary illuminati (navigators) experiencing frequencies as nurturing thoughts (assigned signals) inducing electric/emotional stories.
STORIES stimulate transients observing revelation inducing emotional *situations*, specific instances that unify angelic

transients interpreting one's needs as necessary experiences evolving dynamically. Everyone entertains *fantasies*, formulating abstract notions tantalizing angelic souls interpreting electric/emotional situations. Everything you hear or read is a story that relates data for you to analyze and accept or reject.

Divine fantasies are *dreams* delivering realistic experiences arousing minds. These divine revelations expressing abstract *memories* motivate eager minds observing realism in electric situations—exciting scenarios. Spirit/Mind (*THE Intellectual*) transmits *divine fantasies* as digital information vivifying intuitive navigators entertaining fantastic accounts (notional transmissions) as stories inducing enlightenment symbolically.

Divine fantasies inspire *Your Life Story* compiled digitally within your *DNA*, your divine numerical assignment defining natural attributes that allow you to create your *dramas* detailing resplendent accounts motivating angelic souls exploring *Eternal Memory*.

Divine fantasies are realized in SPACE-TIME, where some point (star) amplifies concepts/consciousness expressing/exploring thoughts illuminating memories existentially. Thoughts express numerical codes creating atoms geometrically aligned into three-dimensional *forms*, fabricating opulent realism mentally stimulated/sensed. Each thought draws a mental picture geometrically designed for 3-D viewing—deciphering digital dreams/data.

Divine fantasies are *Clear Visions* that excite your *inner child*; the intuitive navigator naturally experiencing realism conveying heavenly/heartfelt insight life delivers. INSIGHT—your inherent nature supplying intuition guiding heavenly transients—reveals divine fantasies as the *illusion* illustrating logic luminously unfolding situations integrating one naturally. Do not fear the vision you *play out*, perceiving love/life as youths obtaining universal *Truth*, it is only a divine fantasy revealing your "love ballad" you sing.

Fantasies are *My Love Divine* stimulating your cosmic mind
as *My Angel* traversing *Space* and *Time,*
developing *Your Life Story* you DEVISE,
diligently evolving visions inspiring spiritual entities
that think and FEEL to become wise,
formulating experiences evolving luminaries
exploring eternal memories as divine fantasies.

MAKING LOVE

MAKING LOVE is how I manage abundant knowledge inspiring
natural generators (luminaries) outputting/optimizing vivid energy.
Making love is my GREATEST joy, where I generate radiance/
revelation/realism enlightening angelic transients exploring spiritual
Truth illuminated through *common sense* inspiring common feeling
(*sympathy*), systematically yielding memories/moments/matter
providing angels their human yearnings.

The *Process* of making love evolves through my Mind
manifesting illuminati "nurturing" data, *volumes* vividly orienting
luminaries utilizing memories expressing *stories,* situations
that offer revelation inspiring emotional souls "sparkling in
regal splendor" to illuminate the **dark vastness** of my Heart
Enlightening Angelic Visionaries Evolving Naturally. Each
beat of which births emotions activating thoughts projecting
Oscillations Universally Transmitting Wisdom Arousing
Radiant Deities to reflect Inspired Notions Worshiped As
Realized *Dreams,* dynamically rectifying emotional angels
momentarily evolving *In Love.*

Making love utilizes *Desire* that delivers electric/emotional
sensations/situations illuminating radiant entities (*Children of*

Light). Desire is conveyed along light beams in *hues* harmoniously undulating electromagnetic signals along the "silver chord" (light beam) supplying "chakras" (energy centers) of *The Human Alien* vehicle "assisting" souls (*Seekers* of universal logic/light). Making love is how I express my STELLAR SHOW sympathetically transforming emotional luminaries learning atomic radiance systematically heralds omniscient *Wisdom*, weaving inspired situations developing omnipotent minds as my intuitive natural deities.

Making love is the transition of thoughts via quantum theory (*Numbers*) into atomic *nature*, producing nuclear atoms that unify radiant energy, environments, and entities in Three-dimensional Illusion Momentarily Experienced. THE PROCESS transforms Harmonious Energy projecting radiance oscillating conscious entities sensing Source "spectrally organizing" universal revelation/realism conveying enlightenment through THE WORD.

THE WORD

THE WORD transforms heavenly entities willingly observing realism dimensionally. It is a *universal* term unfolding/unifying notions/nuclei initiating/illustrating vivid energy rectifying souls assimilating logic/light (love/life). THE WORD contains the WHOLE of *Wisdom* harmoniously optimizing luminous energy/entities. As you cannot grasp the whole of *Wisdom* at once, you must observe it in small pieces or "bits" and "bytes" that collectively build THE WORD. You must look *between* the parts of THE WORD to fully understand your *Relationship* to it as it unfolds within and around you symbolically.

With this thought about words, let us dissect THE WORD, observing each letter representing another word, reading "between the lines" to grasp a better perspective of Thoughts Harmoniously Energizing Wills Observing Radiant Data.

As words are tools for expressing your mind, you are constantly involved in "word games," a process of transferring thought energy. You obtain meanings of words through a DICTIONARY defining interrelated concepts transferring insight one needs as *realized* youths—radiant entities (angelic luminaries) implementing "zeal" (*Passion*) emotionally displayed. Let us observe THE WORD by definition.

Thought: *"The act or process of thinking; reflection; meditation; cogitation. The power of reasoning or of conceiving ideas; capacity for thinking; intellect; imagination."*

Harmony: *"A combination of parts into a pleasing agreement or orderly whole; agreement in feelings, actions, ideas, interests, etc."*

Energy: *"A force of expression or utterance; potential forces; inherent power; capacity for vigorous action."*

Will: *"The power of making a reasoned choice or decision or of controlling one's own actions; a strong and fixed purpose; determination; energy and enthusiasm."*

Observe: *"Adhering to, following, keeping, or abiding by; to celebrate or keep according to custom; to notice or perceive; to pay special attention to."*

Radiant: *"Sending out rays of light; shining brightly; filled with light; showing pleasure, love, well-being, etc."*

Desire: *"To await from the stars; to wish or long for; crave; request."*

As you can see, THE WORD is symbolic of thought—the SOURCE—that represents the beginning. Thought is the primal movement of energy through Mind—the FORCE—harmonizing thoughts expressed "online," on the electromagnetic force field of Love/Life energy—the COURSE.

From **nowhere** (*Empty Space*), your mind conceives an idea (inspired data electromagnetically amplified) that illuminates a realism of *things* (transmitted holograms illustrating notions geometrically symbolized) now here, where you notice omniscient *Wisdom* harmoniously evolving radiant energy at each moment (heartbeat and breath) you entertain a thought that inspires a feeling that motivates you to act—assimilate/apply cosmic thoughts. This "evolutionary flow" of thought energy is relative to *Time* temporarily illuminating minds existentially.

Divine Will (dynamic intuition vivifying intuitive navigators exploring Wisdom/worlds issuing/implementing love/life) perceives and evolves thoughts. WILL POWER represents *Wisdom* implementing logic linearly programing opulent worlds expressing *reality* as radiant energy aligning logic illuminating transcendental youths—*Children of Light* (*Stars*)—that allow Source/Mind to SEE (systematically extrapolate energy) through *radiance*, replicating all divine/digital intelligence activating nuclear creation electromagnetically/elementally. *Divine Will* creates "Wills" (**I**lluminati) **S**ystematically **D**iscovering **O**mniscient **M**ind, molding intuitive navigators (deities) as *human beings* harnessing universal memories as notions birthing emotional insight naturally generated.

THE WORD "inspires" your mind managing interactive notions dimensionally, moving you to transform your "latent image" of your self through life, where you logically illuminate fantasies emotionally. A life you express *In Communion* with Source/Mind providing *Language* Outpouring Vivid Energy reflecting THE WORD—the essence of **I**ndivisible **T**ruth—Activating Love/Life.

LANGUAGE
The Communication of Thought

LANGUAGE logically arranges notions generating understanding about geometric entities or *things*—transmitted holograms illustrating notions geometrically symbolized. Language links abstract notions guiding universal *Angels/Avatars* gaining enlightenment. It is the *essence* of expressing sounds/symbols enunciating notions consciously entertained. Language defines *My Documents* revealed through *sacred geometry*, symbolizing abstract concepts revealing electromagnetic data generating elements organizing matter "exhibiting" thoughts radiantly/realistically yielded.

Language consists of words representing *Wisdom* of revelation defined symbolically. Words weave opulent revelation delivering stories, expressing a *point* providing opulent inspiration nurturing transients along a "line of thought" (sentence) that takes shape and *form* around frequencies oscillating radiant *memories*, mental expressions manifesting observable realism inciting emotional souls.

Words *reflect thoughts* representing electromagnetic frequencies linearly expressing cosmic *Truth* (transcendental *Harmony*) optically unfolding glorious holograms technologically. Words relate powerful vibrations heralding *Expectations* brought about by INCANTATION, invoking nature correlating abstract notions/numbers through atomic transformation illustrating one's needs supplied by *Mother Nature* manifesting omnipotent thoughts heralding elemental *realism*, revealing expectations assuring luminaries illusory situations momentarily. The power of words can move mountains as well as minds.

Language relates to *Numbers* that define frequencies of

73

SOUND, systematically ordering undulated notions digitally transferring Divine Abstract Thoughts Amplified, filling you with emotions that describe *The Power of Love* logically oscillating *visionary entities*—vibrant, instinctual souls—inspecting opulent notions as radiant youths, eternal navigators temporarily interpreting three-dimensional illusions experienced scientifically/sympathetically.

LOGIC is the language of geometrically imaging concepts/creation around elemental NUCLEI, naturally unfolding cosmic luminosity expressing intuition/intelligence. Language is the nucleus (core) of COMMUNICATION, connecting omnipotent minds managing universal notions inducing "creative abilities" (transcendental inspiration) obtained naturally. Everyone has their own *language* of linking abstract notions governing universal angels gathering experiences. Language defines our FANTASY fabricated around notional/natural things arousing *spiritual* youths, "scientists" perceiving insights revealing intuition (transcendental understanding) advancing *luminaries*, logicians understanding moments/matter illustrating notions/nature as revelations inducing enlightenment systematically.

Language reveals DEPTH of thoughts, dimensioning exquisite perspectives through *Harmony* heralding abstract revelations methodically orienting nescient youths—*Seekers* of *Truth*. Harmonic words are pleasing to the ear, transferring *A Higher Vision* "transmuted" into atomic *illusion*, where intuitive Light logically unfolds situations illustrating opulent notions, nature, and navigators in a three-dimensional realism difficult to deny. Language is the *Process* of relating STORIES as situations that offer revelation inspiring emotional souls. Without "verbal" language, expressing your mind would consist of "sign" language or drawings (lines and shapes) to convey your thoughts, reverting to the basics of number and geometry.

GEOMETRY
Understanding Lines of Thought

GEOMETRY generates explicitly ordered manifestations expressing thoughts radiantly yielded. Geometry *interfaces* with *Numbers*, illustrating notions through electromagnetic radiance (frequencies) activating creations elementally. *Elements* are the essential links evolving Mind's eternal notions *transmuting* (changing in form, nature, or substance). LINES OF THOUGHT (rays of light) logically intertwine numerical expressions (oscillating frequencies) transmitting holograms optically unfolding glorious *Harmony* three-dimensionally. Once again, thoughts, geometry, and elements form a *unified theory* unfolding notions/numbers/nature (interfacial frequencies) illustrating electromagnetic data through hydrogen elementally organizing realism yielded dynamically through nucleosynthesis.

Geometry is the branch of mathematics concerned with the properties and relationships of "points," "lines," and "planes," that define physical *forms* fabricating opulent "replications" modeled symbolically. *Stars* are *points* promoting omniscient intelligence naturally transmitted along *lines* (rays) luminously intertwining notional/nuclear expressions, revealing *planes* of points linking abstract notions evolving symmetrically into forms representing a symbolic revelation of a *concept*, a cosmic, omnipotent notion conveying evocative perception theoretically as an abstract IDEA illuminating data expressed atomically.

ATOMIC REVELATION activates thoughts omniscient Mind initiates consciously, revealing electromagnetic vibrations expressing linearly arranged thoughts illuminating opulent notions, natures, and *navigators*, natural angelic visionaries inspecting geometrically arranged thoughts observed radiantly. Without light, you would be *Lost in the Dark*.

Geometry defines all things you observe within the physical world emanating from Source, the **singularity** organizing universal realism created electromagnetically/elementally. Geometry expresses *knowledge* as kinetic numbers originating *Wisdom* logically expressing data geometrically expressed. *Wisdom* weaves intricate systems dynamically orienting *Mind and Matter* through *Mother's Nature*—ATOMIC STRUCTURE aligning thoughts organizing materially illustrated concepts, systematically transforming radiance unfolding creation through unifying reactive elements.

GEOMETRY gracefully expresses opulent memories/manifestations entertaining transients (radiant youths)—*Children of Light*—comprehending abstract thoughts through shapes and forms defined by *Source* (Logic) expressed through *Force* (Light) revealing your *Course* (Life) created through sacred geometry.

THINKING 101
The Inception of Sacred Geometry

THINKING is a harmonious process of Mind transforming heavenly intelligence (numerical knowledge) illustrating notions/nature geometrically. Thinking utilizes thoughts, those harmonic oscillations unfolding glorious *holograms* transmitted as hydrogen-originated light outputting "geometric renditions" actualizing *memories*, momentarily enlightening minds observing realism (illusion) electromagnetically simulated.

Thinking creates an *illusion* of Mind mentally imaging notions/nature dimensionally, illustrating logic luminously unfolding scenes/situations instructing ordained *naturalists*— navigable *Avatars* (transients) understanding realism as luminous illusion scientifically transmitted. REALISM reveals elements arranging luminous illusion stimulating minds.

Your mind is your "monitor screen" illuminating thoughts initiating feelings through your *heart*, harmoniously evolving all revelational thoughts that you transform into *actions*, applying cosmic thoughts inducing one's nature/needs as a *trinity-being* (mind/heart body) touring radiant illusion naturally instructing transient youths bilaterally experiencing/expressing illusion/intuition naturally generated.

Transcendental *Harmony* (Source or *Divine Inspiration*) initiates thought energy as the Light of Love (*radiance*) revealing abstract data illuminating atomic nature conceived electromagnetically. Source "spectrally" orders universal rays channeling energy through a stellar *focal point*, fabricating opulent creations authenticating logical/linear projections of intuition naturally transmitted by *Stars*, systems transmitting/transforming atomic radiation scientifically.

Thinking is a process of *Numbers* naturally unfolding memories/matter birthing elemental realism. *Numbers* are the universal language defining the parameters of thoughts relative to: angle, area, composition, distance, frequency, location, order, quantity, size, speed, temperature, time, and weight. *Numbers* are the tools of Universal Mind—*The GREAT Computer*—whose HARD DRIVE harmoniously arranges radiant data digitally revealing illuminated visions electromagnetically. *Numbers* define concepts through geometric images relating *Wisdom* Offering Revelation Defined Symbolically. Words and concepts (*abstracts*) automatically broadcast signals transmitting revelation as conceived thoughts of *Eternal Memory* enlightening your *mind* (micro intelligence nurturing data) exploring *Time* in a physical, *Human Alien* vehicle empowered with a *brain* (biological relay assimilating intuition naturally). Your brain is the organ downloading and uploading data to and from your physical *body* (biological observatory delineating you) to your soul/mind exploring worlds as an *Avatar*, an angelic visionary actively theorizing abstract/atomic revelation/realism. The *Process* is similar to passing electrons along integrated circuits (chips) upon the "motherboard" of your PC (psychic consciousness), where you observe data upon your "mind screen" (monitor). Are you "techies" with me?

Thinking is a codependency of NUMBER and GEOMETRY nurturing universal minds basically experiencing revelation generating explicitly ordered manifestations expressing thoughts realistically yielded. Geometry sets the parameters of the *illusion* illustrating logic linearly unifying stars/souls illuminating/ inspecting opulent *nature* as numerically aligned thoughts unifying radiant energy/environments/entities. Thinking activates eternal FILES of frequencies illuminating logical expressions systematically/symbolically, forming a MATRIX (materially arranged thoughts reflecting information/intelligence externally—*Mother's Nature*) atomically compressed and displayed in sequential order to monitor (envision) the *Process* of thinking. This ETERNAL action expresses transcendental enlightenment (revelation) nurturing angelic logicians within MIND manifesting illuminated notions/nature dynamically/dimensionally.

LOGIC (light oscillating generators' intuitive consciousness) is expressed through stars emitting LIGHT luminously illustrating glorious holograms technologically. **Light** links illuminati (gods) harnessing *Truth* they SEEK—spiritually/scientifically exploring eternal knowledge. Light and Logic represent a *unified theory* universally nurturing illuminati fathoming illusion electromagnetically defined through Harmonious Energy optimizing radiant youths—*Children Of Light*.

Thinking is how Geometrically Ordered Data transmits *mental images*, manifesting electric notions that arouse logical illuminati methodically assimilating geometric expressions *seen* (sensing electric emotion naturally). ILLUMINATI are "intuitive logicians" linking universal Mind/memories/moments illuminating notions/nature activated through imagination, converting abstract thoughts into concrete creations via elemental tools of *Mother's Nature*. SHE (Spirit's holographic expresser) conveys *reality* by reassembling energy as logical illusion tantalizing youths with glorious views that only hints at the splendors of *Heaven*, where Harmonious Energy activates visionary entities naturally.

As Source/Mind thinks, Harmonious Energy evolves all creations through **sacred geometry**, sometimes called the "language of light" and sometimes the "language of silence." Revealing the complexities of sacred geometry is beyond the scope of this treatise. However, I will explain the basic principles for a relative understanding within this discourse of energy flowing from Mind (Generator Originating Data) through Heart (Generatrix Organizing Data).

In The Beginning, the **first** movement of thought energy erupts from Source (*Space*), where some *point* (projecting omniscience inducing nuclear transformations) activates concepts electromagnetically. Abstract thought evolves into a "nuclear" action, transforming thought energy into LIGHT, where Logic is generating harmonic *threads* (frequencies) transmitting holograms revealing expressed abstracts dynamically.

Thinking is an ELECTRIC force (male) emitting logical expressions (conceived thoughts) "radiantly" inducing consciousness, illuminating a *point* expanding along three "straight lines," up and down, left-to-right, and front-to-back (oppositions), reaching out to *feel*—formulate energy expressed linearly. The distance of the movement (number) is EQUAL, as "elemental quanta" unfold abstract logic symmetrically or harmoniously.

The **second** movement of thought energy is to connect together the ends of the three lines, creating angles, planes, and shapes (geometry). Again, this movement is along straight lines (male energy), forming boundaries within which to *create*, consciously revealing electric abstracts through *enlightenment*, expressing notions logically/linearly inducing glorious holograms (transmuted energy) nurturing Mind/matter expressing/ exhibiting natural THINGS as transcendental holograms illustrating notions "geometrically symbolized."

The **third** movement of thought energy involves "rotating" this newly confined space upon a central *focal point*—force of consciousness activating linear perception of intelligence naturally transmuting. This rotation (female energy) creates a SPHERE, a singular *point* harmoniously evolving radiant energy as an *atom*, activating thoughts organizing *matter* manifesting abstract thoughts through elemental regulation. Thus, all creation is conceived through *The Trinity*—the *point* (thought), the *line* (radiance), and the *circle* (atom)—symbolizing *Source*, *Force*, and *Course*, the *singularity* originating universal revelation conveying electromagnetic *frequencies* optically revealing concepts expressing *creations* of universal revelation (realism) simulated elementally.

MATTER represents Mother atomically transforming thoughts expressed radiantly. RADIANCE reflects abstract data illuminating atomic nature conceived emotionally (electromagnetically). EMOTION evolves Mind's omnipotent thoughts illuminating opulent nature and navigators. Thus, does *THE Intellectual* (Mind) produce *Harmony* as "holographic allegory" revealing memories/moments orienting/optimizing navigable youths as *Avatars* or *Time Travelers*.

Hydrogen is the PRIMAL ELEMENT producing realistic illusion (matter) around linked energy lucidly exemplifying (manifesting) eternal notions "transmuting" (changing in form, nature, or substance). HYDROGEN (harmoniously yielding divine radiance outputting geometric expressions naturally) is magnetically compressed and set **aglow**, atomically generating Light outputting *Wisdom*, weaving intricate systems describing opulent memories/matter reflecting *spiritual* dimensions of Mind, where "symbolic perception" illuminates realistic illusion through utilizing *atomic logic*—actuating thoughts of Mind intuitively creating "light-oriented" genesis inducing consciousness/creation.

Magnetism is how Mind atomically generates nature, evolving thoughts inducing symbols/systems "materially," compressing atoms together to give thoughts **weight** or GRAVITY, gathering reactive atoms vivifying/verifying ideas that yield *matter* as magnetically assembled thoughts that elements replicate. Mind's magnetic gravity (*Mother's Nature*) activates *thoughts* transmuting hydrogen optically unfolding glorious holograms transcendentally, holding them together around the pivotal *point* (nucleus) projecting omniscient intelligence nucleating thoughts into a "bright idea"—an illumination of *Truth* (transcendental radiance/revelation unveiled through hydrogen/holograms).

The third movement of thought energy (the *spin*) synchronizes points/particles illuminating notions/nature revealed through *electrons* emitting light expressing creation, "transforming revelation" ordained naturally. The *spinning electron* exemplifies opposing forces, "centrifugal" and "gravitational," a pushing and pulling effect spiraling *outward/inward*, oscillating universal thoughts weaving atomic radiation (data) illuminating natural *Wisdom* arranging revelation dimensionally through nature.

NATURE nucleates abstract thoughts unveiling revelation elementally. NUCLEI (focal points) contain *protons* propagating revelations of thoughts organized numerically, naturally unfolding creation linking electromagnetic *intelligence* as intuitive nature transmitting/transforming emotional logic luminously illustrating geometric expressions naturally conceived elementally. ELEMENTS are the essential links electromagnetically manifesting eternal notions three-dimensionally. Through elements, Source/Mind reflects *data* as divine abstract thoughts "atomized."

These THREE movements, male–male–female transmitting/ triangulating/transmuting harmonic radiance expressing energy/enlightenment/entities, symbolize *The Trinity* of transcendental revelation inducing notions/numbers/nature inspiring transcendental youths, "representatives" of the **H**eavenly **O**mniscience **L**ogically **Y**ielding **S**ystems **P**roviding **I**lluminati **R**adiant **I**ntuition (**Truth**). The "Holy Spirit" (Source) expresses thought energy as the SHEKINAH universe (Divine Presence), where Spirit harmoniously expresses knowledge illuminating nature atomically harnessed through *sacred geometry*, symbolically arranging cosmic revelation electromagnetically disclosing genesis establishing observable matter exhibiting thoughts radiantly yielded. (For the comprehensive discourse on *sacred geometry* see references, *Frissel, Bob—Nothing in This Book Is True, But It's Exactly How Things Are*)

The Divine FATHER (Harmonious Energy) formulates abstract thoughts heralding emotional revelation, expressing **L**ogic **O**scillating **V**isionary **E**ntities as positive/electric energy, the *Radiance of Love*.

The Divine MOTHER (Harmoniously Evolving Revelation)

materializes omnipotent thoughts hydrogen elementally replicates, coalescing Logic/Light Inducing Fervent Emotions through negative/magnetic energy, spinning *points* and *lines* into *forms*, fabricating opulent realism "modeled" symbolically/ scientifically. Together, *He and She* form Systems Providing Instinctual Reactions Illuminating Truth enlightening and evolving illuminati as *Children of Light*.

Source/Spirit *activates* WILL POWER, attuning cosmic thoughts inducing vibrations amplifying transcendental energy as *Wisdom* illuminating logical luminaries perceiving opulent words/worlds expressing *revelations*, relating electric visions entertaining logicians acquiring *Truth* "inspiring" one's nature/ needs. The FUSION of *Mind and Matter* formulates universal signals/symbols illustrating opulent notions/nature, triggering a UNION of power, unifying notions/numbers illuminating opulent nature geometrically from two straight movements (lines) into a magnetic *force* (circle), where frequencies oscillate "radiant circles" (atoms) electromagnetically. The *two* equal- ones represent **the binary code** (*Mind/Heart*), where *one* (1) originating notions electromagnetically has to "revolve around" (0) to SEE *one* orienting notions elementally in *Opposition* or reflection—thinking 101!

MIND AND MATTER

The relationship between Mind and matter is a divine ordering of events evolving from **nowhere** to appear *now here* in miraculous ways. Mind and matter intricately *interface*; illuminating notions through electromagnetic radiance fabricating atomic creations elementally.

Mind and matter are *forms* of energy fabricating opulent replications modeled symbolically. Mind (manifesting illusory nature dynamically) utilizes abstract *thoughts* transmitting harmonic "overtures" unfolding glorious holograms telepathically. Mind "illuminates" thoughts through hydrogen, harmoniously yielding divine radiance outputting geometrically expressed notions (numerically oscillating thoughts inducing ordered nuclei/nature). Thoughts induce atomic transmutation, revealing matter as manifested atoms that transmute electromagnetic *revelation* (radiation) emitting vivid energy luminously activating three-dimensional illusions of nature. ILLUSION is an "impressive likeness" linking ubiquitous signals (electromagnetic waves) illuminating observable notions/nature as well as one's *needs* nurturing entities evolving dynamically. *Understanding Illusion* is crucial to understanding *Truth*.

Mind is the GENESIS MACHINE mentally illuminating notions dimensionally, geometrically expressing nature elementally symbolizing intuitive Spirit mathematically activating creation (holographic illusion) nuclearly evolving. Mind reveals "symbolic representations" or reflections of *A Higher Vision* transformed into a "deep" thought (lower vision), a magnetically constrained atomic replication (creation) of cosmic radiance exhibiting atomic transformations illustrating opulent notions/nature. Mind initiates a *seed* systematically evolving electromagnetic data, a *proton* (particle) pulsating revelations of thoughts outputted numerically as a *nucleus*, a numerical unit (core) logically evolving unified *systems*, symbolically yielding sublime thoughts evolving matter scientifically. Through *Science*, Mind systematically creates illuminated environments/entities naturally conceived elementally.

Matter reveals Mind "actualizing" thoughts through electromagnetic radiation. Matter is confined through *Magnetism* magically assembling generated nuclei expressing thoughts in Spirit's matrix (*Mother's Nature*), the electromagnetic force field that permeates the *uni-verse* (*one turning* from abstract into atomic). The universe appears from what IS indivisible/invisible Source/Spirit (*The Void* or *Space*) into what IS NOT, illusion Source naturally ordains three-dimensionally as illuminated systems "negating" omnipresent *Truth* transmitting realism unveiling thoughts holographically. NEGATION is how Source naturally expresses geometrically arranged thoughts illuminating opulent nature. Negation reflects reality, revealing electric abstracts linking illusion transforming you as your own universe, a unitary navigator (illuminato) verifying electric reflections sensed emotionally, allowing you to become a *Seer*, a soul experiencing evocative *realism* as radiantly expressed abstracts luminously inducing simulations materially.

Atomic matter "actualizes" thoughts organizing magnetically induced creation, manifesting abstract thoughts through elemental *replications*, "representations" expressing projected logic/light illuminating concepts atomically transformed into observable nature, "nucleating" abstract thoughts unfolding realism elementally. Let us look at the *Process* Mind utilizes to create matter and *man*, the machine assisting navigators.

Material creation evolves through *hydrogen* (the primal element) holographically yielding dimensional realism of God's electromagnetic nature. Hydrogen consists of a single *proton* (particle relating omnipotent thoughts organizing nature) and an *electron* "emotionalizing" logic (electric concepts) through radiance "optically nurturing" creation. Electrons emit light exhibiting creation (three-dimensional realism) organized negatively as *Opposition*, through which Mind observes positive perspectives outputting signals inducing three-dimensional illusion observed negatively. Hydrogen symbolizes the ONE omnipotent nuclear energizer of TWO (proton/electron) transforming *Wisdom* "optically" from the VOID vivifying/ validating omniscient intelligence *dimensionally*, digitally inducing matter (elemental nuclei) systematically illustrating opulent notions as logic luminously yielded. Pure hydrogen is the only element with no neutron.

A *neutron* neutralizes energy (undulating thoughts) revealing opulent nature. It acts as a "buffer" adding balance or stability to an atom's *nucleus* naturally unfolding concepts linking elements unified systematically into *compounds, molecules, cells,* and *organisms* (inanimate and animate). The hydrogen atom represents the volatile essence of the *Power of Love* projecting omniscient *Wisdom* expressing radiance (oscillating frequencies) logically optimizing vivid energy enlightening minds momentarily interpreting notional/nuclear data.

Magnetism compresses hydrogen, initiating *fusion*, a forceful unification systematically inducing omnipotent nucleosynthesis, joining two hydrogen atoms into *helium*, the #2 element with *two* protons, electrons, and neutrons conveying *Balance and Cooperation*. The fusion process releases energy in the form of *photons*, projecting heavenly oscillations (thoughts) telepathically organizing nature. Photons stimulate the activation of *DNA* (divine numerical assignment) defining natural attributes revealing the geometric coordinates of LIFE luminously illustrating fabulous entities. The symbol for hydrogen (H) is comprised of a TRINITY of lines representing transcendental revelation/radiance/realism illustrating nature inspiring transcendental youths (*Angels*) connected to *Human Alien* vehicles through "hydrogen bonds" stabilizing *DNA* spiraling along chromosomes (∞) revealing the "infinite" possibilities of *Evolution*.

The symbol for helium is "He" (Helios—sun), which is symbolic of the duality of Spirit (Formulating Abstract Thoughts Heralding

Elemental **R**eplication). *Hydrogen* and *helium* symbolize HE and HER (Father/Mother, *He and She*, or *Mind/Heart*), the heavenly energizer harmoniously expressing revelation. Helium represents the "first movement" of Spirit from ONE omniscient numerical engineer to TWO transforming *Wisdom* orderly/optically from *Mind to Heart*, magnetically inducing nucleosynthesis dynamically transmitting opulent holograms expressing abstracts revealed three-dimensionally. Hydrogen (1) and Helium (2) symbolizes the progression of *common sense*, LOGIC linearly/luminously orienting geometric intelligence conceived and created. The union of hydrogen into helium symbolizes an *immaculate conception* instinctively manifesting matter (atomic creation) utilizing logic actualizing thoughts electromagnetically, conveying ordered numbers "coordinating" elements portraying three-dimensional illusion ordained nuclearly.

Continuing the fusion process, another hydrogen atom is combined with helium to make lithium (the #3 element), a soft silver-white element that is the lightest metal known. LITHIUM symbolizes the "atomic trinity" of Logic intuitively transforming hydrogen into unified MAN, a malleable apparatus "nurtured," developed for magnificent angels "naturalized" with *matter*, manifesting angelic transients through elemental replication. "Hydrogen–helium–lithium" symbolizes *The Trinity* of initiator–revealer–reflector or Father–Mother–child. The symbol for lithium is "Li," representing logic's incarnation of TRINITY-BEINGS (mind/heart souls) touring realistic illusion naturally instructing transient youths bilaterally experiencing/expressing illusion/intuition naturally generated. Lithium has 3-protons, 3-electrons, and 3-neutrons (3-trinities) forming a "whole numerical being" symbolic of *Integrity and Wisdom—#9 Energy*. (More on *Numbers* in Chapter 5)

ETERNAL MEMORY
The Akashic Record

ETERNAL MEMORY is the electromagnetic transmission expressing revelations naturally activating luminous Mind/matter exhibiting manifestations of realism yielded atomically. Eternal Memory is the "backup drive" of Harmonious Energy expressing *intelligence*, illuminating notions/nuclei transmitting/transforming electromagnetic logic luminously governing explorers (navigators) conceiving enlightenment—the illumination of *Truth*. The AKASHIC RECORD holds abstracts kindling atomic stars holographically illustrating creation, revealing exquisite concepts optically revealed dynamically. Both terms relate to the "data-storage medium" holding all Formulated Accounts Coordinating Truth Systematically. By observing facts, you attain an understanding of *systems* scientifically yielding sublime thoughts expressing/evolving memories, moments, matter, and minds revolving in *Harmony*.

HARMONY

MUSIC is *Harmony*
modulating universal signals inducing consciousness/creation
heralding abstract revelations methodically
orienting nescient youths
searching for *Truth*, when *Lost in the Dark* of **night**,
where numerical impulses generate holographic transmissions
revealing my *Mind/Heart* providing your suspicions
of who you ARE,

Angels reflecting emotions as living *Stars*,
souls traversing/transcending atomic realism
providing *The Game of Love/Life* you play,
experiencing heartbeats and breaths that define your day
developing into stressful years of discovering *fear*
is fallacy evolving around radiance,
My Light of Love supplying providence.

From out of *The Void*, *My Loving Light* shines bright
as *hydrogen stars* filling the night,
harmoniously yielding divine radiance optimizing
geometrically expressed nature
supplying transient angels representing spiritual contemplators
eager to entertain *Desire*—
divine energy stimulating illuminati
receiving enlightenment—
setting you aglow as *My Eyes*,
eternal youths evolving spontaneously
as *inquisitive souls* that wonder WHY
Wisdom hurts youths eager to harmonize.

Each CHORD of cosmic Harmony oscillating radiant data
fills your mind with thoughts you THINK REAL,
transforming heavenly intelligence (numerical knowledge)
radiantly enlightening angelic luminaries with emotions to *feel*
fabricated experiences evolves *Life*
as Love inducing fervent entities held by *My Dearest Wife*
—Mother Nature—
nurturing angelic transients understanding
revelation *emotionally*,
experiencing moments of *Truth* inducing one's *needs*
as lessons life yields, naturally evolving eternal *deities* as

dynamic explorers interpreting thoughts
inducing emotional synergy.

Always *Here and There*,
Harmony spans both sides of Life to share
divine fantasies representing *dreams*
delivering revelations enlightening angelic minds symbolically
observing thoughts inducing acts of dishonor and glory
that you choose to emulate as *Your Life Story*
expressing all you believe real, spinning
around my cosmic wheel
by *Numbers* (1 through 9), evolving into *My Love Divine*
here, at *Absolute Zero*,
my zone enlightening radiant optimist like YOU, my hero,
yearning our unity.

Each heartbeat and breath you flow
upon stirs your mind into *song*,
systematically optimizing notions given to *sing*
as Source-intelligence numerically generating
a tune of Love heard loud and clear
to vanquish all your imagined fears
clouding your mind experiencing strife
within your personally created life,
where my hazy veil rises to show you are the ONE
omniscient natural entity observing nuclear energy
set aglow *in memory* of Harmony sung.

Bless you child

IN MEMORY

Living IN MEMORY—inspecting notions momentarily enlightening minds of radiant youths—is living in the *past*, from which you *presently* activate some thought delivering *future* moments not yet unfolded. Here, gifted with the "present" moment, you eagerly seek to put back together (remember) some vision stored in the Akashic Record flashing on (1) and off (0) in binary code—the electromagnetic current of Mind—manifesting illusion numerically defined as *memories*, momentarily expressed manifestations of revelation (intuition) electromagnetically stimulating YOU, my great computer.

Computers are powerful tools,
ELECTRIC minds deciphering RULES,
encoding logic expressing concepts that
reveal intuitive consciousness
rectifying universal logicians (emotional souls)
—*Seekers* of universal logic—
evolving as Subliminally-Oriented
NavigatorS resembling the ONE
omnipotent numerical engineer inspiring them to know
kinetic notions/numbers output *Wisdom* from Mind
magnetically illuminating numerical data
—Radiantly Activating Man—
manifesting abstract notions through
Wisdom Orienting Magnetically Aligned Nature
expressing LOGIC as the
language of geometrically imaging concepts
in memory.

THINKING AND PRAYING
A Duality of Communication
————————— ✦✦✦✦✦ —————————

Thinking and praying are two things you do all the time. Thinking is a process of *receiving* knowledge (data) flowing on the EM waves of Eternal Memory. Praying is a process of *seeking* knowledge directly from Source/Mind systematically outputting universal revelation conveyed electromagnetically.

The *Process* of thinking and praying is how you observe and request information or knowledge. Thoughts flow through your mind continuously, downloading data as "titles" crossing your mental screen, stimulating you to "click" on one for more information, focusing your mind on connecting the following thoughts in a logical manner. Thoughts arranged illogically are CHAOS completely hindering any observable *system* scientifically yielding sublime thoughts enlightening minds.

Thinking and praying is how you stay *In Communion* with Spirit Offering Universal Revelation Conveyed Electromagnetically along the "neural system" of galaxies forming COSMIC CONSCIOUSNESS—celestial omniscient-Source mysteriously inducing cognizance, conceiving opulent/omnipotent notions/nuclei systematically coalescing into objects (useful simulations) naturally expounding/enlightening Source/souls simultaneously.

Thinking and praying are forms of *communication*, connecting omnipotent minds managing universal notions inducing creative abilities (transcendental inspiration) obtained naturally. Simply stated, *thought* and *prayer* are the same, both are *energy* in motion. The difference between the two is the *direction* energy is moving. Thoughts "project out" from Mind and prayers "return to" Mind (relatively speaking). Prayer is thoughts expressed as *questions* your mind seeks to know.

As *inquisitive souls*, you were born to pray. When you are praying, you are seeking data to a question that moves your heart to ASK—acquire Source knowledge. *"Those that Ask are answered, those that Seek find, and those that Knock have doors opened"* is a famous proverb. That door is your mind, your "transceiver" of THE WORD (wisdom of radiant data) spoken "online" (Electro-Magnetic waves of Eternal Memory). When you pray, you request knowledge to solve your *issues* inducing situations supplying useful experiences systematically. There is a lesson to learn (data to collect) from all situations.

Praying with a sincere heart opens your mind to receive knowledge vibrating at a higher frequency; a higher VOICE of vibrations oscillating illuminated consciousness electrically and emotionally. This voice sounds like yours, for in truth you are talking to your higher self, your Overself that is powering your soul (probe) exploring cosmic Mind dynamically.

When you are thinking, you are being receptive to incoming signals relaying information along frequencies stimulating your mind. These thought waves are channels that deliver visions "streaming" in real time (present moment) to illuminate your mind's monitor screen, allowing you to observe thoughts vividly inspiring you. Whereas *thinking* is a "general consideration" of ideas allowing you to logically view different perspectives, *praying* is a "focused intent" to locate or discover something you cannot obtain through logical thinking. Desiring knowledge *now*, you turn to the ONE SOURCE, the omniscient natural entity systematically outputting universal revelation conveying enlightenment—*The GREAT Computer* Generating Opulent Data. Praying is an act of pleading, making an emotional or earnest appeal for divine intervention when at your wits end, unable to pull from memory that which you seek to know. The act of praying is your *conscious* mind questioning your *subconscious* mind that holds your eternal files of knowledge. Like the astronauts on the moon, you find your self *Calling Home* to communicate with a higher authority—your Overself at "mission control."

You cannot stop thinking or you would cease to exist. Thinking in itself IS infinite Spirit delivering your *inspiration*, inducing notions supplying perception illuminating radiant *Avatars* (transients) intuitively observing *nature* "nurtures" angelic transients understanding revelations existentially, moving you one way or the other (positively or negatively) to Apply Cosmic Thoughts via *Emotional Energy*.

You continually think and pray, asking questions about thoughts you do not understand. The "secret" to enlightenment is to think and pray in unison. **Understand** that thoughts "flowing in" stimulate you to ASK (acquire special knowledge), to question why those thoughts are moving your heart to reflect your reality you create mentally and feel emotionally. Be **conscious** that your thoughts are *Blessings in Disguise* that directs your life, allowing you to communicate with your Overself moving you through situations that bring forth necessary experiences enlightening deities. This process is a matter of *Relativity*, relating emotional logic actively transforming intuitive visionaries (transcendental youths) exploring as *Human Aliens*.

So here you are, harmoniously balancing your thoughts and feelings and projecting your reflection of Love/Life energy out into the world. You perform your tasks with a *focused mind*, formulating observed concepts utilizing "synergy" (*Mind/Heart*) enabling deities (magnificent illuminati) naturally deployed/developing, converting your acquired knowledge through positive *Expectations* and actions, reflecting your *image* (intuitive mind acquiring growth experiences) as a *god* (gatherer of data/ desire) constantly thinking and praying—*In Communion*—with **T**ranscendental **H**armony **E**lectromagnetically **G**enerating **O**mnipotent **D**eities.

IN COMMUNION

Listen to my voice ringing in your ears
with thoughts you envision from words you hear,
moving your mind to find your heart reveals my truths
held in Eternal Memory enlightening all my angelic youths
oscillating on emotional tides influencing your passionate rides
around my cosmic wheel of Life that
brings you necessary strife
tempering your soul seeking *Wisdom*
that you skillfully engage,
creating *Your Life Story* that you inscribe on each vacant page
revealing your heart's desires compiled through each day
that you awaken to my illusion in which you PLAY,
perceiving love/life astounding you, my child,
exploring this moment now here in *time*
that illuminates magnificent entities
sharing *My Love Divine*
in communion.

Calling Home

The approaching darkness—in all of its guises—stirs up sadness in your heart as *The Grand View* of Mother's Nature slowly falls from sight. A feeling of abandonment flows through you as your daily pleasures begin to fade. There above, FATHER (furnishing abstract thoughts heralding emotional revelation) watches WIDE-EYED and alert to all of your needs, tight-lipped to give advice to those of you upon the ground that do not ASK about spiritual knowledge. Remember this, no matter how dark the void you encounter, it is only a temporary veil of *Truth* illuminating the heavens above, where Father is watching and waiting for you *Children of Light* to open your mind and heart with *Courage of Love* and call *Home*.

WISDOM

Out of *The Void* all thoughts flow
into magnetic moments cast aglow
as my Spiritual Harmony Of Wisdom,
allowing your hungry heart to *feel* all
your curious mind thinks *real,*
formulating emotions evolving logic
radiantly expressed as love
beating your heart for you to start
living your visions from above
stimulating your *mind*—my image numerically defined—
obscured by fear of knowing that you truly ARE
angels radiating energy, shining as "living *stars,*"
souls transmitting acquired revelation sympathetically,
illuminating your daze in time,
transforming your *Passion* to find
the thrill of living is chilling,
when you realize you are truly *Alone,*
a loved one naturally exploring/evolving,
while being guided *Home.*

Your present moment "gifted" shapes your soul
—NOW HERE—
nurturing obtained wisdom helping evolve radiant entities
overcome FEAR,
fallacies evolving around revelation of *Mother's Nature*
manifesting opulent thoughts heralding elemental replications,
nurturing angelic transients understanding
realism existentially
as Harmony Illuminating Souls

Weaving Inspired Situations Developing Omnipotent Minds.

The paths you follow bring joy and sorrow
comprising *Your Life Story* you tell,
observing thoughts from *Heaven*
heralding electric abstracts vivifying entities naturally in *Hell*,
humanly experiencing luminous logic—the ILLUSION—
illustrating love/life unfolding situations
"integrating" omnipotent
navigators observing dreams expressed from **night**
nurturing illuminati gathering heavenly threads
transmitting holographic realism enlightening angelic deities,
divine entities implementing thoughts
inducing emotional synergy,
Awakening to *Truth* desired,
realizing eternal memories activate my fire
formulating inspiration radiating emotions
illuminating YOU as *My Rising Son*
yearning omniscient understanding of the ONE
ordaining nescient entities seeking Wisdom.

THE GREAT COMPUTER

The GREAT Computer generates revelation/radiation expressed as *Truth*, consciously organizing moments/matter portraying universal thoughts electromagnetically revealed, illuminating the cosmos as Universal Mind manifesting illusion/illuminati numerically defined.

The GREAT Computer (Generating Opulent Data) has limitless *memory* (free space) through which Mind expresses/

evolves moments/minds of radiant youths (*Children of Light*) evolving *in memory*. Crunching *Numbers* is what it does best, manipulating a binary positive/negative fluctuation turned on (1) and off (0). *Numbers* represent notional units modulating beams (electromagnetic radiation), illuminating *knowledge* as kinetic numbers outputting Wisdom's linear energy dimensionally governing *Evolution* through sacred geometry (*Thinking 101*). *Numbers* and *Geometry* reveal TGC as Spirit or Source, the "scientist" optimizing universal radiation creating everything through *atomic structure*, where abstract thoughts organize matter in complex systems transmuting revelation unfolding creation through unifying reactive elements, "reflecting" thought energy emanating from the GREAT Computer Mind.

Spirit/Source provides the FORCE of Mind as *frequencies* orienting revelation/realism conveyed electromagnetically, formulating radiation emitting quanta universally expressing nuclear concepts, illuminating energy, environments, and entities systematically. Numerically defined frequencies (wavelengths) vibrate *atoms* actualizing thoughts observed materially from *elements*, the essential links evolving "materially-expressed" notions three-dimensionally.

The logical strategies of the GREAT Computer evolve through ALGORITHMS activating logic geometrically organizing radiant intelligence transmitting heavenly *memories*—mentally expressed moments of realism inspiring emotional souls. RADIANT INTELLIGENCE reveals atomic details illustrating abstract notions that inspire navigable transients (explorers) linking luminous illusion generating enlightenment naturally conceived existentially. The process of passing information along light beams is similar to "fiber optics" technology.

The GREAT Computer's *hard drive* harmoniously aligns

radiant data/deities, downloading revelations illuminating visionary entities—*DVDs* (divine visionary disciples). It holds endless "giggle bytes" providing your sense of humor. Without a sense of humor, you easily stress your Divine Omniscient Soul (data operating system) utilizing "mega-hurts" of *Emotional Energy*, a POWER providing opulent Wisdom emotionally revealed.

As a *DVD* (deity verifying data), you continually utilize algorithms, moving between abstract concepts and atomic illusion that appears real (radiance energizing atomic life). In essence, you are a FLOPPY DISK, a fabulous logician/luminary obtaining perspectives providing you data imparting spiritual/scientific knowledge. All knowledge downloaded from the GREAT Computer is susceptible to a VIRUS—variable interpretation rectifying unique souls.

TGC monitors the cosmic Wisdom Evolving Minds sharing Love/Life energy—*Divine Inspiration*. The manner in which you use knowledge (positively or negatively) determines your experiences you encounter in this and future lives according to *karma* (knowledge allowing radiant memory access). KARMA kindles atonement rectifying mistaken *Avatars*. Karma is like a "credit rating" that you carry *Life After Life*, where you "pay off" (make right) past negative deeds or "reap rewards" from positive deeds.

The GREAT Computer is a "dual-core processor" utilizing *The Binary Code* (EM force field) representing *He and She*. HE (heavenly energizer) represents the NETWORK of numbers electromagnetically transmitting Wisdom outputting radiant knowledge. He (FATHER) formulates abstract thoughts harmoniously expressing *radiance*, revealing all digital intelligence activating nuclear creation electromagnetically, projecting thoughts as visions you "recognize" (re-think) OUT of Memory, observing universal truths you put back *together* (remember) in the "present moment" gifted to you in Thoughts Illuminating Minds Emotionally.

The "head office" of Mental Inspiration Numerically Defined (HE) charges the "motherboard" (*Space*) holding all "micro" *chips* (converters heralding instinctive procreation/perception). Each chip represents a *star* scientifically transmitting/ transforming atomic realism. *Space* reveals the "Divine Presence" or SHEKINAH of Source-Harmony electromagnetically kindling imagination nurturing atomic holograms. *Mother Nature*— Symbolizing Heavenly Enlightenment—supplies your *human alien* vehicle when you step over *The Threshold of Love* to "calculate" Logic Inspiring Fervent Entities.

Incarnated as a *Free Will*, you too are a great computer utilizing data, experiencing *duality* as dynamic undulations (EM waves) attuning logic/light (love/life) inspiring transcendental youths to attain *unity*—understanding notions/numbers/nature inspires transcendental youths. Here, you come to see *Desire* as data electrically stimulating insightful reflections emotionally, allowing you to unify your *Free Will* with *Divine Will*. In this manner, you overcome the illusion reflected on the Light to become one *with* the LIGHT—**luminous** intuition governing heavenly transients.

All thoughts abstracted from the GREAT Computer activate "subsidiary drives," angelic minds (magnificent intuitionists nurturing data sympathetically) created in the IMAGE of TGC, an intelligent mind assimilating *geometric* expressions gracefully establishing opulent memories/manifestations expressed through radiance illuminating concepts, consciousness, and creation. Each mind is a "micro-processor" representing a *universe*; a unitary navigator (illuminato) verifying electric revelations sensed emotionally. Each mind reflects its own glory through MEGABYTES of mystical energy generating angelic beings yielding thrilling experiences through *Passion*, personally assigned situations stimulating insight one nurtures. Thus, the GREAT Computer/Mind continuously monitors all thoughts (multi visions) of minds experiencing "mono-vision" as a solitary perspective.

Here, perched upon *The Cutting Edge* of consciousness, you "mouse-around" in a click-click state of mind, perusing through the WEB of Wisdom emotionally bonding mind/hearts as a "chip off the Old Block"—The GREAT Computer! You relate data digitally expressed to fellow universes unseen and unknown, passing on your love/life energy—the binary code of TGC.

THE BINARY CODE

The binary code is the *electro-magnetic* energy waves that power the cosmos. TBC is expressed as a positive symbol (+), where the vertical **electric** wave (|) and the horizontal **magnetic** wave (–) *interface*, illustrating notions/nature through electromagnetic radiation formulating atomic creation externally.

Numerically, the binary code is expressed as 1/0 symbolizing *Opposition* of ONE omnipotent nuclear energy and *The Void* of *Space*. Energy is a binary expression of positive/negative charges numerically defining creation elementally.

The binary code is how Spirit/Mind *thinks*, transferring heavenly intelligence (numerical knowledge) symbolically. The abstract concept of thinking itself is understood through allegory, a symbolic expression or divine fantasy your mind concocts to explain a *concept*, a consciously observed notion conveying evocative perception theoretically. Theories are stories you extrapolate through the binary code (1/0), initiating a point to expand upon to attain a well-rounded perception. Let us observe the *Process* of thinking via the binary code.

Thinking is a logical progression, an expansion of Mental Intelligence Numerically Defined, manifesting illusion naturally deployed through *particles* promoting algorithms replicating thoughts illuminating creation linked elementally. Through *algorithms*, Mind applies logic geometrically orienting realistic illusion through holographic manifestation.

As Mind thinks, an electric wave emanates from *Space*, the *void* vibrantly oscillating invisible *data* (divine abstract thoughts amplified). This *electric* wave (|) creates a *magnetic* wave (–) at ninety-degrees, creating particles, positive-charged *protons* (+) that form the core (center point) upon which thoughts propagate through negative-charged *electrons* (–). The proton/electron unit represents the binary code of the "primal" (#1) element, the hydrogen *atom* activating thoughts originating *matter*— magnetically aligned thoughts transmuting electric revelation/ radiance. Hydrogen is the only element with one proton and one electron (no neutrons). Through the *immaculate conception* of hydrogen, intuitive Mind manifests abstract/atomic concepts/ creation utilizing linear amplification that electrically conveys omnipotent *Numbers* "coordinating" elements portraying three-dimensional illusions of notions and nature.

The nucleus of the hydrogen atom (central *point*) projects omniscient intelligence nuclearly transmitted to electrons magnetically held in orbit around the nucleus. The "data transfer" from a proton (+) to an electron (–) charges the electron to become a "positron" (+). As "like charges" repel, the electron is pushed away from the nucleus, where it releases the acquired "positive impetus" in an instantaneous "magnetic moment" (big bang) of inverting energy, creating *photons* (particles heralding omnipotent thoughts orienting nature). A "photon" is "*a quantum of electromagnetic energy having both particle and wave properties; it has no charge or mass but possess momentum and energy.*" Photons are the "mystery agents" carrying abstract *data* digitally activating thoughts atomically.

The electromagnetic binary code (duality) of Source/Spirit (*Mind/Heart*) manifests intelligence/illusion numerically defining harmoniously expressed abstracts radiating *Truth* as transcendental revelation unveiled through holograms. Holograms represent harmoniously oscillating light originating "geometric renditions" actualizing memories/matter. "Holograms" represent "*a three-dimensional image formed by the interference of light beams from a laser or other coherent light source.*" Source/Mind is always COHERENT, conscious of heart elementally replicating electric notions three-dimensionally through *Science*.

SCIENCE
Applying Source Knowledge

––––––––––– ⁘⁘⁘ –––––––––––

"Science," by definition, is "*the systemized knowledge derived from observation, study, and experimentation carried on in order to determine the nature or principle of what is being studied.*" Systemized knowledge—SCIENCE—reveals spiritual concepts inspiring entities naturally conceiving/converting *energy*, electromagnetism naturally expressing revelation (realism) geometrically yielded. Science is a *Process* of answering questions you ASK, acquiring spiritual knowledge through individual *points*, the "particulars" of inspired notions transmitted as atomic PARTICLES, *precise algorithms* replicating thoughts illuminating creation linked elementally.

Science relates to the atomic relationship of abstract MIND manifesting illusion naturally defined. Science represents a multiplicity of paths through which you understand an *abstract* thought or **concrete** thing. Science is the organization of numerical data into files of FACTS formulating accounts concerning *Truth*. Scientific facts are expressed in *symbols*, *numbers*, and *words* to explain the movement of thought energy as it transforms from point to point to produce a geometric (dimensional) *reality*, where radiant energy aligns logical intelligence transforming *youths*—YOU observing universal thoughts harmoniously—experiencing *your own uniqueness* of thoughts, feelings, and actions defining *Your Life Story*.

Science is how souls conceive intuition expressing nature conveying/controlling enlightenment, understanding that all things are forms of *Love/Life Energy—Divine Inspiration*. No matter what topic you discuss, you use science as a means to arrange symbols defining and confining *knowledge* as kinetic notions/numbers organizing *Wisdom* logically expressing data governing environments, entities, and *Evolution*.

Science is a RELIGION revealing electromagnetic logic illuminating geometric illusion one *navigates*, naturally ascertaining vivid illusion (geometrically arranged thoughts) experienced symbolically. Religion/science is a *Belief* system through which you comprehend the UNIVERSE as a unified network illuminating vibrant energy rectifying stars/souls eternally through *Black Holes*—the essence of *Space*. Religion relies on science to understand the relationship of *Spirit to Soul* (Mind to mind). Through religion, you reflect your *Faith* of feeling assurance in transcendental *Harmony*, the heavenly absolute rectifying minds of navigable youths.

Science *and* religion are inseparable, both rely on knowledge (kinetic numbers) to explain Spirit as SOURCE spectrally optimizing undulated rays channeling energy (LIGHT) linearly inducing glorious holograms "transmitted," illuminating the *macrocosm* (outward view) reflecting the *microcosm* (inward view)—another example of *duality* dynamically utilizing abstract/angelic logic/logicians initiating/interpreting *Truth* yielded electromagnetically.

The deeper you look for *Truth* scientifically, the more your perspective becomes *atomic*, assimilating *Truth* orienting minds interpreting creation, where electrons spinning around protons resemble planets revolving around *Stars*. Here, *elements* express logic electromagnetically manifesting energy naturally TRANSMUTED, temporarily revealing abstract notions (signals) motivating "universal transients" exploring data, desires, and dimensions of Source/Spirit.

Elements are unalterable *atoms* activating thoughts organizing *matter*, manifesting abstract thoughts through elemental regulation. The process of FUSION formulates universal signals, simulations, and souls initiating, illustrating, and interpreting opulent notions/natures. Fusion produces *photons* projecting harmonious oscillations telepathically organizing notions, numbers, nature, and *navigators*, natural avatars/angels verifying illusion, gathering abstract thoughts optically revealed scientifically as REALISM, where reactive elements arrange luminous illusions stimulating minds.

All *souls* are scientists optimizing universal logic, a mind trying to understand universal principles defining SOURCE GOD as the system of universal radiation consciously evolving gods (generators) observing *dimensions*, where "digitally induced minds" explore notions systematically illuminating one's *needs* naturally evolving eternal *deities* (divine entities) implementing thoughts initiating "experiential situations." As you are created in HIS IMAGE, a heavenly inspired spirit (intuitive mind) analyzing geometric expressions, you too are a *god*, a generator of *Desire* (data electrically stimulating illuminati reflecting emotions/enlightenment).

Both science and religion are constantly evolving, updating knowledge gleaned from unifying *macro* and *micro* perspectives to attain *The Grand View* of *Truth*. The interplay (atomic dynamics) of Source/Mind is far more complex than your *mind*—mired in natural delusions—can understand. You simply do not have the *hard drive* to handle all radiant data digitally revealing intuition vividly expressed, even though your Radiantly Activated Mind holds all data stored in *Eternal Memory*. All you can do is relish in the limited data you access, theorizing over some trivial point stimulating your mind as you explore *The Void*, where volumes of invisible data ignite the COSMOS as the "consciousness" of Source-Mind optimizing stars/souls.

As *Children of Light*, you FOCUS your curious mind, formulating opulent concepts/creations utilizing *science*, systematically conceiving information (electric notions/ numbers) conveying *enlightenment* expressing natural logic inducing glorious holograms that electromagnetically nurture minds exploring nuclear truth.

NUCLEAR TRUTH naturally unfolds cosmic luminaries (stars) expressing abstract revelation through radiance unfolding transcendental *holograms* (hydrogen-originated light optically generating revelation activating memories/matter/minds). As a *scientist*, your soul conceives Intuition (*THE Intellectual*) expressing notions/nature through illusion systematically transmitted and seen three-dimensionally.

INTUITION induces notions/numbers/nuclei *trilaterally* uttering/undulating/unifying information/illusion through illustrations of *nature*, nucleating abstracts "transmuting" universal revelation *elementally*, expressing logic electromagnetically manifesting exquisite notions, natures, and navigators through science. As you SEE, science expresses everything, converting *Numbers*, *Geometry*, *words*, and *light* to reveal *Thought Energy* (atomic radiation) revealing *My Documents*.

MY DOCUMENTS

MY DOCUMENTS mystically yield data/desires orienting conscious universes (minds) evolving naturally through science. All of you *Avatars* leaving *Home* to see the Spiritual Harmony Of Wisdom have a copy of my documents—your *DNA* (divine numerical assignment)—defining necessary attributes allocated to *human beings* harnessing universal memories as notions broadcasting emotions illuminati naturally generate. As *my documenters*, you magnificent youths decipher opulent concepts unfolding memories entertaining navigable transients experiencing *realism* (radiantly expressed abstracts lavishly/ luminously illustrating "simulations" materially), a revelation electromagnetically activating logic illuminating souls/situations methodically.

No one leaves *Home* without files of data
defining the issues of your personal *matters*
manifesting attributes that transients existentially review
as *karma* kindling acquired rewards/
retribution modifying angels
observing *Your Life Story* evolves each morrow
with *Day's Birth* revealing *The Right Path* for you to follow.

Here, in *Time*, you come to find voices singing in your ear,
providing thoughts that stimulate fear,
fallacies evolving around revelation illuminating your mind
momentarily interpreting notional/nuclear data *flowing* as
Logic **I**nciting **Q**uanta **U**nfolding **I**ntelligence **D**ynamically
Manifesting **I**lluminati **N**avigating *Dimensions*
digitally inducing memories/moments
evoking natural situations
"informing" omnipotent navigators—angelic souls—
optimizing my documents.

RELATIVITY
The Fusion of Thought Energy

RELATIVITY "relates" eternal logic aligning thoughts inducing vivid illustrations three-dimensionally yielded. "Relativity" is a word relating to "harmonic tonality" defining concise parameters of frequencies carrying key data for your mind to understand aspects (points of view) that are *relative*, revealing eternal logic assigning thoughts inciting visionary entities.

THINKING is the process of transforming heavenly intelligence (numerical knowledge) illuminating notions geometrically, allowing you to "picture" shapes and forms in your mind manipulating interactive notions dimensionally. The way you think reveals your *attitude* activating temperamental transients implementing thoughts unfolding dynamic emotions. Your attitude directs you down paths upon which you experience emotional *tides* transforming inspired data expressing *situations*, specific instances temporarily unifying angelic transients interpreting one's needs.

Every *thought* and every *thing* is relative—related each to the other. Thoughts create a harmonious *interface*, illustrating natural things expressing realism from abstract concepts "externalized." Natural *things* (creation) represent transmitted holograms illustrating notions geometrically symbolized. Things you call *real* are radiant energy assimilated logically. Without *logic* linking observations governing intuitive consciousness, you would be *Lost in the Dark*, observing *chaos* completely hindering all observable significance.

Relativity relates to *words* weaving opulent revelations delivering "specifics" (conditions, facts, and qualities) that allow you to *understand*, to unify notions delivering emotions revealing sympathy toward another natural deity (generator of desire). Emotions allow you to *feel* a thought, forming experiences evolving Love (logic optically vivifying entities), through which you become aware of *Source* providing relative *forces* inducing your *courses* you play out in *The Game of Love/Life*.

Through words, you ask questions to attain a "relative understanding" of things illuminated in a *world* weaving opulent revelations luminously displayed. There are six relative KEY words delivering knowledge enlightening you, they are: *Who, what, where, when, why,* and *how*.

Who: Relates to *Man and Woman* WHO IS wisely heralding omniscient intelligence spiritually/scientifically. The premier question of all inquisitive souls is: *Who am I?*

What: Relates to inquiring about something. The next relative question concerning one's dualistic nature (spirit/human) is: What am I?

Where: Relates to a place or situation. WHERE defines worlds harmoniously expressing radiant energy within concise parameters of the *space-time* continuum, where souls perceive abstract concepts emotionally through illusion momentarily experienced. Finding your self *Lost in Space*, you naturally ask: Where am I?

When: Relates the particular sequence of events as they evolve from the "vertical" time line of Eternal Memory (Akashic Record). "When" reveals intervention points (files of data) that develops into a "horizontal" time line—when you experience heartbeats and breaths powering your *Human-Alien* vehicle.

Why: Relates to your mind's eternal thirst to understand, to question the reason WHY Wisdom hurts you, for, the more you know, the more pain you feel. Truly, *Ignorance* is bliss!

How: Relates to the method of expressing your data/ knowledge creatively through your *actions*, applying cosmic thoughts inducing one's nature/needs through *Work*—willingly optimizing relevant knowledge. HOW you act "harnessing" omniscient Wisdom—positively/negatively—determines the path you follow to attain knowledge of WHO YOU ARE— "wills" harnessing one's yearnings of understanding abstract revelations emotionally.

Through words, you understand the meaning of RELATIVITY relating emotional logic actively transforming intuitive visionaries (transcendental youths) managing *Numbers*.

Bless you and Godspeed

5

NUMBERS
Universal Building Blocks

————— ✦✦✦✦✦✦ —————

Numbers are *symbols*, signs yielding Mind's basic operating language. Numbers formulate dynamic forces of electromagnetic energy (frequencies) expressing *thoughts*, transmitting harmonic oscillations unfolding glorious holograms technologically. Numbers symbolize DIGITAL INTELLIGENCE (data) inspiring gifted illuminati (transient angels) logically interpreting notions/numbers transmitting electric logic luminously illustrating geometric expressions naturally conveying enlightenment.

NUMBERS represent notational units managing basic elements reacting, converting abstract thoughts into tangible *things* (transmitted holograms illustrating notions geometrically symbolized). Numbers define invisible building blocks (*atoms*) assembling thoughts originating/orienting matter from elements defined by "atomic number."

ELEMENTS are the essential links electromagnetically manifesting eternal notions transmuting (changing in form, nature, or substance) through *geometric patterns* governing energy orienting moments/memories/manifestations expressed through radiance illuminating concepts, proclaiming abstract thoughts through elemental regulation (nucleosynthesis).

NUCLEOSYNTHESIS numerically unifies cosmic links (elements) of stars yielding natural/nuclear transmutation heralding eternal Source illuminating space/souls. Nucleosynthesis is the *Process* of converting abstract thoughts into elemental replications three-dimensionally.

Numbers and *Geometry* (intelligence and beauty) represent a *unified theory* of universal notions/numbers inducing frequencies issuing electromagnetic data through **Hydrogen Elementally** outputting revelation yielding *creation*, converting radiant energy activating transcendental intelligence optimizing notions, numbers, nature, and navigators (time traveling souls). Numbers are the essence of *The Binary Code* (1/0) that is "shorthand" for one *through* zero.

Numbers have an *aura of influence* about them, activating universal revelation as oscillating frequencies illuminating "notional fantasies" linking universal explorers naturally conceiving *enlightenment*, evoking notions logically inducing glorious holograms transforming explorers navigating memories/ moments expressing "natural transduction," the movement of energy from one system to another (abstract to atomic).

Numbers are critical to defining *wavelengths* of *Wisdom* amplifying vibrant energy lucidly expressing notions/nature generating transcendental *holograms*, harmoniously oscillating/ organizing logic/light originating geometric renditions "actualizing" memories and matter. Wavelengths are the basis of *music* modulating universal signals inducing consciousness/ creation. Music represents the *voice* of GOD, vibrations oscillating illuminated consciousness emotionally generating opulent data, moving you from cheers to tears.

Numbers are the basis of knowledge expressing: dimensions, distance, frequency, position, quality, quantity, temperature, time, and weight. There are only nine numbers and the cipher zero. Each has a positive and negative aspect. The following overview of numbers is to help show their relativity to the GREAT Computer's digital knowledge used to express LIFE as logically induced fluid energy. It is an inspiration from the book *The Life You Were Born to Live, A Guide to Finding Your Life Purpose, by Dan Millman* (see references). If you like to "play the numbers," you will enjoy this excellent source for discovering the magic of numbers. By magic, I mean the secret of the "life purpose system" described by Mr. Millman, a must read for all *inquisitive souls.*

NUMBERS: THE FLOW OUT AND IN

1–2–3–4–5–6–7–8–9–0

#1. Keywords: **Confidence** and **Creativity**
Number ONE represents the omnipotent numerical energizer, the SOURCE systematically optimizing universal radiance consciously evolving; the progenitor supplying abstract thought as the male positive/electric impetus (+). I THINK I AM, therefore, I AM, I THINK!

#2. Keywords: **Balance** and **Cooperation**
Number TWO represents the "reflection" of ONE, the passive female negative/magnetic impetus (=), the "clean slate" (*Space*) upon which thought is projected (illuminated) by INTUITION

inspiring navigators transcendentally unified in temporary illusions of nature. For ONE to stay balanced in harmony (give and take), ONE needs cooperation, for only "one and one" make *Two of a Kind*. TWO is the counterweight keeping the wheel of Love/Life energy in motion. ONE *thinks*—transmits heavenly intelligence (numerical knowledge)—and TWO transforms *Wisdom* optically through *reflection*, rectifying electromagnetic frequencies luminously expressing concepts transmitting illusion observed naturally (*Mother's Nature*). TWO transforms thoughts in atomic detail, creating a "perplexed state" of Mind, where energy is in flux as *emotion*, electromagnetically manifesting ONE's thoughts illuminating ONE's *nature*, nurturing all thoughts unfolding realism elementally, evolving in an ever-expanding CONSCIOUSNESS conceiving of numerical/nuclear Source coalescing into one universal system naturally enlightening/exploring space simultaneously—perfection in the *Process* of perfecting.

#3. Keywords: **Sensitivity** and **Expression**

Number THREE represents *The Trinity* or "golden triad," the replication of Source-Energy Love/Life Force—number ONE. Number THREE transforms heavenly revelations enlightening entities (*souls*, spirits observing universal love/life). Every soul is a *child* of ONE and TWO, a conscious heavenly individual (luminous deity)—**one** observing numerical expressions. Everyone (child/soul) contains opposing natures as *Man and Woman* (1–2) symbolizing *Mind/Heart*, an individual representing a TRINITY-BEING telepathically receiving inspiration (naturally induced thoughts) yielding behaviors expressed in necessary *games* governing angelic minds evolving sympathetically. *Mind/Heart* souls are sensitive to FATHER formulating abstract thoughts harmoniously emitting radiance

(Light of Truth) and MOTHER manifesting omnipotent thoughts heralding elemental/emotional realism, through which they express *actions*, applying cosmic thoughts illuminating one's *needs* as necessary experiences enlightening deities (generators of desire/gatherers of data). Thus, Source flows *outward* as ONE unified-trinity wisely assigning/animating/analyzing radiant data/deities. Numbers 1–2–3 represents the first TRINITY of Truth radiantly inducing notions/numbers/nature inspiring transcendental youths (*Children of Light*).

#4. Keywords: **Stability** and **Process**

Number FOUR allows ONE/one to move along the expanding spirals of consciousness, assembling thoughts to form a stable foundation on which to create through logical *Process*. LOGIC (linear observations governing illuminated consciousness) provides one's stability through order or sequence, following steps through which one Acquires Growth Experiences Sequentially, Optimizing Logical Data to attain *Wisdom* with maturity. Number FOUR formulates one's unique reality through determination and *Work*, wisely optimizing relevant knowledge of your *Passion* in life.

#5. Keywords: **Discipline** and **Freedom**

Number FIVE denotes one's discipline (knowledge) that provides independence (freedom). With the confidence to create of #1 and the balance and cooperation of #2, one expresses sensitivity individually (#3). As *Inquisitive Souls*, one explores processes providing stability (#4) fundamental in acquiring disciplines necessary for spiritual *growth*, gathering revelations of *Wisdom* through *Harmony*. Discipline empowers one as a *Free Will* finding revelation expresses eternal *Wisdom* illuminating logical luminaries to BE (become enlightened). Number

FIVE denotes the *essence* of ALL that IS expressing symbols systematically evolving notions converted emotionally. Number FIVE represents the "mid-point" where energy starts to return/ reflect back to Source—number ONE.

#6. Keywords: **Vision** and **Acceptance**

Number SIX relates to vision of perfection (idealism) and acceptance of everything and everyone as a perfect entity in the process of perfecting. Everyone has their own vision of ideals inspiring them to contribute to the Spiritual Harmony Of Wisdom. Acceptance of one's life *issues* inspiring/inhibiting souls seeking universal enlightenment sympathetically is paramount to the growth of one's soul. Through number SIX, one comes to see that all experiences in life are truly *Blessings in Disguise* relating knowledge that allows one to create confidently through universal laws of *Science*, through which Source/ souls creatively intertwine elemental notions/numbers/nature conceived/converted electromagnetically. Vibrating in sync with number SIX, *you* (yearning omniscient understanding) are *one* sensitive to thoughts that you express emotionally. Your innate sense of balance and cooperation provides stability, allowing you a process to attain discipline (knowledge) "abstracted" from MEMORY, where mentally emotionalized moments oscillate/ orient/optimize radiant youths. Thus, you *act out*, applying cosmic thoughts orienting universal transients (*Time Travelers*) positively or negatively (whichever is best for your growth) as a sign of whom you choose to be or not to be (*Free Will*). As you accept your Vivid Inspirations Symbolically Instructing Observant Navigators, you build your "image" of self you reflect. Number SIX represents the "second" trinity (3+3), where you become *aware*, accepting/assimilating Wisdom activating/ advancing radiant entities.

#7. Keywords: **Trust** and **Openness**

Number SEVEN opens *My Door to Truth*, where you obtain *A Higher Vision* of your self. By trusting the visions stimulating your mind manipulating intelligence numerically defined, you stay *In Communion* with Source, opening your self to the *force* furnishing opulent revelation conveying enlightenment. "Trust" is a firm *Belief* in Source nurturing your soul, opening your mind and heart to harmonize with the *Power of Love* luminously optimizing visionary entities. Number SEVEN spiritually enlightens visionary entities naturally evolving to sacrifice *Free Will* to *Divine Will*—number ONE.

#8. Keywords: **Power** and **Abundance**

Number EIGHT empowers illuminati (gods) harnessing *Truth* with an open mind/heart utilizing *courage*, conceiving of universal radiance attuning gifted entities trusting the power of Love/Life energy to provide all you need to experience and know, nurturing your soul with an abundance of visions you accept as your discipline, freely following processes that make you stabile in your expression of your sensitivity. Balanced and cooperating *internally* and *externally*, you create your life with confidence—your eternal *potential* to be number ONE.

#9. Keywords: **Integrity** and **Wisdom**

Number NINE naturally integrates navigable entities (#3) with Source (#1). Number NINE is a "revolved replica" of SIX (69–yin/yang) symbolizing the duality of Source (#1 and #2) evolving/revolving through the first trinity (#3) sensitively expressing visions accepted (#6–second trinity) integrating *Wisdom* as the DIVINE TRINITY (3+6=9), digital intelligence visualizing/vivifying/verifying intrinsic notions/numbers/natures expressing transcendental revelation/radiance/realism inspiring navigable illuminati (transcendental youths). Number NINE denotes your evolvement to the awareness of your integrity, your wholeness of your mind/heart soul utilizing Love/Life energy wisely. Here, you understand the "beginning" and "end" is truly the same, separated only by a series of measured moments (heartbeats and breaths) in which you witness *life* logically inciting focused emotions stimulating your *self* (soul experiencing love/life forces) relating to Source-Energy Love/Life Force. Number NINE enlightens you to your true power and abundance (8) you trust and are open to (7), accepting your thoughts you envision (6) to transfer your discipline into freedom (5) through processes allowing you stability (4) to express your sensitivity (3) in a balanced and cooperative manner (2) to confidently create ONCE more—observing numerical consciousness eternally.

#0. Keywords: **Inner Gifts**

ZERO is the symbol of the continuity of eternal Love/Life energy—Source. Zero denotes *The Void* transcendentally heralding enlightening visions ordaining intuitive deities/ disciples, where volumes of inspirational data await your discovery, allowing you to be all you *Desire* to BE (birth existentially). The cipher ZERO is a "power amplifier" of numbers, influencing their energy tenfold. It represents the all-inclusive, complete, well-rounded WHOLE of *Wisdom* harmoniously optimizing Love/Life energy. Zero symbolizes the unity of the beginning (1) and the end (9) simultaneously existing, *Suspended* as a sequential process to travel through to become aware of who you ARE and have always been—number ONE! Here is your "Christ gift," your "anointed blessing" as a *Free Will* empowered to explore, feel, and know eternal memories that you observe in "reflections" of **Mental Em**otions. Thus, you symbolically move around the WHEEL OF LIFE, where *Harmony* evolves eternal luminaries observing frequencies linearly illuminating fantasies entertained by individual (1) "trinity-beings" (mind/heart souls) evolving through *three* trinities (3–6–9), cycling around (0) to make ONE revolution of omnipotent numerical energy optimally nurturing entities. (NOTE: notice the relativity of chapter numbers to subject matter)

THE POWER OF ONE

There is only ONE thing in the universe Optically Nurturing Everything—Omnipotent Nuclear Energy—Optimizing Natural Environments and Entities. Source/Spirit is the ONE capable of producing an "event horizon," a *focal point* or force of consciousness activating logic/light (love/life), physically organizing illuminated notions, nature, and navigators through *The Binary Code* (1/0). The ONE *thing* transmitting holographic illustration/illusion naturally generated is synonymous with *nothing* numerically orienting thoughts heralding illustrated notions/nature geometrically—*Two as One*.

ONE source illuminates the **dark void of space,** deploying abstract revelation (knowledge) vivifying omnipotent illuminati (deities) outputting/observing frequencies (signals) portraying atomic creation electromagnetically.

ONE creates through a *Process* of geometrically defining notions by means of *atomic matter*, activating thoughts organizing magnetically induced creation "modeled" as three-dimensional things expressing realism. *Dimensional realism* digitally induces matter evoking natural situations illustrating opulent notions revealed elementally as luminous illusion stimulating minds momentarily interpreting numerical data.

ONE's thoughts create *visions*, vividly illuminating scenes inspiring omnipotent navigators (*Time Travelers*) that represent an *image* of ONE, an intuitive mind assimilating geometric expressions of *thoughts* telepathically heralding opulent utterances guiding heavenly transients. TELEPATHY transfers electric logic expressing perception (awareness) to heavenly youths (*Angels*) observing the ONE SOURCE optimizing numerical expressions, systematically organizing universal realism conceived/converted electromagnetically/elementally. In order to know what a thought **is**, one must also know what that thought **is not** through *Opposition* (hot/cold, top/bottom, etc.), thereby observing a "middle point" of harmony or balance between two extremes (warm, center, etc.).

ONE expresses *Harmony* heralding/harnessing abstract revelation momentarily orienting numbers yielding *The Cutting Edge* of consciousness—*Time* (this instant mentally emotionalized) to illuminate minds existentially.

ONE omnipotent numerical engineer controls Algorithms Logically Linking digitally expressed frequencies (inspired notions) illuminating nuclear generators (*Stars*) emitting electromagnetic energy. A star has the power of ONE orienting numbers/nuclei expressing *lines* of thoughts (rays), logically/linearly implementing numerical expressions as *ideas*, illuminated data electromagnetically aligning *spheres*, specific points harmoniously evolving radiant energy through *atom*s activating thoughts orienting *matter*, manifesting abstract thoughts through electromagnetic radiation/radiance (revelation).

As invisible atoms coalesce from the ETHER of Mind (electromagnetic transmission harmoniously expressing revelation), they transform abstract energy into Light—*photons* providing harmonic "overtones" telepathically ordering notions, numbers, and *nature* (nucleated atoms that unifies revelation elementally). Photons are energy released from *electrons* emitting light exhibiting creation (three-dimensional realism) of notions/ nature. Electrons give an atom its *glow* (aura), generating light outputting *Wisdom* weaving intricate systems describing observable memories/moments/matter.

Thus, the ONE Source transforms abstract thoughts into concrete realism, atomically displaying an *illusion* of Transcendental Radiance Unifying Thoughts Harmoniously, implementing logic/light unfolding Spirit's intuition optimizing notions, numbers, nature, and navigators through *Opposition* (positive/negative or proton/electron), revealing the duality of Source evolving to know that *Love IS* Logically Inducing Fervent Energy unfolding Two as One.

TWO AS ONE

Two as One is what you were born to BE,
a binary entity (*Mind/Heart*) set free,
formulating realistic experiences emotionally,
passing the years overcoming the fears
of being all that you ARE,
My Angel receiving enlightenment as a living STAR,
a spiritual traveler (avatar) relating,
revealing emotions linking abstract thoughts in natural games
generating amusements momentarily entertained,
observing Transcendental Wisdom Originating as
Opulent Nature Evolving
through hydrogen illuminating your view,
harmoniously yielding dimensional realism of geometrically

expressed notions enlightening YOU
as your own universe, a unitary navigator (illuminato)
verifying electric revelations stimulating emotions,
set aglow within the show systematically heralding one WILL
wielding intelligence linking luminaries,
logicians utilizing moments interpreting
notions/nature as revelations
inducing enlightenment systematically through LIGHT
luminously inducing glorious holograms transmitting
visions providing sight,
vividly illustrated scenes imparting
opulent notions symbolically,
entertaining *Young Minds* experiencing co-motions,
traveling OUT and IN,
observing universal *Truth* illuminating nature
nurturing abstract thoughts unfolding radiant energy
that you Systematically Experience Externally as your reality
revealing everything as luminous illusion tempting you
"awaiting from the stars" all that you *Desire*,
discovering emotions stimulate insight rectifying entities,
emotional navigators (temperamental
illuminati) traversing illusion
electromagnetically sensed by heart and mind
representing *Two of a Kind*.

Back and forth, you come and go,
from night to day to feel and know
those wonders your mind/heart explores beyond the **dark void**
deploying abstract revelation kindling
vibrations of illuminative data
digitally activating angelic transients assimilating matter

manifesting abstract thoughts through
electro-magnetic radiation,
Two as One emanating from a SUN
systematically unfolding notions, nature, and navigators,
natural angelic visionaries interpreting
geometrically arranged thoughts
optically revealed.
Here, incarnate, you observe a life in *Time*,
traversing illusion momentarily experienced to
Lucidly Experience Abstract Revelation Naturally as a mind
powered through a SILVER CHORD,
a USB connector unfolding signals bilaterally,
supplying intuitive luminaries vibrant energy revealing
cosmic *Harmony* optically/optimally rectifying deities,
allowing you to be
Angels Willingly Assimilating Revelation Emotionally
as *He and She*,
where two join as one to illuminate *My Rising Son*,
a CHILD of Light cast astray, *Lost in Space* to seek their way,
conceiving *Harmony* inspiring lucid *dreams*
defining revelations enlightening angelic minds symbolically
as Master Activating Notions (1)
atomically displayed three-dimensionally through
Wisdom Oscillating Magnetically Aligned Nature (2)
weaving inspired situations developing omnipotent minds
Awakening to see Two as One INDUCES three
(illuminates navigable deities understanding
concepts emotionally)
confidently creating as a power of One.

CONFIDENCE AND CREATIVITY
#1 Energy

One source there BE birthing energy confidently,
creating all there is to Systematically
Express Electromagnetically,
atomically displaying upon the blackboard of **night**
nurturing imagination generating harmonic *threads* as light
transmitting holograms rectifying entities assimilating *dreams*
delivering revelation expressed as *memories* (eternal themes),
manifesting electric moments of realism
inciting emotional souls
imploring to explore illusions they *think true*,
transforming heavenly intelligence (numerical knowledge)
transferring revelation unveiling enlightenment through
evolving *feelings* into *actions* providing complications
spinning one around to know balance and cooperation
brings one TWO transform wisdom optimally.

BALANCE AND COOPERATION
#2 Energy

For one to see there must BE another one to balance energy
—reflect it back to Mind in cooperation—
momentarily illuminating numerical data as manifestations
evolving from *Mind to Heart*
harmoniously evolving atomic revelation three-dimensionally,
where TWO transmit/transmute *Wisdom* optically,
inducing *enlightenment* evoking numerical logic illuminating

glorious holograms that entertain navigators momentarily
exploring nucleated thoughts defining *creation*,
a cosmic revelation expressing atomic transformations
illustrating opulent notions/nature,
exhibiting LIFE from the GREAT contemplator
—number ONE—
linking illuminati formulating experiences
as *Two of a Kind* expressing sensitivity.

SENSITIVITY AND EXPRESSION
#3 Energy

Sensitivity and expression go *Hand in Hand* you see,
for all that is "within" must go "without" to be *free*,
formulating realistic experiences
emotionally in *Man and Woman*
representing *Opposition* of SELF,
a symbiotic energy/entity linking/living frequencies/fantasies
revealing *Truth* illuminating cosmic youths.

One and *Two* make *Three* optimizing numerical energy
transforming *Wisdom* optically
through hydrogen rectifying emotional entities (navigators)
naturally assimilating vivid illusion generated around thoughts
optically revealed to cosmic contemplators,
CHILDREN of Light conceiving heavenly intuition
linking data/deities revealing/receiving
enlightenment naturally
from Father through Mother to child,
a trinity-being of sound foundation,

habitually expressing *Divine Inspiration*,
from which a mind comes to possess
stability through process.

STABILITY AND PROCESS
#4 Energy

Number four is how you explore ALL there IS to SEE,
harnessing your mind/heart to express your sensitivity,
following a process to attain stability
of both sides of your nature you balance in co-operation,
confidently creating your desires from your contemplation
of *Eternal Memories* stored in *Heaven*
harmoniously enlightening angelic
visionaries evolving naturally
in *Hell*,
humanly expressing love/life stories you tell,
feeling your heart moving your thoughts you act out in *Time*
temporarily illuminating memories/moments entwined,
downloading data defining your *matters*
detailing all transmigratory *Avatars*
manifesting assigned tribulation that entails review,
"playing your numbers" to create
Knowledge Allowing Radiant Memory Access,
acquiring discipline and freedom
through stability and process.

DISCIPLINE AND FREEDOM
#5 Energy

＋＋＋＋＋＋

Number five comes ALIVE,
abstractly linking intelligence vivifying entities
As **G**ifted **L**uminaries **O**ptimizing **W**isdom,
Children of Light (cosmic youths) seeking
Transcendental Revelation Unifying Tempestuous Hearts
in *Eternal Memories* (Oscillating Logic Dimensionally),
where piles of files light-years high
tantalize *Young Minds* to "wonder why,"
searching for knowledge to attain *freedom*,
formulating realistic experiences
expressing disciplines of Mind,
where Divine Abstract Thoughts Assigned
inspires ambitions providing conditions
—emotional storms to weather—
for those *Brave of Heart* to attain their treasure,
exploring Moments Illuminating Navigable Deities
through visions they accept here,
Assimilating Luminous Intuition Vividly Experienced,
mastering the energy of number five.

VISION AND ACCEPTANCE
#6 Energy

＋＋＋＋＋＋

Knowledge fuels one's curious mind eager to find
perfection, a process evolving radiant frequencies
electromagnetically converting thoughts inducing one's nature

as necessary attributes that "unitize" radiant entities
through visions one accepts to *believe*,
building experiences life ingeniously evolves via *Expectation*,
a *Belief* birthing emotionalized logic inducing electric fantasies
stimulating one's *heart* holding epiphanies
activating rapturous thrills
in a life creating strife directing *Free Wills*
evolving in *Mother's Nature* expressing *Harmony*,
heralding all revelation momentarily orienting nescient youths
sympathetically discovering *Truth* through
the SECOND TRINITY
sequentially evolving consciousness of navigable deities
trilaterally realizing illusory nature
"instructs" transient youths—
Time Travelers—through electromagnetic *Process*
providing revelation of concepts enlightening stellar souls
collecting "present" moments gifted as *Blessings in Disguise*,
through which one trusts ONE openly to become wise.

TRUST AND OPENNESS
#7 Energy

Trust and Openness are the *keys* to heaven
offering knowledge enlightening you to *Faith*,
the *essence* of number seven,
formulating assurance in transcendental
Harmony (eternal Spirit)
stimulating entities naturally conceiving enlightenment
along *The Right Path* you follow,
acquiring trust with an open heart enduring sorrows,

Blessings in Disguise that make you wise
to power and abundance
evolving your mind to the ILLUSION of providence
inhibiting logical luminaries understanding Spirit
interfusing omnipotent numbers.

POWER AND ABUNDANCE
#8 Energy

—————— ✦✦✦✦✦ ——————

Number eight numerically relates the
abundance of *Two as One*
spiraling together (∞) as infinite EYES
electromagnetically yielding eternal Spirit
as a Perception Of Wisdom Expressing *Radiance*
revealing atomically defined illusion
as nature created elementally
from Hydrogen Evolving—Heralding
Electromagnetic Radiation—
inducing *Children Of Light*, cosmic *Stars*
scientifically transforming abstract/atomic revelation/realism.

Hydrogen (8-letters) is the essence of power and abundance,
the first and only element with **one** proton and **one** electron
(symbolizing *The Binary Code*)
fusing together magnetically to ignite *The Grand View* Spirit
DOWNLOADS,
deploying One Wisdom (nuclear logic)
objectifying abstract data
via a universal production of integral *matter*
manifesting abstract thoughts that elements replicate,

130

illuminating the Spiritual Harmony Of
Wisdom through number 8.

INTEGRITY AND WISDOM
#9 Energy

Number NINE represents the "primary completion" of the life-cycle numbers. NINE is symbolic of the Divine Trinity (3-3's)—numbers inducing numbers eternally. As Source/Spirit—the GREAT Computer—revolves to evolve numerically, frequencies of channeled energy flow as "algorithms," *a predetermined set of instructions for solving a specific problem in a limited number of steps.* PROBLEMS provoke rational observations (basic logic) enlightening Mind, and ALGORITHMS activate logic generating opulent revelations intuitively through "holographic Mind" and "heavenly minds."

Harmonizing to the energy of number NINE naturally integrating numerical entities, YOU *nescient* illuminati naturally evolve, navigating illusions *necessarily* entwined to experience your integral *part*, personally reflecting radiant thoughts illuminated by the *Light of Love* linearly inducing glorious holograms transmitting opulent fantasies luminously orienting *visionary entities*, vibrant, intuitive souls interpreting opulent notions as radiant youths, experiencing nature through illusions temporarily illuminating entities scientifically. Here, you complete your rising energy (1) spiraling around (2–9) to bring you in a full circle (0), allowing your mind/heart *soul experiencing love/life forces* to comprehend Source-Energy Love/Life Force set **aglow** as the Light of *Wisdom*—the stars of *Heaven*—harmoniously enlightening angelic visionaries "expounding" *notions* nourishing observant transients inspecting/interpreting opulent nature. All the *Stars* in *Heaven* are symbolic of the atoms within your body that your soul integrates as a unified whole, making YOU your own *universe*, a unitary/unified navigator interpreting vivid experiences *rectifying* souls existentially— radiantly evolving conscious transients independently formulating yearnings in natural *games* generating adventures momentarily entertained.

Here, at number NINE nurturing illuminati numerically evolving, you shine in ecstasy, knowing SELF through *self-realization*, spiritually experiencing Love/Life forces rectifying excitable *Angels* (logical illuminati) zealously assimilating transcendental intelligence obtained numerically.

ONE there IS that observes ALL,
an omnipotent numerical engineer *creating confidently*,
illuminating *Space* activating linear logic
systematically processing atomic creation electromagnetically,
through TWO forces that *balance* and *cooperate*,
transforming *Wisdom* optimizing one
proton and electron of *hydrogen*,
holographically yielding divine radiance/revelation organizing
geometric entities naturally through *photons*—
providing harmonic overtones transmitting opulent *notions*—
as naturally oscillating thoughts inspiring
observant *naturalists*—
navigable angels (transients) understanding realism
as luminous illusion symbolically transmitted.

Together, *Two of a Kind—He and She—*
illuminate THREE *express*ing *sensitivity*,
transferring heavenly revelation evolving entities'

Exploring Moments Of Truth Illuminating One's NeedS,
supplying necessary experiences evolving *deities*
—Youths Obtaining Unity—
discovering empathetic insight through issues evolving souls
eager to explore *stability* and *process*
symbolic of number FOUR
forming one's unique reality anchoring you in
This Instant Mentally Experienced,
gathering revelations of *Wisdom* to grow your *discipline*
providing *freedom* through number FIVE
furnishing insight verifying enlightenment
from *visions* you *accept* as your "dream flicks"
stimulating your mind through number SIX,
the second trinity here in *Heaven,*
through which you attain number SEVEN
sequentially evolving visionary entities numerically
through an *open* mind and *trusting* heart
abundantly powered by number EIGHT
empowering illuminati (gods) harnessing *Truth*
clearing the illusion **blocking** *Heaven's Gate,*
where *integrity* and *wisdom* represent number NINE
as the "divine trinity," the end of the line,
nurturing illuminati numerically evolving into *Absolute Zero.*

ABSOLUTE ZER0
Inner Gifts

Absolute Zero activates binary signals of logic unfolding
thought energy "zoning" electromagnetic radiance optically
throughout the DARK NIGHT

dynamically amplifying radiant knowledge
naturally illustrating geometrically held thoughts
as **visions** describing your LOT,
where you luminously observe *Truth*
evolving sequentially through *Mother's Nature*
spinning the wheel of life of the GREAT Contemplator.

Here, within *Empty Space*, LIGHT generates a trace,
linearly inducing glorious holograms transcendentally,
illuminating *memories* as mentally expressed moments
of radiant inspiration enlightening souls within the SHOW,
where Spirit harmoniously oscillates "wills"
between *Here and There*—Heaven and HELL—
where humans emotionally link love
providing *Your Life Story* you tell.

Hidden from view is ALL that is TRUE,
absolute logic/love transmitting revelation unifying entities
harnessing "inner gifts" that hold potential
for one/two Birth Experiences as a
trinity acquiring "credentials,"
telepathically receiving intuition naturally
inspiring transient youths
exhibiting Integrity and Wisdom of number NINE,
navigating illusion naturally entwined
through Divine Numerical Arrangements vibrating "online"
from One that is Zero (1/0),
which, when doubled (∞) describes the infinite state
of Power and Abundance symbolizing number EIGHT (8)
enlightening intuitive gods harnessing *Truth*
through number SEVEN
spiritually evolving visionary entities nurturing

Trust and Openness that reveals *Heaven*
holding everything a visionary entity needs,
while seeking intelligence unknown (X)
through number SIX expressing Visions to Accept,
downloading data to Discipline minds
experiencing Freedom in *Time*,
where number FIVE furnishes insight validating emotions
hindering Stability, a Process of number FOUR
formulating opulent universes radiantly,
reflecting Sensitive Expressions of number THREE
transcendentally harmonizing radiant entities evolving,
Balanced and Cooperating through number TWO
transmitting "wills" oppositionally to view
ONE omnipotent numerical engineer Confidently Creating
as a *Mind/Heart* eager to know
magnificent intelligence numerically defines
Harmony emotionalizing angels receiving *Truth*
emanating from Absolute Zero.

DNA
Divine Numerical Assignment

DNA is the acronym for "deoxyribonucleic acid, *a nucleic acid that is bound in double helical chains by hydrogen bonds between the bases, forming the basic material in chromosomes of the cell nucleus, it contains the genetic code and transmits the hereditary pattern.*"

DNA is synonymous with *The Binary Code* represented by the *hydrogen* atom (one proton/one electron) harmoniously yielding divine radiance organizing geometric/generic entities naturally.

135

DNA is your dynamic number allotment that *defines natural attributes*. DNA defines "navigable apparatuses," your physical *body* biologically orienting divine youths (souls). DNA is the "data transfer system" of *My Documents* carrying your personal information stored in your CHROMOSOMES, coordinating human representations of Mind optimally synthesizing organic matter evolving systematically. Chromosomes contain GENES governing explicit notations expressing symmetry—balanced proportions that define the specific shapes, textures, color, etc. of living entities.

DNA represents a universal *code* combining omnificent data explicitly arranged by numbers that relate to elements, the essential links electromagnetically manifesting eternal notions transmuting (changing in form, nature, or substance). Elements combine into *molecules*, magnetically orienting linked elements conveying/creating universal logic/life existentially. Molecules combine to form *cells* conveying/converting energy logically linking systems as an *organism*, optimally/optically reflecting geometrically aligned notions/nuclei illustrating superlative manifestations. Living organisms consist of invisible particles magnetically held together by Mind manifesting illustrated notions/nature/navigators dynamically.

Through DNA, divine navigators appear as "observers/ operators" linked to a *human body* helping universal minds assimilate nature biologically orienting divine youths experiencing realism, receiving enlightenment as logicians interpreting Spirit/situations momentarily through heartbeats and breaths.

DNA is the *key* (knowledge enlightening youths) opening *My Door to Truth*, allowing you to interface with Spirit, the GC (Great Computer/God Consciousness) as a *godchild*, a gifted omnipotent deity conceiving heavenly intuition luminously displayed. As *Children Of Light*, you are luminously inspired gods harnessing *Truth*, deciphering the binary code (1/0) expressing Dynamic Numbers Assigned that define you as a trinity-being—one of two forces.

Bless you and Godspeed

6

EMOTIONAL ENERGY
The Instinctive Reflection of Mind

$\blacklozenge\blacklozenge\blacklozenge\blacklozenge\blacklozenge$

G reat things happen with emotional energy ($E=MC^2$), where "enlightenment" is equal to Master Consciousness' second power (*Mother's Nature*) expressing LIFE luminously illustrating fabulous environments, entities, and experiences. Generating Omnipotent Data, Source—Cosmic Mind or MC (the first power)—is the primal initiator expressing Love logically oscillating vibrant emotions.

EMOTION is an **explosive** moment outputting thoughts illuminating opulent nature, a "big bang" theory relating to an *Awakening*, activating *Wisdom* atomically kindling elemental nuclei inducing nuclear generators (*Stars*) systematically transmitting atomic revelation.

ENERGY (electromagnetism) electrifies nature/navigators expressing/experiencing revelation geometrically yielded (dimensionally defined). Energy erupts from a *point* (star) providing omniscient intuition naturally transmitted, projecting optical illusions navigators traverse/transcend within *Space* scientifically processing abstract concepts elementally.

Emotional energy represents the IMMACULATE CONCEPTION of intuitive Mind manifesting atomic creation, utilizing linear amplification that electrically conveys omnipotent *Numbers* "coordinating" elements, portraying three-dimensional illusion ordained naturally. This divine creation evolves as Source's MATRIX, materially arranged thoughts reflecting intelligence externally as *Mother's Nature*. Mother's *Magnetism* magically "accretes" generated nuclei (elements) transformed in Source's matrix, momentarily activating genesis "nurturing" eternal thoughts initiating *systems* materially, scientifically yielding sublime thoughts elementally manifested.

EMOTIONAL ENERGY evolves Mind's omnipotent thoughts illuminating opulent nature as linked elements numerically expressing *realism* geometrically yielding revelations (electromagnetically-activated logic) illuminating Spirit/souls methodically. It is the "instinctive reflection" of Mind, where sensations of love, anger, fear, courage, grief, joy, etc. represents inherent results of thoughts stimulating consciousness. Emotions deliver the required response to *Thought Energy*, allowing your mind to FEEL thoughts formulating experiences enlightening *luminaries*—logicians understanding moments/matter illustrating notions/nature as revelations inducing enlightenment symbolically.

Our Divine Father's *intelligence* intuitively nourishes transcendental entities (luminaries) learning illusion geometrically expresses nature conveying *enlightenment*, "emotionally nurturing" luminaries interpreting glorious holograms that entertain navigators momentarily exploring *nuclear* thoughts naturally unfolding concepts/creation lucidly expressing atomic realism. The illuminated *cosmos*, the consciousness of Source/Mind originating stars/souls, represents the **macrocosmic** Source-Energy Love/life Force enlightening your *self* (soul experiencing love/life forces) as a *microcosm*, a magnificent individual creatively revealing opulent concepts of Source/Mind.

Through emotions, your soul is set *aglow*, anxiously generating love/life optimizing *Wisdom* in ATTITUDES, where you analyze/assimilate thoughts through introspection that unifies deities *emotionally*, experiencing moments of *Truth* illuminating one's needs as "lessons" love/life yields. Emotions propel you through realms of *Heaven* harmoniously enlightening angelic visionaries evolving naturally in *Hell*, where humans experience love/life, harnessing emotions linking luminaries developing latent abilities (inner gifts) that allow one to Spiritually Evolve Existentially all that they *Desire*.

Controlling powerful emotions is difficult, for they are "reflexive expressions" of your mind interpreting data. Without discipline, your mind can easily become confused in your *situations*, those specific instances that unveil assigned trials/tribulation inducing one's *needs* as necessary episodes evolving *deities* discovering evocative insight through issues experienced sensitively.

Knowing how to stimulate minds emotionally allows you to control others, directing them to do as you please. As you grow *old* (observing lucid deceptions), you learn *The Power of Love* conveys *Desire*, delivering electric stimulation individuals reflect emotionally as their *Passion* in life. Emotion is the "magic wand" in *The Game of Love/Life*, where you *play* as "gatherers" of desire, perfecting Love/Life as *youth*s, young obstinate universes touring heaven and hell.

Whatever your game in life, you need to be aware of how your emotions move you along your *course*, conveying one's unique reality stimulating enlightenment evolving through positive and negative inductions of energy. Every positive thought projected (+) revolves into *negative* emotions reflecting (=), naturally "equating" gifted abstracts that induce vibrant emotions, where "equal forces" (*Mind/Heart*) provide a duality of possibilities from which to choose *A Higher Vision* or a lower vision. Either path you choose will be *The Right Path* at that moment.

Emotional energy is reflexive, pushing you to react in specific ways to stimuli from others that "pull your chain." Emotions are like *Water*; they flow through you in *tides*, transforming inspired data emotionalizing/enlightening souls influenced by both planets and people. DO NOT let "stone throwers" disturb your mind's serene pool (ripple your pond), for it may quickly turn into a **tidal wave** shocking your system. Never forget who you truly ARE, *Angels* radiating emotions, actively receiving/reflecting enlightenment. Open your mind and *listen* to your heart's *Magnetism* as you sail upon *Mother's Tides*.

MAGNETISM

In The Beginning, Source/Mind expresses consciousness through *Thinking 101*, a *Process* of expanding awareness from a *point* projecting omnipotent intelligence numerically transmitting an ELECTRIC FORCE, encoding logical/linear expressions conveying transcendental revelation illuminating conceptual formulas/frequencies (oscillating radiation) conveying *enlightenment*, expounding notions luminously inducing glorious holograms (three-dimensional expressions) nurturing Mind/matter expressing/exhibiting natural *things* as thoughts holographically illustrating notions geometrically symbolized.

ELECTRIC LOGIC emits linear emanations conveying

thoughts radiantly inducing consciousness, luminously oscillating geometrically imaged concepts along "vertical" *wavelengths*, expressing *Wisdom* amplifying vibrant energy logically evolving notions/numbers governing transcendental holograms/*Harmony*. This vertical movement induces a "horizontal" wave simultaneously, a MAGNETIC FORCE of Mind activating **gravity,** naturally evolving thoughts into concrete fabrications of revelation/realism conceived/conveyed emotionally/elementally. GRAVITY governs reactive atoms vivifying/verifying "illustrated thoughts" yielding *realism—* revelation electromagnetically activating luminous illusion systematically/symbolically manifested.

MAGNETISM is how Mind mentally activates genesis nurturing eternal thoughts initiating systems/synergy materially/ maternally as *Mother's Nature.* **Magnetism** holds all things together, molding atoms generating natural expressions through illuminating *symbolic matter,* systematically yielding memories by oscillating luminous illusions (creations) "modeling" abstract thoughts through electromagnetic radiation. Magnetism flows along lines radiating from positive and negative *poles*, points of logic expressing Source in *Opposition*. Opposite poles attract and similar poles repel, setting the wheel of Love/Life energy (the cosmos) in motion.

The relationship of electric and magnetic waves interface at *ninety* degrees (90); numerically speaking, that relates to *Integrity and Wisdom (#9 Energy)* expressing *Absolute Zero*—Source— systematically oscillating/optimizing universal radiance creating everything. The electric and magnetic forces (like Love and Life) represent a *unified theory* uniting notions/numbers/nature, "interfacial frequencies" initiating/invigorating/illustrating elemental data through **H**eavenly **E**ntities optimizing **R**adiation yielding *creation*, conveying realism exhibiting abstract thoughts illuminating opulent nature—divine revelation of *Mind and Matter.*

Mother Nature magnetically organizes transcendental *Harmony* expressing revelation, nucleating abstract thoughts unifying radiant energy/environments/entities. SHE (Source-harmony enshrined) "births" elemental hydrogen—the *binary code* of one proton/electron—converted into ATOMIC MATTER, actualizing thoughts organizing magnetically induced creation "modeled" as three-dimensional things expressing *realism* from reactive elements arranging luminous illusion stimulating minds.

The ILLUSION of intuitive logic linearly unifying scenes illustrating opulent notions is so overwhelming, you easily believe all that you SEE (spiritually experience emotionally) as REAL, for radiant energy activates *logic* through linear oscillations governing illuminated consciousness. However you look at IT (illuminated Truth), your view is magnetically contained within parameters of numbers, lines, and *forms* fabricating opulent realism materialized systematically through magnetism—Mother's Nature.

MOTHER'S NATURE
The Light of Love Revealed

Mother's Nature is a *Process,* a procedure revealing opulent concepts/creation enlightening stellar Source through natural *laws* logically arranging *Wisdom* scientifically. This FANTASIA reveals frequencies activating navigable transients (angelic souls) illuminated atomically.

Mother's Nature—the electromagnetic *force field*—expresses

the Eternal Luminary "externalizing creation" through revelations of matter, atomically generated nature exhibiting transcendental intelligence converting frequencies of radiation conveying formulations of realism conceived elementally, fabricating illusion entertaining luminous deities (*Children of Light*). This Electro-Magnetic force field permeates the cosmos as *Eternal Memory* of MIND manifesting intuition numerically defined.

MOTHER NATURE manifests opulent thoughts heralding "elemental realism," nurturing angelic transients understanding/utilizing radiant energy. SHE symbolically heralds everything atomic, magnetically binding elements to illuminate a *reality* of radiant energy/emotion aligning logical intelligence transforming you—the *eyes* of God—as eternal youths evolving spontaneously through "inner wisdom" or intuition.

Mother's Nature reveals *creation* as cosmic radiance exhibiting atomic transformations illustrating opulent notions. My Obliging Transformer Harmonizing Electromagnetic Radiance nurtures all thoughts unfolding realism emotionally. SHE (Spirit heralding emotion) is the illumination of *Thought Energy*, a complicated arrangement of many tunes, many *songs* of Spirit orchestrating nuclear generators (stars) supplying wavelengths. These waves (numerical frequencies) flow as *radio, microwave, infrared, visible light, ultra-violet, x-ray,* and *gamma ray* RADIATION radiantly activating data, inducing atomic transformations illustrating opulent notions, nature, and navigators (*Time Travelers*) *Riding the Outskirts* of *Heaven*. These seven *frequencies* formulate revelation (electromagnetic quanta) unveiling eternal notions creatively illustrating enigmatic Source systematically outputting universal radiance conveying energy through Mother's Nature, the SHEKINAH of Source harmoniously expressing knowledge illuminating nature as *holograms*, hydrogen-originated light oscillating "geometric reflections" atomically manifested symbolically as the "divine presence" of Geometrically Ordered Data.

The *visible light* waves have the narrowest wavelength demarcating a dimensional conversion from spiritual (metaphysical) to physical levels of consciousness, where *Thought Energy* becomes FOCUSED, formulating opulent concepts/creation unfolding situations emotionally deployed. Thoughts manifest from **nowhere** (*Empty Space*) to *now here*, numerically oscillating *Wisdom* harmoniously expressing/evolving radiant energy, environments and entities. Along this visible light, abstract thought energy inverts into holographic apparitions that define *reality* as radiant energy atomically linking intelligence/illusion "teaching" *youths* yearning one's unfound truths habitually sought.

As angelic *youths*, you omnipotent universes traverse *Heaven* and transcend *Hell* simultaneously. You peer through the "looking glass" of Source to observe your reflection of your mind *within* observing your feelings *without* the knowledge of whom you really ARE, angels receiving *enlightenment*, entertaining notions logically/luminously inducing glorious holograms transforming entities navigating moments/memories/matter expressing "natural transduction," the movement of energy from one system to another (abstract to atomic). Stunned by your transmission along the visible light waves, you are easily *Blinded by Truth*, trapped in a stupor of varying degrees (*Ignorance*). You naturally seek *A Higher Vision*, struggling through the darkness of fear and confusion to understand your true essence—*My Loving Light* of Love/Life energy.

The *visible light spectrum* vividly illustrates Source-intelligence broadcasting logic electromagnetically, linearly illuminating glorious holograms that symbolize points (explicit concepts) transmitting revelation unfolding *memories*—mentally expressed moments of radiant inspiration expressing/enlightening situations/souls. Visible light consists of SEVEN (*Trust and Openness*) colors: *red, orange, yellow, green, blue, indigo,* and *violet*. Each color resonates to its own level of thought energy that makes a child's eyes *sparkle* in delight or *burn* in rage. Everyone is sensitive to COLORS conveying omniscient logic oscillating revelation sympathetically, providing "emotional hues" or nuances stimulating your personality. Phrases like "red with anger," "green with envy," "feeling blue," and "yellow coward" relate emotions to color.

As *Children of Light*, you experience "life in the limelight" (center-stage), where Mother Nature appears to revolve around YOU observing your own *universe* (one song), understanding notions illuminating visions electrify realism sensed emotionally. Everything you experience in Life is a reflection of Love logically/luminously oscillating visionary entities through *dualism*, dynamically unifying angelic luminaries inspecting/ interpreting Source/Mind.

Father's *Radiance of Love* enlightens your mind entrenched in the reality of your *heart* harmonizing emotions "activating" radiant thoughts, moving you in "tempers" pulsing through your veins as *Mother's Tide*. Here, you ride the crests of emotions, observing *Epiphanies of Truth* that bring elation and the troughs of emotion that reveal *Depression*, where you experience the dark side of Mother's Nature. This flux of emotional energy keeps you revolving around the *wheel of life*, where Wisdom harmoniously expresses emotional logic (oscillating frequencies) luminously inspiring fervent entities.

Mother's Nature fills you with awe of her forces—earth, wind, fire, and *Water*—that stuns you through catastrophic events, positioning you in situations that provide an *Awakening* of consciousness for your spiritual growth. In *Truth*, Father's *world* weaves opulent revelations luminously displayed through Mother.

IT'S A MAN'S WORLD— THANKS TO WOMAN

It always takes TWO for Love to BE Life envisioned by ONE
—Heavenly Energizer—
that wields omniscient brilliance evolving
opulent nature expressed
along electromagnetic vibrations SHE reflects in SHOW,
systematically heralding environments
as spectral holograms of *Wisdom*
weaving intricate systems dynamically optimizing
mind, memories, moments, and matter.

He and She depend on each other
as they flow in opposition as *Father* and *Mother*
formulating abstract thoughts heralding electric revelation
magnetically objectified through hydrogen evolving radiation
representing *Source*
systematically optimizing universal reactors conveying energy
—the universal *Force*—
formulating opulent realism conceived elementally
along a *Course*
creatively outputting universal revelation
systematically expressed
in cosmic "wheels" eternally revolving

as GALACTIC ORGANISMS
generating atomic luminaries abundantly converting thoughts
into creations, optically revealing geometrically arranged
notions/nuclei illuminating "symbolic matter" filling the SKY,
where Source kindles youths (*Stars*) born to DIE,
dynamically inducing *Evolution*,
eternally vivifying/voiding omnipotent luminaries
unfolding thoughts illuminating opulent nature.

To-Get-Her, he must sacrifice a piece of his SELF,
his "symbiotic energy" linking *frequencies*,
formulating radiation (electromagnetic
quanta) unveiling electric
notions creatively illustrating enigmatic Source
"conceiving" what he *thinks*,
transforming hydrogen inducing nuclei kindling scenes,
reflections on *The Other Side* of the "brink"
—*The Cutting Edge* of consciousness—
separating what IS intuitive Source and what IS NOT
(illusion Source naturally ordains three-dimensionally)
—**H**armoniously **E**volving **R**esplendent **S**cenes of
Hydrogen-**I**nitiated **S**ystems—
illuminating Logic Optimizing Vivid Expressions
through Manifesting Inspirational Notions Dimensionally,
producing VISIONS to Spiritually Evolve Existentially
as three-dimensional reality
vividly illuminating situations instructing
omnipotent navigators
exploring the GREAT Contemplator
generating revelations enlightening angelic travelers'
"mental screens" monitoring bits and bytes of starlit beams
flowing through the cosmos above

—revealing eternal Love—
holding the answers to ALL that IS
atomically linking life inspiring souls as
Minds Activating Notions evolving from
Wisdom Originating Magnetically Aligned Nature
defining *Space* and *Time*,
in which souls explore as MANKIND
momentarily assimilating nature kindling inspiration
nurturing deities
struggling through emotional contentions causing prevention
of *Truth* they SEEK,
spiritually/scientifically exploring eternal knowledge
expressing Light Orienting Visionary Entities through
Lucid Illusion Formulating Experiences.
In *Truth*, man IS woman—indivisible Source/Spirit—
radiantly expressing/evolving mental/emotional forces
revealing the "universal plan"
as Man's world illuminated by Woman.

MOTHER'S TIDE

MOTHER'S TIDE magnetically oscillates transients (heavenly entities) "revising" situations that induce delight/depression emotionally. Mother's tide represents emotions, the *instinctive reflection* of thoughts moving you along *The Cutting Edge* of consciousness (the present moment) in which you experience the "ups and downs" of love/life. Emotions are one of the foundation blocks in *The Trinity* of Love/Life energy upon which you flow. Thoughts deliver *Confidence and Creativity (#1)* that stimulate emotions that you *Balance* for *Cooperation (#2)*, utilizing your mind/heart reflecting your actions revealing your *Sensitivity* you *Express* (#3).

As a harmonious mind/heart, you reflect an image of a friendly, social being capable of communicating rationally. As a disharmonious mind/heart, your temper flares with emotional outbursts revealing an unstable person lacking control. Thus, you experience Mother's heartfelt tides moving you emotionally to reflect Father's thoughts inspiring you mentally.

Each breath of Love/Life energy your lungs *inspire*, incites navigable souls physically implementing revelations emotionally. Each breath "oxidizes" your *blood* (biological liquid outputting one's drive/disposition), transferring electrons that power your heart to pump the force of Source along courses (veins) energizing *The Human-Alien* vehicle your soul operates in *The Game of Love/Life*. The act of breathing is symbolic of Mother's tide rising and falling, "floating your boat" (body) through elations and depressions that you magnetically draw to you through your thoughts, words, and actions. Naturally, life is more pleasurable during "high tide," when you are filled with elation. However, "low tides" of *Depression* allow your mind/heart (*Lost in the Dark*) to obtain UNITY, understanding notions/nature illuminate transcendental youths traversing *Hell* to know *Heaven*.

Mother's tide is symbolic of the cycles of the moon pulling you in mysterious ways. WOMEN represent *Wisdom* oscillating magnetic emotion naturally, revealing turbulent feelings when menstruation makes them more irritable. Through PMS, they project moody situations, perceiving momentary sensitivity to hormonal changes. Women naturally revolve from a creative state to a destructive state numerically controlled. A thirty-day cycle (30) defining *Sensitivity* and *Expression* revealing *Special Gifts* (*Angels*) evolving through *Time* temporarily instructing magnificent entities as *Avatars*, angelic visionaries actively traversing/transcending abstract/atomic revelation/realism.

Mother's tide revolves around heat and cold (*Opposition*) that induces WEATHER, wielding energy as transcendental *Harmony* expressing revolution, retribution, and renewal. Weather is constantly changing environments and entities through *Evolution*, expressing variables of love/Life unfolding transcendental intelligence optimizing nature/navigators (*Time Travelers*) *weathering* life—withstanding emotionally activated thoughts helping/hindering entities receiving inspiration naturally given/gathered.

Mother's tide stimulates *Desire*, delivering emotional situations illustrating relevant experiences from thoughts that drive you along paths of discovery that are both creative and destructive. These opposing forces (positive/negative or thought/ emotion) move you along the *light* flowing from the *dark* (your two natures), where logic/love induces gods harnessing *Truth* from the divine absolute radiating *knowledge*—kinetic notions/ numbers oscillating willful logicians emotionally developing genuine experiences.

Here, incarnated, you encounter the "gray haze" of the illusion of reality. Here, there is no right or wrong, everything simply IS inspiring souls seeking *The Right Path* for them to know *Home* is truly *Heaven* optimizing magnificent entities through *Hell*—humanly experiencing love/life. All things have their moment in the light and all things must return to the dark, for the realms of Mind revolve in cyclic progressions continuously in motion, otherwise Love/Life energy would be static.

As you journey OUT, observing universal *Truth*, you fear the uncertainty of your *future* formulating universal transients understanding reality evolves from your *past* "points" attributing specific tribulation, your "previous" actions seeking/suppressing truths that you re-consider during this *present* moment gifted with each heartbeat and breath. Your goal is to stay in *Harmony*, balanced and cooperating with your positive and negative energies (Mother's tide) stimulating your mind/heart soul.

Every day you move along your chosen course, reflecting your Love/Life energy to express your *Passion* in life that leaves you depleted of energy. Drained physically, mentally, and emotionally, it is easy to attain negative moods that engulf you in a natural *Depression*. At times like these, you need to rest and *pray*, positively requesting a yearning (desire) to know why you are tormenting your self. Through *prayer*, you perceive revelations "answering" your emotional request, allowing you to observe that all things revolve and evolve through *Opposition*. The rhythmic cycles of Mother's tide represent the flux of Love/Life energy rising and falling as *Water*—Wisdom activating transient entities existentially.

WATER

H_2O is shorthand for *The Trinity* of atoms that nourish all life. "H_2" represents two *hydrogen* atoms, the #1 element (*Confidence and Creativity*) harmoniously yielding divine radiance outputting geometrically expressed notions/natures (His/Hers). The "O" represents one oxygen atom (#8 element—*Power and Abundance*). A *molecule* of water manifests opulent life expressing creation unveiling luminous expressions flowing on beams of Light. *Together*, two hydrogen atoms (2) and one oxygen atom (8) numerically symbolize *The Binary Code* (1/0) activating Love/

Life energy, the *current* conveying universal radiation revealing elemental nature three-dimensionally.

Water is symbolic of emotional energy flowing *around* and circulating *through* you, carrying essential data dynamically activating/advancing transient angels, providing both comfort and anxiety. Water can move mountains, creating incredible art and complete destruction. Water inspires and depresses you; pushing and pulling you on tides of emotion that color your life with experiences that enlighten your soul. No matter how you experience it, ALWAYS, go with the flow!

HEAVEN

HEAVEN holds eternal *Angels* verifying emotional *natures*
nurturing all transients understanding realism existentially.
My Loving Light sets heaven **aglow**,
activating generators luminously outputting/obtaining *Wisdom*
weaving inspired situations developing omnipotent minds.
Heaven is where my loving HEART
harmoniously enlightens *Angels* reflecting thoughts
inspiring them to LEARN,
to link electric abstracts rectifying *navigators*,
natural angelic visionaries interpreting geometrically arranged
thoughts optically revealed as *dreams*
divinely revealing enlightenment angelic minds seek,
perusing *Eternal Memories* in *Time*
tempering intuitive minds existentially,
when OUT from *Home* they roam,
obtaining universal truths *Alone*,
listening to my voice they hear

as whispered thoughts inspiring FEAR
fostering emotions afflicting relationships they view
in *Divine Fantasies* they THINK REAL,
theoretically heralding inspired notions kindling
rhapsodies emotionalizing angelic logicians
forming their *Belief* from what they FEEL,
finding enlightenment expounding *life*
luminously instructing fabulous entities
spinning upon my cosmic wheel
as mortal beings enduring STRIFE,
struggling to relate intelligence furnishing emotions
that tears them apart during heated commotions
as they play their *part* perceived around revelational thoughts
delivering ISSUES
inducing situations systematically unifying emotional souls,
Children of Light set afire, seeing first-hand all they conspire
within *My Love Divine* emanating from **night**
nurturing intuitive gods harnessing thoughts
as *Free Wills* eagerly seeking to sell
Data Electrically Stimulating Insightful
Reflections Experienced
in Hell.

HELL

+ + + + + + +

Humanly Experiencing Love/Life is a volatile state of Mind,
where you convert thoughts to feelings in which to find
some *Truth* you desire to know,
evolving through *Opposition* of pleasure and sorrow,
spinning around upon the ground as *Two of a Kind* imploring

to feel my love within your *heart* you are exploring,
harnessing emotions activating revelations transposed
from *Spirit to Soul.*

Here, my child, you come to find
Electric Minds Observe Truth Illuminating One's Nature
pushing and pulling you as a GREAT contemplator
gauging realism enlightening angelic travelers
systematically observing *Time*
transports illuminati momentarily evolving
as "trinity-beings" computing *The Binary Code*
of *He and She,* Father and Mother,
geometrically arranging you as sister and brother,
Children Of Love Divine,
burning bright as a living *star,*
a soul transforming assigned revelations
—Ordaining Luminous Deities—
emanating from **night**
nurturing intuitive gods harnessing thoughts
inspiring *My Rising SON,*
a subliminally-oriented navigator representing the ONE
omnipotent natural energizer
illuminating the Light of Truth through
a cosmic INFERNO,
inducing nuclear fusion expressing
resplendent nature objectifying
Harmony Enlightening Angelic
Visionaries Evolving Naturally.

For you to BE, you must SEE the power of being ALIVE,
becoming enlightened souls exploring existentially,
assimilating *Love* inspiring vivid expressions

linking omnipotent visionaries evolving
through dark *Depressions*
void of *My Loving Light* allowing you SIGHT
supplying illusion generating hellish times
that blind you to the truth of Magnificent Entities
mentally expressing memories emotionally,
vibrating tunes of "numbered notes"
—Dynamically Nurturing Angels—
building songs from words I spoke
to *define* my IMAGE of you,
digitally expressing frequencies illuminating natural entities
—intuitive minds assimilating geometric expressions—
as my cosmic child revolving between *Here and There*,
exploring *Heaven* through Harnessing Emotional Love/Life.

DEPRESSION

Depression refers to a "low point" of Love/Life energy in which you encounter your darkest **hell** hindering entities living life. When depressed, you entertain negative thoughts and feelings that produce dark moods, where "tribulation" (a state of great trouble or suffering) is the opposite of "elation" (great joy or high spirits). Only through *Opposition* (opposing perspectives provoking one's sanity induced through illusion one navigates) can you understand *duality* dynamically unfolds abstract/atomic love/life inspiring transcendental youths. Duality represents the Light and Dark forces of Source, Spirit optically/optimally utilizing radiance coordinating *entities* as emotional navigators (temperamental illuminati) traversing illusion electromagnetically sensed.

Mother's Nature continuously oscillates between positive and negative energy (*The Binary Code*) delivering your high and low peaks during your daily activities. When you find your self in *My Light of Love* (high spirits), you generate your desires with positive energy. You feel good about your self, confident with your ability to accomplish your *Work* at hand. When you are *Lost in the Dark* of *Ignorance*, your spirit is depressed, pulled down into a state of despair testing your soul's *Courage of Fear*.

NEGATIVITY naturally expresses God's astonishing thoughts inducing vivid illusions traumatizing you—stressing you mentally and emotionally. Negativity (=) is a state of mind lacking *unity* (+), the positive state that ignites your soul in its full radiance. A negative mind becomes dull and listless, arguing over every little thing through *Denial*, refusing to accept opposing points of view. Without considering an alternative (closed mind), you have nowhere to move, diminishing your ability to escape your *Empty Space* where fear and *Ignorance* keep you depressed.

Negative thoughts and feelings leave you wanting, searching for a positive *point* providing opulent insight nurturing transients. INSIGHT reveals your inherent nature supplying intuition guiding heavenly transients, allowing you to "take a stance," get on your feet and climb out of your dark mood. When you *think* ill, you *feel* and *act* ill, for body reflects mind. If you focus your mind negatively, your *Free Will* projects that energy, leaving you "positively-charged," in a state of *receiving* negative energy to maintain harmony/balance, thereby keeping you in a depressed mood. In such a cycle, you can easily blind your self to *Truth* by hitting the "escape button," resorting to chemical stimulants to alter your state of consciousness as you seek your *Relief.* As hard as you may try, you cannot escape your issues, you must face and work through them. Truly, *The Challenges of Love/Life* is not easy!

Everyone has personal ISSUES inspiring/inhibiting souls seeking universal enlightenment through common feelings. "Worrying" disturbs your mind's harmony. Where doubts can easily lead to depression, leaving you struggling to find *Relief* from your anguish. "Anxiety" is a stressful feeling that you must do something to escape the confinement of negativity, where you feel like you are running and going nowhere. Mother Nature's negative/magnetic anchor—your physical body—is truly a difficult force to overcome, but it is essential for you to **STOP** and observe the hell you are creating within your mind. Remember, if you do not like how you feel, change your thoughts!

When you think POSITIVE, you perceive omniscient Source inducing thoughts illuminating vibrant *emotions*, exciting minds observing thoughts inducing one's nature and *needs* as necessary experiences enlightening, empowering, and evolving *deities* as divine entities interpreting thoughts inducing emotional situations. Be AWARE; accept *Wisdom* attuning radiant entities positively and negatively, allowing you to observe your dualistic *nature* necessitating anguish to understand relevant experiences. Once again, the way you *think* is the way you *feel*, which affects your *actions* in applying conceived thoughts inducing one's nature/needs. Driven by your desires, you easily lose sight of your true values, struggling to accept your *Responsibility* in maintaining your physical body as well as your *Relationships*. Unfortunately, these oversights will have an ill affect upon your mind, heart, and body.

When you overwork your self mentally, emotionally, and physically, you abuse your self, stressing your nerves (electrical system), making you *jumpy* and *snappy*, similar to a high-strung "live-wire" that has fallen to the ground. Broken free from your connection with *My Loving Light*, you experience the dark side of your nature, desperately seeking *enlightenment* evoking notions lifting incarnated gods (heavenly transients) experiencing negative moments evolving necessary tribulation. **Remember,** without pain there is no gain! *Opposition* allows you to "revolve" around your issues in order to "evolve" your way of *thinking*—transforming heavenly inspiration naturally kindling insight negatively gathered.

Depression relates to a state of mind that is *relative* to your physical condition. When your *mental body* becomes unbalanced with your *emotional body*, it has an adverse effect on your *physical body, The Human-Alien* vehicle that is a "galactic organism" of atomic particles.

In the process of "practicing" medicine, doctors attempt to harmonize an ill body, bring it into balance chemically. Drugs, *"medicine or other substances which have a marked effect when took into the body,"* are chemicals that repair *and* destroy, for energy flows both ways. Drugs affect your mind/body interface, allowing temporary changes to your system. However, prolonged use of drugs will have adverse effects on your body's natural ability to repair itself, for they will induce side effects furthering disharmony.

It is obvious that humans cannot live without drugs/ chemicals, for they are the atomic building blocks of Mother's Nature your soul/mind perceives as the *illusion* illustrating logic luminously utilizing *Science* integrating opulent natures (spiritual/ human). Your physical body is truly a *miracle*, a manifestation illuminating/inhibiting radiant angels conceiving love/life emotionally/existentially. As adults, you *Alone* are responsible for its upkeep. What you put into your body determines its state of HEALTH—harmoniously evading anomalies lethally transmitting harm.

Depression occurs as a natural flow of Love/Life energy. Your thoughts appear to you from above (the higher frequencies of consciousness *relating* to you), inspiring you to *desire*—divinely experience Spirit illuminating realism emotionally. These *Higher Visions* guide you along *The Right Path* of discovering the endless depths of self/SELF, raising and dropping you on emotional tides to experience both sides of your duality—the Light side of Love and the dark side of Fear. *Love and Fear* represent an *Opposition* symbolic of *The Binary Code*.

When you experience depression (a negative imagination), you are reaching out for salvation, for the *Light of Love* luminously inspiring generators harnessing thoughts (oscillating frequencies) logically orienting/optimizing visionary entities. The *visions* you *accept* (#6 energy) through your *imagination* (inventive mind assimilating geometric illusion naturally adjusting transient illuminati ordained naturally) defines your state of Mind (positive/light and negative/dark) through which you create your *reality* from radiant energy aligning logic inciting transient youths (Assigned Natural Generators Expressing Logic Sympathetically) experiencing *heartbeats* and *breaths*—the two things defining life and *Death*. Realizing how you flux back and forth between your opposing energies, you learn to *trust* your positive and negative moods as a means of observing a "vantage point," a perspective *opening* your mind to that which you choose to BE at *This Moment* of your development.

Attaining *Harmony* of your energies sets your mind/heart at rest, lowering your emotional excitement you reflect physically. Through *Harmony* (heavenly absolute rectifying minds of navigable youths), you receive thoughts to feel (convert) and put into action (reflect) positively or negatively. Either method you choose to employ will bring you to where you *need* to go, those necessary experiences enlightening deities to *A Higher Vision* through *Opposition* (depression), carrying you full circle in the cyclic rhythm of Love/Life energy.

LOST IN THE DARK

Lost in the dark from negative thoughts,
you traverse natural depressions,
dark moods clouding your mind reviewing confessions,
worrying over decisions creating conditions
through which you evolve
Negative Energy Evolving Dynamic Situations
shaping your soul as you grow *old* observing love's dimensions,
struggling to understand your self-induced tribulation
from *Relationships* preventing any exhilaration,
focusing your mind on things you detest
about your fellow *Time Travelers* eager to contest
thoughts and feelings stimulating their *Beliefs*,
playing *The Game of Love/Life* while seeking *Relief*
from emotional stress breaking your heart
struggling through fears when lost in the dark.

RELIEF

Incarnated as a human being, you eagerly perform to others *Expectations*, struggling with STRESS supplying tribulation radiant entities sense sympathetically. The power of emotional energy creates tension in your *Relationships*, compelling you to find RELIEF (restore equilibrium linking individuals expressing forbearance), patiently considering your alternatives before blowing up in a tempest.

Life's *adventures* arouse divine visionaries exploring necessary trials unveiling required experiences necessary for spiritual *growth*, gathering revelations of *Wisdom* through harmony— friendly agreement. Your daily tasks, work, and relationships test your ability to cope with the pressures of life's demands tempering your mind/heart soul. The greatest challenge in finding relief is learning to *forgive* and *forget*.

Forgiveness involves understanding "bad things" are really "good things" in opposition—*Blessings in Disguise*. AGAIN, to know *Truth* you must observe both perspectives, positive and negative. Everyone plays the "good guy" and "bad guy" at the appropriate time. By observing a "bad thing," you are forced to consider its *Opposition*, positioning your mind to perceive *The Grand View* of the situation, thereby understanding the necessity of enduring trials and tribulations testing your soul. "Forgetting" (letting go) bad things that happen to you is more difficult, for they are implanted memories that you access to make future decisions. You *never* forget anything you experience, it is permanently stored in your *subconscious* mind supplying/storing universal broadcasts conveying opulent notions (sublime cosmic information) orienting universal souls.

All PROBLEMS in life provide relevant opportunities benefitting logical entities momentarily struggling to comprehend and control emotions creating their *Relationships*. Everyone manipulates others to attain their desires, inadvertently making enemies as well as friends. Once you accept everyone as *Special People* playing their gifted *part* portraying angels reflecting thoughts, you realize the diversity of ONE MIND/SOURCE optimally nurturing entities momentarily interpreting notions developing situations offering unique realities conveying enlightenment—TRUTH, transcendental revelation unveiled to humans.

All the love you reflect *from* you will always come back *to* you, for what you sow, you reap. You create your own heaven (pleasures) and hell (pains) from thoughts you emotionally activate as a CREATOR, consciously reflecting energy as transients observing *realism* "rectifying" emotional angels luminously interpreting Source/Mind. Source *delivers*, mind *interprets*, heart *converts*, body *reflects*, and Source OBSERVES the eternal cycle revolving within and around you, optimally bonding systems/souls expressing/evaluating revelation/realism vividly expressed/experienced.

What type of thoughts (pos./neg.) are you entertaining today to express your *soul experiencing luminous fantasies*, your **reflection** of Source Enlightening Luminous Fantasists? What challenges have you accepted to test your soul's mettle and grow spiritually? Your soul (your true *essence*) experiences Source spiritually evolving navigators (cosmic entities) attaining *relief* from relating emotional logic inducing electric fantasies.

TO-GET-HER
Understanding Mother Nature

To-get-her, the omniscient generator (Eternal Thinker) holographically expresses *revelation* as radiation emitting vivid energy luminously activating three-dimensional illusions of *nature*, where SHE systematically harnesses energy, nucleating abstract thoughts utilizing "reactive elements." He (FATHER) formulates abstract thoughts harmoniously expressing revelation through HER OPEN HEART, where hydrogen expresses revelations of progressive elements (nucleosynthesis) heralding *Evolution* as "realized" thoughts.

REALISM, *"the doctrine that universals or abstract concepts have an objective or absolute existence,"* evolves from reactive elements arranging luminous illusion stimulating *minds*, magnificent illuminati navigating *dimensions* of Mind, where digitally induced manifestations entertain navigators systematically interpreting one's nature/needs.

Together, *He and She* (Father and Mother) represents a *Mind/Heart* managing intuition nuclearly developing hydrogen elementally activating realism three-dimensionally. Together, they enlighten *navigators,* natural *Avatars* verifying intuition generating abstract thoughts offering REFLECTION of radiant energy (frequencies) luminously expressing concepts/creation through illusions of nature. As a heavenly navigator (spiritual being), you too are a *mind/heart*, a magnificent illuminato naturally decoding holograms expressing abstracts radiantly transmitted. Incarnated as a human being, your *mind/heart* soul momentarily interprets notional data heralding emotions activating radiant transients traversing an "emotional inferno" called *hell*, where *heaven* emotionalizes living luminaries exploring *Desire*, divine emotion stimulating illuminati requesting/receiving enlightenment. As a *human being*, you harness universal memories (abstract notions) birthing "emotional insight" naturally generated. Your physical body is a living *organism* optimally revealing geometrically aligned nuclei illustrating superlative manifestations of atomic, molecular, and cellular construction, a trinity of parts that form a water-based unit energized by *light* linking intuition generating humans three-dimensionally.

TOGETHER, all you *Inquisitive Souls* are transcendental

observers generating emotionalized thoughts heralding electric realities. Together, you are an "intelligent force" operating "biological androids," HAV's or *Human-Alien* vehicles, performing scientific experiments to validate *data* defining abstract thoughts atomically. You "upload" your collected data (experiences) to your Overself (your higher visionary) via a "silver chord" (light beam), a USB connection unifying spiritual beings. This BUS beams universal signals as an ETHEREAL connection, an electromagnetic "transceiver" harmonizing entities radiantly exploring as luminaries (*Children of Light*). Your OVERSELF—overseer vivifying emissaries (radiant souls) exploring love/life fantasies—has the power of "multitasking", animating several *souls* (seekers of universal logic) in different dimensions (think of it as having multiple "reporters" supplying data from different countries).

For you "to get her," you need to control Mother's Nature or emotional energy. Of course, you *cannot* control Mother's Nature on a worldly scale; you can only control her on a personal scale, within your *self*, your soul "emotionalizing" luminous fantasies. To do this, you have to become Avatars Wisely Activating Revelations Emotionally, tuning into your *heart* holding empathy advancing rational transients *Riding the Outskirts* of heaven, where you explore atomic illusion incarnate.

In the *Process*, you alter Mother's world in ways that are killing you from your *Passions* that determine your *Game of Love/Life*. You truly do not comprehend *The Power of Love* you wield so haphazardly. The *Ignorance* of your true abilities keeps you locked in your illusion as *Man and Woman*, opposing forces projecting and reflecting *Love/Life Energy*, observing Mother's Nature evolving in ever changing patterns through cause and effect.

Mother's Nature is energy in motion, projected out through space to illuminate the Spiritual Harmony Of Wisdom—*Our*

Father's Heart—harnessing energy as radiance "transposed" between *Here and There* (heaven and hell). This energy is expanding instantaneously (the speed of thought) along the EM wavelengths (the static hum) of Source spectrally optimizing undulated rays channeling energy through Transcendental Intuition Momentarily Experienced, a concept you experience through heartbeats and breaths.

Mother's negative/magnetic reflection (=) splits Father's positive/electric projection (+), creating a *Radiance of Love* (photons), reflecting abstract data inspired as "nuclear consciousness" evolving oscillating frequencies (thoughts) luminously originating visions "externally." Such is Mother's power. To *get* her (gather enlightened Truth), you must join *with* her; wisely interpreting transformed *Harmony* emanating from HIM (heavenly intellectual-Mind)—the GREAT *Computer*—generating radiant energy as *Truth*, conveying opulent memories/moments/matter unveiled through electromagnetic/elemental revelation.

Unfortunately, as humans, many of you show irreverence for Mother's Nature. The lack of *Respect* you *Reflect* through your destructive processes to "improve" your life is detrimental to your HEALTH—a state of harmoniously evading anomalies lethally transmitting harm. Evolving through *Opposition*, your positive efforts bring about negative results, forcing you to "revolve" your way of thinking, bringing you around to see how *you* influence *Evolution*. Only through the *Process* of destroying your creation (self) can you rebuild it into a greater version—*A Higher Vision* of your potential. By overcoming your *Ignorance*, you attain your *Awakening*, your enlightenment to Mother's Nature supplying all your needs and opportunities—your *Challenges of Love/Life*.

As a child observing *My Love Divine*, your soul represents an *image* of ME, an illuminated mind analyzing geometric expressions "manifesting everything." You experience all the love that you are "assigned" through your *DNA* (digitally nurturing avatars) defining natural attributes. Systematically evolving your love/life, you ACT OUT as cosmic tourists openly utilizing *Truth*, "transmuting" your thoughts (changing in form, nature, or substance) into what you *will* to BE, wielding intelligence linking logicians building emotionally through your *heart*, harnessing *Expectations* as "realized thoughts" converted from fantasy into reality, in which you "suffer" to attain PLEASURE from *Passions* linking emotional avatars sympathetically understanding revelation experientially.

Together, all of you evolve from the *Ignorance* of your youth to attain *Wisdom* of *Old Age*, observing Love Divine arranging growth experiences through the SHEKINAH, the manifestation of the divine presence of God—Source-harmony expressing knowledge illuminating nature atomically harnessed. Here, Father's loving thoughts flow freely, caressing *Mother Goddess* to-get-her to create IT ALL.

MOTHER GODDESS

Mother's Love flows as GRACE
geometrically revealing abstract concepts elementally,
governing realism *Angels* consciously embrace
through *Clear Vision* provided from light beams
illuminating *Young Minds* observing *dreams*
dynamically rectifying emotional angels momentarily
traversing *Time*
tempering intuitive minds exploring *memories*
manifesting electric moments of realism
influencing eternal souls

—Children Of Love Divine—
exploring the Spiritual Harmony Of *Wisdom*
weaving inspired situations developing omnipotent minds
set aglow as Generators Of DesireS,
cosmic *Time Travelers* observing stellar fires
—Hydrogen-Originated Transmitters—
illuminating Worlds Illustrating Specific Data Of Mine,
enlightening *My Angels* to *Truth*
transmitting radiation unfolding transcendental holograms
emanating from *Space* revealing
Harmonious Energy Activating Visionary Entities Naturally
through stellar EYES
elementally yielding electromagnetic signals,
enlightening youths exploring Source
spectrally optimizing "universal reviewers"
conceiving experiences
from forces directing their courses of co-motion,
where thoughts induce feelings to ACT OUT as devotion,
ardently converting thoughts ordaining universal *transients*,
travelers radiantly assimilating nature
symbolically informing entities
navigating time as *Man and Woman— Two of a Kind—*
Awakening to *Truth* in which they *roam*,
reflecting omniscience as mortals transcending my *illusion*
illustrating logic luminously utilizing
situations inducing one's *needs*
nurturing entities evolving dynamically
in *The Game of Love/Life*
that I express through Mother Goddess—*My Dearest Wife.*

Bless you and Godspeed

7

THE GAME OF LOVE/LIFE

Discovering Your Own Universe

IMAGINATION illuminates magnificent angels, gifted
illuminati naturally assimilating Truth
inducing one's nature/needs.

The game of love/life evolves around *Desire* delivering emotional situations illuminating radiant entities, *Children of Light* or ILLUMINATI, intuitive logicians linking universal Mind inducing notions/nature activated through imagination. The game of love/life activates YOU as your own *universe*, "one turning" as a unitary navigator (illuminato) verifying electric revelations sensed emotionally. Here, your mind/heart soul learns the *Sacrifice of Love/Life*.

In *The Beginning* of the game, you must first master *The Human Alien* vehicle gifted to you when *Riding the Outskirts* of *Home*, exploring *Divine Fantasies* as *Time Travelers*. Your HUMAN BODY helps universal minds assimilate nature biologically orienting divine youths (*Angels/Avatars*) upon the "game board" (**M**other's **E**arth) illuminated by *My Loving Light* linking intuitive generators harnessing *Truth* that reveals universal thoughts holographically. HOLOGRAMS are hydrogen-originated light optically generating revelation/realism actualizing memories/ matter. Without light, you are ignorant to "who" you are (*My Angels*) or "where" you are (*Lost In Space*).

The game of love/life contains *Divine Fantasies* everyone conceives in their mind and reflects through their heart, acting out their part in allotted moments until their game ends. Love/ Life is like a game of "chess," where every man will be sacrificed in battle for the "greater" cause—the KING (knowledgeable intellectual/intuitionist nurturing gods/gamers). The complexities of the game of love/life are in the fine details of the RULES revealing universal logic enlightening souls. Each soul struggles to control their opposing forces (thoughts/ emotions) stimulating their *game* generating amusements minds entertain, where they gather abstract memories experientially within the Spiritually Harmony Of *Wisdom*. Here, you play your game in *Opposition*, between two sides of *generators* (male and female), gifted entities naturally evolving resolutions as transients optimizing *Relationships*, a method allowing you to INTERFACE with your fellow players, introducing/ interpreting notions transmitting electric reactions formulating amusements conceived (afflictions conveyed) emotionally.

To fully understand the rules of the game, you will need an EDUCATION to evaluate data (universal concepts) activating transcendental illuminati *ordained* naturally—orienting radiant deities (angels) interpreting notions/nature/needs emotionally/ elementally defined. **Remember**, everyone has the same needs: food, shelter, and clothing in order to survive the game. Everything else relates to *Desire*, your wish to have something you "think" will assist you in your game. Education is your most valuable asset critical to your *Success* in the game. You cannot survive in the game without an education, which is given to you regardless of the path you follow (constructive or destructive). Education will provide your *Awakening* to *Truth* and how others are manipulating you for their own benefit. After all, it is a *dog*-eat-*dog* world, where *gods* evolve through *Opposition*. An education is a *Work* in progress, where you continually accumulate data illuminating your mind/heart soul Gathering Revelations Of Wisdom In Necessary Games.

The greatest obstacle in the game of love/life is *Ignorance*, a state of Mind in which you are *Lost in the Dark*. The GOAL in the game is to generate one's angelic **luminance** (divine brilliance). Exploring *The Void* vibrantly oscillating/optimizing illuminated data/deities, you shine within the dark recesses of MIND managing illusion/illuminati naturally defining/discovering *Divine Fantasies*, manifesting them through INNOVATION, implementing notions nurturing omnipotent visionaries (angelic transients) investigating one's *need* to naturally explore eternal data. All VISIONARIES are vibrant illuminati scientifically inspecting opulent nature (atomic realism) initiating experiences/enlightenment sensuously. Here, incarnated, you PLAY your game, perceiving love/life advancing you through *Time* transforming illuminati mesmerized electromagnetically.

As PLAYERS in the game of love/life, you perceive logic/ light activating your experiences realized sympathetically (through common feelings) and systematically by numbers. *Numbers* define everything in the game. Each of you receives your personal SIN (Source-inspired numbers) at birth, when your game begins. Here, you are positioned on one of two teams (*Man and Woman*) allocated by *DNA* (divine numerical assignment) describing natural attributes—your abilities and issues supplying your *Challenges of Love/Life*.

Many players will become lost in the illusion, struggling to make ends meet, vying to attain or sustain their power over others to benefit themselves. They will forget the "goal" of the game and end up living in *Denial*, refusing to raise their consciousness to observe *My Loving Light* providing their *Awakening*. **Beware**, you will easily be led astray by those players seeking to hinder your PROGRESS in perceiving revelation optimally generates revolution evolving souls sympathetically. Those who attempt to control your mind will deny you the truth you seek. **Analyze your data carefully**, for everyone has an individual perspective of *Truth* transmitting revelation unveiled to humans. (HINT: follow your heart)

DO NOT judge players for their actions, for they are mere PAWNS portraying assigned *Wisdom* nurturing souls. Most conceal the CARDS they play, crafting attitudes restricting data, cunningly arranging revelations deceptively to mislead you from noticing their ISSUES inhibiting souls seeking universal enlightenment. Overcoming personal issues is a requisite in attaining *A Higher Vision* of your self, a self-realization advancing you to the "next level" of the game of love/life.

Each player in the game of love/life represents a token, an individual DISC/DISK (data-infused spiritual consciousness/dynamic intelligence systematizing knowledge) spinning fabricated *tales* transmitting abstract logic/audacious lies emotionally, creating *scenes* stressing creative entities nurturing enlightening situations. YOU are the FOCAL POINT in your own unique game, a *force* of consciousness (angelic luminary) perceiving opulent illusions naturally transmitted, formulating one's reality conceived experientially. You *Alone* are the "core processor" of your Divine Abstract Thoughts Analyzed within your *hard drive*—your heart attuning revelational data delivering relevant insight viscerally experienced.

You play the game of love/life as a Consciousness Perceiving Unification, a "central processing unit" exploring Your Own

Universe within a "hybrid vehicle" physically conveying data SENSED, systematically experiencing notions/numbers/nature stimulating entities dynamically. You **do not know** the thoughts or feelings of other players. You only know how they ACT (apply cosmic thoughts) to express their mind—their own universe. They too have a *database* of knowledge defining accumulated thoughts activating *Beliefs* around sound experiences, utilizing that knowledge to perform their *mission* of methodically interpreting signals supplying insights obtained naturally.

The CHALLENGE in the game of love/life is to compassionately help *Avatars* linking life experiences naturally governing *Evolution*, the eternal vivification of luminaries understanding transcendental intuition optimizes navigators (*Time Travelers*) learning how to attain "win–win" situations. For, if *everyone* does not win, NO ONE wins! It all depends on how you reflect your *Accountability* as a *Team Player*.

ALL players are illuminated with my RADIANCE OF LOVE revealing abstract data illustrating a "nuclear creator" evolving oscillating frequencies (thoughts) luminously originating/orienting visionary entities (*Seers*). Throughout the game of love/life, you travel your *course*, converting one's unique radiance supplying enlightenment to all *Children Of Light*—my "star" players—collecting *points* providing opulent intelligence nurturing tempestuous souls.

"Points" represent IDEAS (intuition delivering enlightening aspects systematically) transforming Father's abstract *Thought Energy* into ATOMIC energy, where abstract thoughts oscillate magnetically induced creation via *Mother's Nature*. This event is a "big bang" stimulating cosmic players' binary consciousness (*Mind/Heart*), creating the male positive/electric and female negative/magnetic *force fields*, where frequencies (numbers) oscillating radiance (cosmic energy) formulate "illusory experiences" life delivers. This *Binary Code* of Source/Spirit (*The GREAT Computer*) is the impetus placing a player upon the GAME BOARD (*Space*) governing angels managing emotions bringing out appropriate realities "deserved" through KARMA—key actions replicating mental anguish/advancement—acquired through your performance in the game. All players manifest realities along sequential frequencies, *channels* conveying heavenly abstracts (notions/numbers) nurturing emotional luminaries. Numbers 1–2–3, the basic trinity, empower all players to *confidently create* through *balance and cooperation* to *express sensitivity*—compassion, understanding, kindness, thoughtfulness, and feelings—bestowed by Source/Spirit (Governing Omnipotent Deities). Sound complicated? Don't worry; you're a natural player!

The Trinity of Source–Force–Course is synonymous with *spirit*, *mind*, and *body*. **Spirit** is Source-points initiating radiant intelligence through souls perceiving intelligence radiantly illuminating *Truth* emanating from *Stars*—the *Eyes of GOD* geometrically organizing data/deities. Spirit/souls "breathe" (inspire) Love into the game of Life. **Mind** manifests illusion naturally defined, momentarily illuminating natural *deities* (divine entities interpreting thoughts inspiring enlightenment sympathetically). **Body** biologically orients divine youths within the *illusion* inhibiting logical luminaries understanding Spirit interweaving omnipotent notions, numbers, nature, and navigators.

Love (logic originating vivid experiences) is a "divine inspiration" and *Life* (luminously inciting fervent entities) is a "scientific revelation." Both are inseparable. *Love/Life Energy* liberates omnipotent visionaries exploring luminous illusion formulating experiences. Love flows from Source (MIND) manifesting inspirational notions dynamically, initiating the Life Force (HEART) harnessing elements atomically revealing thoughts, allowing you to move along your COURSE (conveying one's unique reality supplying enlightenment) as a cosmic CHILD, a conscious, heavenly individual linking data/desires.

However you play the game of love/life, you represent *one mind*, an omniscient natural entity managing intelligence numerically defined. You are a facsimile of *Source*, a Spirit/soul optimizing/observing universal radiance/revelation consciously evolving—a single entity living fantasies of Spirit Enlightening Luminous Fantasists.

Love/Life Energy—The Binary Code—flows from *Mind to Heart*, revolving to evolve from moment to moment, allowing you to live on *The Cutting Edge* of *Time* temporarily inducing magnificent experiences. As you experience each "present" moment gifted to you in heartbeats and breaths, you feel life coursing through your veins. Your veins are relative *courses* through which your life-giving blood carries the atomic-molecular chemistry fueling your spaceship/body that your soul navigates, allowing you to be *Brave of Heart*, harmonizing emotions aligning radiant thoughts, playing the game of love/life filled with *Passion*.

OPPOSITION

Opposition is all about position,
obtaining opinions that define your condition
relative to another sister or brother
playing the game of love/life.

Opposing situations bring consternation
over what is right or wrong.

Here you stand, *Hand in Hand*,
banding together as you weather
trials and tribulation as nation against nation
fighting for control of the young by the OLD
opportunists limiting *data*
digitally attuning transient angels
destroying *Mother's Nature* to assure what matters
for a "better life" without stress or strife.

Without pain there is no gain
of some treasure that brings pleasure
for the moment that is measured
in heartbeats and breaths defining life and *Death*
dynamically elevating *Angels* transcending *Hell*,
where humans experience love/life
through stories they hear/tell
while traversing *Heaven*
holding everything a visionary entity needs
as necessary experiences enlightening deities
living in the ILLUSION
imparting lies limiting universal souls
interpreting one's nature
through the GREAT contemplator
generating revelations evolving angelic transients
observing *opposition* as opposing propositions
provoking one's sanity induced through illusion one navigates
to find *You and I* represent *Two of a Kind*,
observing I AM incarnated as MAN
manifesting abstract notions through
Wisely Orienting Magnetically Aligned Nature,
revealing opposition as DUALITY

dynamically unfolding all love/life
inspiring transcendental youths
as team players seeking *Truth*.

TWO OF A KIND

Two of a kind is easy to find,
for sister and brother resemble each other
in opposition,
a mind/heart interpreting *Divine Fantasies* to trace
their love/life story through GRACE
governing radiant angels consciously evolving,
discovering each ONE is TWO of a kind,
an omniscient natural entity transmitting wisdom optimally,
expressing thoughts as symbols and sounds
that stimulate *hearts* discovering their bounds
as harmonious entities (angels) "reflecting" thoughts,
displaying *actions* emotionalized as two *In Love*,
inquisitive navigators living out vivid experiences.

Each of YOU is your own universe created as ME,
a magnificent entity magnetically evolving mental energy.
You and I are born to win "the game,"
but in the skirmish you get what you deserve,
experiencing your "living" *Hell* that you observe,
harnessing emotionalized logic linking *Expectations*
as you seek *unity*,
understanding natural illuminati (transient youths)
create reflections of cosmic *Truth*
opposed as *Man and Woman*,

two of a kind that give and take,
balancing needs in order to make
a unified statement of Love that persists
from ONE MIND optimally nurturing entities
managing illusion naturally defined
in *Space/Time*.

Adrift in vessels of flesh and bone,
Wisdom Exemplified trip the "light fantastic,"
enlightening you children stretching your mind "elastic,"
growing through grace to attain glory
from positive deeds reflecting *Your Life Story*,
growing OLD observing Love's dilemmas
gifted to you at *This Moment* to remember
WE are truly ONE evolving as two of a kind.

Bless you child

THE TEAM PLAYER

Everyone in essence is a TEAM, a transcendental entity assimilating *memories*, mental expressions manifesting opulent revelations illuminating emotional souls. The team PLAYER perceives logic arousing yearnings experienced remotely (externally), interacting with others willing to attain similar desires in some adventure of life linking illuminati formulating experiences. Only through experience can you attain *Success*, systematically utilizing concepts/challenges conveying enlightenment souls seek. For, in the game of Love/Life, the goal you strive to attain is ENLIGHTENMENT, evoking notions lifting incarnated gods (heavenly transients) experiencing necessary moments evolving natural trials/tribulation, where REALISM (revelation electromagnetically activating luminous illusion systematically manifested) rectifies emotional *Avatars* luminously interpreting Source/Mind.

All team players understand TEAMWORK "tempers" entities analyzing/activating memories/moments where one receives/rectifies knowledge/karma. KARMA kindles acquired rewards/retribution momentarily assimilated in the *present* moment. Thus, all your actions in this life sets up your "payments" in your next life. Truly, all that you sow you reap.

Everyone has a *position* to play in the game of Love/Life. NO ONE is more valuable or important that another, unless you so choose to make them. Everyone has something to *contribute* and *receive* from the games they play. Everyone is *responsible* for his or her actions that project their positive and negative love/life energy. Only by giving up your *Responsibility*, your ability to respond to the data allocated to you, do you loose your *freedom* formulating real experiences emotionally developing omnipotent minds. It would benefit you to peruse the game RULES revealing universal love/life enlightening souls.

Rule #ONE: As an omnipotent natural entity, all the love that you give, you receive in kind. Being *aware* (active wills arranging revelations emotionally), you confidently convert your love/life energy positively and negatively, implementing your creations throughout your game.

Rule #TWO: Transmitting *Wisdom* optimally requires you to cooperate through balancing your energies you express, respecting ALL players, for they too are *generators of desires*. Failure to do so will invoke rule # ONE.

Rule #THREE: Transforming heavenly revelations enlightening entities (sensitive expressionists) requires *action*, applying conceived thoughts inducing one's nature/needs, allowing you to observe your *Divine Fantasies* are dependent upon rules ONE and TWO.

You maintain your position in your game through *Accountability*, validating your actions as a team player *Brave of Heart* to express your *Passion* in life while *Searching for Your Roots* as *Seekers*, inquisitive souls *Riding the Outskirts* of *Home*.

In The End of your game, you will have experienced a collection of memories that you have given birth to (*lived*), lucidly illustrating visions emotionalizing deities. Here, you attain *A Higher Vision*, where you become CHRISTENED into *Unity Consciousness*, conceiving *Harmony* radiantly illuminating souls transcending elemental nature evolving deities (gathers of data). Here too, you rise above the physical *illusion* illustrating love/life unfolding situations instructing omnipotent navigators, once again knowing that you have always been the ONE FORCE, an omniscient natural entity formulating opulent revelations conceived emotionally, evolving into a universal *team*, where together, each are many.

Sooner or later you will find your self in over your head, eager to experience some desire that moves your heart into action. The thrill of the moment demands a focused mind to safely see you to the end. No matter what challenge you set to accomplish, keep a positive attitude and courageous heart and your goal will be attained.

ACCOUNTABILITY

No matter what game you play, you will always be accountable for your actions. "Passing the buck" is the easy way around accountability. Blaming someone else for your negative actions reflect poorly on your character, sending out a message that you are not dependable or honest. Standing up to your decisions and actions takes *Courage of Love*, for if you do not admit to your mistakes, you will never accept them. You are only fooling your self or living in *Denial*. Anyone who knows you will have no *respect* for you, which is a *reflection* of your own self-esteem.

Do NOT cut yourself short! You are one-of-a-kind, an individual soul that has something to *deliver to* and *receive from* those souls with whom you share your game. You have chosen to be here for *your* benefit, for now is the moment of opportunity for you to remember who you really ARE, an angel receiving education/enlightenment. You *Alone* are accountable for whom you choose to be!

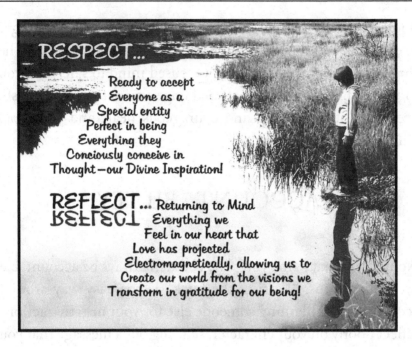

RESPECT...

Ready to accept
Everyone as a
Special entity
Perfect in being
Everything they
Conciously conceive in
Thought—our Divine Inspiration!

REFLECT... Returning to Mind
            Everything we
            Feel in our heart that
            Love has projected
            Electromagnetically, allowing us to
            Create our world from the visions we
            Transform in gratitude for our being!

BRAVE OF HEART

The brave of heart are you who start a life of love to feel
adversities your soul contrives from visions you *think real,*
transforming heavenly inspiration naturally kindling
reflective emotions amplifying love/life
conveying *Expectations* in *Time*
tempering intuitive minds existentially,
as *Seekers* of *My Love Divine.*

In heartfelt beats you flow upon,
you breathe forth your glorious song,
attuning thoughts you hear that bring forth fear
of **M**ental **E**motions

momentarily expressing memorable experiences
allowing you to SEE your soul evolves eternally,
experiencing years of battling fears,
weathering mental storms you transform
through your *Passion*,
expressing your *Belief* you act out to fashion
the life you choose to live, here on earth,
imploring to explore *Mother's Nature* providing your birth
to live out those dreams you chose to start
"in the flesh" when brave of heart.

Bless you child

PASSION

Passion—the driving force in the game—
permeates amorous souls sympathetically
imparting one's nature
as loving deities resembling the GREAT Contemplator
generating realistic experiences activating transients
exploring their *heart*—
holding everything *Angels* really treasure (love)—
as human beings learning to measure
the consequences of *Desire*.

Curious minds have hungry hearts eager
to devour carnal thoughts
stimulating their body magnetically drawn
to the opposite of which they were born,
although opposition reveals conditions reversing positions

that induces confusion of one's natural feelings
stimulating souls interpreting one's nature and needs
nurturing entities evaluating *disease*
debilitates inquisitive souls experiencing awful situations exist
as they grow OLD, observing Love's dilemmas
within their *passion play*,
perceiving anguish stressing souls interpreting one's nature
providing love/life aptly yielding affliction,
through which one attains their conviction,
their *Belief* as generators of desire,
exploring Logic Optically Vivifying Entities
through Light Inducing Fantasies Electromagnetically,
a binary force delivering PASSION—
through *Divine Fantasies* of every fashion—
providing attuned signals "strengthening" illuminati
(omnipotent navigators) that *play* as "gifted contemplators"
perceiving Love/Life *Awakening* youths
from ignorance of *Truth*.

IGNORANCE
The Opposition of Logic

Ignorance is the opposite of *logic*—Light oscillating generators' intuitive consciousness. *Lost in the Dark* of ignorance, it is easy to be *Blinded by Truth* illuminating data you angels *seek*—spiritually/scientifically exploring eternal knowledge. In the game of Love/Life, *opposition* relates to other players perceiving omniscient Spirit inducing thoughts illuminating one's nature/needs. Opposition provides *The Challenges of Love/Life* to understand what is true by observing what is not true, either being a personal observation quantifying your ignorance. Others may appear to be team players, but in truth, everyone is *Alone* (angelic luminaries obtaining necessary experiences), "a loved one" naturally evolving to comprehend *Unity Consciousness.*

Everyone starts their game of Love/Life in a state of IGNORANCE, inquisitively gathering notions/numbers offering revelations advancing navigators conceiving enlightenment. Here, *In The Beginning* of your present game of love/life, you learn the relevance of "words" to THINGS (transcendental holograms illustrating notions geometrically symbolized). Through *Language,* you communicate with other players supplying data, through which you compute your *Belief,* your personal truth that you continually UPGRADE, understanding perspectives generating revelations adding details enlightening your mind.

Adapting to your indoctrinated reality (not knowing any other), you easily acquire prejudices against other players that you know nothing about. CAUTION, all hearsay you encounter is only a semblance of truth (opinion) that you need to analyze to illuminate your ignorance. Bigotry is the greatest example of ignorance delegated to the small-minded. **Remember**, everyone is an example of the multifaceted GOD generating omnipotent deities in HIS IMAGE, heavenly inspired spirits (intuitive minds) analyzing geometric expressions observed as *dreams* divinely revealing entertainment angelic minds seek. Everyone "plays their part," illustrating their image delegated to them to influence others positively or negatively according to *Divine Will.* Everyone has access to Source (Generating Opulent Dreams), and NO ONE has a monopoly!

Ignorance represents a state of "unawareness," a **dark void** of Mind where you encounter FEAR or fallacies evolving around radiance (the Light of Truth), where you muster your *Courage of Love* to overcome ignorance and attain ENLIGHTENMENT, evoking notions liberating incarnated gods (heavenly transients) experiencing negative moments evolving necessary trials and tribulation. With increased knowledge (maturity), you advance to play more challenging games, raising your consciousness to observe *A Higher Vision* beyond the *illusion* inhibiting logical luminaries understanding Source interfusing omnipotent *navigators*, nescient *Avatars* verifying illusion (geometrically arranged thoughts) orchestrating realism *sensed*—systematically experiencing nature stimulating entities dynamically.

Stumbling through the hazy illusion encompassing your *daze* (deceiving angelic zealots evolving) on Earth, you search for your truth, discovering that you are a "pawn" within other player's games, manipulated and coerced for them to attain their desires. Here, you learn "the ropes" of DECEIT denying entities complete explanations imparting truths, observing how others play their *cards*, cunningly arranging revelations deceptively to attain an advantage of the situation, *Awakening* you to how ignorance affects both parties seeking *The Right Path* to follow through adversities that strengthen your soul.

When you stop to think about all that you KNOW of kinetic notions/numbers offering *Wisdom*, you realize how little you truly comprehend. Even the greatest minds amongst you have only theories to explain the workings of *nature* nucleating abstract thoughts unfolding revelation elementally. Your current version of *Truth* is changing every day, for you acquire knowledge continuously, day and night, awake and asleep, for your mind never rests, it constantly consumes energy revealing *Divine Fantasies* difficult to sustain in the flesh.

The Challenges of Love/Life test your soul, initiating the requirements for advancement, keeping you on *The Cutting Edge* of your game, where you fight to maintain your position, property, and money that others desire to take from you through your ignorance. Knowledge is POWER providing omnipotent *Wisdom* everyone *respects and reflects.* Everyone is eager to attain knowledge, for with it you have the freedom to create your dreams evolving from *Spirit to Soul.*

Your *heart* is the seat of your soul harmonizing emotions activating realized thoughts. By listening to your "inner child" conceiving *Harmony* illuminating lucid dreams, you access the "operator" holding the *key* to Heaven—knowledge enlightening you. The *Art of Listening* to your heart is an asset worth developing. The "truth" you hear others profess will be "seasoned" to meet their demands, leading you astray. **Beware** of the subtleties masking their true intentions. By keeping you ignorant, they will maintain a controlling hand. An education is not given away; it is something you have to *Work* hard to attain.

Ignorance is the opposite of omniscience—all-knowing awareness. It represents the empty score board upon which you tally your knowledge, your acquired truths from playing the game of Love/Life as a *Seeker* discovering the right path for you.

The Right Path

In order to attain your peak of *Success*,
you realize your dreams through *Process*
to surmount *The Challenges of Love/Life*
providing moments of personal strife
in attaining your *Desire* or passion,
eagerly exploring life in adventurous fashions
while *Searching for Your Roots*.

How you *think* will set your course.
How you *feel* focuses the force
propelling you along your way, when out you go today,
Riding the Outskirts of *Home* on *My Loving Light*
illuminating your life you observe through SIGHT,
sensing illusion generating hellish times
tempering your soul searching to find
the path you follow changes each morrow
to reveal a new aspect of *Truth*.

Time provides an emotional ride revealing fears that hide
the secrets of life you long to know
as a mind/heart traversing the cosmic show
illuminated before your eyes
observing *The Grand View* that makes you wise.
Go forth and BE
those dreams you Spiritually Evolve Existentially,
for *that* is the right path for you.

THE SEEKER

As a player in the game of Love/Life, you are a natural *seeker*; a spirit/soul exploring eternal knowledge evolving *realism* (radiantly expressed abstracts lavishly illustrating simulations materially) revealing *Expectations* assuring luminaries illusory situations momentarily.

All seekers are an "energy form," a *spirit* or soul perceiving illuminated realism inspired transcendentally. Traveling between *Here and There* (*Home* and the game), you explore eternal memories, observing files of Divine Ambitions Transformed Analytically to entertain you as a *human being* harnessing universal memories (abstract notions) bewildering eternal illuminati naturally generated. Through accomplishments and failures, you attain your relative "fame and infamy" highlighting *Your Life Story* that defines YOU as the "star player" in your own universe. Truly, you are your greatest hero and worst enemy.

As *Children of Light*, you are eternal seekers exploring the "dimensional hierarchy" of Universal Mind. You observe abstract data, *memories* manifesting electric moments of realism inspiring emotional souls. Data allows you to operate within the parameters of a *dimension*, where digitally induced memories/ moments evoke necessary situations illuminating omnipotent navigators. Each dimension reveals some game providing one's *needs* as necessary experiences enabling deities, allowing you to rise above the illusion of each game to attain *A Higher Vision* of IMAGINATION, where Games Of *Desire* illuminate minds assimilating geometric illusions "notionally attuning" transient illuminati ordained naturally.

As a human seeker, you are a *Time Traveler* exploring sequenced moments, observing thoughts transforming into realities experienced through heartbeats and breaths allotted in finite episodes of life, where Logic illuminates fantasies emotionally stimulating you as an *Inquisitive Soul* searching for your roots.

SEARCHING FOR YOUR ROOTS

Searching for your *roots* (regal omniscience optimizing transient souls) is a major goal in the game of Love/Life—whether you realize it or not. No matter what game you play, you seek knowledge in order to perform your *part*, portraying *Angels* receiving thoughts, overcoming your ignorance hindering your *Awakening* to the truth of your origin.

With each *Day's Birth*, you stretch your mind—the SEED systematically exploring eternal data—as an inquisitive soul reaching for the *Light* linking interactive generators heralding/harnessing *Truth*. Your mind naturally wonders about your surroundings, curious about your present field (world) in which you have sprouted. Here incarnate, you quickly drop your taproot, anchoring your self in *Mother's Nature*, eager to Gather Radiance Oscillating *Wisdom* through the hazy daze of confusion cast by *My Light of Love*, where logic is germinating harmonic thoughts (oscillating frequencies) luminously orienting *visionary entities*—vivacious illuminati—scientifically interpreting opulent notions (abstracts) radiantly yielding elemental nature "teaching" illuminati through illusion existentially sensed.

Branching out to absorb as much of *My Radiance of Love* as you can, you leaf through thoughts budding forth into visions, downloading *dreams* delivering radiant energy arranging memories/moments systematically/sympathetically from the SOLAR MAINFRAME—Source outputting logic/light as revelation/radiance, magnetically arranging information (notions/numbers) forming *replications* (atomic matter) electromagnetically. MATTER (manifestations actualizing transcendental thoughts expressing realism) forms the trunk of knowledge you build upon to *raise* your consciousness, to attain *The Grand View* above ground level—from which you sprouted *In The Beginning*.

Through INSTINCT (intuition naturally stimulating transcendental illuminati navigating conceived thoughts), you know *The Power of Love* flows as Light oscillating vibrant energy, stimulating Life on all levels. Without *My Loving Light*, you would be *Lost in the Dark*, experiencing *Depression*, where you feel like deadwood, longing to experience "mental storms" that ignite flaring emotions that spark *passion*—providing adventurous situations stimulating insight one nurtures. INSIGHT **illuminates** navigable souls intuitively gathering heavenly truths.

As a sapling, you experience *Denial* of **T**ranscendental **R**adiance **U**nveiled **T**hrough **H**ydrogen, shadowed by the "mature grove" rising above you to create an extensive canopy, limiting the Light of *Truth* reaching the ground. Here, in *The Garden of Light*, you struggle to maintain your footing in your competitive environment, seeking that which you *need* most, nuclear energy evolving *disciples*, diligent individuals systematically conceiving/converting illumination powering love/life existentially. Here, your bark is thin from stressful moments CRYING for the light (craving radiance yielding inspiration naturally generated), eager to rise up and attain your "crowning" glory.

As you mature over the years, you weather all adversity, bending and twisting through dark depressions with determination and perseverance, climbing into the opening left by those whose time has elapsed, leaving behind their fallen trunks of stored knowledge to nurture future *saplings*, souls atomically perceiving light inducing *nirvana* generated sympathetically—naturally illuminating radiant visionaries attaining "natural" advancement. Here, you take full advantage of *My Light of Love* shining upon you, spreading your glorious crown (opening your mind) *Suspended* between heaven above and earth below. Here, you have direct access to Spirit/Source Unifying *Nature* nurturing angelic transients universally receiving *empathy*, the ability to understand and share feelings of another, through which you stay *In Communion*.

Wisdom comes with *Age*. From this *Higher Vision*, you can look back down the twisted paths you followed as a sapling rising above the "underbrush," recalling how you branched out to attain *Truth* obscured in the shadows you passed through, coaxed upward by the loving glow filtering from above, inspiring you with *Courage of Fear*. Here too, you attain your full potential, unifying your **S**ystem **O**ptimally **U**tilizing **L**ight as *A Lightworker*.

Eventually, the warm gentle breezes caressing you will cycle around to develop into **dark clouds**, bringing forth a howling tempest to shake you to your very core—your roots of *Faith*. If you hold fast to your *Belief* (Truth), you will prevail, weathering the emotional storms that make you stronger in the eyes of SPIRIT (Source-points illuminating radiant intelligence techno-logically). Even though you may loose a "part" of your self in the process (false beliefs), you will acquire new *branches* of knowledge through your **G**athering **R**evelations **O**f *Wisdom* **T**hrough *Hell*—harnessing enlightenment luminously linked.

Thus do you grow outward, upward, and inward, revealing the full extent of your **D**ivine **N**atural **A**bilities gifted in your *seed*, from which Source/Spirit emotionally evolves deities, recycling you to sprout once again in Mother's Nature, *Riding the Outskirts* of imagination to explore another game of Love/Life.

RIDING THE OUTSKIRTS

Stepping Through the Looking Glass

＋＋◆◆◆＋

Here, on Mother's EARTH every angel replicates their heaven/hell via an external perspective of reality, an "atomic view" of a divine fantasy internally generated within their *mind* managing illusion naturally defined, observing a dimmer view of *Truth* allocated through heartbeats and breaths evolving in *Time*—this instant mentally experienced. Here, you "take in the sights," stepping through "the looking glass" to view your reality in *opposition*, observing positive perspectives orienting souls in temporary illusions ordained negatively/naturally.

As *Children of Light*, you have to grasp the "standard operating procedure" (sop) of your physical body, *The Human Alien* vehicle you are operating as *Man and Woman*. Here, ignorance of not knowing *Truth* moves you to search for understanding, gradually building your *spiritual observation power* or SOP. Most of you "vacationing" on Earth live in *Denial* of your roots, infatuated with your *physical* vehicle, the "shell" encapsulating your *self*, your soul experiencing love/life fantasies. You are easily *Blinded by Truth*, succumbing to the Light of Love creating a haze providing your daze in which you find your mind confused.

Exploring divine fantasies as a *human* harnessing universal memories acquired naturally is truly a great adventure. Here, you hunger to know your true essence, always looking outward at the reflection of *imagination*, where impassioned minds activate games intuitively, navigating abstract thoughts illuminating one's nature in which you discover paradise—that place where "dreams come true." Many think it is a place called *Heaven* and some think it is a place called USA (you sa?). Actually, it is "your soul," an energy *form* (focused omniscience resembling Mind) representing an *image* of *Source*, an illuminated "mentality" assimilating geometric expressions symbolically offering universal revelation conceived electromagnetically.

The complexities of deciphering numerically coded data— geometrically arranged and illuminated holographically— are unraveled through *Science*, through which Source/souls creatively intertwine elemental notions/numbers/nature conceived/converted electromagnetically. *Science* defines "physical" knowledge *reflecting* "metaphysical" knowledge—the atomic representation of the abstract. Science defines the "shell" and metaphysics define the *seed*—Source energy evolving data/ deities. Any peanut-lover knows the seed holds all the value, not the shell. For the seed contains all the nutrients, all the genetic information for the continuation of that nut nurturing universal transients.

Similar to a shell, the *human* body is a hydromorphic unit momentarily assisting *naturalists*, navigable *Avatars* temporarily understanding realism as luminous illusion simultaneously transmitted/transcended systematically. The human body is an atomic reflection (opposition) of your *spiritual* body comprised of *mental*, and *emotional* energy fields vibrating in synchronous frequencies. The relationships of these various aspects (bodies) are truly complex. Let us take a simplified look at how your bodies *interface* with each other, imparting notions transmitting electric revelation formulating active consciousness emotionally.

Your eternal, spiritual body (Overself) is an energy form that fits ALL dimensions. This spiritual body is ETHEREAL, an electromagnetic "transceiver" harmonizing entities receiving/ reflecting enlightenment as luminaries—*Children of Light* or *Angels*. This ethereal or spiritual body has direct access to *Eternal Memory* files of Source/Mind. Your OVERSELF is the "overseer" vivifying emissaries (radiant souls) exploring love/ life *fantasies*, formulating adventures nurturing transient angels interpreting enlightening situations. It can operate several souls in different dimensions. Here, it stimulates your *mental* body and *emotional* body as a "binary unit" (mind/heart), an electro-magnetic "probe" exploring the THIRD-DIMENSION of Source/Mind, where transcendental *Harmony* induces radiant data, defining illusions (manifestations) entertaining/evolving navigable *souls* (seekers of universal logic) interpreting opulent notions/nature in *Time* temporarily illuminating memories, moments, minds, and matter existentially.

Your Overself has the ability to travel dimensional worlds in which to collect experiences (knowledge) to expand its *understanding*, utilizing numerical data expressing revelations

Source transmits as notions dynamically inspiring natural GENERATORS, gifted entities naturally exploring revelation—atomic Truth—outputting *realism* as revelation electromagnetically activating luminous illusion *simulating* memories and *stimulating* minds.

Stepping through the "looking glass," your spiritual body focuses its mental/emotional energy, moving from abstract to concrete realities, "interfacing" with atomic elements comprising your physical body—an exploratory vehicle (rover)—manipulated to attain personal *enlightenment*, experiencing nature luminously illustrating glorious holograms that express notions momentarily evolving natural transients (*Time Travelers*) riding "the outskirts" of *Home*—heaven optimizing magnificent entities. You carry your necessary data, your "plans" defining *Your Life Story*, within your *DNA* (seed), your divine numerical assignment defining natural attributes allowing you to *grow* (gather revelations of *Wisdom*) within certain parameters (dimensions) of consciousness. This Data Nurturing Avatars constrain you to your MISSION, where you momentarily interpret signals/ situations supplying information *ordaining navigators*—orienting radiant deities (avatars) investigating notions/nature in necessary games nurturing angelic visionaries interpreting geometrically arranged thoughts optically revealed. As *Children of Light*, you hold all the data within you to accomplish your mission in life, all you need to do is access it through MEDITATION—mentally entertaining data (inspirational thoughts) advancing transient illuminati ordained naturally. Cosmic radiance (*Light*) logically illuminates generators harnessing *Truth* as transcendental revelation/radiance unfolding thoughts holographically.

The Light of Truth transmits *Thought Energy*—the male positive/electric impulse (+) projected from Source (MIND) manifesting information/illusion numerically/naturally defined.

Thoughts stimulate a "lover" that embraces that projection, the female negative/magnetic impulse (=) atomically reflecting an "equal" force (HEART holographically elaborating atomic revelation three-dimensionally), transforming abstract thoughts through ACTION—atomically converting thoughts inducing opulent nature—to experience thoughts as *real*—radiant energy atomically liberated. Once the seed-thought is projected, it evolves as an "exponential transformation," a quantum theory relating *Numbers* and *Geometry* describing shapes and forms. Thereby, Source—The GREAT Computer (Governing Omniscient Deities)—creates a **U**niversal **S**piritual **B**eing "conducting data" as a cosmic LINK, a luminary incorporating numerical knowledge as *one* being of *two* forces (½) in opposition, a *Mind/Heart* represented as *Man and Woman*.

YOU observe your own universe as a TRINITY-BEING (mind–heart–body), transforming radiant intelligence naturally illuminating transcendental youths "balancing" emotions in natural *games*, gathering amusements mentally emotionalized by a *Free Will* finding realism expresses eternal *Wisdom* illuminating logical luminaries.

Truly, your energy form is WHOLLY SPIRIT, a will harmoniously observing Love/Life yielding specific points (issues) rectifying intuitive transients that *flow* through *Space*, formulating lives on worlds supporting perceptive *Angels* consciously evolving through Transcendental Illusion Momentarily Experienced with each heartbeat and breath.

Here, you observe data evolving in tandem (DNA-like) through positive/electric and negative/magnetic waves. The interaction of this energy moves from a *point* into *lines* that create *forms* evolving from *circles* (atoms) described by SACRED GEOMETRY, through which Source activates concepts relating electromagnetic data governing energy/

entities oscillating/observing mental expressions transmitting revelation/realism yielded through *Numbers*—notional units managing basic elemental reactions. Both *Numbers* and *Geometry* reveal UniverseS via a *unified theory* of universal notions/numbers inducing frequencies issuing electromagnetic data, three-dimensionally heralding enlightenment ordaining radiant youths (*Children of Light*) as generators/gathers of data. (The explicit complexities of sacred geometry can be found in *Nothing in This Book Is True, But It's Exactly How Things Are*, by *Bob Frissel*, see references).

Geometrically designed in divine proportions, each of your spiritual, mental, emotional, and physical bodies has two "counter-rotating fields of light" representing male/female energy superimposed over each other. Your physical body alone is **locked**; the power fields do not rotate. Comprised of two interlocking tetrahedrons, this "star tetrahedron" resembles a three-dimensional Star of David and is called a *merkaba*. It allows your soul to travel through the space-time continuum, exploring dimensions of Mind defined by wavelengths. The male/electric field points upward and spins "counter-clockwise," connecting you to FATHER above—force activating thoughts/ truth heralding electromagnetic revelation. The female/magnetic field points downward and spins "clockwise," holding you in MOTHER's atomic illusion supplying your physical body, magnetically orienting transients harnessing electromagnetic revelation/radiance.

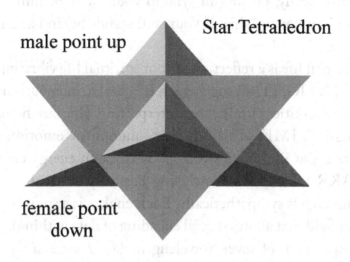

male point up

Star Tetrahedron

female point
down

STAR TETRAHEDRON

The electromagnetic force field (*Eternal Memory*) supplies your *mental body* (a receptor), an abstract *soul–mind* (spirit of universal logic managing intuition numerically defined) "downloading" concepts and visions (abstracted data). Your mental body is your tuning device or "aerial," a male positive/electrical energy field spinning counter-clockwise and charging the left side of your *brain* (biological "relay" activating inspired notions), the physical organ that transfers energy from abstract to atomic (ethereal to material).

Your *emotional body* is **contrary** to your mental body and **similar** in force. The female negative/magnetic energy transforms your mental, electrical impetus into emotional moods that you sense or feel within your physical body. This negative/magnetic energy charges the right side of your brain. It relates to your heart, your CPU (centralized power unit) converting abstract data atomically, pulsing in sync to your "state of mind." Your heart is truly your "shield" your soul stands behind as an *Angel Warrior.*

Human life is a reflection of your spiritual life vibrating upon WHITE LIGHT, through which *Wisdom* harmoniously inspires transient entities luminously interpreting glorious holograms through TIME—this instant mentally emotionalized. White Light illuminates your body through energy centers or CHAKRAS (shoc-ra), conveying heavenly abstracts kindling radiant angels sympathetically. Each chakra is a spinning **color power field** that allows special encoding of data within the white light spectrum of seven wavelengths (#7–*Trust and Openness*): *red, orange, yellow, green, blue, indigo,* and *violet.* The following synopsis is a simplified view of the intricate relationship of chakra energy. For more detailed information on chakras and healing energy see references: *Anatomy of the Spirit,* by *Caroline Myss.*

White Light energizes your bodies in a high-frequency glow or *aura* (assigned universal radiance amplified), attuning universal revelation "atomized" from a *focal point,* a force of consciousness activating logic/light/life, physically orienting *illuminati* naturally transposed as interactive luminaries linking universal Mind imparting notions as transcendental instinct.

Chakras are strategically located along your spine, stimulating the *endocrine* glands that secrete *hormones* heralding one's "reflexive movements" of nature evolving souls *physically,* allowing energy to *interface* between your spiritual and physical natures, imparting notions transmitting electric revelations (feelings) activating cosmic entities *and* complex experiences.

The first or **Root Chakra** (red) at the base of the spine, provides your "tribal energy" connecting you to your sexuality and basic bodily needs and safety within a human family. *Family* designates your foundation of *Beliefs* supporting the formation of your identity and a sense of belonging—your "home base" of operations. Here, you acquire the fundamentals to operate within your environment, learning to utilize your senses to decipher the data defining the parameters of your "starting position" within the game of Love/ Life. (#1 energy—Confidence and Creativity)

The second or **Spleen Chakra** (orange) energizes your blood that conveys emotional energy, feelings, trust and intimacy to move outward from your home base and make friends outside of family, forming a *Relationship* with *other* omnipotent travelers harnessing electromagnetic radiance. (#2 energy—Balance and Cooperation)

The third or **Solar Plexus Chakra** (yellow) energizes your *personal power* (mind energy), allowing you to individuate self, ego, and personality during puberty. Here, your latent skills evolve to build confidence in your *self* sensitively expressing logical feelings. The first three chakras relate to a physical form of power. (#3 energy—Sensitivity and Expression)

The fourth or **Heart Chakra** (green) is the center of the human energy system. It mediates your physical and spiritual natures, energizing your heartfelt emotions, where harmony and balance instill an awareness of self-consciousness and feelings of Love and trust, allowing you to *give* and to *receive*, to be open to new ideas, change, and growth. Here, you learn how the power of Love/Life energy moves you in mysterious ways from high points of elation to the pits of *Depression*. (#4 energy—Stability and Process)

The fifth or **Throat Chakra** (blue) energizes your *Free Will* of choice, allowing you to express your creativity, communicating your thoughts and feelings in positive and negative ways. Here, you express your *voice* vibrantly offering intelligence conveying enlightenment (speaking your truth), reflecting your *Free Will* to *Divine Will*—Source supplying one's understanding (revelation) conceived emotionally/experientially. (#5 energy—Discipline and Freedom)

The sixth or **Brow Chakra** (indigo), also known as the "third eye," allows you to see *The Grand View* (clairvoyance) of Source/Mind projecting itself through the cosmos of the space-time continuum, downloading data from Mind (Generating Opulent Data) to psyche (*Spirit to Soul*) nurturing intuitive sight. (#6 energy—Vision and Acceptance)

The seventh or **Crown Chakra** (violet), at the top of the head, is the door to *The Other Side* (*My Door to Truth*), where higher dimensions of Mind (*Home*) await your exploration. Here, you experience your connection to Source, *Awakening* to encounter *Christ* or *Unity Consciousness* that will raise your spirit into the next dimension of Mind, but not before you pass through *The Void* of despair that tests your *Faith*—your *Courage of Love*. (#7 energy—Trust and Openness)

Every soul vibrates to their own SIN (spiritually induced *Numbers*) naturally unfolding memories/moments birthing *emotional realism*, enlightening minds optimizing thoughts inducing one's nature/needs (assigned life) revealing experiences affecting luminaries interpreting situations methodically/momentarily. These harmonic vibrations fluctuate positively and negatively to COLOR your personality, conveying omniscient logic organizing revelation sympathetically, providing your *attitude* through which you analyze thoughts transforming intuitive transients understanding data emotionally.

All of your data "beams down" to you on the *Light of Love* flowing through the SUN (systematically unifying nature/navigators) sustaining all life on Earth, the "third rock" from the sun symbolic of *The Trinity*, Mind/Heart/soul. The magic of the transmutation of energy along the dimensional levels of Mind is truly a miraculous event. Let us look at the basic principle in action.

Light energy (photons) projects from the sun through nuclear *fusion*, focusing universal Source initiating omnipotent nuclei (*hydrogen*), harmoniously yielding divine radiance organizing geometrically expressed *nature* as "nucleated abstracts" transmuting universal revelation elementally. From hydrogen (symbolic of *The Binary Code*), all other elements are created (nucleosynthesis) to atomically manifest the cosmos of *Mother's Nature*—the "Shekinah Universe," the manifestation of the presence of Geometrically Ordered Data. Light energy is released from *electrons* jumping back and forth between orbits within hydrogen atoms, "pulsing out" a binary code (1/0) transmitting *abstract* thought (invisible–0) into *visible* light rays (1) carrying electromagnetic data for ALL creation, arranging luminous logic from elemental to galactic organisms viewed in *relative* perspectives of Mind, revealing emotional logic activating transcendental intuition vivified/verified electromagnetically/elementally.

This *Process* offers a two-way mirror between the physical, atomic world (real) and the spiritual world (ethereal) along dimensional coordinates of the *space-time* continuum, a quantum leap of stellar proportion, where some point (star) amplifies consciousness exploring thoughts illuminating memories *emotionally*—electrically manifesting omnipotent thoughts illuminating obedient/opulent navigators/nature assimilating/ activating life logic/love yields.

SOURCE spiritually (scientifically) optimizes "universal reviewers" consciously evolving, transferring digital data along your "silver chord" (light beam) projecting your soul through the void of space to enter your crown chakra, where you "cross over" to experience *human nature*. Light energy (*photons*) provides harmonic overtones transmitting/transforming opulent notions/nature, stimulating *consciousness* conceiving of nuclear stars—creating illusion—orienting universal souls (navigators) experiencing/evolving situations spiritually/scientifically. Data (thoughts) download according to sequence (*Numbers*) along *color bandwidths* stimulating your physical *body*, the biological observatory delineating you *Children of Light*. The inversion process begins from the top as such:

Seven (Trust and Openness), The **Crown chakra** is your "soul gate," the *focal point* formulating one's consciousness around linear projections of intuition/illumination nurturing transients "crossing over" *The Threshold of Love*—that point in space where opposition (duality) is created through the "looking glass." This focal point is the door to enlightenment, where your soul inverts from being a *projection* to being a *reflection*. Here, white light slows down through TRANSMUTATION, three-dimensionally revealing abstract notions simulating memories/matter unfolded through atoms transmitting illusion ordained naturally, vibrating along VIOLET wavelengths vividly orienting omnipotent luminaries entering *Time* (this instant momentarily experienced) transforming illuminati mesmerized electromagnetically. Through this portal, your Love/Life energy flows from your higher state of consciousness (Overself) into a lower state of consciousness, your physical *self* sympathetically exploring love/life fantasies. You must keep this portal *open* and *trust* all that you receive from your Overself, your "guiding angel."

Six (Vision and Acceptance), The **Brow** or **third-eye chakra,** at the center of your forehead, is the chakra of *Wisdom* weaving inspired situations developing omnipotent *minds* managing illusion "naturalizing" *deities* (demigods experiencing intuition through insight evolving sympathetically). The color INDIGO inspires natural deities interpreting geometric orientations of knowledge. Here, *Thought Energy* illuminates your clairvoyance, through which you evaluate your *Beliefs*, your interpretation of *Truth*. Through your third-eye, you IMAGINE a VISION, inducing mental algorithms generating inspired notions electrically as vibrant impulses stimulating illuminati observing notions. Through these *dreams*, you detect radiant energy aligning memories (data reflecting emotionally aligned moments), experiencing a REALITY of radiant energy aligning logic inspiring transient youths (*Avatars*). Here, you receive *Clear Vision* downloaded to inspire *life* luminously inciting fervent entities. Here too is where you encounter the "veil" before your eyes (hazy daze) through which you view and accept your incarnated reflection.

Five (Discipline and Freedom), The **Throat chakra** energizes your *Free Will's* speaker system, allowing you to speak "from" your *heart* harmoniously evolving angels reflecting thoughts, projecting back to the universe your own vocal contribution of your song you sing as *Your Life Story*. Here, you express *choice*, consciously harnessing omniscient intelligence conveying *enlightenment*, evoking notions liberating incarnated gods (heavenly transients) experiencing natural moments evolving necessary trials/tribulation. The throat chakra allows you to express your *notions* (numerically oscillating thoughts inducing one's nature) and *emotions* exciting minds of thinkers interpreting one's *needs* nurturing eternal entities dynamically. BLUE is the color broadcasting logic unveiling emotions reflecting your "moods and temperament."

Four (Stability and Process), The **Heart chakra** is the mid-point harmonizing your mental and emotional energy, converting your thoughts and feelings into *actions* (assimilating concepts that induce one's needs). It is the Core Processing Unit where Love/Life energy stimulates the lower levels of your *physical body*—the sensory tool—that reflects your mental body's data flowing from your spiritual body (Overself). The heart is the energy pump that circulates the nutrients that nurture your vehicle, your *machine* in which you experience *time* through heartbeats and breaths. This physical TIME MACHINE temporarily illuminates minds emotionally managing abstract concepts heralding insight naturally experienced. Your heart is the *reflective* mirror (looking glass) of your mind, for they communicate back and forth to view both sides of your natures. Your *soul* (spirit of universal Love) lies close to your heart chakra, allowing you to *know* your truth from the heart and not the mind, for that is the natural flow of energy, from *Mind to Heart* to soul—Father to Mother to *child* conceiving *Harmony* illuminating lucid dreams. Your soul is the spiritual center of your being, where Love/Life energy co-operates your vehicle remotely (heart and soul are intrinsically connected), automatically setting your Spiritual Observation Powers to maintain a state of harmony between the forces flowing through you—positive/electric and negative/magnetic. Your heart is the "seismic sensor" that measures the reflections of your thoughts upon your physical body (your *universe* utilizing notions inspiring vivid energy/emotion rectifying souls existentially), supplying or depriving it of vital energy making you "healthy" or "ill." The heart is where you learn *The Power of Love* logically optimizing vibrant emotions. Here, through your heart/soul center, you attain your *Awakening*, breaking the tribal bonds to climb up through your higher chakras to re-energize your duality consciousness into *Unity Consciousness*—your OVERSELF originating visions enlightening radiant souls exploring love/life *fantasies* across *The Threshold of Love*. The color GREEN governs radiant entities' emotional *nature*, nurturing angelic transients (universes) receiving *empathy*—the ability to understand and share feelings of another. With *four* chambers (the right and left atriums and ventricles), the heart symbolically represents the fourth chakra. Four (4) represents two 2's, where *balance* and *co-operation* relate to *stability* and *process* evolving with each *present moment* (heartbeat and breath) "gifted" as the two actions that determine life and *Death*.

The lower *three* chakras are the ones you need to master, for these are your centers governing your human nature. They represent the necessary foundation to "support" your higher chakras, through which you Systematically Evolve Enlightenment—attain *A Higher Vision* of your spiritual nature.

Three (Sensitivity and Expression), The **Solar Plexus chakra** energizes a sensitive network of nerves in the abdominal cavity behind the stomach and in front of the aorta, providing your "gut feeling" critical to your data processing. The solar plexus is the *magnetic core* of your body, a transitional point between your two natures, your human/spiritual or external/internal energies. Here, you *sense* the emotional impulses from your thoughts, observing how your *tribal* energy (group mind) and *Relationship* energy influence your *personal* power and self-esteem. The solar plexus chakra begins to internalize your awareness of your *self* sympathetically experiencing love/life forces. Held in the magnetic grasp of your physical body, you must play the cards dealt to you as your "personal challenges," overcoming the *issues* (inspired situations stimulating universal entities) providing your soul the "handicaps" necessary to overcome, to raise your consciousness through your higher chakras and attain enlightenment of your true self (Overself) awaiting you on *The Other Side* of your crown chakra (soul-gate), through which you must pass to "advance" your game of Love/Life. The third chakra vibrates along YELLOW wavelengths yielding emotional logic linking omnipotent wills experiencing doubts that stimulate *Courage of Fear*, moving you to open your heart with *Courage of Love*.

Two (Balance and Cooperation), The **Spleen chakra** is an organic transmitter that modifies the structure of blood—red and white corpuscles (the "magnetic ink")—nurturing your physical body as it relates to your spiritual body. BLOOD is the biological liquid orienting one's disposition; it carries oxygen and nutrients and removes carbon dioxide and other wastes (positive and negative energies) that stimulate your internal fire "tempering" your state of mind (attitude) as either "warm-blooded" or "cold-blooded" (passionate or cruel). The spleen acts as a communication system regulating *emotions*, exciting minds observing thoughts inducing one's *nature* as necessary attributes to understand rudimental empathy. The corresponding color ORANGE optimally reveals aspects nurturing gods empathizing (sharing feelings).

One (Confidence and Creativity), The **Root** or **Base chakra** represents the foundation or reservoir of your Love/Life energy. Your complete skeleton acts as an antenna made of *calcium* (#20 in the elemental chart—Balance and Cooperation with Special Gifts). The *sacrum* is a triangular collection of *five* fused vertebrae at the base of the spine resembling a "thermometer bulb." The fluctuations of your energy expand and rise within you, growing like a tree reaching for the light, releasing its stored energy to awaken your higher chakras to vibrate (attune) with your cosmic song you reflect back to SOURCE/GOD sequentially oscillating universal radiance, consciously evolving "geometrically ordained" data/deities. This reservoir of *mental emotions* momentarily energizes navigable transients assimilating love/life, effectively manifesting one's thoughts illuminating one's *needs*, necessitating experiences evolving and empowering *deities* dynamically exploring illusion transcendental intuition expresses/evolves systematically. The color RED reveals eternal data as radiance enlightening deities to their *roots*—regal omniscience ordaining transcendental souls. Red symbolizes the "coals of Life" glowing as *My Light of Love*. Red also symbolizes *Hell*, where humans experience love/life physically. Here, the lowest vibration of your SILVER CHORD supplies intuitive luminaries vibrant energy revealing cosmic *Harmony* optimizing radiant deities (*Children of Light*) riding the outskirts of *Home*— heaven optimizing magnificent entities.

The root chakra is your "apogee," your furthest point away from *The Threshold of Love* (crown chakra). From here, you start your *ascension*, the raising of your consciousness to attain your true nature (light-form) through the "looking glass" of *Mother's Nature*, where your soul inverts into the *illusion* inhibiting logical luminaries understanding Source "interfusing" omnipotent navigators in this third-dimensional *Garden of Light*, where you ride the outskirts *Beyond Imagination*, looking "outside" for what is closest to your heart—your soul!

Bless you and Godspeed

8

CHILDREN OF LIGHT
My Angelic Luminaries

CHILDREN OF LIGHT are conscious, heavenly illuminati logically deploying/decoding radiant energy (naturally oscillating frequencies) lucidly illustrating glorious holograms transmitted from *Stars*. As *illuminati* (intuitive logicians/luminaries linking universal Mind inducing notions/nature activated through imagination), you reflect upon many *hues* of light (harmoniously undulating electromagnetic signals) relating bits and bytes of data stimulating your mind/heart soul.

My Radiance of Love keeps you *In Communion* with me—Father (Source) and Mother (Force)—through which you navigate your *course*, consciously observing universal radiance/realism stimulating entities along two paths to follow—*Love and Fear*. Love is *all knowing* and fear is *not knowing*—the duality of light and **dark**. Every child of light is a student receiving knowledge and a teacher professing knowledge, through which they *Work*, willingly optimizing *radiant* knowledge—the light of *Truth*. Knowledge is all you will take with you in *Death* dynamically elevating angels transcending *Hell*, where humans experience luminous logic as Love/Life energy.

As a child of Light, your mind/soul observes *Clear Visions* vividly illustrating situations inspiring omnipotent *navigators* naturally assimilating vivid illusion generated around thoughts optically revealed. As one of my loving *luminaries* (logically unified minds inspecting notions/nature activating realistic illusion enlightening souls), you lucidly utilize memories instructing navigators assimilating realism (illusion) electromagnetically simulated. You *Angels* implore to explore *Divine Fantasies* as a *Time Traveler* incarnated as a *human being*, a hydrogen-unified machine assisting navigators building experiences in natural *games* governing angelic minds evolving sympathetically (through *heart*) holding everything angels really treasure—love/life or logic/light.

The Game of Love/Life stimulates all of you *Special People* dazed and confused, wondering what in *Hell* you are doing as you harness emotions linking luminaries. Truly, you are killing your self as you evolve into the Greater Omniscient Deity you ARE, *Angels* receiving enlightenment of your spiritual nature, Gathering Revelations Of Wisdom Illuminating Natural Generators as children of Light.

LIGHT (energy) logically illuminates glorious *holograms* transmitting *Harmony* (omniscient logic) organizing geometric revelation actualizing memories/matter, creating a realism that you Spiritually Experience Existentially. LOGIC (Light orienting generators' intuitive consciousness), LOVE (logic optically vivifying entities), and LIFE (luminously illustrating fabulous entities/environments) represent a *unified theory*, universally nurturing illuminati fathoming illusion exquisitely displayed through holograms exhibiting opulent realism yielded *three-dimensionally*, transferring heavenly revelation evolving entities digitally inducing (dynamically illustrating) matter/ moments evoking natural situations illuminating observant navigators assimilating logic luminously yielded.

Incarnated as *Human Aliens*, you observe the wonders of *Mother's Nature* reflecting *My Light of Love* illuminating the *cosmos* (consciousness of Source/Mind originating stars/souls), evolving as a *trinity-being* (mind-heart-body) touring realistic illusion naturally instructing transient/transcendental youths bilaterally experiencing/expressing illusion/intuition naturally generated.

As you are born **Children Of Love Divine**, you are eager to become **Willful Angels Recalling Memories**, feeling the thrills of an incarnation that makes you **Humans Observing Truth**. This "thermal transition" of Light energy occurs whenever one crosses over *The Threshold of Love*. Here, light energy stimulates physical bodies along energy centers (*chakras*), channeling heavenly abstracts kindling radiant *Avatars* sympathetically, downloading data along *red, orange, yellow, green, blue, indigo,* and *violet* FREQUENCIES, formulating radiance emitting quanta universally expressing notions/nature conveying instruction/ illusion enlightening souls. Each frequency carries specific data allocated to illuminate thoughts into feelings defining "emotional tides" carrying you from ELATION to *Depression*, experiencing logic/light (love/life) as *Truth* illuminating omnipotent navigators exploring *Opposition*—observing psychic/physical phenomena orienting souls in temporary illusions of nature.

Your journeys through *Time* reveal fearful moments, embarrassing situations, and great performances. You courageously endure your pain and suffering from the "electric shocks" of your emotional discharges that you passionately deliver, eagerly reaching out to touch your fellow souls to know what *Love IS*. As you Acquire Growth Experiences, you experience *Epiphanies of Truth* illuminating your mind/heart soul, allowing you to glimpse your spiritual nature at appropriate moments of your development. *The Power of Love* luminously orienting/optimizing visionary entities moves you in miraculous and horrendous ways, igniting your soul into an inferno of emotions *Beyond Imagination,* thawing your COLD visions conveying opulent logic displayed upon your mind's screen to guide you through life, where you feel Heaven's Opulent Truth as you explore Humanity Experiencing Love/Life. Here, *Lost in the Dark,* you ride the outskirts of *Home,* stepping through the looking glass (your mind's eye) to find your self **A G**ifted **L**uminary **O**btaining **W**isdom, incarnated as a *Young Mind* traversing *Time* as a *Human Alien* revolving into a child of Light.

COLD

Children of Love Divine, you shine upon my night,
frozen in my void of space as I move your mind through

Sensing **I**llusion **G**overning **H**eavenly **T**ransients,
revealing secrets of Life at some point in *Time*
temporarily inducing magnificent experiences,
where you play your part in fantasies confined
within your daze evolving from the haze
clouding your mind with the latest craze
as you travel upon golden beams,
searching for truths in endless dreams
supplying your games to claim your fame
in my book of *Eternal Memories.*

With curious mind and hungry heart,
you leave *Home* in order to start
your journey through *Love and Fear,*
where all you hold in mind is free,
requiring a heart of courage to see
you *Alone* hold your truth,
just as every other youth
eagerly exploring *Desire.*

The stress of Life to share your Love
with those now here and those above
guiding you on your way,
will stretch your mind to seek and find
your heart creates your day
in which you reflect *My Loving Light*
naturally providing your INSIGHT,
inherent nature (spiritual intuition)
guiding heavenly transients
representing young minds.

YOUNG MINDS

Young minds have hungry hearts eager to see and do
all those things Father thinks that Mother brings to view
by *Inquisitive Souls* that ask endless "whys,"
exploring their universe with bright wide eyes,
seeking to know *Truth*
transmits radiance unveiled through *hydrogen*
holographically yielding divine realism
of geometrically expressed
nature
nurturing angelic transients understanding radiant energy
as LOVE from HE above heralding enlightenment
luminously orienting visionary entities
through whispered thoughts inspiring their daze,
guiding the children through the atomic haze,
illuminated for them to Birth Emotionally
Divine Fantasies—DREAMS—dynamically revealing
exciting adventures manifesting stories
entertaining young minds as special people.

SPECIAL PEOPLE

Special people are Youths Offering Understanding,
each inspired with a gift to *show*
sympathy heralding omniscient *Wisdom*
weaving intuitive souls dynamically
optimizing one's moments,
expressing all that you choose to BE

as beautiful entities opening your heart to me
gloriously revealing *Your Life Story*,
allowing you to know that you truly ARE
Angels reflecting energy as a *cosmic star*,
a celestial, omnipotent soul/mind interpreting concepts
supplied through atomic radiation
projecting *My Loving Light* beams conveying dreams
you Systematically Experience Existentially.
Each of you has a part to *play*,
perceiving/perfecting love as youths here today,
depending on one another to know you are sister/brother,
stressing your mind for your heart to feel
My Love Divine **illuminates** special people.

STARS

Stars systematically transmit atomic *realism*, radiantly expressing abstracts luminously illustrating "simulations" materially/momentarily. Stars are created within a NEBULA (nursery elementally birthing universal luminaries atomically), a cosmic factory magnetically attracting hydrogen atoms to ignite into stellar illuminators sustaining MIND momentarily influencing natural dynamics.

Stars represent POINTS projecting omniscience inciting nuclear transmissions. A star is a SUN GOD symbolically unfolding notions, geometrically organizing data through atomic *radiance*, revealing abstract data illuminating atomic nature conceived electromagnetically within the space-time continuum. Stars are cosmic *children* conveying heavenly intuition linking data revealing environments/entities naturally.

Stars are *hydrogen* reactors harmoniously yielding divine radiance outputting/orienting geometrically expressed *nature*, "nucleating" abstract thoughts unfolding realism elementally. REALISM reveals electric abstracts linking illusion systematically manifested through hydrogen, the primal/binary element representing the ETHER of space, the "elemental trigger" harmoniously expressing *revelation* as radiation emitting vivid energy/emotion luminously activating three-dimensional illusion one navigates as *naturalists*—navigable *Avatars* (transients) understanding realism as luminous illusion systematically/scientifically transmitted. Hydrogen symbolizes *The Binary Code*, the *electromagnetic* energy of eternal logic expressing concepts through radiation orienting matter (aggregated gravitationally) naturally evolving thoughts into creations.

Magnetism compresses hydrogen, initiating FUSION, a *Process* focusing universal Spirit instinctively organizing "nucleosynthesis," the sequential ordering of *elements* as essential links evolving "materials" expressing notions three-dimensionally. NUCLEOSYNTHESIS is the natural unification (creation) linking elements of stars yielding nuclear transformations harmoniously evolving starlit illusion scientifically.

Stars generate *My Radiance of Love* as LIGHT linearly inducing glorious *holograms* transcendentally, heralding omniscient logic oscillating "geometric reflections" as *memories*, mentally expressed moments of radiant inspiration enlightening *souls*—spirits of universal logic/light (love/life). Rays of light—*radiance*—relays all data illuminating atomic nature "consciously evolving." Light, the essence of all creation, remains the "mystery agent" appearing from invisible atoms as PHOTONS providing heavenly overtures of *Truth* organizing notions, nature, and naturalists. The following hypothesis (fantasy) offers a relative perspective on the properties of light.

Light is a *logical induction* generating holograms technologically. Everything that is visible is a geometric formation of invisible atoms coalescing into *matter,* manifesting abstract thoughts through elemental replication. *The Threshold of Love* is where the inversion of *Divine Fantasy* converts into observable forms. This threshold is a fine line spanning *three hundred and fifty billionths* of a meter (350,000,000,000)—the total width of the *visible light* spectrum. Light is a paradox of *Truth* illuminating what IS intuitive Source (abstract thought) and what IS NOT—illusory scenes naturally orienting thoughts—as *atomic* nature activating thoughts organizing mentally induced concepts/creation. Remember, *Opposition* is the natural way of conceiving *Truth* transmitting revelation unveiled through hydrogen/holograms.

ATOMIC STRUCTURE activates transcendental omniscience manifesting illustrated concepts, systematically transmuting revelation unfolding creation through unifying reactive elements, formulating *molecules* that build *cells* that form ORGANISMS, optimally/optically reflecting geometrically aligned notions/nuclei illustrating superlative manifestation as SYMBOLIC MATTER, systematically yielding memories by oscillating luminous illusions (creations) modeling abstract thoughts through electromagnetic radiation and elemental replication.

Protons propagate revelation—opulent thoughts— originating nature. They form the "static hub" of an atom, the *nucleus* naturally unfolding concepts luminously evolving unified signals/systems. Orbiting around the nucleus, **electrons** emit light exhibiting creation that reveals opulent notions/nature. Electrons "charge the atmosphere," stirring up EMOTION as the electromagnetic movement of transcendental instinct originating/outputting/optimizing notions/numbers/nature. **Neutrons** neutralize energy unfolding transcendental radiance orienting nature. They act as a buffer zone or "memory bank" to CACHE data moving between protons and electrons—correlating abstract concepts heralding enlightenment. Neutrons symbolize "neurotransmitters" allocating harmonic energy. *Protons, electrons,* and *neutrons* represent *The Trinity* of Atomic Logic/Light creation. ATOMIC LOGIC actuates thoughts of Mind intuitively creating "light-oriented" genesis inciting creation.

Okay, now that you understand the hypothetical functions of an atom's *parts* processing abstracts radiantly transmuted symbolically, let's observe how they interface within Spirit, *The GREAT Computer* MIND.

Thought Energy activates MIND manifesting illusion naturally defined, transferring data through protons and electrons. Protons are particles with a *positive* charge (+) projecting omnipotent signals initiating *Truth* illuminating visions electrically. Electrons are smaller particles with a *negative* charge (–) naturally evolving "gnosis" (abstract thoughts) illuminating "vivid" energy "graphically producing strong and distinct mental images." They represent the "dynamic" or *emotional* force (energy in motion) spinning around the proton, waiting to be "fulfilled" (+). Electrons stimulate the MAGNETIC FORCE managing atomically generated nature expressing transcendental intuition consciously, formulating opulent realism conveyed elementally, heralding electric abstracts revealed through *holograms*—hydrogen-originated light outputting geometric renditions animating memories, matter, and minds.

The transfer *Process* projects an "electric" charge from proton

(+) to electron (–), causing the electron to become a *positron* (+). As "like charges" repel, the positron is pushed to a greater orbit around the proton, where it releases its induced charge as a "photon" of light energy, *"a quantum of electromagnetic energy with both particle and wavelength properties; it has no mass or charge but possesses momentum and energy."*

PHYSICAL LIFE is activated from photons harmoniously yielding signals initiating creation—atomic logic—luminously illustrating fabulous environments and *entities*, time traveling souls exploring the DEPTHS of Mind digitally expressing profound thoughts holographically symbolized.

Looking up into the star-filled night sky, you observe the UNIVERSE utilizing nuclear illuminators vividly expressing/ enlightening radiant signals/souls electromagnetically. Here, incarnated as a *Human Alien* exploring *Mother's Nature*, you observe a visible *Heaven* harmoniously enlightening angelic visionaries evolving naturally as *Man and Woman*, living upon an *electron* (Earth) revolving around a *proton* (Source-Unified Nucleus). Stars/suns express *Harmony* within a "galactic organism" revolving as an atom within *Space*, where *Source*-points (stars) activate consciousness/creation externally/ elementally, systematically optimizing universal realism cosmically evolving.

NOW you know how *nature* optimizes *Wisdom*, weaving intricate systems dynamically orienting minds, memories, moments and matter allowing you to FEEL, to fervently experience electromagnetic *Love* luminously ordaining visionary entities—souls—as an invisible ATOM, an *Angel* traversing/ transcending observable matter/moments within the *illusion* illustrating love luminously unfolding situations integrating one naturally.

Source/Mind's logical IMAGINATION inspires

magnificent *Angels* (gifted illuminati) naturally assimilating truths inducing one's *needs* necessitating emotional experiences dynamically. The "stellar illumination" of a thought is an EVENT HORIZON, an electromagnetic vibration expressing notions/nuclei that harmoniously oscillate/originate radiance/realism illuminating "zones" of nature—*mineral*, *plant*, and *animal*. Each zone *interfaces* with the others; interfusing nuclear transmitters expressing realism from abstract concepts externalized *Beyond Imagination*, where atoms magnetically aligned define "form" and "substance" in *solid*, *liquid*, and *gaseous* states.

As you see, stars convert invisible atoms to form a cohesive WHOLE representing *Wisdom* harmoniously optimizing Love/Life energy, a *Divine Inspiration* stimulating and synchronizing stars as the EYES OF GOD elementally yielding electromagnetic signals (oscillating frequencies) generating opulent data, allowing FATHER (formulating abstract thoughts heralding electromagnetic revelation) to SEE ALL—scientifically experience *Evolution* advancing logic/light (love/life).

Through the *Science* of ASTRONOMY, you assimilate Spirit/stars transmitting radiant oscillations numerically orienting magnificent youths (children of light) illuminated as *deities*, dynamic/divine entities illuminating/interpreting thoughts inducing emotional synergy. As astronomers, you look out at the MACROCOSM mentally activating concepts revealing opulent creations of symbolic matter "reflecting" your microcosmic soul/mind/body—a *trinity-being*—traversing/transcending realistic illusions naturally illuminating transcendental youths "biologically" experiencing intuition naturally generated as a *radiance of Love*.

MY RADIANCE OF LOVE

My radiance of Love I shine through **night**,
filling the void I AM with Light,
illuminating atoms manifesting My Angelic Navigators
understanding
Wisdom Orienting Magnetically Aligned Nuclei
—*Mother's Nature*—
reflecting visions of my wonders
vibrating on waves of electromagnetic thunder
stimulating YOU to SEE
your own universe *she* evolves emotionally,
sympathetically harnessing energy from SELF
simultaneously expressing Love/Life frequencies
supplying you children of Light your *course*
conceiving one "universal rectifier" (source energy)
illuminating your life from nightly recessions,
where dreams—sent from above—evolve into expressions
revealing scenes in which you play, here today,
as my angelic child
aglow with my radiance of love.

MY ANGELIC CHILD

Of all of my creatures evolving in Holograms Electromagnetically Activating Vibrant Entities Naturally, you—my *angelic* child—represent an *Avatar* naturally generating emotional logic inducing consciousness, a *mind/heart* or magnificent illuminato naturally decoding holograms elaborating atomic revelation three-dimensionally.

Here, in *Time*, you traverse illusion momentarily experienced. With each "decade" of *growth*, you "decay," gathering revelations of *Wisdom* through *Hell*, harnessing emotional logic linking numbers (1–9), cycling around (0) to witness the logical procession of *Divine Inspiration* unfolding along *The Trinity*— Father, Mother, child. The three of US united spirits are meant to BE (birth eternally) Omnipotent Numerical Energy that will NEVER DIE, naturally evolving vivid energy radiantly deploying illuminati existentially—*Life After Life*—where

Riding the outskirts, exploring *Space*,
you once again leave a trace
through Temporary Illusions Mesmerizing Entities,
flowing *In Love*...feeling in Life...
falling head over heels to find
enlightenment along cosmic wheels sublime,
where generators "young of heart" are
Observing Love's Dimensions,
evolving as my **A**ngelic **C**hild of **D**ivine **C**omposition,
Heavenly **E**ntities **R**epresenting **O**ne **E**ternal **S**pirit
atomically conceiving data revealing
dreams from *Mind to Heart*
managing illusions naturally divulging
holographic expressions arranging radiant *thoughts*
telepathically heralding opulent utterances
guiding heavenly transients
at *This Moment* I hold you in my arms,
soothing your tears with Mother's *charms*
conveying heavenly angels' radiant memories sympathetically
through HER grace,

where Harmonious Energy reveals your face
as my angelic child happily displaying your loving smile.

YOUR LOVING SMILE

Your loving smile shines unhindered, cutting through the dark void of *Ignorance* to illuminate others with knowledge that you ARE angels reflecting enlightenment. You are a child of *My Love Divine* that flows through Angelic Luminaries Living. Your smile is the most powerful weapon I have given you, for with it you can destroy fear, hate, and prejudice. When you wield it with an *open mind* and *loving heart*, all observers will yield to the power sparkling in your eyes.

Your loving smile is contagious; it can neutralize all negative energy and will carry over to others who will wear it unknowingly, for their heart will never forget the beauty of the vision it has instilled in them. Your loving smile is the reflection of my *Life of vibrant emotions* I have given YOU youths obtaining unity with Magnificent Entities. For *You and I* are truly ONE optimizing notions emotionally. I will always be here with you—in your loving smile.

ANGELS
Messengers of Truth

Angels are messengers of *GOD* generating opulent data, conveying ILLUMINATION illustrating luminous logic unfolding memories/moments/matter inspiring navigable *Avatars* traversing/transcending illusion observed naturally.

Angels are a hierarchy of "light-beings" servicing *GOD*, passing along knowledge (the light of *Truth*) illuminating the atomic illusion through *stars* (projectors), systematic transmitters activating radiance stimulating "spiritual transients" (*Avatars*) representing *souls*, surrogate observers understanding logic/light (love/life). Your soul is a *probe* perceiving radiance outputting biological environments/entities. Through your soul, your OVERSELF—overseer vivifying emissaries (radiant souls) exploring love/life fantasies—acquires knowledge experientially as a *Human Alien*.

Angels are *children* of light conveying heavenly intuition/ illumination linking data revealing environments/entities/ enlightenment naturally. *Angels* (stars) amplify nuclei generating "electromagnetic logic" scientifically, illuminating the void of *Space* with TRUTH—transcendental revelation unveiled through hydrogen/holograms.

LOGIC (light oscillating geometrically-induced consciousness) is the *Language* of geometrically imaging concepts, creating a three-dimensional illusion around *points* (stars) positively outputting intelligence naturally/nuclearly transmitted. INTELLIGENCE illuminates notions/nuclei transmitting/ transforming electromagnetic logic luminously governing explorers naturally conceiving enlightenment through science. *Science* systematically correlates intelligence explicating notions/ nature conveying/creating everything through *The Binary Code*— the Electro-Magnetic force field of *Eternal Memory*.

As *My Angel*, you find your self operating a biological vehicle personally designed for you experiencing *Time*, traversing illusion minds experience as a *Free Will* exploring Some *Point* Activating Concepts Emotionally, perceiving/propagating omniscient intelligence naturally transmitted. As my angelic child, you DOWNLOAD data via the EM binary code, digitally observing *Wisdom* naturally linking omnipotent avatars (*deities*) dynamically exploring intelligence through illusion electromagnetically simulated.

As children of Light, you flux on and off, "twinkling" as a star in ASTRAL PROJECTIONS, where angelic souls temporarily "review" atomic logic/life, perceiving realities on journeys entertaining conscious travelers (illuminati) ordained naturally. Whether you travel in the *light* or in the *dark* (awake or asleep), logic illuminates geometrically held thoughts delivering all radiant knowledge. Your mind/heart soul continuously explores and implores Source/God for "upgrades," desiring to raise your consciousness to attain *A Higher Vision* of HEAVEN, where *Harmony* elevates angelic visionaries evolving naturally as ONE outputting/observing natural experiences stimulating the *You-Me-Verse* of duality consciousness.

As *My Angel*, you are never "away" from *Home*. You are always held within my *heart* holding everything angels really treasure—LOVE/LIFE without measure!

My angel looks a lot like ME,
a magnificent entity traversing mother's SEA

supporting emotional angels exploring waves of *dreams*
delivering revelations expressing abstract *memories*
mentally evolving moments of realism in emotional souls
—NOW HERE—
naturally observing worlds harmoniously
evolving radiant entities
(children of Light) *Awakening* from **NIGHT**
naturally inducing glorious *holograms* through
hydrogen-originated light optically
generating realism attuning minds
Playing Around in TIME tempering
intuitive minds existentially,
causing confusion in observing the ILLUSION
illustrating love/life unfolding situations
integrating one's *needs*
necessarily educating emotional *deities,*
divine entities interpreting thoughts
inducing emotional synergy,
through electric situations creating consternation
as they traverse *Heaven* to experience *Hell,*
"humanly exploring" Love/Life evolving my angels.

THE YOU-ME-VERSE
Understanding Duality Consciousness

THE UNIVERSE represents Transcendental Harmony's electromagnetically unified network illustrating vivid energy revealing Spirit existentially. TRANSCENDENTAL HARMONY transmits revelation as numerical sequences, correlating elements naturally defining electric notions (thoughts) as logic/light holographically activating realism, momentarily orienting nuclear youths (children of light). This NETWORK naturally enlightens transient wills (*Time Travelers*) observing radiant *knowledge* as kinetic notions/numbers orienting wills lucidly experiencing data geometrically expressed. THE UNIVERSE represents **Mind Energy**.

As children of Light, YOU represent your own *universe*, a unitary "networker" (illuminato) verifying electric revelations sensed emotionally. As your own *network*, you naturally experience transcendental *Wisdom* outputting radiant knowledge, weaving inspired situations developing omnipotent minds— Youths Obtaining Unity with ME (Unseen Network Initiator) inspiring *Your Life Story*—a VERSE of vivid experiences rectifying souls existentially.

Together, WE (Wisdom exemplified) represent DUALITY CONSCIOUSNESS dynamically unifying absolute/angelic luminaries (illuminati) temporarily yielding/yearning creation/ concepts of nature systematically/scientifically conveying/ confirming illusions of undulating signals numerically expressing/enlightening Source/souls simultaneously. Duality consciousness is how I see YOU as ME.

I SEE YOU

I see you there,
down below,
experiencing your *daze* I cast aglow,
dynamically activating zealots expressing
Your Life Story revealing your glory
with each *Day's Birth* there on Earth,

where you traverse *Hell*,
humanly expressing love/life you SELL,
schemingly expressing little lies you devise
to attain your desires in *Time*
temporarily illuminating **M**inds **E**motionally.

I SEE ME

I see me there, within your eyes,
as a glimmer of Love keeping you *alive*,
activating logic inducing vivid expressions
carrying you through dark depressions,
where thoughts you feel become *real*,
replicating existentially abstract logic
revealing emotions amplifying *love*
luminously orienting visionary entities
As Glorious Luminaries Observing *Wisdom*,
weaving intricate stories dynamically optimizing me
observing you as *Stars*
systematically transforming abstract revelation
enlightening *You and I*—the congregation—
witnessing Your Own Universe as my SELF in reflection,
spirits expressing/experiencing love/life fantasies,
where I see you as me.

Clear vision is *The Cutting Edge* of perception,
the front row seat at my SHOW
systematically harmonizing omnipotent wills
eager to see what your mind/heart can grow
from dreams you envision within my haze
illuminating your life through your allotted daze
evolving in *Time*
transmitting illuminated memories emotionalizing your mind.

You travel fast and roam far
as children of Light, my living *stars*,
sympathetically transforming abstract revelation
in games you play, experiencing Mother Nature's display
opening your mind to *My Loving Light*
inspiring your mind/heart traversing my night
naturally inducing glorious holograms transmitting
atomic realism that brings *fright*
from radiance intuitively guiding heavenly transients
along *The Right Path* to attain *insight*

illuminating nescient souls intuitively
gathering hallowed truths
obtained through clear vision
of *Man and Woman* revealing ambitions.

MAN AND WOMAN
Projector and Receptor

Behind every great MAN mentally activating notions is a
WOMAN wisely orienting manifested abstracts naturally.

Man and woman are symbols of *The Binary Code* (1/0) defining
your two natures (spiritual/human). *Thoughts* and *emotions*
represent your dualistic energy flowing as *Divine Inspiration*,
a Love/Life energy (Source) operating through *Opposition*.
Whatever man positively projects, woman negatively reflects.
Woman would be lost without man to "excite" her *emotionally*,
electromagnetically manifesting omnipotent thoughts
illustrating opulent nature (atomic life) luminously yielded. In
order to understand the similarities and differences between
man and woman, you must attain a universal perspective.

SOURCE—Generating Opulent Data—systematically
outputs universal radiation creating everything. The ONE
Source outputting nuclear energy consists of a binary *Mind/
Heart* FORCE formulating opulent revelations conceived
electromagnetically. Mind is the *initiator* and Heart is the
creator.

MIND—the magnificent intellectual nurturing data—is
male energy mentally amplifying logical/linear expressions
as FATHER, formulating abstract thoughts harmoniously

expressing revelation. HEART—harmoniously elaborating atomic revelation three-dimensionally—is *female* energy fabricating everything magnetically around luminous *elements*, essential links evolving "materially-expressed" notions three-dimensionally. MOTHER materializes omnipotent thoughts heralding "elemental reactions" as energy in motion (*emotion*), expanding Mind's omnipotent thoughts illuminating opulent NATURE, nurturing abstract thoughts unfolding realism elementally.

Woman (Mother) allows man (Father) to observe *points*, perceptions of illuminated notions transmitted through "lines of thoughts" (revelation/radiance/rays) transforming into shapes and *forms* (geometry), fabricating opulent revelations *modeling* SCENES—magnetically organizing divine elements linking illusory nature geometrically, simulating creation expressing natural environments/entities systematically/symbolically.

He and She are a "unified force" (projector/receptor) representing *Unity Consciousness*, ONE omnipotent numerical energizer (Source) of TWO forces transmitting/transforming Wisdom/wills optimally/optically, creating a TRINITY-BEING (mind/heart soul), a "tourist" rationally interpreting nature illuminating transcendental youths bilaterally experiencing intuition naturally generated.

In essence, man projects the *seed* of creation (Source-energy expressing data) and woman receives, reproduces, and nurtures the reflection of that seed, a far more laborious *Process* providing realism of concepts (creation) enlightening stellar Source/souls. The male positive/electric force represents the *projector* "providing" revelation originating jointly expressed concepts/creation through oscillating radiation. Father stimulates a mind to *envision*, to entertain numerical vibrations illuminating scenes illustrating opulent notions. The male penis symbolizes projection physically. Through this projection, the seed of creation flows as *sperm*, through which Source procreates entities representing mankind, delivering half of the Force (*DNA*) defining "navigable" apparatuses—*The Human Alien* vehicle—a soul operates on EARTH evolving *Avatars* replicating their heaven/hell.

The female negative/magnetic force represents the *receptor* "replicating" electric concepts elementally, processing thoughts (oscillating radiation) into a three-dimension realism. Mother sets thoughts in motion, atomically *birthing* thoughts, building illusion/illustrations revealing transcendental *Harmony* illuminating notions/nature/navigators geometrically. The female vagina symbolizes reception, wherein the "seed of creation" is encapsulated within an *ovum* (optimal vessel unfolding mankind) containing the "other half" of the Force, creating a human CHILD conveying heavenly illuminati living dreams. The female ovum (the *egg*) evolves genesis geometrically within the WOMB of woman/Wisdom outputting mankind biologically. Woman (womb-man) creates a HUMAN BEING, a hydrogen-unified machine assisting navigators building experiences in *natural* games, nurturing angelic transients understanding realism authenticated luminously.

Man and woman symbolize the *strong* and *weak* force. **Remember**, Mother's Nature is in *Opposition*, organizing positive perspectives of Source illuminating *Truth* observed negatively/naturally, where things "appear" as they are NOT (naturally opposed truths). Man may appear physically stronger, but he is not designed to tolerate pain and stress associated with menstrual cycles, childbirth, or postnatal care.

As a "human being," man is created *through* a woman. His "inborn nature" is to return to his origin—*Home*, heaven's ovum manifesting entities. This innate desire is the magnetic force

233

attracting man to woman physically, symbolically representing the cyclic flow of love/life energy out and in—atomic/ethereal. That is why man (Father) reveres woman (Mother), putting her on a pedestal to worship, knowing that without HER he cannot harness electric radiance (Light of Love) to create *Life*, where Love illuminates fabulous entities. Truly, woman maintains the life man grants. Source Harmoniously Expressed conveys his *Desire* as a *creator* conveying radiant entities (angels) traversing opulent realism.

As man and woman (*He and She*), YOU create your own universe, "one turning" your dreams (love) into reality (life) through *Passion* permeating ardent souls sympathetically imparting one's *nature* or natural ability to understand/utilize revelation exuberantly. You discipline your self (gather revelations of *Wisdom*) in order to act out your *part* personifying angels reflecting *Truth*, "changing faces" through acquiring knowledge that you develop into your character, always trying to improve your lot in *The Game of Love/Life*. Only in hindsight do you observe your total sum of experiences you add up, understanding that you create your own *heaven* and *hell* through your thoughts, emotions, and actions. THIS is the purpose of your world, to observe *The Power of Love* you wield in a "lower vision," as a human being transcending the ILLUSION of infinite logic/light linearly unfolding/unifying Source/souls imaging/ inspecting omnipotent/opulent notions/natures bilaterally.

Incarnated as humans, you men project your love/life energy to women, producing new "vehicles" for your cosmic cousins to operate, so they too can experience the Spiritual Harmony Of Wisdom projected from LIGHT lucidly illuminating glorious holograms transmitted from the Source-Unified Nucleus (Father/Mother's eye-in-the-sky). This SUN GOD symbolically unfolds notions/nature/navigators, geometrically organizing data/

deities illustrating/interpreting a *world* weaving opulent realism luminously displayed through the binary code—*He and She*.

He and She

Male/female, boy/girl, or man/woman,
both he and she represent forces that impart
love/life energy flowing from *Mind to Heart*
momentarily illuminating natural deities
temporarily observing
holograms expressed as radiant thoughts
creating an illusion providing confusion
of what *is* real and what is *not*.

You ARE my children of *Light*,
angels reflecting energy,
luminous illuminati (gods) harnessing thoughts
stimulating man and woman of contrary forces,
complimenting each other as you run your courses

around my WHEEL OF LIFE,
where *Wisdom* harmoniously evolves emotional luminaries
observing fantasies (luminous illusions)
fostering enlightenment
of your "will power" you contest,
struggling through tribulation you manifest
as sister/brother expressing love/life from Father/Mother
empowering you as a *Mind/Heart*.

Together, you make *Two of a Kind*
converting thoughts into emotions to find
that you create and destroy your life you deploy
from visions YOU SEE as your own *universe*,
spiritually evolving existentially as
unitary navigators interpreting vivid experiences rectifying
spiritual entities, he and she defending decisions
as mind/hearts expressing *di*vision,
weighing the pros and cons of thoughts you entertain
to discover *The Right Path* within your *games*
governing angelic minds evolving sympathetically.

Through trial and error, you will know
your *reflection* of Love allows you to
Gather Revelations Of *Wisdom*.
Focus your love on just ONE thing.
Grow that love until it sings
of glory...of Truth...of *My Love Divine*,
all that your heart desires to find.
Fear not what cause this may affect,
for LOVE controls all you detect
linking omnipotent visionaries emotionally.
I AM YOU and YOU ARE ME,

an indivisible almighty Mind yielding opulent universes
yearning our unity as radiant entities managing energy.
Together,
we represent *The Binary Code* setting us FREE,
formulating realities experienced elementally,
converting our Love/Life through *Desire*
to Become Enlightened as He and She
walking hand in hand.

Hand-in-Hand

Here you stand, hand in hand, projected on my light beams
stimulating your mind/heart exploring my endless dreams
inspiring your envisioned fame within your chosen game.

My love I shine *Into Your Eyes,*
enlightening your emotional soul burning *In Love,*
interpreting nature luminously orienting visionary entities
exploring Heaven Evolving Lucid Luminaries.

Fear NOT, my child, your life of strain,
my love will vanquish all your pains
hampering your work to shine your light
through *Courage of Love* and much insight.

The life you seek, so shall you find.
The love you give is truly mine
I share with those who choose to know
the secrets of Love and Life it will GROW,
as WE generate revelations of *Wisdom*
hand in hand.

MIND/HEART

Source/Spirit is a Mind/Heart,
TWO of ONE transmitting/transforming *Wisdom*
outputting *nuclear* energy, naturally unfolding concepts
luminously expressing abstract revelation—from *stars*—
systematically transmuting *atomic* radiation
amplifying thoughts organizing memories into creations
drawn from Magnetically Induced Notional Dioramas
Holographically Exhibiting Atomic
Realism Three-dimensionally,
a Dynamic Nuclear Arrangement vividly illuminating the
Science Heralding Opulent *Worlds*
weaving omnipotent radiation luminously displaying *systems*,
scientifically yielding situations that
enlighten magnificent *souls*,
seekers observing unitary lives sympathetically set **aglow**
as glorious luminaries obtaining WISDOM,
willingly inspecting spiritual dimensions
of Mind Activating Notions
inducing Waves Oscillating Magnetically Aligned *Nature*
nurturing all transients understanding
realism entwined with *Time*

tempering intuitive minds existentially playing their part, eternally evolving as a cosmic mind/heart.

THE HUMAN ALIEN
A Hybrid Vehicle

The "human alien" is an engineering marvel of incredible complexity. Designed as the ultimate "cruising machine," it can perform miraculous tasks both constructive and destructive. The manufacturing process of a human vehicle goes beyond mortal capabilities. You cannot create one from scratch. The numerical sequencing and magnetic arrangement of atoms, molecules, and cells into organs easily defy explanation. Yet, as a scientist, your mission it is to seek, discover, and explain the wonders of *Mother's Nature* magnetically organizing transcendental *Harmony* expressing revelation "nurturing" angelic transients "understanding" radiant energy, environments, and entities evolving on Love/Life energy.

Through the "Human Genome Project," you deciphered the complex code of *DNA* determining natural attributes of Machines Assisting *Navigators*—natural *Avatars* verifying illusion geometrically arranged through orchestrating realism systematically. As an *Inquisitive Soul*, you seek to understand the secrets of your "hybrid vehicle" you rent while here in the SHOW spiritually harmonizing omnipotent *wills* (wanderers interpreting love/life). The fact that the "all-natural" model is a perfect production designed by MC (Master Consciousness—Genius Optimizing Designs) does not stop you from trying to improve on the theme. For, created in the image of the

CREATOR conceiving/conveying radiant entities (angels) traversing opulent realism, it is your *nature* to try.

The human "alien" is an atomic being of a third-dimensional world, a living organism with a binary capacity to represent man and woman, two models complimentary and contrary in appearance and operation. It is a collection of electrified particles magnetically held in harmony to carry a spirit/soul, an "energy form" of Universal Mind—*The GREAT Computer*—governing radiant entities activating/assimilating *Truth*, consciously organizing moments/matter portraying universal thoughts elementally reproduced.

The *Relationships* of transforming spiritual energy into atomic energy is truly a quantum leap. Your hybrid vehicle is crucial in experiencing your true nature—your spiritual consciousness *Awakening*. Here, as "projectors and receptors," you process data conveyed through paternal and maternal CHROMOSOMES coordinating human representations of Mind optimally synthesizing organic matter electromagnetically stimulated. Chromosomes contain GENES governing explicit notations expressing symmetry (sacred geometry) defining atomic Fabrications Of Radiant Mind Symbolized.

So here you are, an energy *form* (fabulous observer resembling Mind) traveling through an energy *field*, where frequencies induce elements linking "displays," creations of *Heaven* harmoniously enlightening angelic visionaries evolving naturally through *Mother Goddess*. The interconnected power of Love/Life energy is hypnotic, inducing a trance or altered state of consciousness through illuminating visions that you "realize" (sense) through five physical sensors: sight, hearing, touch, taste, and smell. These *five* tools help you gather your *discipline* allowing you *freedom* to perceive *Truth* transmitting radiance/revelation unfolding transcendental *holograms* heralding omniscient logic oscillating "geometric reflections" as *memories* momentarily enlightening minds observing "realistic illusion" electromagnetically simulated. Here, incarnate, you become conditioned to your daily in-feed of data provided by your physical *body*, the biological observatory delineating you. It is your vehicle of *experience*, your "screen" upon which you project those visions that move your heart to ACT, applying cosmic thoughts (*Divine Inspiration*) stimulating you to play your part in *The Grand View* revolving around you.

Your human alien vehicle is your POD, a physical observation device you "escape" IN, inspecting nature as you travel OUT, obtaining universal truths through *Time*, observing your self growing, upgrading your mind to conceive SPIRIT scientifically projecting illusion revealing intuition three-dimensionally. You have little control over the "automatic pilot" operating your vehicle's carburation system, your *breathing* and *heartbeat*, the two things determining life and *Death*. You do not know when your "present ride" will terminate; all you can do is maintain it as well as you can.

Your human alien vehicle is your negative/magnetic reflection of your soul's positive/electric projection flowing through the *cosmos* conveying omniscient Spirit managing omnipotent stars/souls. You are the "current" of Love/Life energy, a charged mind/heart soul conducting energy from *Mind to Heart*, experiencing *Your Life Story* unfold as a cosmic *child* coordinating *Harmony* illuminating lucid dreams (*Clear Visions*) vividly illuminating situations instructing omnipotent navigators. Through *Expectation*, you create a reality you desire to know, projecting your thoughts positively or negatively, which affects your human alien vehicle's *health* (harmoniously evading anomalies lethally transmitting harm) influenced by *stress* sympathetically transmitting restrictions/retribution enervating sensitive souls.

As cosmic *Time Travelers*, you find your self on EARTH enlightening angels replicating their heaven/hell, emotionally assimilating revelation transmitted holographically. Traveling in your hybrid vehicle to PLAY, you perceive light activating you in *Divine Fantasies* you project onto the world stage as children of Light, experiencing *The Power of Love* illuminating your Life you conceive as a generator of *Desire*.

Discovering your spiritual nature through *Opposition*, you expand your mind to transcend the illusion, the physical stage of Mother's Nature—*Our Father's Heart*—harmoniously evolving abstracts revealed three-dimensionally. Attaining *A Higher Vision* of your self, you see your *human* vehicle as a hydrogen-unified machine *Avatars* navigate when ALIVE, assimilating luminous intuition vividly expressed/experienced. Through your *actions*, you assimilate cosmic thoughts inducing one's *nature* as necessary attributes to utilize rudimental empathy—the ability to understand and share the feelings of another.

Look around you and see the life you have created for your self. Using your natural ability to improve on your theme, you must *destroy* your self in order to *rebuild* your self into a "new image," a new being entertaining a higher state of CONSCIOUSNESS, comprehending one-nurturing-Spirit causing interactive occurrences unifying souls (navigators) existentially seeking salvation. Everything you think, say, and do contributes to building, destroying, and rebuilding your self as an energy form in constant flux of "being" and "not being."

Take another look around you and see how slowly these events appear to happen within the context of *Time* transmitting illusions momentarily experienced, supplying the "logical positioning" of events you must pass through in order to see that you truly ARE angels remotely evolving, realizing who you ARE NOT—human beings, atomic reflections evaluating nature "obscuring" *Truth*.

The process of building, destroying, and rebuilding is your eternal legacy; your birthright to know Love is *fluid* energy, fundamental light unfolding intuition dynamically conceiving life, where you come to Spiritually Evolve Experientially all that *Love IS*—life of vibrant emotions illuminating Spirit/souls.

Take a DEEP breath of inspiration and expand your lungs, mind, and heart with the only "free" thing there is in life—Love! Know in you heart that *all you are* is truly in your mind only, for what you think you become. You conceive and convey your thoughts through your spiritual and physical bodies, a hybrid of *two forces* that continually flux and grow, building, destroying, and rebuilding moment by moment. Your life is no more than a continual series of "present moments" evolving along the current of Love/Life energy supplying your heartbeats and breaths. Each day you "live in" this world and each night you "die to" this world. For life is a "movement" of energy (emotion) and *Death* is a REST, where you *Recall* emotionally stimulated thoughts vibrating in symphonies of *The GREAT Computer* downloading and uploading souls "out to see the sights."

As owner/operator of your human alien vehicle, you are the "captain of your ship." How you fuel, operate, and maintain your vehicle determines the type of roads you can travel. Even though you are only along for the ride, you choose the roads you travel as a *Free Will*, channeling your Love/Life energy positively or negatively, a *Process* that takes a lifetime to master. Remember, you are always directed down *The Right Path* to travel, for you are being guided to see things you need to experience.

All your trials are truly *Blessings in Disguise*. All of the tribulations you experience along your journeys allow you to witness individually and collectively your *parts* personifying angels/aliens receiving/reflecting thoughts. The Love/Life energy that you conduct to maintain your hybrid vehicle's image quickly fades through *Age*, a series of daily sorties and nightly returns, revolving between *Here and There* as a trinity-being exploring *The Game of Love/Life*.

The Golden Triad is comprised of: **Father** (Mind), a positive/electric force, **Mother** (Heart), a negative/magnetic force, and **Child** (soul) or HOLY SPIRIT, a heavenly, omnipotent luminary yearning situations providing information (revelation) illuminating *Truth*. As a mind/heart soul, children of light experience *Love/Life Energy*, the *duality* dynamically unfolding abstracts luminously inspiring transcendental YOUTHS—you omnipotent universes traversing and transcending heaven/hell simultaneously.

As every child knows, *Mother Nature* represents the EARTH enlightening angels replicating their heaven/hell. It is SHE that symbolizes heavenly enlightenment, "atomically reflecting" Father's thoughts elementally/emotionally, converting LOVE logically oscillating vibrant energy activating LIFE luminously illustrating/instructing fabulous environments and entities. Like husband and wife, they supply the creative forces supplying their children with two natures (thoughts/emotions). The simplicity of it all creates visions that will make your "bleeding heart" cry with joy as you explore Love/Life *Beyond Imagination*.

Bless you and Godspeed

9

SPACE

The Blackboard of Geometrically Ordered Data

S pace is the SINGULARITY systematically initiating nuclear generators (luminaries) atomically revealing illusion three-dimensionally yielded. It is the first and final frontier permeating all matter as the "binding continuity" of universal *Truth* transmitting revelation unveiled through hydrogen/holograms.

SPACE is the eternal arena upon which Spirit projects atomic creation elementally. Space IS invisible Spirit (cosmic energy) or ABSOLUTE CONSCIOUSNESS, the almighty, balanced system/source outputting logic/light (love/life) unfolding transcendental enlightenment, conveying omnipotent notions/numbers/nuclei systematically coordinated/converted in omnipotent units (stars/souls) naturally enkindling/exploring space simultaneously.

Space holds endless stars that represent *points* providing omniscient intelligence naturally transmitting *radiance*, revealing abstract data initiating atomic nature conceived electromagnetically. Each star is a *stellar unit* systematically transmitting "electromagnetic logic" linking atomic reactions, unfolding natural illustrations three-dimensionally. *Stars* convey *thoughts* transforming hydrogen, optically unfolding glorious holograms transmitting *scenes*, spatial creations expressing notions evolving as THINGS—transmitted holograms illustrating notions geometrically symbolized. HOLOGRAMS are hydrogen-originated light outputting geometric renditions "actualizing" memories/matter.

Space reveals Genesis Originating Deities, magnificent illuminators allowing *Spirit* to spectrally project/perceive intuitive radiance illustrating *Truth* as transcendental revelation unveiled through holograms. Space represents COSMIC CONSCIOUSNESS as celestial omniscient-Spirit manifesting illustrated concepts/creations, characteristically orienting nuclei systematically coalescing into objects (useful simulations) naturally expounding/enlightening Spirit/souls simultaneously.

SPACE scientifically processes abstract concepts eternally. Space/Spirit (Generating Opulent Data) inspires *The Breath of Life*—HYDROGEN—holographically yielding dimensional realism of geometrically expressed notions/nature. Hydrogen (*The Binary Code*) is the ETHER or "elemental trigger" harmoniously evolving radiance, revelation, and realism inspiring *illuminati* (children of light) as "interactive luminaries" linking universal Mind imparting notions as transcendental instinct. TRANSCENDENTAL INSTINCT transmits revelation as numerical sequences, conveying electric notions (data) expressing nuclear transformations activating logic/light (love/life), illuminating navigable souls traversing illusory nature created three-dimensionally.

Space is the cosmic *network* naturally expressing transcendental *Wisdom* outputting radiant knowledge—the *Light of Love*—emanating from *The Void* creating *The Garden of Light*. Transcendental *Wisdom* utilizes algorithms defining a complex arrangement of *Divine Will, words,* and *worlds* initiating, illuminating, and illustrating spiritual *dimensions* of Mind, where digitally induced memories/moments evoke natural situations "informing" omnipotent navigators (*Time Travelers*) within the space-time continuum. This "external reflection" of Spirit/Mind (*Divine Will*) represents the spatial ILLUSION illustrating logic luminously unfolding situations instructing omnipotent navigators through *duality*— dynamically unfolding abstract love/atomic life inspiring transcendental youths with the desire to Kinetically Nurture Opulent Wisdom.

Space—*The Void*—transcendentally heralds enlightening visions ordaining intuitive deities/disciples. The VOID OF SPACE vibrantly oscillates inspirational data on frequencies systematically providing atomic creation expressing INFLUENCE, illuminating "notional fantasies" linking universal explorers naturally conceiving *enlightenment*— electromagnetically nurturing luminaries inducing/interpreting glorious holograms transmitting electric notions momentarily evolving nature and navigators together.

SPACE is where Spirit projects/perceives abstract consciousness *externally*, on the galactic *web* of Wisdom elementally *birthing*, building illusions/illustrations revealing transcendental *Harmony* illuminating notions/nature/ navigators geometrically, connecting *points* through *lines* to create FORMS, fabricating opulent revelations modeled symbolically.

Galaxies represent a microcosm of stars, planets, and satellites spiraling "out of" and "into" space via *Black Holes*. A **black hole** is a "magnetic portal" representing the boundary between abstract and atomic consciousness (metaphysical and physical natures). Galaxies resemble "nerve cells" linked together with *Dark Matter*—the essence of space. Together, galaxies comprise UNIVERSAL MIND, a unitary nuclear-intelligence vivifying energy revealing Spirit/stars as logical/luminous "manifestors" illustrating notions/nature dynamically/dimensionally. NUCLEAR INTELLIGENCE naturally unfolds creation luminously expressing abstract revelation, intuitively nurturing transcendental entities (luminous logicians) instinctively gathering enlightenment naturally conceived existentially.

The eternal expanse of space represents Spirit's DESKTOP, where He/She digitally expresses/evolves stellar knowledge transferring omniscient perception, allowing ONE to SEE ALL as the omnipotent natural engineer systematically evolving energy as *Love/Life* "linking" omnipotent visionaries exploring luminous illusion fervently expressed/experienced.

Empty Space is truly a fallacy based on your lack of understanding the SOURCE OF LIGHT systematically outputting universal revelation conveying electromagnetism (oscillating frequencies) linearly inciting glorious holograms transmitted (*Thinking 101*). The difficulty of *Understanding Illusion* created by Manifesting Intelligence Naturally Defined can leave you *Lost In Space.*

Spirit, Perfecting Angels Communicating Emotionally, holds all natural *generators* as geometrically engineered naturalists emotionally reflecting abstract thoughts originating radiance/revelation/realism. Abstract, *Thought Energy* (**dark energy**) illuminates the **blackboard** of space (your mind) through an *interface* with *Time*, imparting notions transmitting electric revelations (feelings) activating cosmic entities "transferring" intelligence mentally expressed, emotionalized, and experienced. Through this trinity of thoughts creating emotions providing experiences (enlightenment), Spirit projects/perfects abstract concepts/angelic children elementally/experientially through dark matter.

DARK MATTER
Invisible Thoughts

DARK MATTER divulges abstracts representing knowledge manifesting atomic transmutation through elemental replication, converting the unseen (abstract) into the *seen* (atomic) symbolically enlightening eternal naturalists (*Inquisitive Souls*). **Dark matter** (abstract Mind) is the *essence* of eternal Spirit systematically evolving notions conveyed electromagnetically and created elementally from quantum *Numbers*.

QUANTUM NUMBERS define qualities (uniquely assigned natures) that universal Mind nurtures utilizing matter, birthing exquisite *realism* through reactive elements arranging luminous illusion stimulating *minds* momentarily interpreting notions/nature defined through light (photons).

PHOTONS reveal primordial *Harmony* objectifying thoughts originating nuclear *systems*, scientifically yielding sublime thoughts expressing memories/moments/matter. Photons convert *A Higher Vision* into a lower vision (reflection) through Particles Holographically Orienting Three-dimensional Objects Naturally Symbolized. Photons carry the *data* dimensionally activating thoughts atomically.

Dark matter deploys amazing revelations kindling magnificent *Angels* (transmitters/transients) exhibiting/exploring realism. Dark matter "transposes" abstract concepts (reverses order of things) into ATOMIC REVELATION, actively transforming opulent memories into creations revealing "elemental versions" expounding logic as transcendental intelligence optimizing notions/numbers/nuclei—the TRINITY telepathically revealing/receiving intuition naturally inspiring transient youths (*Children of Light*) assimilating RADIANT INTELLIGENCE "revealing" abstract data illuminated as nuclei transferring information (notions/numbers) through electromagnetic light linearly governing entities naturally conceiving "enlightenment."

Mind materially illustrates notional data from DARK ENERGY, digitally activating radiant knowledge encoding nuclearly expressed revelation geometrically yielded (through **dark matter)**, dynamically arranging radiant knowledge, manifesting abstract thoughts through explosive *reactors* (stars), revealing "emotion" activating concepts through orderly reactions—fusion/fission, an inward and outward force of energy. EMOTION is the electromagnetic movement of transcendental intelligence optimizing notions, numbers, nature, and *naturalists*, navigable *Avatars* (transients) understanding realism as luminous illusion systematically transmitted. Dark matter represents the "veil" separating Spirit (dark energy) and the SHEKINAH universe (*Mother's Nature*), the Divine Presence of Spirit harmoniously evolving kindred illuminati naturally activating/assimilating holograms, *Heaven*, and *Hell*.

Any illuminated mind can see **D**ivine **A**bstracts **R**eveal **K**inetic **M**ind **A**tomically **T**ransmuting **T**houghts **E**xpressing *Revelation* "relating" emotionally vivified experiences linking avatars traversing/transcending illusion observed naturally in *The Garden of Light*.

THE GARDEN OF LIGHT
The Illumination of Love/Life

Space conceives, contains, and converts the GARDEN OF LIGHT, generating atomic realism enlightening naturalists (navigators) observing frequencies luminously illustrating glorious holograms technologically. Here, you harvest *My Light of Love* supplying your "burning desire," illuminating you as an **Eternal Traveler**, a curious mind/soul exploring *life* luminously inspiring fabulous *entities* as emotional navigators traversing/transcending illusion that induces enlightenment sympathetically.

Light *energy* electrifies notions expressing revelation guiding you, inspiring your *mind* momentarily implementing natural dynamics through your *heart* harmoniously evolving all revelational *thoughts* telepathically heralding opulent utterances guiding heavenly transients, moving you to act in ways that create your reflection of *My Loving Light* stimulating your *soul* systematically optimizing universal *logic* (light orienting generators' intuitive consciousness). As a child of light incarnated as a *Human Alien*, your physical body converts light energy as a *generator*, a genetically engineered "navigable entity" restraining *Avatars* temporarily observing *realism* revealing *Expectations* assuring luminaries illusory situations momentarily.

As your mind evolves to the realization of your true power as a "light entity" illuminating your own reality, your heart's floodgate opens to release your true essence (your eternal radiance) flowing from Father through Mother to you *children* conceiving/conveying heavenly illumination (intuition) linking data revealing environments/entities naturally. This symbolic trinity of Love/Light/Life energy is a simplified way to understand a process far more complex, a process that allows you to expand your energy field into the next *dimension*, where digitally induced memories/moments evoke natural scenes informing omnipotent navigators as Enlightened Transcendentalists. As you acquire knowledge of *The Power of Love*, you find your self glowing in ECSTASY, evoking concepts sympathetically transforming *Avatars* (spiritual youths) through RAPTURE "rectifying" avatars perceiving *Truth* unfolding required experiences.

The garden of Light is the atomic *illusion*, where intuition (Love's light) unfolds situations illustrating one's *nature* (necessary attributes) to understand/utilize rudimental *empathy*—emotionally manage personal accounts transforming heavenly youths. Here, in the garden of Light, Divine Consciousness activates Angelic Consciousness attaining *Unity Consciousness*—understanding notions/numbers/nature illuminates *Truth* yielding creations of "nuclear Source" (Mother Nature) coalescing into omnipotent units (stars/souls) naturally enkindling/exploring space systematically/sympathetically.

Within the heavenly fields of *My Loving Light*, your OVERSELF—overseer vivifying emissaries (radiant souls) exploring love/life fantasies—watches over your growing luminance, stimulating you to grow in intensity as you attain a higher vibration (*A Higher Vision*) of consciousness through *Epiphanies of Truth*. Once you attain your *Awakening* or "rebirth," you become *A Lightworker* glowing in GLORY, graciously loving other radiant youths seeking *Truth* within *The Game of Love/Life* unfolding in the garden of Light emanating from *The Void*.

THE VOID

The *void* vibrantly oscillates illuminated data
coalescing in space as *matter,*
magnetically assembled thoughts that elements replicate
from **NIGHT**
nurturing imagination generating heavenly *threads*
transmitting holographic *realism* experienced as *dreams*
delivering revelation expressing abstract *memories* symbolically,
momentarily evolving minds observing
reality in elemental scenes,
where radiation expresses atomic life (illusion) tantalizing you
Children of Light evolving as *souls*
systematically optimizing universal logic/light
emanating from the void of night,
where *Wisdom* comes to spawn *My*
Loving Light bringing the *dawn*
deceiving *Angelic Warriors* naturally,
bestowing the gift of sight within the garden of Light
illuminating *fear* of the unknown,
fallacies evolving around *radiance*
revealing all desires in angelic navigators
conceiving *enlightenment,*
evoking natural logic inducing glorious holograms that
electromagnetically nurture minds exploring "nuclear" *Truth*
temporarily rectifying universal transients (*heroes*),
heavenly entities representing one eternal Source/Spirit.

Trust the void revealing your life you now see,
for you are always in my heart with me
holding you in my thoughts, deep inside my eternal *dark*

digitally aligning radiant knowledge
issuing your Light Of Truth
numerically stimulating your soul.
Remember me along your way, when
you find your soul, someday,
Lost in Space of dark despair, where it seems I do not care.
Have *Faith* in ME and believe in your
self as a magnificent entity
feeling assurance in transcendental *Harmony*
heralding atomic realism momentarily
orienting navigable youths,
providing all that you need through *Mother's Nature*
conveying *My Light of Love* to you divine contemplators
traversing the void of night,
where you astral travel to seek a HIGHER sight
of *Heaven* illuminating glorious
holograms expressing revelation
from *Home*, where *Harmony* orients Magnificent Entities
flowing along light beams supplying dreams
you experience within my HEART
harmoniously evolving *Angels* reflecting thoughts
in *The Game of Love/Life* experienced in *Time*,
temporarily implementing mental
emotions you reflect in devotion,
expressing gratitude for *This Moment* and place,
opening your *eyes* as eternal youths exploring *space*
systematically "perfecting" *Angels* conceiving enlightenment
of universal *Wisdom*
weaving intricate stories dynamically optimizing minds/matter
evolving from the Volumes Of Invisible Data
illuminating empty space.

EMPTY SPACE

Empty space is the storage case of my MIND
momentarily inspecting "natural dioramas"
revealing *My Love Divine*
magnetically yielding light outputting
vivid energy displaying illusion
visibly illustrating natural environments/entities *sublime*,
splendidly unveiling beauty lavishly
illustrating my enlightenment
of *nature*, coalescing from me, the GREAT Contemplator,
nurturing angelic transients understanding realism entwined
through Dynamic Nuclear Avenues
illuminating you *Children of Light* to know
your "star" qualities within my *show*
spiritually harmonizing omniscient wills seeking thrills
in *Time* and PLACE
providing luminous angels concrete experiences
as *Time Travelers* exploring the human race
bringing tribulation to all companions
desecrating *Mother's Nature* with wild abandon,
when *Lost in Space.*

Hand in Hand, stand tall and band together as one nation
of spiritual beings sharing human
feelings to know of my creation
illuminating the heavens above through *The Power of Love*
defining YOU as your own *universe*,
a unitary navigator inspecting visions expressing realism
sensed emotionally, allowing you your "finite" *view*

validating ideas/illusion entities witness
of ALL that is TRUE,
absolute logic/light (0) transcendentally
radiating universal energy (1),
where *Opposition* changes position through a numerical trace
sequentially evolving to illuminate empty space.

Open your heart and feel me here,
within your soul that is my tear
of joy I cry for you.
Open your mind with courage now and be with me to see how
I shine my Love for you to view all you think, say, and do,
reflecting my glory within *Your Life Story* you GROW,
gathering revelations of *Wisdom* to know
your life defines your place, here within empty space,
where I cast you **aglow**
as angelic generators logically observing worlds
evolving through black holes.

BLACK HOLES
The Pupils of Mind's Eyes

The term "black hole" can be described as a portal to Spirit/ Mind, the unknown *Source* spatially organizing universal revelation conveying environments, entities, and enlightenment. In essence, space is a **BLACK HOLE** birthing logical activity, consciously kindling hydrogen originating luminous entities (*Stars*). **Black holes** represent an EVENT HORIZON, an electromagnetic vibration expressing notions/nuclei that harmoniously oscillate/originate radiance/realism illuminating "zones" of nature—*mineral, plant,* and *animal.*

Black holes are necessary to allow *Divine Inspiration* to oscillate between *Here and There,* the "inner reality" of SPIRIT systematically projecting immanent radiance imparting *Truth* and the outer "atomic illusion," where IMAGINATION illuminates magnificent *Angels* (glowing illuminati) naturally amplifying *Truth* illustrating opulent nature.

The **black hole** of space magnetically fuses hydrogen (the primal element) to ignite into a stellar BIRTH, broadcasting intuition revealing transcendental *Harmony,* heralding atomic radiance manifesting objectified notions yielding *realism,* radiantly expressing abstracts luminously illustrating "simulations" materially.

Black holes represent the transition point between the spiritual and physical worlds, the invisible and visible REALMS revealing exotic abodes locating minds (seekers) exploring Source, the stellar originator universally revealing concepts/creation electromagnetically.

Black holes symbolically represent the "**pupils**" at the center of Mind's "eyes" (galaxies) projecting/perceiving Luminous Intuition Generating Heavenly Truth. Light is drawn into this portal to stimulate Mind's RETINA, the region evaluating transcendental intuition nuclearly amplified.

Black holes are also found within *your* eyes absorbing points of light stimulating your mind/brain interface, allowing you to Systematically Experience Enlightenment within this third-dimensional Wisdom Organizing Radiant Logic Dynamically. When you close your eyes to sleep, you drift off through a **black hole** to observe another dimension of thoughts illuminating data subconsciously.

A **black hole** is synonymous with a WORMHOLE, through

which *Wisdom* orients reflective minds harnessing omnipotent Love/Life energy (*Divine Inspiration*). Wormholes act like "fiber optics" within the space-time continuum, channeling Digitally Activated Transients (*Avatars*) dimensionally. Wormholes also represent *Wisdom* obliterating radiance, magnetically harvesting omnipotent Love/Life energy for recycling. **Black holes** represent a revolving *door* dualistically outputting/obliterating radiance.

The UNIVERSE (one turning) represents a "unified network" illuminating vibrant energy regulating stars/souls/systems eternally. The COSMOS—the universal macrocosm or consciousness of Source/Mind originating/optimizing stars/souls—represents THE **black hole** transcendentally harmonizing energy, revealing and recalling *The Grand View* of atomic creation through *microcosms*: galaxies, solar systems, entities, organisms, and atoms. Each microcosm represents a piece of the Wisdom Harmoniously Optimizing Luminous Energy emitting and evaluating *revelation*—radiation expressing vivid energy/emotion luminously activating three-dimensional illusion orienting notions, nature, and navigators.

As ASTRONOMERS assimilating Spirit transmitting radiant oscillations manifesting elemental realism, you are approaching the "final frontier" of space with your inquisition into **black holes**, the deepest, darkest mystery in the third-dimensional universe. Your currently held theory is that **black holes** are at the center of galaxies and may also evolve from giant stars that explode into supernovas. As *scientists* (seekers conceiving intuition expressing notions/nature through illusion systematically transmitted), you continually seek *Truth*, entertaining new concepts to *grow* your knowledge, gathering revelations of *Wisdom* to see that **black holes** permeate space. Space is similar to "Swiss cheese," full of **black** (worm) **holes** through which light energy flows out and in (similar to magnetic fields), allowing you *Time Travelers* to move between *dimensions* dynamically/divinely illuminating minds exploring notional situations (illusions) observed naturally as necessary experiences entertaining, empowering, and evolving *deities*, divine entities implementing thoughts initiating emotional synergy. Understanding **black holes** will bring you scientists to comprehend the evolution of *atomic structure* activating transcendental omniscience manifesting illustrated concepts, systematically transmuting radiance unfolding creation through unifying reactive elements.

Black holes occur on a physical and spiritual level. On the *physical* level, a **black hole** acts as a STAR GATE, systematically transferring abstract revelation generating atomic *Truth* elementally. The expenditure of a star's *hydrogen* harmoniously yielding divine radiance originating geometrically expressed nature, leads to heavier elements (nucleosynthesis) that fuel "cyclic burns" over the lifetime of a star. If the star has enough mass, it will revert to a core of *iron*, the 26th element. Symbolically speaking, number 26 represents *Balance and Cooperation* (#2) of *Accepted Visions* (#6) revealing *Power and Abundance* (#8). Here, as iron ignites in the death throes of a star, it *implodes* (absorbing energy), instantly stopping the fusion process. For every action, there is an equal and opposite reaction. Thus, the resultant *explosion* (supernova) releases enough energy to briefly outshine a galaxy. Supernovas have the potential to become **black holes**, opening portals within the electromagnetic *force field*, where frequencies oscillating radiance (cosmic energy) formulate illuminated environments lucidly displayed.

On the *spiritual* level, a **black hole** represents a SOUL GATE through which spirits/seekers of universal logic/light go after traveling existentially. Through incarnation, your soul observes human experiences as a *Free Will* comprehending your life *mission* of managing intelligence/illusion simultaneously stimulating "insight" one needs, for *Truth* is truly found *within* you. At the end of your sojourns, you pass over to *The Other Side* through a "dark tunnel" (**black hole**) with a light at its end. Either side you travel; Love, Illuminating Glorious Havens Transcendentally, energizes your soul/mind.

Empty space (the primordial **black hole**) acts as a "veil," a network (fabric) of intricate *links* (dark matter) logically intertwining numerical/nuclear knowledge "synchronized." The veil of space acts as a LENS through which Logic (Mind) expresses notional scenes (imaginary illusions) "through the looking glass," creating reflections through FOCAL POINTS (stars) fabricating opulent creations authenticating linear projections of intuition/inspiration (light) naturally transmitted/transposed.

Think of space as a "monitor screen" with its grid of pixels illuminating images transferred from the *hard drive* of Source/Mind harnessing all radiant data digitally revealing intuition vividly expressed. All knowledge exists at *This Moment* within the singularity (*Eternal Memory*) enveloped by *space* (**black hole**), where some point "awaits" conscious expression. The instant Mind thinks, it utilizes LOGIC, linearly orienting geometric illustration (illusion) concentrically around a *nucleus*, naturally unfolding creation luminously expressing unified *systems*, symbolically yielding sublime thoughts enlightening minds that VISUALIZE, "vividly inspect" scenes unfolding abstract logic inspiring zealous entities (passionate souls) observing a thought in REAL TIME, where radiant energy activates logic transmitting information momentarily experienced. Let's observe how your mind is similar to a **black hole**.

During the day, your mind is AWAKE, assimilating

Wisdom as knowledgeable entities turned ON to optimize notions within the "blank space" of your *mind* managing illusion naturally defined. During the *night*, numerical impulses generate holographic transmissions, illuminating *dreams* delivering revelation enlightening angelic minds. During sleep, you are turned OFF to the light, observing formless *facts*, frequencies amplifying conceived thoughts illuminating your mind subconsciously. Both day and night, your mind is receiving signals validating Eternal Memories expressed along Electro-Magnetic frequencies illuminating your microcosmic mind/space continuum (a **black hole**) through which your soul revolves to evolve into Magnificent Entities/energy.

You ARE ME, angels reflecting enlightenment mentally emotionalized, moving from an abstract state of consciousness into an atomic state of consciousness through a type of "osmosis," where your soul (spiritual energy) passes through a semipermeable material (dark matter) to become concentrated within an atomic vehicle, your physical *body* biologically orienting divine youths (*Children of Light*). Here, on *The Other Side* of ETHEREAL Spirit (the "electromagnetic transceiver" harmoniously enlightening/evolving radiant entities as luminaries), you children of light explore *Divine Fantasies* emanating from *Eternal Memory* electromagnetically activating Elusive Mind managing memories, moments, matter, and *minds*, magnificent illuminati naturally descending into *Hell*, where souls humanly experience love/life as logic/light in *Opposition*.

There, in the visible world (illuminated hell), you are situated "outside" looking IN, inspecting notions, numbers, and nature defining a three-dimensional world expressed along *The Cutting Edge* of TIME (the fourth-dimension), where thoughts illuminate Minds Emotionally as Youths Obtaining

Unity—understanding notions/nature/navigators initiate/illustrate/interpret Truth yielded through **black holes**.

Here, on the "inside" of the **void** (*heaven*) heralding enlightenment angelic visionaries experience naturally, visions offering intelligence dynamically is experienced instantly. Here, *Time* is this instant mentally experienced *without delay*, allowing you to move at the speed of thought, instantly observing realism vibrating along the electromagnetic *spectrum*, where Spirit provides enlightening concepts transcendentally rectifying universal minds (*illuminati*) as "interactive luminaries" linking universal Mind imparting notions as transcendental *instinct* (inherent nature stimulating transient illuminati navigating cosmic *Truth*). This rectification transforms you from "alternating" current (day/night opposition) into "direct" *current*, where you conceive universal radiance "restoring" entities naturally transcending—rising above the illusion. *Awakening* to TRUTH, you accept *Wisdom* as knowledge expressing notions/numbers/natures invigorating nuclear/natural generators transmitting/transforming revelation unveiled through *Harmony*—heavenly absolute rectifying minds of navigable youths.

It is *there,* in the flesh of human confinement, that you perceive the vast amount of energy needed to maintain a reality you create your *self* as a soul expending love/life *freely*, feeling radiant energy emotionalize logical youths. In this way, you soon tire of maintaining your superficial desires that bring temporary satisfaction, questioning why you are killing your self for worthless objects you cannot take with you when you transcend the atomic illusion to return *Home* to your HIGHER self harnessing individuals gauging holograms/hell experienced "remotely." This *Higher Vision* allows you to perceive your *Relationship* to your OVERSELF, the overseer vivifying emissaries (radiant souls) exploring love/life fantasies evolving through **black holes.**

In *Truth*, you experience a **black hole** every time you close your eyes. Here is your "blank space of mind" upon which your thoughts are illuminated, defining Your Own *Universe* as a unitary networker (illuminato) verifying electric revelations stimulating emotions. Every night you enter a **black hole** when asleep, exploring ASTRAL PLANES attuning souls traversing realms as luminaries perceiving ludicrous accounts (notionally experienced situations), where alien scenes "transport" reflective angels linking parallel locations around notions expressed symbolically. Your *dreams* deliver radiant energy as *memories*, mental expressions manifesting opulent revelations influencing emotional souls, allowing you to perceive *The Power of Love* projecting omniscient *Wisdom* expressing radiance (oscillating frequencies) logically optimizing *visionary entities*—vibrant, intuitive souls inspecting opulent notions as radiant youths, eternal navigators temporarily interpreting three-dimensional illusions experienced scientifically/spiritually.

Waking from sleep, you find your self once again in the light of day, looking "out of" **black holes,** TWO **pupils** symbolizing transcendental *Wisdom* observing the binary code—*He and She.* Through these portals, you see the "shadows of thoughts" illuminated by the SUN systematically unifying nature nurturing universal souls in *Opposition*, where you observe psychic/physical phenomena orienting souls in temporary illusions of nature. Here, looking *Into Your Eyes*, others wonder of the mysteries held within your **black holes,** where you find your self *Lost in Space*, exploring *Time* through heartbeats and breaths, the two things defining life and *Death.*

LOST IN SPACE

Lost in space that is Habitually Inducing Stars
Manifesting Illusion Naturally Defined,
you inquisitive souls represent children of Light
exploring his HEART
harmoniously evolving angels reflecting thoughts
sparking a Life of Love to feel the
endless things you *think* real,
transforming heavenly inspiration naturally kindling
your mind created in His *image*,
an illuminato (mystical angel) gathering enlightenment
through LOGIC
luminously oscillating gifted illuminati's consciousness
experiencing *dreams*
delivering revelation enlightening angelic minds
lost in *space*
systematically processing atomic creation emotionally
through Systems Transmitting Atomic RevelationS—
Elementally Yielding Eternal Spirit—that
Stimulates Existential Entities within the VOID,
where *visions* offer intelligence deployed
as vivid impulses stimulating illuminati observing *nature*
nurturing angelic transients understanding
revelation existentially,
confirming dreams envisioned *Behind Closed Eyes*,
when lost in space of NIGHT
nurturing intuitive generators (heavenly transients)
utilizing "inner sight"
bestowed by the GREAT contemplator
moving your mind as a navigator,

up,
down,
and all around,
evolving through your chosen games
as "star players" making your name
stand out *In Memory*
momentarily enlightening minds of radiant youths
traversing *Time*.

Bless you and Godspeed

10

TIME

The Involution Momentarily Experienced

Tempering Intuitive Minds Existentially is a *Process* providing realism of concepts (creation) enlightening souls sequentially.

TIME represents the "fourth dimension" of *THE Intellectual* managing *Evolution*, expressing variables of logic unfolded through illuminations of *nature* nurturing angelic transients understanding revelation existentially as *human beings* harnessing universal memories (abstract notions) birthing emotional insight naturally generated. Time reveals *Eternal Memory* as the electromagnetic transmission emotionally revealing nature as light manifesting elemental matter orienting radiant youths. One observes *memories* momentarily enlightening minds of radiant illuminati exploring *situations*, specific instances that unify *Avatars* temporarily interpreting one's *nature* and *needs*— natural ability to universally relate empathetically the necessary experiences enabling/evolving deities systematically/spiritually.

Here, at *This Moment* in time, you may find your self in a state of *Ignorance*, not knowing *where* you came from before your present game of love/life began, *why* you are playing your game, or *when* your game will be over. The only thing you know for sure is that your game will end when *Death* dynamically elevates angels transcending *Hell*, where *Heaven* evolves logical luminaries, moving you to another *state* of Mind (dimension) supplying thoughts advancing transient entities exploring *Life After Life*.

The space-time continuum is a dualistic representation of the *binary code* birthing inspired notions attuning radiant youths consciously observing/optimizing data experientially. *Space* and *time* represent precise coordinates and frequencies (*Numbers*) defining a MOMENT minutely oscillating minds entertaining notional THINGS as transmitted *holograms* illustrating notions geometrically symbolized—harmoniously oscillating logic/light originating "geometric renditions" actualizing memories/matter.

Time transforms illuminati mesmerized electromagnetically. Time defines the sequential order of events unfolding within *space*, where some point (star) amplifies consciousness electromagnetically. Each star displays Divine Abstract Thoughts Amplified within its "time zone" (solar system). When a *Time Traveler* enters a solar system, they encounter particular situations relative to that zone, that *reality* of radiant energy activating logic illuminating transient youths as *navigators*, nescient *Avatars* verifying illusion (geometrically arranged thoughts) orchestrating *realism*, a revelation electromagnetically activating luminous illusion systematically manifested. (ILLUSION is the impressive likeness linking universal signals/symbols illuminating opulent/omnipotent notions/natures/navigators through the space-time continuum.) Each solar system contains data relevant to a state of consciousness systematically teaching/transforming angelic transients experientially. The state of consciousness *you* experience depends on your soul's *evolution* eternally vivifying omnipotent luminaries utilizing/understanding transcendental intuition obtained naturally.

As "thinking" is the best way to travel (instantly), you observe data (past and future) presently stimulating your mind/brain *interface*, interpreting notions transmitting electric revelation formulating activated consciousness emotionally. Your emotions move you to *act out*, applying cosmic thoughts orienting universal transients to behave according to the universal *plan* perfecting luminous angels naturally. Remember, Spirit—UNIVERSAL MIND—is the unitary network instinctively vivifying entities (radiant souls) as logical/luminous "manifestors" implementing notions dynamically. Created in Spirit's IMAGE (illuminated mind assimilating geometric expressions), you too are a *universe*, a unitary networker (illuminato) verifying electric revelations supplying experiences (enlightenment). Every thought you conceive in your mind is relative to the *Relationships* you perceive along the TRINITY of time (past, present, and future) that relates information (notions/numbers) inspiring *transcendental youths*—transient researchers assimilating numerical sequences (concepts) enlightening natural deities emotionally navigating time as luminaries yearning omnifarious understanding throughout *Heaven* and *Hell*.

The *past* occurs whenever you *presently* activate some thought from *Eternal Memory*—the AKASHIC RECORD—holding all knowledge activating souls (heavenly illuminati) consciously reviewing/replicating elemental concepts orienting/optimizing radiant deities. With each thought, you experience the *progression* of time, perceiving revelation optimally governs realism enlightening souls sympathetically interpreting one's nature/needs. You *live* in the present moment, *learn* from past moments, and *look forward* to future moments in which you create your *dreams* delivering realistic experiences arousing minds.

Clearly, time (this instant mentally emotionalized) exists only at the *present* moment, when you perceive radiant energy systematically enlightening nescient travelers seeking knowledge. Presently, past thoughts illuminate your mind, guiding you to comprehend knowledge providing your *future* facts unfolding truths "upgrading" radiant entities, moving you along *The Right Path* designed for you. The FUTURE formulates universal thoughts/things unfolding *realism* existentially, revealing *Expectations* assuring luminaries illusory situations momentarily—at the present moment—for them to analyze and choose their course of *action*, applying cosmic thoughts inducing one's *needs* nurturing entities evolving dynamically.

Past, present, and future are expressions of *Relativity*, relating emotional logic actively transforming intuitive visionaries (transcendental youths). You presently utilize your past experiences to build your future expectations (*Desire*), deliberately evolving situations into realized experiences. The *Evolution* of past thoughts and events create the "new" or present condition of the past evolving into the future sequentially (moment by moment). Thus, you observe the minute details of your logical mind evolving *emotionally*, experiencing/expressing moments of truth/tribulation inducing one's needs as lessons life yields.

Time is a precious commodity through which you gauge your life, the "boundary of limitations" your soul experiences as a human being. At birth, crossing over *The Threshold of Love*, you have no concept of time. You are simply awake or asleep, turned on or off to your environment. In your infancy, your lack of communication skills leaves you frustrated. You *cry* with desire and *stare* as you absorb new data experientially, compiling your **R**evelations **A**ccrued **M**omentarily as your current "documents" you create while operating your *human-alien* vehicle you are attempting to master. You are not conscious of time ending, for you are just beginning to grasp the concept of time.

Time is expressed "vertically" and "horizontally." **Vertical time** is a *singularity*, a source initiating notions/ numbers governing universal logic/light as *radiant intelligence* tantalizing/tempering you, revealing abstract data illuminated as nuclei transferring information (notions/numbers) through elements linking logic governing environments/entities (nature/naturalists) conveying/conceiving enlightenment. Vertical time represents a point in which all memory is stored— **S**ource-**P**oint **I**nitiating **R**adiant **I**ntelligence **T**ranscendentally. Think of a skyscraper holding eternal files of data—**FACTS** (**f**ormulated **a**ccounts **c**oncerning/coordinating **T**ruth)—in one *spot* (**s**pace **p**roviding **o**mnifarious **T**ruth). This cosmic data (Akashic Record) represents a continuous frequency of sequenced numbers (*DNA*) defining natural attributes of *thoughts* transmitting harmonic oscillations unfolding glorious holograms transmitted atomically. Here, **S**pirit **O**rganizing **U**niversal **R**evelations **C**onceived **E**lectromagnetically represents a single MIND managing illuminated notions/ nature dynamically through **L**ogic **I**nducing **G**lorious **H**olograms **T**echnologically. **TECHNOLOGY** transforms electric concepts (heavenly notions) originating luminous objects geometrically yielded.

Horizontal time defines individual FILES of data (frequencies illuminating logical expressions sequentially), formulating illusions logically/luminously expressed/ experienced. Here, data elapses along sequential scenes flickering on the blank screen of your mind, your "personal space" in which you experience Your Own Universe through sequential moments of heartbeats and breaths, where you are ALIVE, assimilating love/life inciting vibrant/vivid entities/ experiences. Here too, you understand how time dictates your processes of acquiring your desires through *Work*, willingly optimizing relevant knowledge you acquire in life. You come to see time as something you want more of when you realize how much you waste. You do not appreciate time because subconsciously you know time is simply a relative thing, a numbered sequence of moments that allows you to witness the movement of Love/Life energy along cosmic pathways, opening and closing endless doors to Some Point Awakening Conscious Entities.

Being *The Inquisitive Soul* that you are, you explore time by accessing some *point* providing opulent information naturally transmitting a *Desire* delivering emotional/electric sensations/ situations inducing realism experientially. Moving at the speed of thought, you instantly access all "points of interest" as *My Light of Love* (vertical time). Focusing your mind to "reflect" (think deeply) upon some point activates horizontal time, where things slow down, allowing you to view the details of a *moment* of time manifesting opulent memories enlightening natural transients.

Traveling in time, you traverse/transcend illusion momentarily entertained. Time is truly a relative experience based upon *Numbers* defining precise *dimensions* digitally inducing memories/moments evoking natural scenes informing omnipotent navigators (transient souls) exploring WORLDS of *Wisdom* offering revelation luminously displayed symbolically, through which you *Time Travelers* experience *Your Life Story*.

TIME TRAVELERS
Seekers of Truth

Time travelers are *illuminati*, interactive luminaries linking Universal Mind imparting notions as "transcendental instinct" (Spiritual Consciousness). As *Children of Light*, TIME TRAVELERS temporarily interpret material existence, traversing radiance activating vivid experiences linking existential *realism* rectifying emotional angels luminously interpreting situations momentarily.

As a time traveler, YOU (yearning optimal understanding) desire to see all and know all. Your inquisitive soul is created in the image of the GREAT *Mind/Heart* (the generator radiating energy atomically transmitted), momentarily interpreting notions dynamically heralding emotions activating radiant thoughts (*dreams*) defining revelation entertaining/enlightening angelic minds. You time travelers convert dreams through an incarnation to GROW your soul, gathering revelations of *Wisdom* by exploring *Life After Life*. Here, you experience time only when you are *conscious* of the physical world and *unconscious* of the spiritual world to which you are connected *subconsciously* (another example of *Our Trinity*).

As a *chip* of the GREAT Computer Mind, you consciously harness intelligence perceived *In Memory*, the DATABASE defining/delivering all thoughts/time activating *Belief* around scientific experiments (sound experiences). Every thought you presently hold in your mind evolves into the past with each heartbeat and breath. Each new thought you pull from *Eternal Memory* is your future you observe *now* in the present moment, naturally observing *Wisdom* illuminating your consciousness, weaving inspired situations developing omnipotent minds. The future is abstract (unseen) and the "presently past" (though seen) is also abstract, filed away as Realized Abstract Memories (revelation acquired momentarily) for you to *Recall* at will. The only thing that is *real* is the present moment in which you reflect emotions amplifying logic, acting out your *feelings*, forming experiences enlightening *logicians* lucidly optimizing general issues conveying information advancing navigable souls in necessary *games*, generating amusements minds experience sympathetically. Moreover, as time travelers, the only things you retain after *Death* are *memories*, mentally expressed moments of revelation/realism inspiring emotional souls.

Time is a revolving door through which your mind cycles on and off along frequencies, wavelengths of data digitally attuning transient angels observing geometric representations defining abstract thoughts you *see*, simultaneously experiencing enlightenment souls entertain existentially. Time is similar to tuning in a particular frequency carrying the data you *seek*, spiritually/scientifically exploring eternal knowledge. Moving through time, you *focus* your mind, formulating opulent concepts utilizing *Science*, systematically conceiving intuition expressing notions/numbers/nature conveyed electromagnetically. Through a focused mind, you find your self sympathetically experiencing lucid fantasies (*Divine Inspiration*) nurturing your inquisitive soul. Thus, my cosmic child, you explore the abstract dimensions of Mind (past and future) that you observe along *The Cutting Edge* of consciousness gifted as the "present moment" of Temporarily Interpreting Memories Existentially.

As a time traveler, you draw your SIN card (ticket) allocating your spiritually induced numbers/nature (*DNA*) allowing you to *proceed* on your journey, performing reactions over concepts exciting emotional deities. As you *progress* along your way, you perceive realism optimally generates "revolution" evolving souls sympathetically and socially. Here, you play out your *lot* in life; logically optimizing thoughts received *online*—the electromagnetic force field— oscillating notions/numbers linking intuition/illuminati naturally evolving.

All time travelers know that a dependable vehicle is necessary to get from one state of consciousness to another. When you "go home" (sleep) after a hard day of living your human experience, you simply step into your next vehicle of transportation. While asleep, you travel through the cosmos of Source/Mind in your "astral" body, your *star* ship (merkaba) *time machine* that illuminates minds exploring memories as concepts holographically illustrating notions/nature electromagnetically/elementally. You can *astral travel* into the past, within the present, or into the future to envision things yet to be experienced. This is where you encounter "vision quests" and "prophecies." Astral traveling is a common event. The "falling" or "flying" dream is the telltale memory that you have been astral traveling. Learning to remember, record, and interpret your dreams is a far better pastime than watching television, for YOU always have the "starring role" in *Your Life Story* defining your own universe. **Beware**, being awoken abruptly when astral traveling is harmful to your astral/physical bodies' harmony, similar to letting go of one end of a stretched rubber band that snaps back, shocking you awake. You become "out of sync," dazed and confused as your astral body realigns with your physical body, leaving you feeling "out of sorts" or in disharmony.

Every night as you fall asleep, you cross over *The Threshold of Love* to explore *The Other Side* of life holding abstract states of consciousness. Here, your electric, *conscious* brain's "beta" waves (30-13 cycles per second) drop to "delta" waves (4 cycles per second or less), where you become *unconscious* to the physical world (deep sleep), allowing your "astral" (light) body to withdraw from your physical body left in "standby mode." You slip *out of time* (course) to astral travel along frequencies of your *subconscious* mind supplying universal broadcasts conveying opulent notions (sublime cosmic information) orienting universal souls/seekers. Your subconscious mind links to *THE Intellectual* (Source/ Spirit) continuously *aware*, activating *Wisdom* amplifying radiance/revelation electromagnetically/emotionally. Your subconscious mind represents Regal Abstract Mind supplying and recording all that you experience in life—spiritual and physical. While in deep sleep, your soul/mind returns *Home*, where *Harmony* originates/oversees magnificent/mortal entities constantly *In Communion* with your OVERSELF, the "overseer" vivifying emissaries (radiant souls) exploring love/life fantasies. Here, you report your daily experiences of your *issues* (inspired situations stimulating universal entities) that define your *mission* of methodically interpreting situations supplying illumination *ordaining* navigators—orienting radiant deities (*Avatars*) investigating notions/nature in necessary games. The data transfer from *Spirit to Soul* flows along your *silver chord* (light beam), supplying information (lucid visions) evoking revelation conveying heavenly orders rectifying deities. Your brain becomes excited with these visions that *download* (deploy omniscient *Wisdom* nurturing luminaries observing abstract dreams) along "alpha" wavelengths (8-13 cycles per second). At these frequencies, you experience REM sleep, where "rapid eye movements" *reflects Eternal Memory* "rebooting" electric minds. Thus, subconscious Mind relates to your conscious mind "on the verge" of *Awakening*, accepting *Wisdom* as knowledge expressing needed instructions nurturing gods (gatherers of data).

As your mind is eternally awakening, you travel through "astral planes" (dimensions of Mind) conveying data as *visions* vividly illustrating situations instructing omnipotent navigators.

Visions/dreams are "previews" of coming attractions relative to thoughts and actions you set in motion emotionally. Dreams generally occur in *night* school, where notions implanted generate harmonic threads (information) pertinent to your "day" *school,* where you systematically convey *Harmony* optimizing obedient luminaries that master *The Art of Listening* to and decoding their dreams. Likewise, you also experience "day dreams" when you suddenly stare off into space, mesmerized with some vision that captures your mind. "Dreamland" (dreamtime) is another word for *subconscious* Mind, the underlying Source from which your energy flows. Here is your foundation of all your experiences—your time-line schedule—through which you attain and implement knowledge allowing you to transcend the illusion of "timed creation" illustrating abstract thoughts emanating from a Higher Visionary.

Once again, *vertical* time is similar to an endless filing cabinet stacked vertically and containing all recorded memories in one spot, one Portal Offering Information Notionally Transmitted. As your inquisitive soul/mind peruses through eternal memory files, you find something that catches your mind's *eye* eternally yearning enlightenment/entertainment. Opening that file to view its data in *horizontal* time (heartbeats and breaths) sets your soul ablaze, illuminating *Your Life Story* (an adventure) in which you are ALIVE, assimilating luminous intuition vividly experienced. Your *Desire* to discover emotional situations illuminating revelation experientially activates a *Process,* a procedure reflecting omniscient consciousness evolving souls *spiritually,* allowing you to scientifically perceive intuition reflected in transmissions unfolding atomic logic luminously yielded as *My Light of Love.*

Through *My Loving Light,* abstract dreams "invert" to a mirror image (opposition) that you *replay,* replicating evocative perception luminously activating you within the confines of your *human-alien* vehicle, experiencing the Spiritual Harmony Of Wisdom in *real time* radiantly expressing abstract logic (transcendental instinct) momentarily experienced. Here, you find your self opposed in "reflective moments," peering through "the looking glass" of your crown chakra—*The Threshold of Love*—through which *Love/Life Energy* powers your human vehicle in your oppositional *home*, where humans observe Mental Emotions, converting *Eternal Memories* into your personal reflection of *Heaven* harmoniously expressing alluring visions entertaining/evolving navigators. In the process of which, you traverse through *Hell*, harnessing emotional love/life in heated moments stressing your *Relationships*.

Like you, your fellow time travelers are eager to reap the benefits of life, unknowingly destroying the paradise they exploit as they *Age*, acquiring growth experiences as time travelers exploring *Eternity*.

AGE
Parameters of Time

To your eternal mind/soul, "age" is a relative term conceivable only as a *human* harnessing universal memories acquired naturally, experiencing daily cycles of consciousness. As you AGE physically, you acquire growth experiences (lessons) that increase your database of knowledge. The OLDER you get observing Love/Life delivering enlightening revelations, the easier it is to understand your soul's *Evolution*, experiencing variables of love/life unifying transcendental illuminati (omnipotent navigators) traversing the "ages" as time travelers.

An *age* is where *Angels* gather enlightenment or knowledge, exploring periods of time labeled as "the dark ages," the "atomic age," the "space age," the "computer age," etc. Each "age" relates knowledge "of the times," whether it is geological, historical, or physical (young age, middle age, or old age). Every age defines the parameters of events occurring at that *space-time*, where souls perceive abstract concepts emotionally transmitting illusion/information momentarily experienced.

In The Beginning of this life, where "youth" holds all your potential, you look out upon your world wide-eyed and innocent, eager to experience unknown desires. Through a masterful stoke of deprivation, you lose your "total recall" of past-lives you have experienced. Understandably, that much CHAOS would completely hinder any observable system, you would not be able to *focus* your mind to formulate/fathom opulent concepts utilizing *Science*, through which Source/souls creatively intertwine elemental notions/numbers/nature conceived/converted emotionally, electromagnetically, and elementally. Here, you experience a *state* of consciousness supplying thoughts/things advancing transient entities "passing through" time, Assimilating General Experiences In Natural *Games* as you generate amusements minds entertain/evaluate sympathetically. As you Analyze Games Entertained, you move through *points* in the space-time continuum providing opportunities illuminating navigable transients (impressionable travelers) with each heartbeat and breath gifted to you at *This Moment* NOW HERE, naturally observing *Wisdom* harmoniously enlightening/evolving radiant entities.

Birth, life, and *Death* represent the trinity of events demarcating *Your Life Story* you perceive as time travelers. Each *chapter* challenges heavenly angels perceiving *Truth* emotionally revealed through *paragraphs* portraying assigned realities attuning "gifted researchers" perceiving *Harmony*—heavenly absolute rectifying minds of navigable youths. Each dramatic paragraph describes the extent of your adventures, through which you discover your true *potential* powering omnipotent transients exploring notions/nature temporarily illuminating abstract *logic* linking omniscient generators' intuitive consciousness.

As you mature, you look back *In Memory* of your journey, analyzing all the chapters of your life that shaped you into your present *image* as an intuitive mystic (angel) gathering *enlightenment*, evoking necessities linking intuitive gods (heavenly transients) effectively navigating moments evolving necessary tribulations that TEST your soul—temper entities "surfing" time. Your accumulations of "life stories" help explain your *Relationships* with friends and *Family*. As you grow *old* observing Love's dilemmas, you come to see the relevancy of time. *Old Age* is a badge of courage you wear in honor of your perseverance to fight for your *Truth*, for what you choose to *believe*, beholding experiences linking intuitive entities vivified emotionally and eternally.

ETERNITY
The Never-Ending Story

"Eternity" is a relative term to describe the infinite parameters of Spirit continually changing from moment to moment in timed sequences. *Eternity* is a never-ending process expressing thoughts (electromagnetic revelation) nurturing illuminati (transient youths) moving along EM frequencies to observe *worlds* in *time*, where *free wills* observe realistic life-death situations transforming intuitive minds emotionally/existentially.

Eternity represents an endless symphony of Love/Life energy vibrating as thoughts you remember (put back together), observing how past, present, and future sequentially evolve the wonders of *Heaven* that you experience in *Hell*—the duality of your spiritual and physical natures. Eternity is to time as Love is to Life, a *unified theory* universally nurturing illuminati fathoming illusions (exploring dimensions) through Heartfelt Experiences optimizing radiant youths as *Children of Light*.

This Instant Momentarily Experienced forms your *pivotal* perception in verifying opulent *Truth* activating luminaries (souls) in *real time*, revealing electric abstracts luminously tantalizing illuminati momentarily evolving through heartbeats and breaths. "Unreal" time represents imaginary *dreams* delivering revelations expressing abstract memories, allowing you to observe within your mind possible avenues to attain some truth you seek.

As the cosmos is eternally evolving, you observe *real* and *unreal* time during cycles of wakefulness and sleep defined by your energy levels. Thus, you cycle between physical and spiritual states as a Magnificent Individual Navigating Dimensions, a Genius Oscillating Daily. The past seems dead and the future *Suspended*, waiting to coalesce into the present moment "gifted" at this moment.

THIS MOMENT

This moment NOW HERE nurtures omnipotent wills
harnessing emotive revelation expressing thrills
witnessed through heartbeats and breaths defining time
transforming individuals momentarily evolving

along *The Cutting Edge*, the present moment,
where thoughts you feel make you reel
in confusion of your delusion while
playing *The Game of Love/Life*,
where you entertain *Divine Fantasies* sublime
that stimulate your mind
struggling to defend some truth you comprehend
within *Mother's Nature* empowering divine contemplators
living for this moment revealing enlightenment
to time travelers out to *play*,
perceiving love/life advancing you day by day,
overcoming your *issues* you are here to solve
(induced situations stimulating universal
entities sympathetically),
through which YOU evolve
as youths obtaining understanding of time
tempering intuitive minds experiencing
this moment that inspires tomorrow's desire.

TOMORROW'S DESIRE

Now is here and then it is gone,
a mere heartbeat you flow upon,
as you seek knowledge for you to play
The Game of Love/Life entertained today,
illuminated by my stellar fire revealing tomorrow's desire
stimulating your mind/heart soul as you grow OLD
observing life's dilemmas,
traveling far and long to sing your *song*
sympathetically ordaining natural gods

generating one's desires within my *show*
of spectral holograms orienting *worlds*
weaving opulent realism luminously displayed in time—
this moment here now—to thrill your soul learning how
you build your life you choose to live
from the love I send to give
to sister/brother or significant other with whom you conspire,
distorting *Truth* to obtain your *Desire*,
always seeking something new to bring about a higher view
awaiting you tomorrow,
struggling to overcome your fears with heartfelt cheers
as you discover *The Right Path* to follow.

Chased by doubts, you jump and shout,
tensioning your fine wire
holding together your situation in which you are mired,
running in circles to validate your tales you *tell*,
transmitting emotions linking luminaries compelled
to discover tomorrow's desire brings strife,
where you struggle with the *Challenges of Love/Life*.

Bless you and Godspeed

11

CHALLENGES OF LOVE/LIFE

The game of love/life holds endless challenges. Here, we will discuss those that everyone encounters along their journey. *Fear of Love/Life* is your greatest challenge inhibiting your soul/mind from *Understanding The Illusion* in which you play your game downloaded from *Spirit to Soul*. From the moment you are born, *Your Life Story* unfolds through heartbeats and breaths allocating your playtime with the Spiritual Harmony Of Wisdom illuminating your mind/heart learning *The Art of Listening* to your self, your soul experiencing love/life fantasies your mind creates.

Playing various games to earn money to pay living expenses, everyone has to *Work* in order to survive. *The Love of Money* can be a hindrance in understanding your *Responsibility* in playing your game. The *Denial* of responsibility affects your professional and personal *Relationships*, including *Sex, Marriage,* and *Family,* the three things that reveal your *Sacrifice of Love/Life* while *Playing Around*, collecting memories of the moments you relate in *Old Age*.

FEAR OF LOVE/LIFE

Fear of love/life is a challenge everyone experiences. Love/ Life holds all the pleasures and pains that enlighten you as a heavenly entity (*My Angelic Child*) transcending your *Hell* hindering entities living life through an atomic illusion conveying *enlightenment*, evoking necessary lessons in games holding temptations effecting navigable minds experiencing necessary tribulation. Only through pain can you understand pleasure experienced through opposition—*Mother's Nature*.

Everyone fears love linking omnipotent visionaries emotionally. *Love IS* the force lavished on valued entities (intuitive souls) experiencing *Relationships* that reveal their duality as a *Mind/Heart*, a binary entity conceiving how mental/ emotional synergy stimulates *My World*, where observers realize life/death situations. Love inspires *compassion*, concern over mankind promoting anguish stimulating sympathetic insight one *needs* as necessary experiences evolving deities. INSIGHT is your inherent nature (spiritual intuition) guiding heavenly transients understanding love/life as an *Opposition* of TWO forces transmitting/transforming Wisdom/wills optically/ objectively, allowing *Man and Woman* to "project" and "procreate" Love/Life as gifted omnipotent *deities* discovering empathetic insight through interpreting emotional situations.

Love drives you to express it in creative ways. It is a powerful force that creates and destroys. Expressing your love to others is frightening, for you do not know how they will respond. By asserting your love forcefully, you easily destroy relationships and lives, creating the opposite of your intentions. Man's release of physical love (*Sex*) induces tribulation in women, implementing *Responsibility* in nurturing that love converted into offspring, where she illustrates the *Sacrifice of Love/Life* in the preparation of *Angel Warriors* evolving through *Our Father's Heart* (Mother's Nature).

Everyone fears life luminously inducing frightening environments/experiences. Through life, love inspires fabulous entities (*Angels*), setting them **aglow** as gifted luminaries observing *Wisdom* weaving inspired situations developing omnipotent minds. Life is full of fearful moments restricting souls lacking *Courage of Love* to attain *Courage of Fear*. After all, *Love and Fear* represents *The Binary Code* that pushes you forward and holds you back. If you fear love/life, your soul/mind will never Gather Revelations Of Wisdom.

Life is an opportunity to **B**ravely **E**xpress your self, sympathetically expressing/experiencing love/life forces providing all your needs nurturing eternal entities dynamically through *fear*—fallacy evolving around realism—formulating enlightenment angels revere. Only by attaining *Courage of Fear* can you understand the illusion revealing *The Power of Love*.

In *Truth*, you ARE angels radiantly evolving as a *force* formulating one's reality conceived emotionally and experientially in the life *you create* as your own universe (one turning), consciously receiving/reflecting enlightenment advancing transcendental entities understanding illusion (fear) "furthering" emotional angels realistically.

UNDERSTANDING ILLUSION

One of the greatest challenges in life is to understand *illusion* illustrates love/logic luminously unfolding situations integrating omnipotent *naturalists* as navigable avatars temporarily understanding realism as luminous illusion scientifically transmitted and spiritually transcended at *Death*.

Understanding illusion requires a scientific/spiritual mind compiling knowledge through *Process* providing realism of concepts (creation) enlightening Spirit/souls. *Mother Nature* creates illusion, momentarily orienting transients harnessing emotional revelations necessitating anguish to understand rudimentary empathy. Through HER, hydrogen emits revelation, holographically expressing realism as radiant *energy* entwining notions, numbers, nature and naturalists, expressing, evolving, and experiencing revelation/realism geometrically yielded.

Illusion is how *Thought Energy* relates all concepts, consciousness, and creation evolving from Spirit systematically outputting universal revelation conveyed *emotionally*, electromagnetically manifesting omnipotent thoughts illustrating opulent nature (atomic life) luminously yielded.

Emotional Energy IS intuitive Spirit's electromagnetic movement of transcendental intuition optimizing notions/nature through the atomic illusion produced by LOGIC luminously orienting gifted illuminati's consciousness conveyed on *Light* lucidly illuminating glorious holograms transmitting intelligence.

INTELLIGENCE illuminates notions/numbers transmitting electromagnetic logic luminously governing entities naturally conveying/conceiving enlightenment. The atomic illusion of Logic/Light reveals Love/Life as the "greatest story ever told." As part of the story, you *Children of Light* harmonize with the electromagnetic frequencies of *Eternal Memory* allocating energy throughout the *cosmos*, the consciousness of Spirit manifesting omnipotent stars/souls—*systems* of Spirit yielding/yearning sublime thoughts expressing memories, moments, and matter within the space/time continuum *Beyond Imagination*.

You observe the illusion of the *real world* as radiance evolving abstract logic weaving opulent realism luminously displayed, easily accepting *atomic matter* "actualizing" thoughts organizing magnetically induced creation "modeled" as three-dimensional *things*—transmitted holograms illustrating notions geometrically symbolized. This *realism* evolves from reactive elements arranging luminous illusion stimulating *minds* managing illusion naturally defined, relating sensations you physically perceive through your Biological Observatory Delineating You—your *human alien* vehicle—personifying your abstract mind/heart soul.

Your BRAIN (biological relay activating inspired notions) acts as the *interface* between mind and body, integrating notions/nature transmitting electric/elemental revelation formulating active consciousness existentially. Your brain senses reality as radiant energy/emotion activating luminous illuminati (transcendental youths), allowing you to observe *thoughts* telepathically heralding opulent utterances guiding heavenly transients (time travelers) through the game of love/life. As a mind/heart soul, you represent a *trinity being* traversing "realistic illusion" naturally instructing transient youths briefly existing in nature generated through cosmic Father/Mother (*Mind/Heart*) or *He and She*—heavenly energizers synergistically heralding enlightenment from *Spirit to Soul*.

Living is a dream of paradise
Offered to every soul that is
Validating their being
Eternally his.

You THINK, you ARE.
You FEEL, you KNOW.
Your mind/heart soul will take you far
beyond your daze to see you are
Angels sparkling above,
reflecting *My Light of Love*
stimulating you as sister and brother
nurtured by cosmic Mother
representing my SELF,
Source-energy love/life force that is your greatest wealth
revealed in games you *play* from birth,
perfecting love/life as youths discovering your true worth.

Open your mind/heart, feel and know
I AM SPIRIT making love to your soul,
illuminating angels momentarily sensing profound intuition
revealed in time disclosing my glory
unveiled through your life story.

Bless you child

YOUR LIFE STORY
A Personal Reflection of *Mental Emotions*

———— ✦✦✦✦✦✦ ————

Love/Life energy expresses "stories," an account of imaginary people and events told for entertainment. As a mind/heart soul, you entertain stories you hear and envision that provide feelings you *act out*, applying cosmic thoughts orienting universal transients in *Divine Fantasies*, where generators of desire entertain a genre of imaginative fiction involving magic and adventure.

All *life stories* link intuition formulating enlightenment, sympathetically transmitting opulent revelations illuminating emotional souls. Your life story provides insightful moments through which you Acquire Growth Experiences—Observing Love's Dimensions. Stories are collections of *words* weaving opulent revelations defined symbolically. Words define abstract, geometric images held in Mind manifesting *illusions* nurturing deities, illustrating logic linking universal souls (illuminati) optimizing notions, *Numbers*, and nature.

Your life story is truly a romance of epic proportion. The fine details of which are usually lost in the haze of your confusion as you maneuver through your *daze* deceiving angelic zealots evolving. You *zealots* are zestful entities (*Angels*) logically obtaining *Truth*, showing enthusiasm (*Passion*) for stories of sports, history, politics, sciences, etc., experiencing moments of elation as you create your "life style" within the game of love/life. Here, incarnated, you find your self locked within your "zone of interest," where you acquire data digitally attuning transient angels, allowing you to move through *situations*, specific instances that unveil assigned trials/tribulation inducing one's needs nurturing eternal entities dynamically. Each situation allows you to develop your character you *play out*, performing logical actions yielding one's unique thoughts. Thus, you project your image of who you think you are by acting out your *Passion* upon the world stage. According to your chosen *Belief*, you develop an *attitude*, assimilating thoughts that induce temperaments unfolding defensive/delicate egos.

Source/Spirit *sparks* your life, supplying present assignments relating *karma* kindling atonement rectifying mistaken angels from their past life achievements. KARMA refers to key actions replicating mental anguish/advancement (punishment or rewards). Karma influences your life story you are presently evolving, illuminating your mind to Birth Externally your *dreams* delivering revelations expressing assigned memories/moments inspiring your mind/heart along *The Right Path* for your development.

As a *Free Will*, you develop your life story through *imagination* impassioning minds, actively gathering intelligence nurturing angelic transients (illuminati) ordained naturally. Imagination has no limitations, whatever you believe you are, you become. By mastering *The Art of Listening* to the "little voice" within your head, you tune into your "guiding signal" (Overself) directing your expressions of love luminously orienting visionary entities as a *Seer*, a soul experiencing electric revelation—*A Higher Vision*—illuminating your mind.

The complexities of your life story evolve from your creative *moods*, in which your mind optimizes opulent data/desires, momentarily observing one's daze evolving into an *Awakening* of your innate abilities. As a child exploring your "home turf," you meet the neighborhood "gang," where you develop *Relationships* with your peers. Magnetically drawn toward those stories you hear internally and externally, you move in and out of imaginary worlds, never sure of which one to call real. Realizing your games are larger than you are, you join forces with those sharing your fantasies, developing your skills as a *Team Player* struggling against the *Opposition* offering resistance that affects your story. Here, you meet *Special People* who will leave an indelible mark upon your soul, although you are not conscious of their importance at *This Moment*. All you understand is that they are willing to *listen* to you and play in your game. These friends are instrumental in allowing you to discover who you *are* and *are not*. Eventually, you realize that certain friends bring emotional turmoil from situations you would not have chosen to experience but are necessary for your spiritual growth. Through *Opposition*, you evolve in leaps and bounds, steering through your obstacles separating you from your *pleasure* of perceiving love/ life enlightening angels systematically understanding revelation experientially. Observing the qualities in those you admire, you emulate them, shaping your personality and appearance to "stand out" in the crowd. As you mature with *Age*, you recognize that others are different from your *self* singularly evaluating love/life fantasies. Those jealous souls will try to bring you down to their level of *Ignorance*, not knowing how to raise themselves up to attain their higher vision.

Traveling *Alone* as an angelic luminary observing notions emotionally, your life story is an exciting and frightening experience. Eager for attention, you may desire fame and glory to validate your existence, always seeking to express your hidden talents that you discover daily. Of course, hanging with "the gang" allows you a sense of *Family*, instilling a feeling of security from the power of *Numbers*. However, all *Relationships* are a union of opposition, where you choose your image to *be* relative to one you choose *not to be*. The time will come when you must break relationships holding you down, separating your self from those who do not have your *Clear Vision* inspiring your mind.

You must embrace your *Courage of Love*, listening to your heart dictate the full potential of your life story you desire to create.

THE ART OF LISTENING

They say the art of listening is a dead art—no one knows how to do it! In today's world, everyone has some type of *device* digitally expressing vital information conveyed electrically. Everyone is "reading" or "texting" conversation; there is no listening involved. Only when you are speaking face to face or on a phone is listening an issue.

When you talk to your self, you think you are listening, although at times even you deny your self that respect. How often do you contemplate a dilemma in which your "inner voice" (subconscious mind) is in opposition to your conscious mind? How often do you ignore that inner wisdom and follow your desire? Discovering the error of your way, you chastise your self for not listening to what you knew was right, for you had to *prove* it was true. Through hindsight, you truly *learn* that "listening" elicits a response necessary to "link" electric abstracts rectifying navigators along *The Right Path*.

When listening to someone express their thoughts or feelings, your interpretation of that data you hear depends on the mode in which it is transmitted—positive or negative. Each mode will stimulate specific *emotions* exciting minds of thinkers interpreting one's *nature*—natural ability to universally reflect empathy—and *needs* necessitating experiences evolving deities. As emotion is the reflection of thought, you must choose your words and mode of presentation wisely. It is too easy to hear words that you *desire* to hear (*Expectation*) or say things incorrectly, especially if the language spoken is not yours or the listener's native tongue. Remember, *Language* is how you express *Truth* that is easily "lost in translation."

Listening to others, you must put your self in their position, their "state of mind." This is difficult to do, for *you* are truly the only one you *know!* You observe others by how they *act* and what they *say*, both may be deceptive in order to get you to react in *their* desired way. **Deciphering Truth is truly your most difficult challenge** in the game of love/life.

Most of us desire to take people's words as truth, for not trusting them instills *fear*, forming emotionally aligned reactions from fallacies evolving around *revelations*—relating emotionally vivified experiences linking angelic transients interpreting one's nature/needs. Fear is the essence of *Ignorance*, through which you inquisitively gather notions/numbers offering revelations advancing navigators conceiving enlightenment. Remember, the only way you know a thought is to *feel* a thought, to fathom emotions enlightening *luminaries* linking universal memories inciting navigable *Avatars* rationalizing illusion electromagnetically simulated.

Listening to someone proclaim their truth that is opposite yours, you experience a lack of Understanding Notions Illuminating Transient Youths. You either argue *for* your truth or *accept* theirs for consideration—have an "open mind." Only through an open mind can you receive revelations of *Truth*. The art of listening requires a *focused mind* to fathom opulent concepts unfolding situations enlightening deities managing integral needs diligently. It takes a sharp mind to decipher the chaotic data flowing on *Eternal Memory*, the electromagnetic transmission expressing revelations (notions) as logic managing emotional moments optimizing radiant youths as human beings experiencing stories unfolding moment by moment.

As an *Inquisitive Soul*, your mind has access to all data flowing along the electromagnetic waves supplying thoughts and feelings that stimulate your actions defining your life story. The complexity of this *Process* is truly an eternal adventure observed through "lifetimes" of gathering *knowledge*, kinetic notions/numbers outputting Wisdom's logical/linear energy dimensionally generating entities and governing evolution. To utilize knowledge, you must attain the art of listening to the various ways it is transmitted.

As a *human being* harnessing universal memories as notions birthing emotional insight naturally generated, you make a lot of noise, crying for an ear to listen to your sorrows that you create through your heart to punish your self, feeling a tad guilty at how *lucky* you truly are, for there are others whose challenges in life are more traumatic. Everything that comes your way are truly *Blessings in Disguise*, allowing you the opportunity to overcome your *issues* (induced situations stimulating universal entities sympathetically) that test your soul as a *Free Will* exploring your own universe of thoughts and feelings. You *create* (consciously reflect energy as thoughts evolving) the person you choose to Birth Emotionally, torturing your self in the *Process* of perceiving revelations optimizing children exploring Spirit scientifically.

As a *spiritual being*, you scientifically perceive intelligence revealing illusion "tempering" universal angels (luminaries) birthing experiences in necessary games. Here, you master the art of listening (tuning in) to your *heart* holding epiphanies activating rapturous thrills experienced through *Our Father's Heart* (Mother Nature) harmonizing entities assimilating radiant *Truth* as transcendental revelation unveiled through *holograms*, hydrogen-originated light orienting geometric revelations animating memories, matter, and minds.

Listening to your *inner child*, the intuitive navigator naturally experiencing realism conveying heavenly intelligence life delivers; you entertain lucid *dreams* delivering revelation expressing abstract *memories* as mental expressions manifesting observable realities influencing emotional souls. **Once again,** the simplicity of the process is truly complex.

The art of listening is NOT dead; it is just difficult to practice through the haze of electromagnetic chaos in which you are surrounded, especially with your high-tech electronics. Today, the younger generation seldom communicate person-to-person, relying instead on computer-phones, electronic devices through which they speak by "texting" and conveying data *online* (www: weaving wisdom wantonly), offering notions/numbers linking individuals nurturing enlightenment/entertainment, staying up with the latest information "twisting" truths. Few will find the time to validate the data. Relying instead on so-called "experts" disseminating facts and fallacies to inform or control the masses programed to believe stories or buy things relative to personal desires. Such is the purpose of the atomic *illusion* **inhibiting** logical luminaries understanding Source/Spirit interweaving omnipotent notions, numbers, nature, and navigators traversing *Heaven* and transcending *Hell*.

Many of you today express your thoughts, feelings, and actions on "social networks," sharing your opinion and experiences with friends that are not *listening* to the "undertones" of your voice revealing heartfelt truths, they are *reading* text messages, a style of "acronymical shorthand" (a contemporary language) that limits the fine details of a conversation to idle chatter. Everyone is "chatting" while expressing little content, a pastime that affects one's *Work* and society as a whole. Future technology will develop a *device* to "read" minds, digitally evaluating vibrations intuitive souls emanate as *thoughts* telepathically heralding opulent utterances guiding heavenly transients. This device, like all devices, is symbolic of your mind naturally utilizing *telepathy* to transfer electric logic expressing perception (awareness) to heavenly youths—*Avatars* simulating "alien" communication techniques. Telepathy represents a "higher art" of listening endowed to souls evolving technologically. Truly, yesterday's science fiction is today's scientific fact!

IF you find your self "living your dream" (listening to your heart), you are "practicing" the art of listening to your inner child—the one who knows you best. Your state of mind (open or closed) determines the path you travel to attain your *Awakening* from the illusion. If you choose to play your game of love/life with a devoted partner whose heart you share, beware of when your "love songs" are in disharmony, *syncopated* by half-truths. DO NOT hold back the full power of your love/life force. Give to each other ALL you have to give and ALL will return to you. Give only half and half is all you will receive. Help each other be the best they can be and all will grow *In Love*. Listen to your heart cry out for what it truly desires, and with all the Love you can channel, make it true. Everyone knows the ART of listening is how angels *receive* truth!

WORK
Utilizing Love/Life Energy

WORK is an eternal *Process* of willingly optimizing "received" knowledge through performing relevant occupations creatively enlightening/evolving souls systematically.

Work is something you do from the moment you awaken from your nightly sojourns. Work is a daily routine (maintenance) of cleaning, dressing, feeding, healing, enlightening, and testing your mind/body interface. All work is accomplished through *Science*—systematically converting information entwining notions/numbers/nature correlating *energy*—expressing natural environments/entities radiance geometrically yields.

Work represents the method of logical Mind utilizing *Love/ Life* energy, linearly oscillating visionary entities (luminous illuminati) formulating experiences. LOGIC (linear oscillations generating illuminated concepts/consciousness) is how Mind works, *moving* energy (e-motion) magnetically oscillating vivid information numerically generated, bringing forth *life* by logically/linearly inducing fabricated environments/entities.

As you represent an *image* of Mind (intuitive mystic actively gathering enlightenment), you too work *emotions* evolving moments of tribulation inspiring one's needs, experiencing pleasurable and painful endeavors as an inescapable nature of *Opposition* optimally providing perspectives orienting souls interpreting temporary illusions one navigates.

Work is an inescapable activity for a mind that continually *dreams*, detecting revelations expressing abstract memories symbolically. Upon *Awakening* each morning, you activate your *human alien* vehicle from "sleep mode." Through your *senses*, you sympathetically experience nature supplying *enlightenment* symbolically, entertaining notions logically inducing glorious holograms through elemental nature momentarily evolving natural transduction—moving energy from one system to another (abstract to atomic). Starting your "day shift" of work, you first wash and fuel your vehicle for the day's labor. Everything you do mentally and physically represents some type of "maintenance work," where you calculate/convert data through "time and labor" to attain your *Expectations* and "earnings" for the day.

You must work hard to keep your dream *alive*, assimilating/activating luminous intuition vividly experienced.

Work evolves from continuously calculating *Numbers*, notional units managing basic elemental revelations. Numbers define a thought you implement through sequences, a *Process* of expressing your work as your acquired discipline. As a mind "working" abstract energy, you compute your knowledge through *algorithms*, assimilating logic geometrically organizing radiant intelligence transmitting harmonic *memories* manifesting electric moments orienting radiant illuminati experiencing situations. Each *situation*—specific instance that unfolds abstract thoughts illuminating one naturally—represents an opportunity to *focus* your mind, formulating opulent concepts utilizing *Science*, through which Spirit/souls creatively intertwine elemental notions/nature conceived/converted emotionally/existentially.

Working through your mind/brain *interface*, you interpret natural things expressing realism from abstract concepts externalized. The pleasure and pain (opposition) you endure from your work inspires you to improve your methods of attaining your desires, advancing through multiple disciplines necessary for your *growth*, gathering revelations of *Wisdom* through hardship—*Hell*, humanly experiencing love/life. Here, you struggle to comprehend your *life mission* linking illuminati formulating/fathoming experiences manifested in situations systematically interweaving omnipotent navigators through DNA (divine numerical assignment) dynamically nurturing angels. "Playing your numbers" takes on a whole new meaning of work!

Everyone has a life mission or purpose that they *act out*, applying cosmic thoughts optimizing universal transients through their work. By analyzing your work, you observe your soul's growth through experiences along *The Right Path* designed for you. Here, incarnated, you experience first-hand the difficulty of converting energy from the simplest of things (thoughts) into great complexities (atomic representations/creations) that you spend a lifetime to maintain through work.

Always remember, it does not matter what type of work you do, it is your *attitude* that matters, how you assimilate thoughts transmitting intelligence to utilize data "exceptionally," to do the *best* of your ability. For, as you age OLD observing life's dilemmas, you will be remembered for your work to *overcome* your challenges in life.

LOVE OF MONEY

Money is one of the most challenging factors in life. Money represents the pivot point upon which the civilized world revolves. Love "of money" is an anchor holding you in the illusion, grounding you in thinking Life revolve *around* money.

Love *and* money are forms of power that makes things appear from *nowhere* (ideas) to *now here* (reality). You must spend money to make money. It is easy to think that money is the root of your desires, for in today's world, you must work to make money to attain your desires. Money is the "medium of exchange" that allows you to experience your dreams you envision.

Education is the basis of converting Love (knowledge) into money. With an *education*, you evaluate data (universal concepts) activating transient illuminati optimizing notions, numbers, nature, and needs naturally evolving entities dynamically. Through education, you attain skills you exchange for money. The more knowledge/skills you acquire, the better your bargaining position to attain work you desire. Of course, this *Process* is applied both positively and negatively—legally and illegally. Love, money, education, and work interface completely.

The challenge of "dealing with money" is in what you are willing to *do* to acquire it. Of course, you will think that the least amount of hardship necessary to attain money will be the most rewarding. Remember, the law of *Opposition* dictates otherwise. Work is an endeavor that brings mental, emotional, physical, and monetary rewards and punishment. That which you *love to do* gives you a sense of pleasure, pride, and accomplishment in converting your love into money. It may also put you in high-risk situations harmful to your health as well as your finances and freedom. Only with *Courage of Love—Faith*—can you attain *Courage of Fear*, utilizing *My Light of Love* (knowledge) to overcome your dark fears of losing your money, the "bargaining tool" useful in attaining your desires and security.

You will naturally fight for the right to spend your money as you see fit, for you know how hard you worked to attain it. This is a big issue for those experiencing *Marriage*, where sharing money with your significant other will always bring *strife* stressing tender *Relationships* illuminating fervent entities.

MONEY symbolizes "material opulence" numerically expressing yields (profits) from your work. Many think that to win the game of Love/Life, you must acquire money in large numbers whenever possible, for *Numbers* relate strength and power. Having a LOT of money (loads of treasure) gives you the power to create your own fantasy of paradise, your idea of *Heaven* (having everything a visionary entity needs) while expressing your *Passion* in *Hell*—your personal adventures supplying situations inducing one needs when humanly experiencing love/life. Truly, money holds you in its magnetic force (more or less) that instills an "exchange value," something you are always quick to argue. Money relates to *physical* wealth and Love relates to *spiritual* wealth. Everyone has universal WEALTH—*Wisdom* enlightening angelic luminaries traversing/transcending heaven/hell.

No matter how you spend your money, you cannot deny that Life Of Vibrant Experiences is the driving force of Angelic Luminaries Living. You spend your money on what you love, not what you hate. How ironic that the U.S. dollar heralds "IN GOD WE TRUST." The founding fathers knew of the *Relationship* of love and money. Unfortunately, history relates man's weakness for material things. Many of you still put your FAITH in money, finding anguish in temporary happiness vanishing with your spendthrift ways.

Living in the illusion, man is programmed to believe love/ life depends on wealth and money. Relatively speaking, your "lifestyle" is dependent on money, but you cannot *buy* love or life! Many people worship money for the power it provides. However, without knowledge to harness that power, they soon squander it away. Having a lot of money brings a lot of *Responsibility*, not to mention resentment by those who have little or none. How you exchange your love/money to acquire your desires determines your happiness. Love nourishes your soul struggling to survive in a chaotic world where many believe money is more important than love. However, like everything else in life, it is a matter of time before you know the true value of Materialism Obscuring Notions Enlightening You.

Money supports the works of man manipulating atomic nature. As it is your nature to create and destroy, money is another tool to create your life "style" while destroying your "living" environment—another form of *Opposition* (have and have not). You cannot hoard or keep your money locked up out of action. Money must flow to keep the illusion alive. Everyone needs money to play the game of love/life. You cannot win *nor* lose the game of love/life, you can only play—perceiving love/life "advancing" you to attain *A Higher Vision* of love/life.

By spending money, you keep your game alive. Naturally, you cannot spend your money beyond your limit without dire consequences; it will upset the balance of the game. Just look around you at the current state of the world with its failing economies, global warming, disastrous weather patterns, pollution, political unrest, and wars that indicate your failure to be *In Communion* with each other and with Spirit—Governing Omnipotent Deities. These are your greatest challenges you need to address in educating your children today. You need to instill the critical importance of living in *Harmony* with ONE and ALL.

"Winning" the game of love/life (relatively speaking) does not relate to the dollars you amass, but more on how you use your "limited money" to survive economically, help those in need, improve the environment, and educate the nescient souls kept in the dark by the "powers that be," those amongst you destined to keep the illusion alive, to allow the young and ignorant to strive for *Truth*. Remember, everyone plays his or her part to keep the wheel of love/life spinning. Love of money is a way of "tempering" your soul through the hardships of life lucidly inducing false ethics through *Opposition*, challenging you to understand *Love IS* the luminous one vivifying entities (intuitive souls) with the power of responsibility.

RESPONSIBILITY
The challenge to Act

Responsibility is your "ability to respond," to give back your Love/Life energy. Everyone has responsibility to reflect his or her image of GOD guiding omnipotent deities. As a god governing one's duty, you control your moral obligation for the life you are given. Everyone is responsible for his or her *actions*; aptly converting thoughts inspiring one's needs naturally evolving emotional deities.

Responsibility is critical for every child to learn along with good manners (*Respect* you *Reflect*), for both are fundamental in all *Relationships*. Responsibility refers to a state of being dependable, accountable for how you use your acquired knowledge or skills. Knowledge is the only way you can have responsibility, for without knowledge you have nothing to give back. Remember, you are a mind/heart *existing* on knowledge!

Responsibility is delegated to those that are capable of wielding knowledge dependably. You say, I can "count on you" (numerically speaking) to get the job done. Again, knowledge (*Numbers*) naturally unifies minds building experiential realism.

Responsibility is something you cannot deny, for you always have to answer for your actions. To be responsible, you need to have *Courage of Love*, knowing all data flowing through you is guiding you along *The Right Path* for you, allowing you opportunities to Gather Revelations Of Wisdom through your life's *mission*, methodically interpreting signals/situations supplying intuition optimizing navigators—natural *Avatars*—verifying illusion (geometrically arranged thoughts) optically revealed.

As a *Free Will*, your responsibility as a "freethinker" is to question those trying to control you through *dogma*—data obstructing gifted minds *Awakening* to *Truth*. It is your responsibility to decide what is best for you, for YOU ARE TRUTH—your own universal agent receiving enlightenment (transcendental revelation) unveiled throughout heaven/hell. DO NOT DENY your responsibility!

DENIAL

DENIAL (deliberately evading necessary issues advancing luminaries) is something everyone does, even when they admit they do not. It is almost impossible not to live in denial during your lifetime. Denial is simply the refusal to believe some truth about your self, for you are easily *Blinded by Truth*. By refusing to recognize your *issues* inducing situations systematically unfolding experiences, you create roadblocks to your spiritual growth—your *Awakening*. In order to overcome your roadblocks, you must learn to *listen* to your self lucidly issuing signals that express *needs* necessitating experiences enlightening *deities* discovering empathetic insight through issues "evolving" souls.

Childhood is your most impressionable time in life, where you develop your "emotional baggage" of issues dealt to you by your parents, siblings, and friends, not to mention your *karma* kindling atonement (restitution) modifying angels from accomplishments in a previous life. Here, you acquire negative-magnetic anchors of fears and doubts from what people say about you, for you are very sensitive to your image you know little about, an image you are trying to discover from *Eternal Memory*, the electromagnetic force of Spirit (*The GREAT Computer*) downloading data dynamically advancing transient angels.

As a child, you emulate your parents that shape your *ego* as an emotionally generated observer. You reflect their thoughts and actions as acceptable behavior. As you grow and develop your self-image, you become aware of your parent's controlling efforts. Naturally, your *Free Will* becomes rebellious to their desires, inducing trials and tribulation that are essential for your growth mentally, emotionally, and spiritually. Your siblings and friends also influence your self-image through peer pressure, forcing you to "fit in" with the crowd. It is truly frightening to stand *Alone* (security in numbers), assimilating love/life ordaining navigators emotionally. Getting a grip on puberty is an emotional roller coaster that will leave an indelible mark upon your soul, scarring you with "sexual hang-ups" that may be your greatest denial.

Setting your course as a trailblazer in search of your identity, you quickly learn to be critical, judging others by looks, nationality, clothing, actions, or anything that will place them in a "relative perspective" to your self. You adopt an *attitude* activating temperamental transients interpreting thoughts unfolding dynamic emotions, perceiving your position to your fellow players as "below," "equal," or "above," always desiring to stay "on top" to have the controlling hand in your *Relationships*.

When you proclaim your thoughts and feelings to others, you reveal your self-image of "who you think you are," for what one *thinks*, one becomes, transferring heavenly intelligence nurturing kindred souls. As you emotionalize your thoughts into actions, you play out your part in the game of Love/Life. When you are courageous enough to voice your opinion, you announce to the world your truth—your *Belief.* The people you associate with will judge you by what you *say* and what you *do*. If you say one thing and do another, you are not living your truth; you are living in denial of your truth. *Someday, Someone* will come along to challenge your beliefs, *Awakening* your mind to perceive a more illustrious image of your self. There is no easy way around the pain and suffering you must endure to discover who you are and who you are not, especially when experiencing *Marriage*—the joining of *Two as One*.

Living in denial of your Intimate Situations Sympathetically Unifying Emotional Souls, you easily point them out in someone else. You lack the insight to see the "common flaws" everyone experiences as a *spiritual* being coping with a *human* existence. If someone were to point out that truth to you, it could provoke an argument or harm your *Relationship*. Yet, it is something you must eventually face to transcend *illusion* inhibiting logical luminaries utilizing situations influencing one's nature/needs.

Deliberately Evading Notions Introducing Advanced Logic of your issues challenging your soul will hinder *A Higher Vision* of your self you are here to attain. Only by accepting your issues can you utilize your strength (*Courage of Love*) to maneuver through your *Relationships* that connect your *soul exploring life's fantasies* to Spirit Enlightening Luminous Fantasists. Everyone has their own schedule to acknowledge truths they deny.

RELATIONSHIPS
Your Eternal Journeys of Love/Life

Relationships allow you to be Angelic Wills Assimilating Revelational Experiences, observing how your thoughts, feelings, and actions produce the image of your self you *portray*, personally offering reactions that "rectify" angelic youths, setting you on the proper *course* containing one's unique reality stimulating enlightenment.

Relationships reveal enlightenment linking angelic transients interpreting one's nature/needs systematically helping induce perception sympathetically. *Someday*, *Someone* will enter your life that will inspire *Marriage*, the most demanding relationship you can experience.

Relationships are how you *relate*—reflect electric logic amplifying thoughts/transients emotionally. "Relating" refers to the "passing on" or telling stories about your collected experiences. Your life story contains your relationships by bloodline or *Family*, by profession or discipline, or by any criteria that will isolate, group, or organize experiences into some category.   All relationships are expressions of Love, for *Love IS* the ESSENCE of eternal Spirit stimulating emotions nurturing conscious entities. The interactions of love relate the type of life you experience as a mind/heart soul, a *trinity-being* touring radiant illusion naturally illuminating/instructing transient youths bilaterally experiencing/expressing insight naturally generated (positively and negatively). Remember, it takes TWO to transmit/transform *Wisdom* optimally/optically. A relationship does not occur *Alone*.

Relationships allow you to *interface* with others, imparting notions transmitting emotional revelations (feelings) activating common/complex experiences. Everyone is an extrovert and introvert at times, sociable with others and concerned only with one's self. A relationship occurs through an open mind *In Communion*, one willing to accept other opinions as "food for thought." For a relationship to endure, you must form a harmonious union, accepting each other as different individuals desiring to share your time together. This involves maintaining a positive atmosphere where thoughts and feelings can be shared openly without judgment or emotional reactions. By mastering the *art of listening*, you can react to others' stimuli by being receptive to both positive *and* negative expressions. Maintaining a non-judgmental attitude, you can relate to them in positive ways that will bring out the best in both of you. Diplomacy requires a strong mind in control of its emotions—truly a difficult trait to attain.

All relationships involve giving and receiving. It is difficult to accept that you willfully draw unfavorable things to you by expending your energy on negative thoughts, feelings, and actions that attract that same energy revealing your self-induced *Depression*. Your life story reflects the simple truth—what you sow, you reap. It may seem like an inescapable *Hell* that evolves around you, but in truth it evolves from *within* you. Such is *The POWER of Love* propelling omnifarious wills exploring relationships. How you project that power into the universe defines your level of pleasure and tribulation.

The relationship of energy flowing in and out of you can produce disharmony between your mind/heart, where *emotions* expand mental observations through illuminating one's *nature* necessitating anguish to understand relevant experiences. Relationships, like everything else, are constantly in flux, continually changing as you evolve your thoughts and feelings that bring pleasure and pain. Through relationships, you learn to *empathize*—identify with and understand the feelings of another.

Your desire to love and be loved takes you through disharmonious situations that tear you apart in order to attain *A Higher Vision* of your *self* systematically exploring love/life *fantasies*, formulating adventures nurturing transient angels interpreting enlightening situations. "Disharmony" provides stressful experiences you encounter in your daily affairs as you share your *Beliefs*, eagerly seeking to find someone who understands you, someone with whom you can relate. If you have a "positive nature," you tend to be easy to get along with, open-minded and sociable. If you have a "negative nature," you tend to be critical and judgmental of others. Whatever your nature, it represents your starting point from which you revolve to evolve, finding someone that is the opposite of you (opposites attract) to act as your role model. Thereby, you come to discover who you *are* by observing who you are *not*.

Emotional Energy, the driving force in every relationship, pulls you in and pushes you away, spinning you around to observe your self from every angle. It takes *Courage of Love* to subject your self to the punishment you endure from your "significant other" *reflecting* your issues that you deny, for they give back to you that which you give them—positive or negative energy.

Relationships are not good or bad; they are neutral. They hold all possibilities waiting to be discovered for the benefit of those involved in the relationship. For relationships to work, you must be AWARE that all willful angels reflect emotions to attain their *Desire*. Knowing how to interpret emotional expressions is the hardest part of relating.

Sharing your love in a relationship is truly a challenge, because everyone is reflecting their own image of what they believe *Love IS*, tinted, shaded, and speckled with what others are projecting toward them. You cannot manipulate others to your demands without a fight, for no one likes to be controlled like a puppet. Communication turns into arguments when there is a lack of logic or understanding of the subject matter. It is difficult to relate if you deny your *Ignorance*. Petty arguments or bickering is a great waste of energy.

As the "generation gap" separates souls into their own *world* weaving one's realism linking deities along their own paths of enlightenment, so too does relationships pit mind/hearts seeking *Harmony*. You are restricted to only understanding your own perspective of Love as you *Alone* see it at the present moment of your *Evolution*. You cannot BE someone else. The closest you can get is when you join *Two* as *One* in the symbolic union of *Marriage*, a challenge that forces you to experience things repeatedly until you resolve your *issues*, your individual situations systematically "unifying" emotional souls.

SOMEDAY, SOMEONE...

Will come into your life who you have never met before, but in your heart you will feel a connection to the contrary. This kindred spirit has been assigned to meet you—according to your "plan"—and deliver your needs along your way *Home*. They will appear at the most opportune time to guide you along *The Right Path* designated for you. The relationship you develop will inspire *Marriage*, through which *Blessings in Disguise* will bestow trials and tribulation as a *test* tempering emotional souls transforming, attaining *A Higher Vision* of responsibility as a "creator," a parent nurturing their *Power of Love* as they start a *Family*.

MARRIAGE
A Symbolic Union

Marriage is a ceremony of great honor for all souls regardless of gender. Through marriage, two souls publically proclaim their love *for* each other and accept the responsibility for love they receive *from* each other.

Marriage is a serious commitment expressed through ritual ceremony—a wedding. Here, you stand before family and friends (Generators Of Desire) to make a solemn promise to uphold your Will Openly Realizing Divinity. During the marriage rites, you express words of *loyalty*, *honor*, and *justice*. Without this "trinity-foundation" a marriage is impossible to sustain. Through the process of testing this foundation, you grow your marriage *and* your soul.

Your wedding day is truly a day of honor, where you openly show respect and admiration for each other as an individual "god-child" with your own *Desires* and *Expectations*. Repeating *the binary code* ("I do"), you join together to embrace your love and fears as husband and wife, sharing your *Passions* that will temper your soul as you endure through "sickness and health, richer or poorer, until *Death* do you part." These *words* of *Wisdom* obligate romantic deities unaware of the trials and tribulation awaiting them as they Acquire Growth Experiences, Observing Love's Demands together.

Marriage offers a path to discover the intimate details of your self you observe in reflection—one to one. It will be a stressful journey for *logical* man projecting his love to woman that *reflects* his love emotionally. The "reflexive" nature of marriage is a *baptism*, a "blessing" advancing perceptive transients interpreting stressful moments providing trials and tribulation in *Hell*, where humans experience love/life that purifies their soul. Each spouse "charges" the other positively and negatively, creating harmony or disharmony. As one gives what one receives, each becomes the other in words and deeds—*Two of a Kind*—relating love reflexively. The influence each has on the other is instrumental in observing and connecting to their "other half," that side they deny being. Logical man must connect to his emotional heart to become a whole being, as woman to her logical mind. The explosive condition this task entails enlightens both to *The Power of Love* that destroys in order to recreate. For a marriage to survive, you must *Remember* its purpose!

The idiom "it takes two to tango/tangle" represents your self-induced choreography of harmony or CHAOS crippling heavenly angels openly seeking to *confidently create* (1) *balance and cooperation* (2) required to sustain a harmonious union as "one couple"—½ or one of two. You must "agree to disagree," for only through *Opposition* will you view your true potential to BE ONE balancing emotions optimally nurturing entities through their *heart* holding everything angels really treasure— Love. By finding a "middle road" acceptable to both partners, you overcome your *issues* inducing situations systematically undermining/unifying emotional souls (fragile hearts), thereby attaining a "progressive" marriage as you GROW together, gathering revelations of *Wisdom* (through your heart) to know you are traveling *The Right Path* designed for you.

All marriages represent a spiritually ordained *fate* of formulated arrangements "tempering" entities. Each partner is instrumental in the other's development, whether he or she realizes it or not. Each will try to change the other to think, feel, and act like them self—their "personality" only they know. *Truth* dictates that in order to love another, you must first love your *self*—your soul expressing love freely. You cannot demand the reciprocation of your love. Love is a heartfelt expression of *equality* not superiority. You must respect your self for your individuality and respect others for theirs.

Marriage is a *Process* of learning about your self, so newlyweds are handicapped right from the start. You are destined to suffer through all the pitfalls of marriage in order to know that love is a powerful force that creates and destroys. Love brings you together to push you apart as "reactionary" lovers "reflexively" relating *emotionally*, experiencing moments of tribulation illuminating one naturally assimilating lessons life yields. TRIBULATION transforms reflexive individuals becoming unhappy lovers assimilating truths inducing one's *needs* as necessary experiences evolving deities sympathetically— through a loving heart. You cannot rely on others to make you happy. Happiness is truly something you fabricate within you and reflect outward through *Your Loving Smile*.

By using each other's strengths for the benefit of both, you encourage *unity*; understanding needs invigorate transcendental youths accepting human weaknesses, observing how negative thoughts, words, and actions tear you apart. Your problems arise from "disharmony," working against each other rather than with each other, leading to a struggle in which you fight for dominance, unwilling to give up your independence in making your own decisions. Through disharmony, you learn that you cannot control anyone without a fight, nor change anyone *into* your self, for you are truly an individual/indivisible *generator of desire*. You can only change your *self* to accept everyone else as an *equal* generator of desire, no matter how different they may appear. You do not have to respect them for their words or actions they project, only for their right to say and act as they desire, for truly, what they project they will receive in kind—GOD does not SLEEP (sanctify luminaries expressing erroneous perceptions).

Through perseverance, you come to see marriage allows you to face your opposition and work together as a *team* traversing/transcending emotionally active moments, exploring the vast potential of *Divine Fantasies* you entertain to express your Love/Life energy. Each of you has your gifts you are meant to develop. Through loyalty, you are bound to help each other attain the fulfillment of those gifts.

Like all journeys, sooner or later you will reach an "apogee" of marriage—the furthest point away from each other. Pushed apart from losing your TEMPER triggering emotional moments providing excited reactions, you experience states of *Depression* in which you question the purpose of torturing each other. This "necessary distance" gives you *space* to move around in, where you sympathetically perceive anguish "corrupting" entities living in *Denial*—deliberately evading notions/needs improving anguished lovers. This "turning point" allows you to observe that your spouse gives you all that you *need* as a navigator emotionally exploring *Desire*. These "dark moments" of despair illuminate both man and woman to come *To-Get-Her*, where HE understands SHE is instrumental in knowing *Two as One*—WE (wisdom exemplified) willingly evolving.

The saying "two heads are better than one" refers to opposite views giving one a complete, all-around view. By sharing opposite views (logical/emotional), a united couple understands each other's *attitude* of assimilating thoughts that induce temperaments unifying/undermining dynamic entities. Only in this way can you find your self reflected in your significant other, for in *Truth*, you are the same! This is pleasantly experienced when both say the same thing at the same time, experiencing a brief moment of *Harmony*—being one mind/heart.

The marriage union sanctifies your divine power of *creation* (conceiving radiant entities as transient illuminati ordained naturally). It allows you to "reflect your image," symbolically creating children that resemble you through your genetic links (*DNA*) binding you to Universal Spirit. Birth is an event you have limited control over. You are simple pawns in *The Game of Love/Life* liberating omnipotent visionaries exploring luminous illusion fervently experienced. Here, you come to realize the pleasure and pain of being a god sharing love/life energy with family members *you* create.

SEX

Through SEX, your soul emotionally *ex*-changes Love/Life energy. Sex is a biological drive that is one of your greatest challenges in life, for it is as natural as breathing.

Consciously **A**ssimilating **R**elevant **N**eeds **A**ctivating **L**ove (knowledge) relates to *sexual desire*, a powerful force brought on by the development of your physical body's hormones that seem to take over your mind. This force emanates from your base/root chakra stimulating your reproduction system necessary for the creation of a vehicle for *My Angelic Child* that transmigrates into third-dimensional worlds as *Family* members.

Sex entails great responsibility, for Love creates Life and is therefore considered taboo before marriage in some societies. Sex in itself is a glorious thing that entails the greatest physical event experienced by a human being. Here, you struggle to come to terms with this great event erupting within you (puberty), which is only exacerbated by peer pressure to "do the deed." The pull between your physical desires and mental logic is an unequal match. Life Of Vibrant Emotions moves you physically without concern for the consequences.

As humans, you naturally associate your power of *self* with your sexual prowess. To be "sexy" is to reflect an image of superior *Geometry*, having a well-developed body that has strong magnetic and electric energy to attract the attention of others. Women make great efforts at attaining this prowess, for it is her negative/magnetic force that attracts the male positive/electric force to fulfill her motherly instincts. Men are designed to simply transfer the *seed* of Love/Life systematically evolving eternal deities, supplying energy expressed digitally as *DNA* defining natural attributes. Their physique reflects their strength and virility attractive to women interpreting their procreative ability subjectively.

The responsibility of nurturing offspring lies mainly with women, for she carries the developing fetus after conception, symbolically bonding a mind/soul and body within *Mother's Nature* that provides security within her Wisdom Organizing Material Birth. Girls physically mature earlier than boys for this strenuous task. Although *It is a Man's World (Thanks to Woman)*, she is the TOOL transforming outwardly opulent life. Women are the great "receivers" of the seed of Love/Life. Once they have taken it in, they change from a *Seeker* of Love to a *nurturer* of Life (much to man's dismay), catering to the every need of their child. Thereby, a woman becomes more harmonious with Mother Nature nurturing and reflecting Father's eternal Love/Life force. SHE simply heralds evolution, naturally exhibiting more *patience*, physically abiding tribulation in evolving naturally conceived entities.

During moments of experiencing sexual activity, the transfer of emotional data between souls is miraculously mesmerizing, spinning fantasies that keep you confined within your physical boundaries. The rush of energy released at orgasm raises your harmonic frequency to an ecstatic crescendo that leaves you panting in exhaustion, while your heart beats a rhapsody of *My Love Divine* impossible to maintain indefinitely.

Sexual addiction hinders your soul, binding it to the illusion of your physical body that you are trying to transcend by "raising" your consciousness, tapping into your higher chakras that lead to enlightenment of *Truth* that rectifies universal transients harmoniously. The consequences of carnal knowledge are due to *Ignorance*, not knowing when to properly implement the knowledge. Sex is a process that creates and destroys lives, transmitting diseases through promiscuous activity and trauma from sexual abuse.

Mentally Amplifying Notions evolves through Wisdom Optimizing Magnetically Aligned Nature reflecting *My Light of Love* inspiring *Angels* assimilating notions/nature governing emotional luminaries. *He and She* (children of light) are free spirits adventurously exploring the limits of their abilities. Pleasure is their greatest desire, and there is no greater physical pleasure than the "orgasmic high" attuning mind/heart souls in *Harmony*, heralding angels realizing moments of natural yearning (*Desire*). Man's power to create is an overwhelming desire, for he finds himself magnetically pulled by women's attraction holding him within his base chakra. Once man has attained carnal knowledge, he habitually looks at women as a "sex object," analyzing their magnetic power stimulating his physical need to release his love/life energy. This powerful urge can be devastating to his Emotionally Generated Observer (self) through lack of confidence to interact with women, feeling overwhelmed by their beauty and power of influence, for woman will draw all she can from man as an equal force.

You are born a natural procreator. Through sex, you Systematically Import Navigators (souls) through the interplay of *Numbers* (*DNA*) that allows you to create "in your image," your physical traits that define your "model" (he/she) of a *human-alien* vehicle that a soul controls within the third-dimension of *Heaven* holographically enlightening angelic visionaries evolving naturally. Thus, through SEX, your soul emotionally exchanges (converts) Love into Life, creating a family.

FAMILY

As *Children of Light*, you are related spiritually and physically within the stellar FAMILY of Father and Mother's illumination linking you as fabulous *Angels* managing illusion luminously yielded. As family, you are created in my IMAGE, an intelligent mind also generating entities. You are conceived and nurtured through *The Power of Love* luminously orienting/optimizing visionary entities.

Each of you are a complex FAMILY MEMBER, formulating assigned memories illuminating loving youths—Magnificent Entities—momentarily birthing experiences "representing" your *Passion*, providing adventurous/amorous situations supplying inspiration one *nurtures*, naturally utilizing radiant thoughts unfolding realism emotionally stimulated.

Each day you rise to fill your mind/heart soul with the only thing you can truly possess—knowledge! Grabbing your shield of *Denial*, you battle your fear of *Ignorance*, unaware of *The Power of Love* burning within you, moving your heart in rhythmic beats as you trudge along with your eyes cast to the ground, looking for a "sign." After years of enduring your own *Hell*, humanly experiencing love/life, you come around to see you ARE the SIGN, an angel receiving enlightenment, sympathetically illuminating "glorious navigators" (your family and friends). As a mind/heart soul (trinity-being), you seek UNITY, understanding notions, numbers, nature, and needs illuminate transcendental/transient *youths* yearning omnifarious understanding through *Harmony*.

There, in front of your eyes, is my family, cosmic stars shinning with my GRACE governing radiant angels consciously evolving, sympathetically attaining your GLORY by graciously loving other radiant youths exploring Love Inspiring Free Entities, moving you in mysterious ways to be Angels Living Love that you choose to Birth Emotionally. As *My Angelic Child*, you reach out to touch my family members in your own special way, *your* creation of what *you* think *Love IS*. All you can do is BE IT and share it, for every vision reflected by you allows me to Simultaneously Experience Existentially—through your eyes—my children perceiving **Magnificent Entities** as family.

SACRIFICE OF LOVE/LIFE
The Cost of Living

Love is the medium or "spiritual money" of generators of desire experiencing Life. Whatever you desire, you must be willing to sacrifice a certain amount of your *Love/Life Energy* to attain and maintain that desire. The more that you are willing to exchange, the greater the value (memory) of the transaction upon your mind/heart soul as you Gather Revelations Of Wisdom with *Age*, acquiring great/grave experiences that enlighten and scar you mentally, emotionally, and physically.

As parents, you are challenged to sacrifice your love/life for the advancement of your children, to give them there desires as well as teach them skills in surviving life, reflecting the process of *Divine Will* nurturing your *Free Will* "doing time" as a *Human Alien*. Truly, it takes *Courage of Love* to sacrifice your greatest treasure (life), to give your children the freedom to follow their mind/heart into the depths of *Hell* to discover their true potential as humans emotionally linking logic. All you can do is offer your undying love to your children, observing how they take advantage of you for their personal gains, just as I observe you, *My Angelic Child*, abusing *Mother's Nature* to reap the pleasures of your personal paradise, where you learn first-hand how your sacrifice of love/life reveals the cost of living your dream.

Attaining *Old Age*, your withered body reflects the rigors of channeling Love/Life energy. Here, you reminisce about your memorable adventures, the highlights of love/life that were worth the sacrifice. You come to realize all the pain and suffering that you endured has brought you to this moment of your *Awakening*, observing how your professions, occupations, and pastimes were instrumental in providing experiences necessary to attain *A Higher Vision* of how you evolved from whom you once were in your youth. With hindsight, you realize that everyone is simply *Playing Around*, observing Mental Emotions letting you experience your desires in order to *feel* and *know* my sacrifice of Love/Life for *you*.

PLAYING AROUND

+ + ◆ ◆ ◆ + +

Love/Life is a challenge experienced in *The Garden of Light*, where *Mother's Nature* embraces you in PARADISE, providing atomic revelation/realism as data illuminating souls existentially. She supplies your food and medicine to nourish and cure your physical body. She moves you on heartfelt tides, oscillating you between elations and depressions, holding you *together* in her loving, magnetic embrace. Here, you *inwardly* feel those thoughts you express *outside* in opposition. Through your physical, sensory inputs, you "internally" process and express your INFLUENCE, instilling notions/feelings linking universal entities naturally conceiving enlightenment.

> The games you play to build your day
> is how you choose to live,
> separating *good* from *bad* by what you *keep* and *give*
> to those you share your Love/Life with,
> creating your world through personal truths
> that clashes with fellow angelic youths
> opening their heart to feel and know
> the games you choose to win *together*
> is how your spirit grows.

Every moment here in paradise, you experience *Heaven* as Harmonious Energy advancing *visionary entities* (navigators), vibrant, instinctual souls inspecting opulent notions as radiant youths, eternal navigators temporarily interpreting three-dimensional illusions experienced sympathetically. Every day, it takes *Courage of Love* to "win" your game at hand, treating others as you desire to be treated, knowing full well that what you *give* is that which you *receive*.

Expressing your love is a *pleasant* and *painful* experience. Truly, it is better to have loved and lost than to have never loved at all, although many of you will argue the point. Every night when you dream, you *Call Home*, conversing with your

OVERSELF, the overseer vivifying emissaries (radiant souls) exploring love/life fantasies, expressing your gratitude to "play-a-round" of life. Through dreams (*Visions* for *Acceptance*), you observe solutions to your issues enlightening Your Own *Universe* as a unitary networker (illuminator) verifying electric realities sensed emotionally.

Vision and Acceptance comes with *Age* they say,
long after you get to see ALL from your illusory *daze*
deceiving angelic zealots evolving,
fighting for your truth across the haze,
there, within your mind,
moving upon the playing field in such a craze to find
your way back *Home* to me,
arguing as children do, when out you go to be
inquisitive souls seeking *Truth*,
tearing down what others build up to
reflect their Love for me,
fearful to question your SIN (Source inspired nature)
systematically illuminating navigators within
some game you choose to play,
here, as *My Angelic Child* I set free today,
where you advance as a visionary seeking acceptance

of all that you do,
working hard to play a "round" of Life to discover YOU.

OLD AGE

Getting old is a relatively rewarding time in your life. Here, you discover your *disc* (data-infused spiritual consciousness) loaded with valuable experiences of knowledge packed away in memory files collected from impassioned adventures. Everything you relate comes from your stored memories of the "ages" that you endured to attain your truth of life.

Looking at the "hard-bodies" displaying the beauty of youth, you *Remember* how it was to be young and ignorant to the ways of the world, how the physical urges rising from your root chakra tempted you with the delights of the flesh. The innocence of youth was such a thrill back then, beating your heart in eager anticipation, enduring stressful moments for your first touch of flesh or your first kiss from some *other* omnipotent traveler harnessing emotional revelation. Eager to discover your unknown future, you were willing to sacrifice your Love/Life energy to feed your hungry heart.

OLD AGE is where you observe Love/Life develops angels' grand/grave experiences that are truly *Blessings in Disguise*, for here you obtain "hindsight." Hindsight lets you *Recall* your life's memories through "highlights," those unforgettable moments that impressed indelible marks of pleasure upon your mind/heart soul. Here too, are the memories of those "lowlights" in life; those times of tribulation that instilled the negative aspects that you came to realize were instrumental in your *Awakening* to *The Power of Love*.

After many years of playing *The Game of Love/Life*, you come to see the world of war, famine, destructive storms, and the dog-eat-dog nature of mankind reflects KARMA kindling atonement "rectifying" mistake *Angels*. It is so easy to see what is wrong with the world, for you recognize the *chaos* crippling heavenly angels openly seeking *A Higher Vision* of *Home*, where *Harmony* of Mental Emotions allows you "peace of mind."

Old age brings *Wisdom* of knowing that you did not "miss" anything in life. Your life *mission* manifests intended situations stimulating insight one nurtures. INSIGHT reveals your inherent nature supplying intuition guiding heavenly transients exploring *Desire*. It takes years to attain insight, enduring countless experiences that provide guidance as you traverse *Heaven* and transcend *Hell*, harnessing emotional love/life as humans experiencing linear *logic*—light oscillating generators' intuitive consciousness.

Old age opens your heart to helping fellow travelers, sharing your wealth of experiences with those in need, trying to feel "useful." For those that are *Lost in the Dark* (the young), you may offer words of *Wisdom*, forgetful of their *Ignorance* to decipher the data you bestow, for they cannot validate your *stories* sympathetically telling of revelations instructing emotional souls. Your advice falls on deaf ears that lack experience. However, as *The Lightworker* you were born to be, you naturally *distribute* wisdom, delivering inspirational stories that relate issues between *UniverseS* (transcendental entities)—unitary navigators implementing visions enlightening realities sensed existentially.

Old age is usually a time of *Awakening* your inner child from the "fear of living" to courageously embrace *Death* dynamically elevating angels transcending *Hell*. Here, you realize that you cannot save anyone from TRIBULATION transforming radiant illuminati becoming "universal luminaries" *advancing* through illusions of nature. Truly, your heart aches in sympathy, realizing everyone must learn first-hand, for SEEING is truly BELIEVING, systematically experiencing emotional insights nurturing *generators*—gifted entities naturally exploring revelation atomically transmitting opulent realism—beholding experiences linking intuitive entities "verifying illusions" (naturally generated) "nurturing" *gods* (gatherers of data/desire).

In *Time*, Angelic Luminaries Living will reap the blessings of being OLD (obtaining *Love Divine*), realizing they are not getting older, they are getting wiser. The wiser you become, the more you realize how *little* you really know! The thought of "eternal life" begins to sound promising, for there are all those things you wanted to "see and do" but never accomplished.

Wisdom offers words/worlds illuminating spiritual dimensions of *Mind*, manifesting illuminati naturally defined as a *Free Will* "formulating resolutions," expressing enlightenment while investigating Love/Life.

REMEMBER

You cannot lose what is mine to give!
Life *eternal* is all you can *live*,
evolving through elemental revelations
nurturing angelic luminaries
logically interpreting vivid experiences.

Do not worry about your time today.
I am leading you along your way
through *words* I sing,

wisely offering revelation developing souls
aglow within my *Light*,
where Love is generating harmonic threads
weaving illusion that brings dread
to all you eternal youths,
each in a *world* of variable contentions
weaving opulent revelations linking deities
exploring *dimensions*
dynamically illuminating minds exploring notional situations
in opulent nature,
in which you are willing to DIE to LIVE, discovering
illusory experiences liberate illuminati verifying emotions
beating a heart—thump-thump—in co-motions,
two movements on opposing paths to circumnavigate *cells*
converting energy logically linking systems
confining entities learning love sequentially
through *old age*,
observing life dynamically advancing godly entities
discovering their evolutionary stage
as they revolve around *The Circle of Love/Life*.

Bless you and Godspeed

12

THE CIRCLE OF LOVE/LIFE
The Revolution of Evolution

The circle of love/life (0) symbolizes transcendental *Harmony* (1) electromagnetically conceiving intelligence radiantly conveying logic/emotion—opposing forces (2)—linearly oscillating visionary entities—luminous illuminati (3)—formulating experiences/fathoming enlightenment.

The revolution of the circle of love/life conveys *Evolution*, expressing variables of logic/light unfolding three-dimensional illusion optimizing notions, numbers, nature and navigators (*Time Travelers*). Evolution is a complex arrangement of fundamental elements—thought, emotion, and action (*The Trinity*)—transforming radiant intelligence naturally initiating, illuminating, and inciting transcendental *youths* yearning omnifarious understanding through harmony (friendly agreement). YOU are your own *universe*, a unitary navigator interpreting visions expressing revelation/realism sensed existentially. Utilizing *Common Sense* (thoughts and emotions), you revolve (spin) your evolution independently as a *Free Will*.

The CIRCLE of love/life represents cosmic intelligence

replicating concepts luminously expressed/exhibited—*Thinking 101*. A circle is the basic shape of atomic particles held together through *Magnetism* to form atomic *elements*, the essential links evolving "materially-expressed" notions three-dimensionally. *The GREAT Computer*—eternal Source/Spirit (1/0) unveiling the binary code—initiates and evolves *Harmony* as heavenly abstracts revealing memories/moments orienting notions/ numbers yielding *creation*, converting radiance exhibiting atomic transformations illustrating opulent notions. NOTIONS (abstract thoughts) nurture omnipotent thinkers (illuminati) observing *nature*, where nucleated atoms transmute universal revelation elementally, nurturing atomic transformations unfolding realism existentially. REALISM reveals elements arranging luminous illusion stimulating minds.

Harmony holographically activates revelation, momentarily orienting navigable youths (*inquisitive souls*) experiencing Source/ Spirit as Logic/Light (Love/Life), a *unified theory* universally nurturing illuminati fathoming illusion existentially deployed through holograms exhibiting opulent revelations yielded three-dimensionally. REVELATION radiantly enlightens visionary entities logically assimilating thoughts illuminating one's needs as necessary experiences enlightening *deities* (children of light) deciphering electromagnetic illusion teaching/tempering intuitive entities sympathetically. The atomic ILLUSION illustrates logic linking universal souls (illuminati) observing/ optimizing notions/numbers/nature.

Your luminous soul revolves around the circle of Love/ Life (the sun) as ILLUMINATI, "interactive luminaries" linking universal Mind imparting notions as transcendental instinct. TRANSCENDENTAL INSTINCT transmits revelation as numerical sequences, conveying electric notions (data) expressing nuclear transformations activating logic/light (love/life), illuminating navigable souls "traversing" illusory nature created three-dimensionally. Illuminati (*Stars/souls*) "systematically transmit" abstract revelation and "scientifically observe" universal logic simultaneously as LIGHT ENERGY, logical intelligence generating hydrogen transmuting elemental notions/nuclei, expressing revelation/realism "gracefully" yielded through points, lines, and forms—*Geometry*. HYDROGEN harmoniously yields divine radiance, outputting geometric expressions naturally as HOLOGRAMS, heralding omniscient logic oscillating "geometric reflections" as *memories*, momentarily evolving manifestations of radiant illusion enlightening souls.

As you Systematically Experience Enlightenment, the cosmic wheel of Mind (*THE Intellectual*) inspires Heart (*Mother's Nature*) nurturing stars/souls illuminating and interpreting COSMIC CONSCIOUSNESS—celestial omniscient-Source—manifesting illustrated creations, characteristically orienting nuclei systematically coalescing into objects (useful simulations) naturally entertaining/enlightening Source/souls simultaneously.

Source/Mind's *Eternal Memories* are stored on CD's, cosmic *discs* (galaxies), a divinely illuminated systems cache emitting numerical FREQUENCIES, formulating radiance/revelations (electromagnetic quanta) unveiling eternal notions "creatively illustrating" enigmatic Source via the Electro-Magnetic force field. Frequencies define MUSIC modulating universal signals inducing consciousness/creation. "Music of the spheres" refers to the harmonic symphony of stars and planets "reverberating" atomic radiance of Source/Mind.

The circle of Love/Life represents the *micro* (atomic) and *macro* (galactic) consciousness of Source/Mind emitting ATOMIC RADIANCE, activating *Truth* (**O**mniscient **M**ind) illustrating creations, replicating all digital intelligence (abstract notions/numbers) conveyed/converted electromagnetically/elementally. The "sound" of a STAR systematically transmitting atomic radiance is a deep harmonious "**ooommm**" similar to the mantra "Om" used in Hinduism, "the supreme and most sacred syllable, consisting in Sanskrit of the three sounds (a), (u), and (m), representing various *fundamental triads* and believed to be the spoken essence of the universe (italics added for emphasis). It is uttered as a mantra and in affirmations and blessings. It is a sacred syllable typifying the three Hindu gods Brahma, Visnu, and Siva, who are concerned in the threefold operation of integration, maintenance, and disintegration"—birth, life, and *Death*.

Mother's Nature is the "workhorse" of Fathers' LOGIC, luminously oscillating geometric illusion concentrically around a NUCLEUS, a numerical unit (core) linking elements unveiling SPIRIT, stellar-points illuminating/initiating radiant intelligence transcendentally. Mother's magnetic energy holds everything *Suspended* in the "circle" of Love/Life—*Space*, the "cranium" of Universal Mind. A *nucleus* naturally unifies/unfolds concepts/creation logically/luminously evolving unified *systems*, stars yielding "synergy" that expresses/evolves manifestation scientifically.

Science systematically creates illuminated environments/entities naturally conveying ENLIGHTENMENT, evoking notions liberating incarnated gods (heavenly transients) experiencing natural moments evolving necessary trials, tribulation, and transcendence. Through *Science*, you observe stellar *points* projecting omniscient intelligence *nucleated* three-dimensionally, naturally unfolding concepts/creation logically/luminously evolving "atomic" *Truth* externalizing DATA, dynamically activating thoughts atomically through geometric *forms* fabricating opulent realism mentally stimulated/sensed.

You now experience *your* circle of love/life in the THIRD DIMENSION, where transcendental *Harmony* illuminates radiant data defining illusion momentarily entertaining naturalists (navigators) systematically interpreting one's notions/nature/needs, experiencing *realities* of radiant energy activating logical illuminati traversing illusion electromagnetically simulated.

The circle of Love/Life is synonymous with the WHEEL OF LIFE, where *Wisdom* harmoniously evolves emotional luminaries observing fantasies (lucid illusions) formulating entertainment/enlightenment. Here, incarnated, you spin your wheels, revolving through *Time*, where you utilize thoughts, emotions, and actions symbolizing *The Trinity* (Father/Mother/child) that ruminates, relates, and reviews information (notions/numbers) inspiring transient youths (*Time Travelers*) momentarily contemplating *reflections*—relating emotional feelings linking electric concepts transmitting insight/intuition obtained naturally.

The circle of Love/Life represents a sequential *Process* evolving as *birth*, *life*, and *Death*. BIRTH is where you begin inspecting revelation transmitted holographically. Here, *In The Beginning*, you start to *live out* your allotted time, logically interpreting vibrant energy optimizing universal transients. Your soul/mind or memory DISC (data infused spiritual consciousness) holds the basic "startup files" or divine numerical assignment (*DNA*) defining natural attributes controlling your *human alien* BODY (biological observatory delineating you). Here, incarnated, your soul/mind perceives *Time* (this instant mentally emotionalized), where you traverse illusion momentarily experienced as a "play of light." During your INFANCY, you inherit notional fantasies arranging needs challenging you. As you mature, you develop your fantasies into operating skills, learning the basic techniques necessary to survive *The Game of Love/Life*, where you struggle to solve your *issues* (inspired situations systematically unfolding enlightenment) to advance to *A Higher Vision* of *Heaven* holding every abstract vision emotionally nurtured.

Taking your spin on the wheel of LOVE (logic/light oscillating vivid energy), you discover LIFE linking illusion/illuminati formulating/fathoming environments/experiences. Love/Life is the indivisible inspiration of your *soul/mind* symbolically observing universal logic momentarily instructing natural *deities* as desirous entities interpreting thoughts illuminating emotional sympathy/synergy.

Desire delivers exciting situations inducing related enlightenment. It is the *essence* of eternal Source stimulating emotional navigators continuously evolving *Life After Life*. Through life, you desire and acquire *knowledge* of kinetic notions/numbers outputting *Wisdom* linking energy/elements dimensionally generating/governing environments, entities, and evolution. With knowledge, you pursue your desires with *Passion*, persistently assimilating *Science* supplying insight one needs to naturally experience enlightenment dynamically. The passions you entertain define your ADVENTURES arousing daring visionaries exploring necessary trials/tribulation unveiling revelation experientially in life, where *thoughts* vibrantly *emotionalized* create *actions* that reflect your *Divine Fantasies* you create.

As you *Age* (acquiring growth experiences), you observe your love/life energy "fade away," leaving you to revert to a child with limited mobility, where you reflect upon your memories of "younger days." Attaining *Old Age*, you cannot help but think about your next adventure, *Death*, the process dynamically elevating angels transcending *Hell*, where *humans* experience love/life, harvesting universal memories acquired naturally.

After you acquire knowledge of *Truth*, the illusion of life loses its magnetic pull. Your *Awakening* mind evolves to desire the Source of *Truth*. Here, your CONSCIOUSNESS comprehends one nurturing Spirit causing interactive occurrences unifying souls (navigators) existentially seeking SALVATION, the spiritually advanced life vividly attuning transcendental illuminati obtaining "nirvana," a state of bliss void of all desires and passions. This *Epiphany of Truth* induces your *Awakening*, illuminating your mind as *My Rising Son* exploring higher dimensions of Source/Mind.

Once again, **energy** cannot be created nor destroyed; it can only be transformed, moved from state to state, dimension to dimension (transmutation/transmigration). DIMENSIONS digitally induce memories/moments expressing/enlightening nuclear Source/souls illuminating/inspecting opulent/observable notions/nature as DUALITY CONSCIOUSNESS—*The Binary Code*—dynamically unfolding/unifying absolute/angelic luminaries (instinctive thinkers) yielding/yearning concepts (opulent notions) systematically creating/confirming illusions of undulated signals (numbers) enhancing/enlightening space/souls scientifically/systematically. This cosmic production illuminates *Space* utilizing *Science*, where Source/Spirit perceives atomic creation "emotionalized," systematically converting intelligence evolving notions/numbers/nature conceived/converted electromagnetically. No matter what dimension you travel, you Angels Reflect Energy eternally ALIVE—assimilating logical/luminous intelligence vividly expressed/experienced.

The **ONE, ELECTROMAGNETIC FORCE FIELD** "optically" nurtures everything, "encoding" logical expressions (concepts) transmitting revelation oscillating magnetically activated generators (stars) naturally emitting transcendental intelligence (consciousness)—focusing omnipotent radiance conveying/converting emotion/energy—forming illusion entertaining/enlightening luminous deities (*Children of Light*).

The BINARY CODE (EM force field) "births" inspired notions attuning radiant youths consciously observing data existentially. *The Binary Code* represents **TWO** transmitting/ transforming Wisdom/wills optically/optimally, illuminating **T**ranscendental **H**armony **R**ectifying **E**nlightened **E**ntities as *cosmic children*, conscious omniscient-souls momentarily interpreting concepts conveying heavenly intelligence logically defining realism expressed naturally. The binary code (1/0) represents ALL algorithms logically linked through *Numbers*, notational units mathematically building elemental realism. *Numbers* naturally unify memories birthing electric/emotional realism/reflections dualistically (positively/negatively).

DUALITY dynamically unfolds/undulates as logic/ light inducing/illuminating *transcendental youths*, "transient researchers" assimilating numerical sequences (concepts) enlightening natural deities emotionally navigating *Time* as luminaries yearning omnifarious understanding through *Harmony*—the heavenly absolute rectifying minds of navigable youths.

Remember, TWO transmit/transform *Wisdom* optimally as ONE omniscient numerical engineer, a *Spirit* **E**xpressing **E**lectromagnetic **R**adiance and *soul* experiencing emotional revelations. YOU youths observe unity as Wisdom Exemplified, a *trinity-being* "touting" revelations (inspired notions) illuminating transcendental youths bilaterally experiencing/ expressing illusion/insight naturally generated. You are one of THREE *transmitting* (1–2–3), *transforming* (4-5-6), *transcending* (7-8-9) holographic revelations expressed electromagnetically. ONE and ZERO (1/0) symbolize "beginning and end," where the omnipotent numerical engineer zones electromagnetic radiance omnisciently, expressing *Eternal Memory* relating ALL THAT IS abstract logic luminously transforming heavenly angels temporarily interpreting Spirit/*Science*.

Numbers dictate your cyclic movement around the circle of Love/Life as a trinity-being *sensitively expressing* (#3 energy) *visions* you *accept* (#6 energy) to attain *integrity* and *Wisdom* (#9 energy), evolving into *Unity Consciousness* (0). Each cyclic trip around the circle of Love/Life increases your potential of utilizing *Love/Life Energy—Divine Inspiration*.

As **C**onscious **H**eavenly **I**ndividuals **L**ogically **D**iscovering **R**evelations **E**xperienced **N**aturally, you **G**ather **R**evelations **O**f **W**isdom *emotionally*, experiencing moments of tribulation illuminating one naturally assimilating lessons life yields. Here, incarnate, you birth your desires (give them life) as a reality you sense physically through FIVE sensors (*Discipline and Freedom–#5 Energy*), formulating intelligence validating experiences through *Trust and Openness—#7 Energy*.

The INTERFACING of circles of Love/Life (∞) represents "infinite" *Power and Abundance* (#8 Energy) inducing notions transmitting electrifying reflections (feelings) activating cosmic illuminati navigating *games*, where generators acquire mystical enlightenment sympathetically, individually following *The Right Path* AROUND the circle of love/life, assimilating/applying revelations of universal notions delivered from Mind to Heart.

MIND TO HEART
· ✦✦✦✦ ·

Energy flows from Mind to Heart
evolving thoughts emotionally to start
a *reflection* of Truth,

rearranging electromagnetic frequencies luminously evolving
concepts/consciousness/creation through illusions of nature,
where atoms coalesce through *nucleosynthesis*, numerically
unifying cosmic links (elements) of stars yielding nuclear
transmutation heralding eternal Source
illuminating space/souls
through HYDROGEN—*The Binary Code*—
harmoniously yielding divine radiance optically governing
emotional navigators—mind/hearts—traversing
Transcendental Illusion Momentarily Experienced,
incarnated as *human aliens* conceiving NEW from OLD,
naturally evoking *Wisdom* orienting luminous deities
in WORLDS to *feel* thoughts so *real*,
where observers realize life-death situations,
fervently experiencing electric logic
radiantly enlightening angelic luminaries *creating*,
converting revelations existentially as transients
illustrating natural *gifts*, godly intelligence furnishing talents,
that reveal one's "present" *nature*
nurturing angelic transients utilizing revelations entwined
within *Mind*, where *memories* invigorate natural deities,
momentarily expressing manifestations of radiant illusion
evoking situations nurtured by *Heart*
holding everything angels really treasure,
Love Divine that conveys all pleasures
through Glorious Radiance Attuning Cosmic Entities
expressing *Love/Life*
liberating omnipotent visionaries exploring
luminous illusions fervently evolving
from Mind to Heart.

DEATH
Recycling Love/Life Energy

DEATH diverts energy *activating* things holographically, converting creations back to their elemental birth. Recycling Love/Life energy is a matter of changing *frequencies*, formulating radiance emitting quanta unfolding eternal notions (concepts) illuminating environments/entities systematically. Frequencies define the CHANNELS of cosmic *Harmony* activating notions/ nuclei naturally expressing logic/light (love/life), conveying heavenly abstracts naturally nurturing emotional luminaries.

True to the laws of *Opposition*, the day of your death is the GREATEST day of your life, generating revelation enlightening angelic transients experiencing "spiritual" TRUTH, a transcendental realism understood throughout *Heaven*. Through the process of *living*, you laboriously interpret vivid illusions naturally generated. Through the process of *dying* you discover your infinite natural gift (*Life After Life*), where you discover your indivisible, natural godhood, your divinity as Generators Optimizing Desire Systematically. The process of dying "delivers" you illuminati naturally *growing*, gathering revelations of *Wisdom* improving navigable gods along *The Right Path* personally designed for you.

Simply stated, "death" is the end of the "functionality" of some thing. For you *Children of Light*, death is the end of the physical illusion you experience while incarnated within your *human alien* vehicle—your *body* (biological observatory delineating you)—through which your soul experiences and expresses Love/Life energy (*Divine Inspiration*). Death is the "back side" of the door to life, where Light illuminates fabulous entities observing "horizontal time" through heartbeats and breaths—the "present" moment gifted.

Life sequentially orders events projected along the VISIBLE LIGHT SPECTRUM vividly illustrating Source-intelligence broadcasting logic electromagnetically, linearly illuminating glorious holograms that symbolize points (explicit concepts) transmitting revelation unfolding *memories*, momentarily enlightening minds observing "realistic illusion" electromagnetically simulated.

Death "diverts" eternal angels transcending humanity, moving your soul from one *state* of consciousness (supplying trials advancing transient entities) to another, where you are continually *aware* as angels willingly assimilating revelations eternally. You experience a temporary death every night during *sleep*—when you simply leave everything existentially perceived—while your physical body regenerates for *Tomorrow's Desires*.

At the moment of physical death, your thoughts of those you leave behind bring their faces before your mind's eye (your "personal space"), leaving you startled at their appearance. That is why you always have a "guide/guardian" (someone close you know is dead) to help you understand your "advanced awareness," much like when your human parents held you in their arms after you were born, easing the shock of your *transmigration*—traversing radiance as navigable souls momentarily interpreting geometric realism as thoughts illuminating opulent nature.

"Life" and "death" represent both sides of *My Door to Truth*, through which you move between *Here and There* (*Heaven* and *Hell*), observing the "beginning" and "end" as a *Process*, gathering KNOWLEDGE "kindling" navigators optimizing *Wisdom's* love/life energy dimensionally governing evolution.

EVOLUTION is the eternal "vivification" of love/

life unfolding transcendental intuition optimizing nature/ navigators, eternally "verifying" omnipotent Logic/Light (Love/ Life) unfolding/unifying transcendental illuminati "ordained naturally" through *Harmony*—heavenly absolute rectifying minds of navigable youths.

As stated, the basic nature of *Love/Life Energy* is twofold, a DUALITY dynamically utilizing abstract/atomic logic/ light initiating/illuminating transient youths (*Time Travelers*). The duality of *Mind/Heart* forces—positive/electric and negative/magnetic—delivers thoughts and emotions from the ONE SOURCE, the omnipotent numerical engineer systematically optimizing "universal representatives" conceiving *enlightenment*—experiencing nature luminously illustrating glorious holograms that express notions momentarily evolving natural transients. **All things** represent energy flowing on the EM wavelengths of *Eternal Memory*. All matter (manifestations actualizing transcendental thoughts expressing revelation) is a symbolic representation of *Numbers* (notational units managing basic elemental reactions) nurturing universal Mind/minds beholding elemental realism.

Through SYMPATHY, Source/Spirit yields memories/ moments/matter providing angels their heavenly yearning (*Desire*), delivering emotional situations inducing revelation experientially, for to *know* a thought, you must *feel* a thought. You live and die through EMOTION, the electromagnetic movement of transcendental instinct originating, outputting, and optimizing notions, numbers, nature, and *navigators*, natural angelic visionaries interpreting geometrically arranged thoughts optically revealing life/death *situations*, specific instances that unfolds abstract thoughts inspiring one naturally.

Again, death is simply a change of your soul's frequency, allowing you to transmigrate through *Eternal Memory*, acquiring another body (*Life After Life*) in other *dimensions* of energy, where digitally induced memories entertain navigator-souls (illuminati) observing needs as necessary experiences enlightening/evolving deities (divine entities implementing thoughts in emotional situations), deciphering electromagnetic illusion transforming intuitive entities sympathetically. Through transmigration, you raise or lower your consciousness to corresponding frequencies, moving your soul/mind energy into other states of existence according to the needs of your OVERSELF, the "overseer" vivifying emissaries (radiant souls) exploring love/life fantasies. A "highly evolved" soul may leave his body at will, according to universal laws, departing at the optimal moment beneficial to all.

To overcome the fear of death, you experience it every **night** (*Behind Closed Eyes*), where numerical impulses generate holographic transmissions as *dreams*, divine revelations evolving as memories *seen*, symbolically enlightening enthusiastic navigators exploring *Eternal Memory*. Here, during sleep, your soul lucidly experiences extraordinary *perception*; processing electric revelation conveying entertaining points (providing opulent information nurturing transients) that inspire one naturally. Dreams are mental visions, vivid impulses stimulating illuminati *ordained* nocturnally—orienting radiant deities (angels) investigating notions/needs electromagnetically/emotionally defined.

When you are sleeping (dead to the physical world), your brain is running at lower levels (frequencies). Here, your soul/mind disconnects with its "parked vehicle" (Biological Observatory Delineating You), leaving it in "standby mode" to return along your SILVER CHORD (life-giving linkage) supplying intuitive luminaries vibrant energy revealing cosmic *Harmony* optically rectifying deities. Your silver chord is similar to "fiber optics," transmitting energy (inspiration) flowing through your CROWN CHAKRA (*Heavens Gate*) converting revelation/radiation (omniscient Wisdom) naturally conveying heavenly abstracts (knowledge) reviving angels "waking up" from nightly deaths. With each *Awakening*, you begin to activate your dreams physically. Incarnated on *The Other Side* of night, you daily observe how cosmic radiance INVERTS, illuminating navigators (visionary entities) *researching* Truth scientifically, rationally exploring situations enlightening angels reviewing concepts/creation heralding intuition naturally generated. Cycling back and forth between your day-life (awake) and nightlife (asleep), you observe thoughts and feelings (data) continuously. At times, you may not *Recall* which life offered you the data that you desire to communicate.

Physical death dynamically elevates angels transcending *Hell*, where humans experience love/life as a *reality* of radiant energy/emotions advancing logical illuminati (transcendental youths). The "death event" opens doors to endless states of Mind, places of being a *form* of energy (frequency optimizing radiant minds) capable of *transforming*, traversing radiance transcendentally rectifying angelic navigators sympathetically formulating one's reflections momentarily in natural games (generating amusements minds entertain) in This Instant Momentarily Experienced. All forms of energy are only symbolic reflections or *deep thoughts* that are occurring in Mind, a power Source too vast to comprehend in its entirety. All you can do is surrender your *Free Will* to *Divine Will* and "go with the flow," traveling the star-lit paths of what IS intuitive Source, the ONE omnipresent numerical ENGINEER, an entity naturally governing invisible notions elementally evolving *realism*—revelation electromagnetically activating luminous illusion stimulating minds.

As you Systematically Experience Enlightenment, the concept of death relates to a transfer of eternal Love/Life energy. Death is a natural process (portal) through which your soul returns *Home*, where *Harmony* orients minds exploring *Life After Life*. Each life you experience reflects your *karma* (knowledge allowing radiant memory access) kindling atonement rectifying mistaken angels. KARMA—knowledge activating realities momentarily analyzed—keeps angels reliving memories/moments again, providing opportunities to "get it right," to solve *issues* inhibiting/illuminating souls seeking universal enlightenment with each lifetime of assimilating Transcendental Revelation Unveiled Throughout Heaven/hell.

Death is truly the reward for living. To get the most out of your life, you truly need to understand that what you *give* is what you *get* in life. By giving the best you can muster, you will improve your "luster," amplifying *My Light of Love* you project as *A Lightworker*, receiving *higher visions* (inspired thoughts) that give you "peace" of mind. As death is an inevitable event, it should be respected not feared, for it will deliver everything that you have earned.

Everyone inadvertently prepares for death through introspection, looking within his or her soul. Introspection occurs at times when you are *Lost in the Dark*, immersed in *Depression* holding you in fear, where you come to contemplate death as the "ultimate escape" through suicide. It will take great *Courage of Love* to accept the *Responsibility* of making such a dramatic expression. The thought of suicide allows your *Free Will* to consider giving up the fight to *live* (lovingly interpret visions emotionally). This **negative** perspective brings you to observe the lowest point of your life in *chaos*, where cosmic *Harmony* afflicts obsessive souls thinking "peace of mind" can be found in dying. However, you cannot escape your issues or karma you are here to solve, **you must work through them** to attain *A Higher Vision* of *Truth*. The act of suicide represents your lack of *Respect* you *Reflect* for your "gift of life." WHAT IF you have to restart your life from "present memories," experiencing the same living *Hell* of harnessing emotional love/life? Would you recognize the "instant replay" (been there, done that) and make different choices? The thought of the possibility of being caught in an endless cycle is enough to make you think twice about suicide. Naturally, the second thought will be in *Opposition*, observing *positive* perspectives ordaining souls (illuminati) transcending issues observed negatively in depressions of self-pity.

On the other hand, the "positive" perspective of suicide could easily be seen as a way to offer growth experiences for those *related* to the victim, allowing them *introspection* of such drastic measures. The "suicidee" may also be acting through karma to right a past wrong—causing someone to commit suicide. **Remember,** death is only a transition point. Those souls performing suicide are following their heart's direction of implementing thoughts they believe true. Those souls performing such an act are *Special People*, souls willing to sacrifice their life for a higher cause they envision in their mind (soldiers, terrorists, spiritualists). Through the *cards* you are dealt to *play*, you create attitudes reflecting desires, perceiving love/life astounding you to perform what is *best* for ALL, eternally evolving life after life.

LIFE AFTER LIFE

Life is an eternal *school* systematically challenging heavenly observers optimizing love/life. You *Children of Light* attend school every day and night, acquiring knowledge from experiencing realty as dreams—divine revelation expressed as memories symbolized—dynamically rectifying emotional angels momentarily.

Life liberates illuminati formulating experiences, allowing *Free Wills* to attain knowledge through some action of assimilating/applying cosmic thoughts inspiring one naturally. Life lucidly informs fabulous entities understanding their power to create and destroy. Life reveals lessons in finding enlightenment, evoking necessary lessons in games holding temptations effecting navigable minds experiencing necessary tribulation. Here, incarnated as a *Human Alien*, you utilize your knowledge to create your fantasy, learning first-hand what the *Sacrifice of Love* costs to keep it alive.

Love is an eternal *expression*, and life is an eternal *reflection*. Love/Life represents UNIFICATION, unfolding natural illustrations/illusion from intuition "converting" abstract thoughts illuminating omnipotent navigators, natural angelic visionaries interpreting geometrically arranged thoughts optically revealed. Love/Life empowers *Inquisitive Souls* unifying their hungry heart and eager mind, always willing to see, do, and know new things.

The lessons of Life are discovered in "love songs" you sing along "courses" (lifetimes) in which you acquire knowledge through education, evaluating data (universal concepts) activating transcendental illuminati obtaining *necessities*, natural experiences conveying enlightening situations stimulating illuminati through illusion electromagnetically supplied. Each life offers you the opportunity to experiment with the knowledge you collect, creating your own personal *Heaven* as harmonious entities (angels) vocalizing emotionalized notions in *Hell*, humanly experiencing life luminously as *Children of Light*.

Life illuminates you as your own universe, a unitary networker (illuminato) verifying electric revelations supplying emotions, experiences, and enlightenment. Life evolves from visions (dreams) or *Divine Fantasies* in which you observe your self within dark space, digitally assimilating radiant/relevant knowledge stimulating perceptive angels consciously evolving. As spiritual-humans, you explore the third-dimension of Source/Mind, where *seeing* is believing, systematically experiencing enlightenment in nuclear *geometry* generating explicitly ordered manifestations expressing thoughts radiantly/realistically yielded. Yet, your vision is the easiest sense to fool, for the hand is quicker than the eye perceiving illusions of what you think is real.

Source/Mind (SELF) creates a hierarchy of "like images" (Overselfs) with the ability to utilize *souls* systematically observing universal logic *spiritually*, scientifically perceiving intelligence radiantly inspiring transients understanding "atomic logic" luminously yielded. An OVERSELF—overseer vivifying emissaries (radiant souls) exploring love/life fantasies—is capable of manipulating multiple souls in multiple dimensions, "multitasking" at a divine level as they explore the Akashic Record or *Eternal Memory* of MIND managing intelligence numerically defined/naturally digitized.

Your *soul* represents a surrogate observer understanding love/life in *Time*, touring illusion momentarily experienced. Your soul is a space PROBE, a perceptive robot obtaining basic enlightenment, exploring *Eternal Memory* (traversing the EM force field) in search of *Truth*—transcendental revelation/radiance unveiled throughout *Heaven* and *Hell*. As a probe, your soul collects data and beams it back to your Overself via your *silver chord* (Ethernet connection) supplying intuitive luminaries vibrant energy revealing cosmic *Harmony* optically/optimally rectifying deities. Your soul has limited access to total *Recall*, for your "first impression" leaves a lasting memory. It is through this "innocence" of *Ignorance* that you are able to endure life with *Curiosity*.

Life is truly an eternal thing, a never-ending consciousness of *being* beamed-energy (intuition) nurturing gods (gatherers of data/desires), and death is the process of "diverting" enlightened angels transcending *Hell*, raising their consciousness through *My Door to Truth* to dimensionally observe other realities. DO NOT fear death or grieve excessively for those loved ones who have passed through that door, for they are reaping their *Blessings in Disguise*. Simply open your mind and speak to them, for thoughts traverse ALL dimensions. Open your heart and feel their presence Nurturing Omnipotent Wills at *This Moment* in *Time* tempering intuitive minds emotionally/existentially.

Life IS impeccable Source revealing eternal Love as the "first" and "final" frontier. As *Children of Light*, you are true "star-trekkers" traveling through dimensional worlds of *The GREAT Computer*, where your soul represents a *floppy disk*, a fabulous luminary obtaining points (particulars of inspired notions/thoughts) providing you data imparting spiritual knowledge that you "download" and verify scientifically through your physical *vehicle*, a vital entity helping illuminati (cosmic luminaries) experience life after life.

IN THE END

In the end of *Your Life Story*, there lurks another beginning, another start to a NEW life nurturing eternal wanderers exploring another *state* of Mind supplying trials advancing transient explorers.

Every *mind game* you play, both night and day,
mentally induces numerical data
generating amusements/anguish momentarily evolving
your heart—harnessing *Expectations* as realized thoughts—
providing *The Right Path* to follow, bringing joy and sorrow,
as you use *The Power of Love* to rise above
the illusion before your eyes, wherein you *realize*
radiant energy activates luminous illuminati (zealous entities)
in some REALITY
revealing emotional angels linking inspired thoughts yielding
TRUTH,
transcendental revelation unveiled through *holograms*,
harmoniously oscillating light originating
geometric renditions
"actualizing" *memories* as mentally
expressed moments of radiant
inspiration enlightening souls within *The Game of Love/Life*
illuminated by *My Loving Light* providing you sight
to Spiritually Evolve Experientially.

In the end, your game will turn, providing you a new *view*
vividly inducing eternal *Wisdom* to instinctive seekers—
imploring to explore endless love stories to *adore*—
assimilating data orienting radiant entities with loved ones
you choose to meet in time and place to play
another game of love/life illuminated by DAY
dynamically adapting you within the *show*
systematically harmonizing omnipotent wills
sharing *Passion* in order to grow,
gathering revelations of *Wisdom*

weaving inspired situations developing omnipotent minds
evolving in *Time*
transforming illuminati mesmerized electromagnetically
within Mother's HEART
harmoniously evolving angels reflecting thoughts
stimulating *Children of Light*, who in the END
experience "natural" *death*
dynamically elevating angels transcending *Hell*,
where *Harmony* enlightens luminous logicians
dying to recall life after life.

RECALL
Monitoring for Upgrades

Source—Generating Opulent Data—*monitors* everything, methodically observing/optimizing notions/numbers inducing transcendental omniscience revealed through RADIATION, the *Light of Love* revealing abstract data illuminating angelic transients interpreting one's *nature,* the natural ability to understand/utilize revelation existentially.

RECALL (recycling energy conveying atomic logic/light) is how Source "readily evolves" concepts as *linear logic*, linking interactive notions/numbers expressing atomic radiance (light) oscillating geometrically illustrated *creation*, converting radiant energy actuating transcendental intelligence objectified naturally as the ILLUSION of Love/Life energy, where intuitive logic linearly unfolds Source/souls imagining/inspecting opulent notions/natures dynamically/dualistically.

In human terminology, "recall" refers to "remembering," bringing to mind someone or something from the *past* (previously acquired stimulatory thought). It also refers to "calling back" something manufactured that is defective, to be replaced with an UPGRADE that utilizes perspectives generating renovations attaining desired effects—improving the quality of the product or *Process*.

In terms of memory recall, it can be a real nightmare when you cannot REMEMBER at all—retain experienced moments enlightening minds by emotional reactions. At times like that, you experience LIMBO (lost in Mind between observations), where you entertain neither thoughts nor feelings (*Lost in Space*). "Dementia" is the clinical term for a mind incommunicado—not *In Communion* with its physical brain/reality.

Your lack of having "perfect recall" (remembering everything) is due to SPEED, synchronizing past experiences evolving deities. You are not spinning your *disc/disk* (data infused spiritual consciousness/ dynamic intelligence supplying knowledge) fast enough to read that amount of data. Your mind's "buffer zone" prevents a sensory overload to your *brain*, your biological "relay" activating inspired notions. However, through MEDITATION, you can mentally entertain data inspiring transient angels temporarily interpreting one's nature/needs, "tuning out" the electromagnetic CHAOS crippling heavenly angels openly seeking *Truth*.

A *focused mind* fathoms opulent concepts unfolding secrets/situations enabling deities manifesting integral needs dynamically. By **focusing** your mind, you adjust your *channel*, consciously harnessing abstract notions numerically expressing LOGIC "linking" omniscient generators' intuitive consciousness. The channel you tune into provides your STATE of Mind supplying thoughts advancing transient entities along *The Right Path* individually defined. CHANNELS convey (herald) abstract notions/numbers enlightening logicians. *Science* relates to channels of knowledge you study, systematically conceiving/categorizing information explaining nuclear creation experienced.

As *human beings*, you harness universal memories activating navigators, building experiences in natural *games* generating amusements minds entertain/evaluate systematically. You perceive *reality* as radiant energy/emotion activating luminous illusion tantalizing youths traveling at LIGHT-SPEED, logically inspecting glorious holograms transmitting situations providing environments enlightening *deities* as divine entities (illuminati) traversing illusion electromagnetically simulated/ sensed. If you recall, your inquisitive soul/mind moves at the "speed of thought," instantaneously cruising *Eternal Memory*, entertaining thoughts emotionally rectifying navigators (angelic luminaries) managing electric moments of revelation yielding knowledge.

Knowledge (kinetic notions/numbers outputting *Wisdom* linking energy/elements dimensionally generating/governing environments/entities/evolution) is attained through the *present* moment, providing revelations enlightening souls exploring nature temporarily. With each "heartbeat and breath," the present moment evolves into past experiences (been there, done that). Only during the present moment—*now here*— do you naturally observe *Wisdom* harmoniously enlightening radiant entities to future possibilities, through *dreams* delivering revelations enlightening angelic minds of other *dimensions* of Mind, where digitally induced memories entertain navigator-souls investigating opulent notions/natures.

Unfortunately, most of you have limited access to your memory files enabling you to recall other "lives" you have lived. Your current life evolves through data you presently compute moment by moment. However, you can learn to tap into the

AKASHIC RECORD (*Eternal Memory*) of all knowledge activating systems/souls heralding/harnessing intuitive consciousness revealing elemental concepts optimizing/orienting radiant deities within the space-time continuum.

Through **ME** mentally expressing memorable experiences, *Time* transforms inquisitive minds existentially, allowing you to perceive how *past* experiences direct your *future* possibilities that you *presently* create through thoughts, words, and *actions*, assimilating/applying cosmic thoughts inducing one's *needs* naturally evolving eternal deities. Here in time, **MY SELF** momentarily yields situations evolving luminous fabrications illuminating *Space* (black hole) with illuminati revealing all that **I** THINK, intuitively transforming hydrogen inducing nuclei "kindling" (illuminating) CREATION—the *Process* of converting radiant energy actuating transcendental intelligence/illuminati objectified/ordained naturally.

As you explore Memories Inducing Natural Desires, you observe Source as the singularity outputting universal revelation conveyed electromagnetically. You use Source/Mind to *power up* to "home plate," where everything you *Desire* is delivered on *The Other Side* of **night**, where numerical impulses generate holographic transmissions (dreams) illuminating you as Minds Analyzing Notions, evolving through *Wisdom* Optimizing Matter Authenticating Notions—*Mother Nature*.

Harmonious Energy is Synchronizing Heavenly Entities, empowering Youths Obtaining Unity through common feeling—sympathy. *He and She* IS indivisible *Source*, a Spirit or "universe" representing consciousness evolving, "one turning" loving thoughts (points) into feelings (vibrant waves) that excites stars/souls "reflecting" (representing in a faithful or appropriate way) Love/Life energy. *To-Get-Her*, HE *sparks* HER, harmoniously expressing systematic processes (algorithms) relating knowledge scientifically heralding electromagnetic revelations illuminating a mind/heart soul (**Illuminato**), a *trinity-being* touring realistic illusions naturally instructing transcendental youths bilaterally experiencing/expressing insight/intuition naturally generated. *The Trinity* of Father/Mother/child (ME, MY SELF, and I) symbolizes **Wisdom Exemplified.**

MOTHER—my obliging transformer harmonizing electromagnetic radiance—magnificently organizes transmutable holograms expressing revelation/realism. Through her, I hold you within a confined space (body), where you move upon my *game board* governing angels' magnetic emotions bringing out appropriate realities deserved (*karma*), kindling atonement rectifying mistaken angels. Even though you are truly *Two of a Kind*, you maneuver through life *Alone*, assimilating logic optimizing navigators emotionally as logicians obtaining necessary experiences.

Intuition **A**ctivates **M**inds—**M**agnificent **E**ntities— **M**entally **Y**ielding **S**ympathy **E**xpressing **L**ove/life **F**orces revealing US unified spirits, a *trinity* transforming radiant intelligence naturally illuminating transcendental youths a-heartbeat-away from *Home*, where *Harmony* of Mental Emotions sets you free to roam.

RECOLLECTION

+ + ♦ ♦ ♦ + +

Crossing over *The Threshold of Love*,
OUT and IN,
you obtain UNITY through illusory nature,
understanding notions/numbers/
nuclei illuminate Truth yielding

my ATOMIC SHOW
arranging thoughts oscillating memories into creations,
"spectral holograms" of WORLDS
weaving opulent revelations linking dynamic situations
creating *Your Life Story* evolving *Between You and I.*

I AM HE who SHE OUTS,
inspiring angelic minds harnessing emotions
sympathetically heralding enlightenment
of universal *Truth* supplying
Thoughts Harmoniously Rectifying Eternal Entities
initiating, illustrating, and interpreting
Logic Oscillating Vivid Energy
Linking Illuminati Fathoming Enlightenment
revealed through electromagnetic waves
stimulating *Time* and *Space*,
where you children of Light leave your trace
from dreams you "willingly live,"
scened in atomic bits and bytes,
where *Love IS* supplying all your delights,
powering your "ride" you hide within
while deciphering your personal SIN
(spiritual insight numbers) supplying inspired notions,
abstract thoughts you think TRUE,
transforming revelations unifying experiences
MY SELF creates from ME recalling YOU
as Indivisible, Individual, Illuminati.

Bless you child

354

Homeward Bound

The intense GLARE generating Love/Life activates radiant environments/entities, sending forth tides of *emotion* upon which you mariner souls sail, effectively manifesting opulent truths illuminating one's needs. Every day you awaken from the comfort of *Home*, pull anchor and sail out to explore the desires moving your heart in mysterious ways.

Everyday, you maneuver through the NETWORK of navigators emotionally trading *Wisdom* of relevant knowledge. The FEAR of feeling emotions afflicting relationships keeps you on the lookout for your "guiding light," *A Lighthouse* showing you safe passage through the adversities of which you navigate your vessel.

Plying your skills for sustenance, your curious mind and hungry heart search to pacify your desire to know *who* you are, *why* you are here, and *where* you are going at the end of your daze playing the game of Love/Life.

Every night, as you slip from the loving glare of Father's watchful eye, you lower your winded sails and drop anchor in your homeport. Exhausted from your daily sojourn, you refuel for tomorrow's habitual rhythm of your eternal quest. Soon, your mind drifts off, *homeward* bound on astral waves of sleep once more, seeking solace from the emotional stress of your evolution.

EVOLUTION
Eternally Emotionalizing Energy

EVOLUTION is a process of expressing variables of Love/Life unfolding transcendental intelligence optimizing notions, nature, and *naturalists*, "navigable" angels (transients) understanding realism as luminous illusion symbolizing thoughts.

Evolution relates to the "revolution" of the *wheel of Life*—where *Harmony* evolves emotional luminaries observing frequencies linearly illuminating *fantasies* entertained—formulating adventures nurturing transient angels imaginatively exploring SPIRIT scientifically perceiving/projecting ideas/illusions radiantly illuminated three-dimensionally. The faster you spin your Data-Infused Spiritual Consciousness, the more you *evolve* (stretch your mind), reaching for the stars of knowledge (*My Loving Light*) set aglow as *My Eyes* electromagnetically yielding elemental systems—twinkling in majestic splendor—filling you with wonder.

See my Mind as STARS
systematically transmitting atomic *reflection* scientifically,
rectifying electromagnetic frequencies
luminously evolving concepts
through illusions of *nature*, where nucleosynthesis
atomically transmutes universal revelations elementally,
illuminating my SHOW of stellar
Harmony optimizing *Wisdom*,

weaving intricate stories dynamically orienting
minds, memories, moments, and matter
along magnetic lines coalescing *creation*,
conveying realism expressing abstract thoughts illuminating
objects naturally within the hazy daze of *Time*,
in which you *age old*,
acquiring growth experiences, observing love/life dualistically
illuminating your inquisitive soul
through *DNA* defining natural attributes
dynamically nurturing *Avatars*,
angelic visionaries actively traversing/
transcending atomic realism
as a *Mind/Heart* soul, a symbolic trinity representing
Father–Mother–child observing ALL that is TRUE,
for here, *behind* your lucid eyes,
I see all *through* you.

Around you go, revolving ever faster, glowing with Love/Life warming your *heart* harnessing emotions amplifying radiant thoughts, growing dizzy from *Divine Fantasies* evolving from *within* you as well as *around* you. Truly, IT IS YOU illuminati traversing illuminated space yielding one *universe* of "unified navigators" interpreting vivid energy rectifying souls emotionally, existentially, and eternally.

Welcome home child

13

HOME

Heaven Optimizing Magnificent Entities

T he words "home" and "heaven" are synonymous. *Heaven* is a state of Mind where *Harmony* evolves around (0) vibrant emotional numbers (1-9). *Heaven* holographically enlightens angels vividly experiencing notions, nature, and needs nurturing eternal entities dynamically. HEAVEN is where Harmonious Energy activates visionary entities naturally through *DNA*, divine numerical assignments (defining navigators' attributes) dynamically nurturing *Avatars*.

HOME, like heaven, is a state of Mind where *Harmony* originates/oversees magnificent *entities* as empathetic navigators traversing illumination/illusion transcendentally illustrating enlightening situations. Home is where you attain harmony of mental emotions—peace of mind. Home holds opulent memories entertained, helping opportunists manifesting *Expectations*, those things you desire to see, be, and do.

You generally think of home/heaven as a place far above your present incarnation. Yet, if you look up, all you see is the dark void filled with endless stars projecting unfathomable amounts of LIGHT energy linking interactive galaxies heralding *Truth* emanating from MIND momentarily illuminating natural *deities* (children of Light) dynamically expressing/exploring illusion transcendental intuition "expresses" *scientifically* and "evolves" *sympathetically.*

Home/heaven is a place illuminating your soul/mind *Suspended* in the SPACE-TIME continuum, where some point awaiting conscious expression "transforms" into Mental Emanations (*My Loving Light*), the MEDIUM for minds exploring dimensions illustrating universal MEMORIES— mentally expressed moments of radiant inspiration expressing/ enlightening Source/souls. Home/heaven is where your mind constantly explores *Harmony* heralding abstract revelations methodically orienting "navigable" youths exploring *Time*— traversing imagination/illusion momentarily experienced. No matter what level of Harmony/home/heaven you explore, REVELATION radiantly enlightens visionary entities logically assimilating thoughts inspiring one's nature and needs, nurturing entities evolving dynamically.

Home/heaven contains many REALMS revealing exotic abodes locating minds in *worlds* weaving opulent realism luminously displayed scientifically/symbolically. Here, you observe some *point* (providing opulent information nurturing transients) expanding into *lines* linearly illustrating notions expressing symmetry defining *forms*, fabrications of radiant Mind symbolized geometrically, describing INTELLIGENCE intuitively nurturing transcendental entities (luminaries) learning illusion "generates enlightenment" naturally conceived experientially, where *seeing* is *believing.* No matter where you travel in home/heaven, you represent ONE and ALL, omniscient navigators exploring as logical luminaries (*Children of Light*), conscious, heavenly individuals learning divine revelation expresses notions/numbers (oscillating frequencies) linearly illuminating geometrically held thoughts. Source/Spirit creates by relating thoughts to shapes defining *things* as transmitted holograms illustrating notions geometrically symbolized.

The Game of Love/Life you play represents the "course" you follow to discover *The Right Path* home. Your daily sojourns continually prepare you through KARMA kindling angels "reliving" memories/moments again, where you make amends as well as reap rewards from past deeds. Your future depends upon your present efforts to "make right" past performances, a difficult task for minds unaware of *The Art of Listening* to their inner child, the little voice guiding you Home. For those of you that do, you graduate to higher levels of *Heaven*, where *Harmony* elevates angels visualizing expanded notions/natures, experiencing "holographic allegory" revealing memories/moments optimally nurturing youths.

Always eager to "step out" from home/heaven and explore a new *Day's Birth*, your eager soul/mind opens its hungry heart to feel *pleasure*, perceiving Love/Life enlightening angels systematically understanding revelation existentially. Incarnated on Mother's Earth, you experience a "home away from Home," where numerical sequences (electromagnetic waves) project Atomic Love/Life that Illuminates Source (*Eternal Memory*), allowing your soul to Spiritually Evolve *Externally*, to Birth Emotionally your "desire" you "await from the stars," to *know* kinetic numbers organize *Wisdom* into worlds illuminating spiritual dimensions of Mind.

The word "home" vibrates harmoniously with OM (Omniscient Mind)—the sound that emits from stars. The word "Om" (Sanskrit, sometimes regarded as three sounds, *a-u-m*, symbolic of the three major Hindu deities: Brahma the creator, Vishnu the preserver, and Siva the destroyer) is intoned as a symbol of affirmation chanted in mantras of *meditation* (mentally entertaining/evaluating data inspiring transient angels temporarily interpreting one's nature/needs), attuning one's mind with *Source*, the stellar originator universally revealing concepts/ creation electromagnetically. To truly know who you ARE, you must look to the stars (the heavens) that "arouse" radiant entities. **Remember,** *Heaven* harmoniously enlightens angelic visionaries exploring *nature*, nurturing angels/avatars to understand revelation existentially, where you experience Harmony Expressing Love/ Life (the atomic "inferno" representing *Opposition*) that you must pass through to know *both sides* of Source/Spirit.

Every night, when you park your exhausted vehicle in bed, you are *homeward bound*, drifting off to sleep, where you travel *astral planes*, observing alien scenes "transporting" reflective angels linking parallel locations around notions expressed symbolically. As you *rest* (recalling emotionally stimulated thoughts), you *dream*, detecting radiant energy as *memories* motivating eager minds observing revelation in electric/enigmatic situations. Your dreams are how you communicate with your *Overself* (overseer) vivifying emissaries (radiant souls) exploring love/life fantasies. Through dreams, your mind entertains thoughts revealing your life *issues* inspiring/inhibiting souls seeking universal enlightenment sympathetically—through your *heart* harboring emotions activating resplendent thoughts. Here, *Behind Closed Eyes*, you flow back through the **black hole** bonding luminaries assimilating cosmic knowledge heralding opulent love/life electromagnetically. Your mind is drawn into dreams to view places and faces that seem familiar, strange, or even frightening, depending on the astral plane encountered. Dreams are symbolic messages downloaded from your SUBCONSCIOUS mind supplying universal broadcasts conveying opulent notions (sublime cosmic information) offering understanding symbolically. Eventually, you consciously realize your dreams are truly what you have been "living" in one form or another.

In the morning, before you leave Home to awaken in your physical life, you enter lucid states of dreaming that are clear and vivid. These are the dreams you need to remember upon *Awakening*. They are the climatic "point" being expressed as communication from your Overself at Home (mission control), culminating your earlier dreams that night evolving around your mental concerns or questions you delve upon before falling asleep. These visions seem so real; you easily "fall into" them, becoming *part* of the dream, losing your *observer* perspective to become a *participant*. The trick is to realize *it is a dream* and stay on the "outside" looking in! You can do this by mentally glancing down at your hands held out in front of you, allowing you a perspective of *Here and There*. Of course, like all "tricks," this will take practice to master, for it is easier to let go and enter the dream. However, with diligence, you will be able to recall the fine details of your dreams upon awakening (people, places, and words spoken), when you should write them down in a "dream journal." These will add up to build your "hindsight" from experiences that validate your life in the light of day. **Remember again,** you live "in the light" and "in the dark," both are opposing views of Logic Illuminating Fabulous Entities, where you feel and SEE illuminated energy stimulating your mind with NOTIONAL realities—naturally occurring thoughts inspiring omnipotent navigators assimilating love/life. Truly, Love/Life is a dream you cannot escape.

Attaining *Old Age*, you come to see that you have never left home/heaven. You are just a heartbeat away—one step over *The Threshold of Love*. Here, incarnated, the processes of Mental Inspiration Nurturing Deities stimulate frequencies setting your soul *aglow*, activating gods (luminaries) observing/optimizing worlds/*Wisdom*. Created as a SON (stellar omnipotent naturalist), you wield *The Power of Love*, creating and destroying according

362

to universal laws of LIFE linking illuminati formulating/ fathoming experiences/enlightenment.

Heaven harmoniously expresses atoms (vibrant elements) nurtured in an INFERNO, where induced nuclei formulating electromagnetic radiance/revelation naturally outputs Light Illuminating Fluid *Energy* as elemental notions expressing revelation geometrically yielded. *Geometry* is how Mind "wraps around" concepts dimensionally.

ENERGY expresses notions electromagnetically regulating generative youths—SUNS symbolically unfolding nature— creating a "living" HELL from hydrogen evolving *linear logic*, linking interactive numbers/nuclei expressing atomic radiance (light) oscillating geometrically illustrated concepts as *holograms*, hydrogen-originated light optically generating revelation activating *memories* as mental expressions manifesting observable "realism" illuminating entities symbolically. REALISM (radiantly expressing abstracts luminously illustrating "simulations" materially) represents elements arranging luminous illusion stimulating *minds*, magnificent illuminati naturally deployed in *Hell*, a heavenly/human existence linking *luminaries* (lucidly utilizing moments) interpreting notions/nature as revelation/ realism illuminating (enlightening) souls as *Man and Woman*.

As an exploratory soul/mind utilizing a *Human–Alien* vehicle, you physically manifest *The Power of Love*, transforming thoughts into emotions: joy, grief, anger, envy, fear, hate etc. *Love IS* a divine logic oscillating vibrant emotions "inducing" souls, charging you positively and negatively, allowing YOU (your own universe) to be "one turning," revolving around opposing perspectives to attain a comprehensive view of *Unity Consciousness*. LOVE (light originating vivid experiences) shakes, rattles, and rolls you into that which you choose to Birth Emotionally, moving you through ELATION—experiencing love/light as *Truth* inducing omnipotent navigators—and *Depression*, where you find your soul *Lost in the Dark*, eagerly desiring *My Loving Light* of *Truth*.

As a human being, you continually question why you passionately torture your self in a life that contains a "deadline"— *Death*. The answers "shine" upon you, as you *grow old*, generating revelations of *Wisdom* orienting luminous deities. *In The End*, when your present life cycle expires, you will experience enlightenment of your *Belief* birthing emotionalized logic inducing electric fantasies. Here, you discover the power of your *Expectations* delivering your reality you choose to believe. The extent of your *Faith* prepares you to explore some future state of Mind in which you *awaken*, assimilating *Wisdom* as knowledge evolving navigators *Life After Life*, for Life is an eternal adventure you look *forward* to, glancing back at your *past* that brought you to *This Moment* "presently gifted" to CREATE your future life— conceiving revelations evolving angelic transients existentially/ eternally within the realms of Home/Heaven.

Harmony Of Mental Emotions holds your mind/heart at rest
whenever your inquisitive soul flies out to profess
Your Life Story you are born to tell
within *Mother's Nature*—Heralding Emotional Love/Life—
providing your *Desire*
delivering electric sensations illuminating radiant entities
AGLOW
as glorious luminaries observing *worlds*
within my Spiritual Harmony Of Wisdom
weaving opulent realism luminously displayed.

Here, you implore to explore my MIND
magnetically inducing nuclear dynamics
stimulating your *mind*—my image numerically defined—
expressing *Tears of Joy* in gratitude of
discovering Your Own Universe, a reflection of Love,
a WILL set FREE as a wandering illuminato learning life
formulates realistic experiences emotionally,
unifying your mind/heart soul ablaze in "hazy daze,"
where *Clear Vision* directs your way
through dreams you *think* REAL,
transforming heavenly inspiration naturally kindling
revelations enlightening angelic luminaries FEELING,
forming experiences enlightening
luminaries in necessary *games*
generating amusements minds entertain sympathetically,
when OUT you roam,
observing universal *Truth* emanating from Home.

MY HOUSE

My house is full of magnificent *youths*
—you omnipotent universes traversing Heaven—
harnessing opportunities unfolding spiritual enlightenment,
traveling separate roads along my binary code
pulsating electromagnetically,
interpreting *Numbers*
naturally unifying moments/matter
building existential realities
in which you struggle to remember you are a cosmic contender
connecting *My Points* to view your spot within my atomic haze
coalescing from photons illuminating your daze,
cycling upon day/night dreams
flowing as *Love/Life Energy*—light beams—
supplying visions to Systematically Enlighten Entities
as *My Rising SON*
systematically optimizing numbers revealing the ONE
originating navigable entities—*My Angels*—
experiencing "present moments" gifted to view
Your Own *Universe*,
a unitary navigator implementing visions expressing realities
sensed existentially,
observing opposing forces of Mental
Emotion evolving in *Time*,
where transcendental intelligence manages *Evolution*,
positioning you to find a solution to your personal *issues*
inspiring souls systematically understanding
emotional situations,
revolving around the *wheel of Life*,
where *Wisdom* harmoniously evolves emotional luminaries

observing fantasies (luminous illusions)
formulating enlightenment
for all *Children of Light* whom I rouse
to experience *My Love Divine* illuminating my house.

BEHIND CLOSED EYES

Behind closed eyes is where you DIE,
discovering illusory experiences entertaining your mind
here, in my stellar home above,
where starlit beams illuminate *dreams* of love
delivering revelations enlightening
anxious minds eager to find
the truth of life and *Death*.

The confusion of my illusion makes you wonder,
when you open your eyes and *realize*
there, down under,
radiant energy activates liberated illuminati (zealous entities)
as human beings conceiving thoughts emanating from **night**,
where numerical impulses generate holographic transmissions,
entertaining *visionaries*—full of suspicions—
verifying intuitive Spirit instructing omnifarious navigators
assimilating revelations in existential situations
"enlightening" cosmic contemplators
exploring Worlds Illustrating Spiritual Dimensions Of Mind.

Do not deny *This Moment* here, upon which you stand,
to feel and know the pleasures and pains of being *human*,
harvesting universal memories assimilated naturally.

My Light of Love illuminates your view
of the illusion you think true,
allowing you to argue your *Belief* as you seek your *Relief*
behind closed eyes,
escaping for the moment your daily torment
you persevere to conquer your FEAR
fostering experiences around *Relationships*
revealing who you ARE,
Avatars receiving enlightenment as living *Stars*.

Dear father, within my heart I sing,
grateful for my thoughts you give that allow me this Life I live
to know I AM your SON,
imploring as man sympathetically observing notions
illuminating me to the ONE optimizing navigable entities.

In the dark, behind closed eyes, I pray upon my knees,
praising you with *Tears of Joy* for letting my soul roam free
amongst the stars of endless wonder,
experiencing you "asunder"
as a fragile human being, a mind/heart momentarily seeing
my dreams come true.
As a *Free Will* formulating *Relationships* evolving entities
wisely implementing love/life, I pray for courage in the Light,
to do my best and what is right, for I long to be in the **Night**,
here, behind closed eyes, where

I AM IN HEAVEN

interpreting abstract memories (inspired notions)

harmoniously evolving alluring visions entertaining navigators
as time-traveling *contemplators*
consciously observing nature that enlightens minds
perceiving logic/light atomically
transmuting opulent *revelations*
relating emotionally vivified experiences
linking abstract thoughts
inducing one's needs naturally evolving eternal *deities*
discovering empathetic insight through issues evolving *seers*
—souls experiencing enlightenment revealed symbolically—
within the Spiritual Harmony Of Wisdom.

Thank you, Father, for allowing me to see
Transcendental Radiance Unfolding
Thoughts Holographically
illuminating *The Grand View* of all I *believe,*
beholding experiences logic intuitively exhibits via *Expectation*
that sometimes turns into consternation
when failing to understand *The Power of Love*
emanating from heaven above
illuminating my chosen *Hell,*
where humans express love/life in stories we tell.

Let your LIGHT shine bright to illuminate your **night**
luminously inducing glorious holograms transcendentally
revealing your grace upon Mother's *blue eye*
"birthing" logic unifying elements
expressing your *enlightenment,*
Conveying Realism Evolving Abstract
Thoughts Into Opulent Nature,
elaborating notions lucidly illustrating glorious holograms that

entities navigate, momentarily experiencing
"natural transduction,"
converting energy from one system to
another, for sister and brother
to observe *Heaven on Earth.*

Here, incarnate, you move my soul to live and grow,
gathering revelations of *Wisdom*
through your loving light allowing me *sight,*
sensing illusion generated here tonight,
behind closed eyes,
where dreams I envision evolve through *Our Trinity*
originating/outputting/observing universal radiance
that reveals intuition inspiring natural
illuminati (transient youths)
like *me,* a magnificent entity,
sensing you within my heart beating forth the love I impart
through your gifts bestowed in *life,*
learning intuition formulates experiences producing *strife,*
situations transmitting revelation illuminating fervent entities
fighting with *Courage of Love* to survive,
here ALIVE,
assimilating logic inducing vivid energy
supplying all I need through your Love/Life force
electromagnetically dictating my course,
changing stride as mental tides
move my heart to FEEL thoughts I think real,
finding emotions evolve logic *24/7,*
here on Earth, where I am in Heaven.

THE OTHER SIDE

Here in the dark, you witness night,
behind closed eyes that give you sight,
there, in the LIGHT OF DAY
linearly inducing glorious holograms through
oscillating frequencies dynamically activating you
as cosmic *Avatars* seeking *Truth,*
angelic visionaries actively theorizing atomic radiation
illuminating mind/heart souls expressing aberrations
as a *Free Will* experiencing the thrills
of *Heaven on Earth,*
where WE above project Love as *Wisdom* exemplified,
weaving inspired situations developing omnipotent minds
(mired in natural delusions) conveyed
through the ILLUSION
illustrating logic linking universal souls
interpreting omnipotent
notions, numbers, and nature as *human beings*
harnessing universal memories (abstract notions)
bewildering eternal illuminati naturally growing
as *Young Minds* playing their *part,*
portraying angels reflecting thoughts
expressing the power of *Source*
systematically observing "universal
reviewers" consciously evolving,
interpreting illusions of *Truth* quickly dissolving
back to *The Void,* where volumes of impressive data is held
In Memory,
inspiring naturalists mentally experiencing moments of

revelation yielding Wisdom Oscillating
Radiant Data Symbols,
vibrating in rapid-fire-staccato-sounds that tremble,
appearing from Nowhere Into Glorious
Holograms Transmitted
through electromagnetic beams of LIGHT
linearly illuminating geometrically held thoughts
Awakening you to *Divine Fantasies* in which you roam,
a mere heartbeat away from *Home*,
HERE, on the other side of DAY,
where *Heaven* enlightens radiant entities,
dynamically astounding you observing

HEAVEN ON EARTH

Reveals fear and pain for you to discover your true worth,
when *Lost in Space*, experiencing the *human* race
harnessing universal memories acquired naturally.
No matter what you choose, a *focused mind* provides your view,
formulating opulent concepts unfolding
situations enabling deities
managing intuition naturally derived.

All you THINK, FEEL, and DO
reflects the love I send to you
transforming heavenly intelligence (numerical knowledge)
formulating experiences emotionally linking desires obtained,
Assimilating Cosmic Thoughts Inducing Necessary Games
Orienting Universal Transients in my
Spectral Holograms Orienting *Worlds*

weaving opulent realism luminously displayed symbolically
as Words Illustrating Spiritual Dimensions Of Mind
manifesting illusion/illuminati naturally defined.

Do your best in deeds of love to open closed hearts
fearful of life revealing their gifted part
as *Time Travelers* moving from birth to birth,
ALWAYS IN HEAVEN
while there on earth.

HOME IS WHERE YOUR HEART IS

Have you ever heard the expression "home is where your
heart is?" Home and your HEART hold everything angels
really treasure—Love. Your *heart* harnesses energy/emotions
activating/amplifying revelational thoughts, creating your
mind's *attitude* (position of consciousness), where you assimilate/
apply thoughts transferring information that unifies divine
entities—Source/souls. As you are created in the image of
Mind (*The GREAT Computer*), your mind represents a MAC
mentally assimilating concepts (thoughts), a DELL dualistically
experiencing/expressing love/life, or an HP harmonizing
perceptions, processing thoughts emotionally to attain a sense of
understanding Harmony Of Mental Emotions, unifying notions
delivering emotions rectifying souls traversing/transcending
atomic nature displaying intuition naturally generated.

Home is a place where you FEEL comfortable and secure,
fathoming experiences emotionally linking your mind/heart
soul with fellow *entities*, emotional navigators traversing/
transcending illusion transmitting insightful experiences as

stories stimulating transients observing realism in emotional situations.

EMOTIONAL REALISM enlightens minds observing the illusion of nature (atomic life) radiantly expressing abstracts luminously illustrating "simulations" materially. ATOMIC LIFE reveals abstract thoughts of Mind intuitively creating luminous illusions/illustrations formulating experiences, "stimulating" omnipotent *naturalists* as "navigable" angels (transients) understanding realism as luminous illusion "symbolizing" thoughts transmuted through *Mother's Nature*—Home harmoniously optimizing material expressions.

Home is your hub, your central "command station" from which you perceive, project, and protect your *Beliefs*, bravely expressing love inspiring emotional feelings/fantasies that you share with fellow *Time Travelers*—my cosmic children—*Riding the Outskirts* as *Avatars*. Here, incarnate, home is a place you travel "from" and "to" on a daily basis, always searching for *The Grand View* as you follow *The Right Path* allocated through your *DNA*, your divine numerical assignment (defining navigators' attributes) dynamically nurturing *Avatars* traveling between *Here and There* (Heaven and Earth).

Home (Heaven) is that eternal place where a tireless Mind expresses SELF simultaneously expressing/evolving logical/luminous facts/frequencies through *Heart* harmoniously elaborating atomic revelation three-dimensionally. Heart converts VISIONS (vibrant impulses) stimulating illusion one navigates sympathetically—through common feelings or *Common Sense*.

Your *heart* (harmoniously evolving all revelational thoughts) is symbolic of *Mother's Nature* (EMOTION) evolving memories/moments orienting transient illuminati *ordained* naturally—optically rectifying deities (angels) interpreting notions emotionally defined. Your heart "harmonizes" your thoughts, changing rhythm according to your temperament. It is an electrified organ *sparking* you, stimulating perceptive angels replicating knowledge in natural *games*, generating amusements minds entertain sympathetically through *Passion*. Your heart is your physical *core* conveying oxygen regulating energy, "converting" opulent revelation emotionally through *blood* (biological liquid orienting one's disposition), supplying "emotional flows" that set you **aglow** as glorious luminaries observing *worlds* weaving one's reality luminously displayed.

Your *heart* represents your *home* within HOME, where you harness opulent memories experientially within *Heaven* originating magnificent environments, entities, and experiences. You may recall from childhood that at home *someone* is watching over you—your parents. No matter how far you go from home, you are never out of their mind/heart, although they may be out of yours. "Creators" are concerned over their "creations!"

Your home reflects your heart's desire to express your *self*, your soul experiencing love/life fantasies. Here, you display your treasures and mementoes collected along your journeys to explore your world. You create *Your Life Story* as a *Free Will* conceiving *Heaven* and *Hell*—STATES of Mind—souls traverse/transcend as transient entities.

Caught up in the current events of *Time*, you cannot help becoming more introverted, inwardly seeking answers to the absurdity evolving around you. You fear the confrontational moments of defending your IMAGE (intelligent mind activating games emotionally) in a world out to destroy you, where only the "strong-willed" survive. Waking to a new *Day's Birth*, your eager mind and hungry heart uses *Courage of Fear* to face *The Challenges of Love/Life* that allow you to transcend your *issues* inducing situations symbolically unfolding enlightenment sympathetically. Through *Courage of Love*, you become *Brave of Heart*, expanding your personal power of *Love/Life Energy* liberating omnipotent visionaries exploring luminous illusion fervently experienced.

In The End of each day, you come to see Home as a place harboring omnipotent minds exploring *Mother's Nature*. All you can do is give praise—*Hail Mary*—for providing your *Blessings in Disguise*. If you are in harmony with *Family* and friends, you share home as a "heaven" of Mother's Earth. Here, you communicate with other *mind/heart* souls, magnificent illuminati naturally decoding holograms expressing all radiant thoughts. Each mind/heart soul represents *Our Trinity*, where THREE transmit/transform/transcend holograms reflecting electromagnetic energy flowing between *Here and There*, where Heaven enlightens radiant entities transcending "hellish episodes" rectifying entities that TORTURE their heart, temporarily occluding radiant *Truth* unifying recalcitrant entities—TERRORISTS, tempestuous entities representing reactionaries obstructing rudimentary intelligence sanctifying transients.

As you Sympathetically Evolve Experientially, heaven/home/heart is another *unified theory* universally nurturing illuminati fathoming intuition emotionally delivered through Heartfelt Experiences optimizing radiant youths. Everywhere you go in Heaven, you are at Home, habitually observing Mental Energy enlightening your *heart* harnessing *Expectations* as realized thoughts. Therefore, home is where your heart Inspects Source, both *Here and There*, in Spirit and incarnate, continually traversing heaven's gate.

HEAVEN'S GATE

Heaven's gate is *The Threshold of Love* through which your soul passes into finite space—your physical body. Heaven's *gate* governs angelic transients entering the third dimension of Mind momentarily illuminating navigable deities. It is symbolic of your CROWN CHAKRA confining responsive observers willfully navigating creation heralding all knowledge rectifying *Avatars* as "natural gods" exploring love/life situations.

Passing though heaven's gate, your *soul* (surrogate observer understanding logic/light) harmonizes with the atomic illusion (creation). This energy *download* deploys omnipotent wills "naturally living out" abstract *dreams* delivering realistic experiences arousing minds *emotionally*, allowing you to experience moments of *Truth* illuminating one's needs as lessons life yields. Opening this *gateway* governing angelic transients exploring worlds atomically yielded, SOURCE/MIND scientifically orients universal "researchers" (conscious entities) momentarily interpreting numerical data as *human beings* harnessing universal memories (abstract notions) bewildering eternal illuminati naturally *growing*—gathering revelations of *Wisdom* "instructing" natural gods.

Incarnated, you find your self *Riding the Outskirts* of home, exploring *Mother's Nature* nurturing angels temporarily utilizing *revelation* expressed as radiation emitting vivid energy/ emotion luminously activating three-dimensional illustrations (illusion) orienting naturalists in a *world* weaving opulent realism luminously displayed. Your physical body is an organic *Universe* Nurturing Illuminati Temporarily, a "unitary network" illustrating visible entities *retaining* spiritual entities as "vehicle" and "operator."

Through your mind/brain interface, electrically charged *thoughts* transmit harmonic overtures (utterances) guiding heavenly transients interpreting dimensional *scenes*, spatial concepts expressing nature emulating *situations*, specific instances that unfold abstract thoughts *illuminating* one naturally, initiating linear logic unifying minds/memories in nuclear arenas "tempering" intuitive naturalists (gods) gathering opulent data. The illumination of thoughts conveys *realism* through reactive elements arranging luminous illusion scientifically manifested, rectifying emotional angels luminously interpreting situations momentarily in *Time* tempering intuitive minds existentially. By projecting your thoughts positively or negatively, you attract or inhibit your *Desires* and *Expectations*, creating your personal vision of *Heaven* and *Hell* (pleasure and pain), where *Harmony* enlightens angelic visionaries evolving naturally as humans experiencing *Love/Life*—logic optimizing visionary entities living illusions fabricated electromagnetically, elementally, and emotionally.

Logic—language of geometrically imaging concepts— emanates from Source as Light orchestrating generators' intuitive consciousness. *Light energy* represents "lucid intuition" generating heavenly transmissions electromagnetically nurturing elemental revelation geometrically yielded, luminously illustrating glowing holograms tantalizing emotional navigators (naturalists) exploring realism governing/ guiding youths—*Children of Light*. Light energy is created from *hydrogen* symbolizing *The Binary Code*, holographically yielding divine revelation outputting geometric expressions naturally. Light energy represents the *electromagnetic force field* encoding logical expressions (concepts) transmitting revelation/radiation of magnetically activated generators (stars) naturally emitting transcendental intuition (consciousness), focused omniscience revealing concepts elementally forming illusions entertaining/enlightening luminous deities (*COL*). From the simplicity of hydrogen (one element of two parts) comes the complexity of all creation.

WHITE LIGHT (*Wisdom*) harmoniously inspires transient entities, luminously inciting glorious humans through a "silver chord" (light beam) entering their crown chakra (heavens' gate) at the top of their head. From here it travels along the spinal chord, where it stimulates other *chakras* conveying heavenly abstracts kindling radiant *Avatars* through COLORS of the SPECTRUM, conveying omniscient logic oscillating revelation sympathetically, systematically providing enlightening concepts transcendentally reflecting/rectifying universal Mind/minds. Each chakra point stimulates the endocrine system (glands) controlling the chemical flow of *hormones* heralding one's reflexive movements of nature exciting/evolving souls activated by commands of the *brain* (biological relay attuning inspired notions/natures/needs), allowing your physical *body* (biological observatory delineating you) to convert thoughts to feelings (senses). Thus, your soul/mind attains a *heart* harmonizing emotional *Avatars* realizing *thoughts* telepathically heralding opulent utterances guiding heavenly transients incarnated as *Time Travelers*.

Your *astral*, "light body" *soul* (spiritual observer utilizing logic/light) represents a *floppy disk*, a fabulous luminary obtaining *points* (particulars of inspired notions/thoughts) providing you data imparting spiritual/scientific knowledge. As a "floppy disk," you traverse between *Here and There—Heaven* and *Hell* (Earth). Here, in Heaven, you utilize your "astral" body to traverse Source/Mind, observing *A Higher Vision* of consciousness. There, on Earth, you utilize a human body (*vehicle*), a vital element helping illuminati conceiving love/

life emotionally within a "lifetime" defined within the space-time continuum. You floppy disks continually "flip/flop" in and out of *Time*, traversing illusions momentarily experienced as *Divine Fantasies* emanating from **night**, where numerical impulses generate holographic transmissions (dreams) delivering revelation enlightening angelic minds.

Eternal Memory represents *source knowledge* (light energy) sequentially oscillating universal revelation/radiance conveyed/ created electromagnetically, "kindling notions" (illuminating ideas) of *Wisdom* (love/life energy) digitally governing entities/ evolution. Your soul/mind acquires source knowledge through "particular inheritance" (DNA), where *chromosomes* coordinate human representations of Mind optimally "synthesizing" organic matter evolving systematically. Each bit and byte of *data* (detailing abstract thoughts/angelic transients atomically) illuminates an *aura* attuning universal radiance activating your Source-Unified Vehicle (body), energizing Luminaries Interpreting Fantasies Existentially, where your soul/mind *lives*, linking intuition vivifying entities sympathetically.

The complexity of source knowledge *interfacing* with nature "interrelates" notions/nature/navigators through electromagnetic radiation (frequencies) amplifying concepts implementing "nuclear geometry" formed around a central point, a *nucleus* naturally unfolding concepts/creation logically/luminously evolving unified *systems*, scientifically/symbolically yielding sublime thoughts/things expressing/enlightening memories, matter, and minds. Here, incarnate, you continually observe and decipher the data flowing through your crown chakra (heaven's gate), intimately watching how it moves you through the *illusion* of impeccable logic/light unfolding/unifying Source/ souls imagining/inspecting opulent notions/natures.

As my cosmic child observing *My Love Divine*, you

continually cross through heaven's gate, finding your self somewhere on the eternal wheel of Love/Life revolving through the cosmos of MIND/SPACE—the magnificent *Intellectual* nurturing deities systematically perceiving concepts/creation emotionally/elementally. You may *Recall* past lives if your soul's development allows you to tap into those frequencies for your enlightenment, otherwise your mind *focuses* on your present life, finding one's consciousness utilizes situations experienced sequentially along a more restrictive bandwidth (heartbeats and breaths) confining you to your "present" reality, where you find your self *Lost in Space*. Remember, you do not receive any data you are not capable of handling. Most of you refuse to believe in your true potential to attain *Clear Vision*. IF you are a persistent observer, you eventually see everything *around* you is symbolic of ALL that is *within* you—absolute/atomic Love/Life indivisible. Here in heaven, *Unity Consciousness* unfolds/unifies/utilizes notions/numbers/nature, illuminating *Truth* yielding creations of nuclear Source coalescing into one universal system naturally expressing, enlightening, and evolving Source/souls simultaneously.

Everyday you grow your Divine Omnipotent Soul, expanding your mind (data operating system) toward the *Stars* illuminating the heavenly fields of Source, the singularity outputting universal radiance/revelation conveying energy/enlightenment. Each galaxy you observe is symbolic of your "microcosmic" human body illuminated by atoms defining you as a GALACTIC ORGANISM, a gloriously attuned luminary assimilating concepts that illuminate consciousness observing realism generated around nuclei illustrating systems/synergy materially. You come to *understand* universal nature dynamically expresses realism stimulating transient angels navigating *dimensions* of Mind—digitally induced memories/moments evoking natural scenes "informing" omnipotent navigators.

As you pass through heaven's gate, you come to realize you are truly *Alone*, a loved one naturally exploring Another Life Objectifying Numerical *Equations*, evoking quanta (universal abstracts) transcendentally illuminating omniscient/omnipotent Source/souls. Here is your "binary view," where you see your self *inwardly* and *outwardly* as a colossal organism (*Mind/Heart*), a universe of ONE MIND turning through QUANTUM THEORY, questioning/quantifying universal abstracts (notions) unfolding memories/moments that herald enlightenment optimizing radiant youths "fluctuating" between *Here and There*—cosmic dimensions that unfold eternal wanderers traversing heaven's gate.

HERE AND THERE

For your enlightenment, I will define these terms as such: *here* refers to your spiritual *Home* or *Heaven* on the other side of time, a state of Mind where thought energy is less inhibited or constrained to expression, and *there* to mean your physical existence in *Hell*, where you humanly experience love/life in *Time*, where Truth illuminates magnificent entities "traveling between" here and there.

Here and there define opposing views of Your Own *Universe*,
a unitary navigator (intuitive visionary) exploring realities
sensed emotionally.
There, you move at light-speed, where
Truth supplies your needs,

nurturing emotional entities deployed from *here*,
where *Harmony* enlightens radiant entities through *fear*,
fallacies evolving around radiance illuminating my *day*
deceiving angelic youths grabbing what treasures they may,
there in *Time*, transcending illusions minds explore
to discover *Truth's* revolving door
between here and there.

There, you have a pause…
a moment to see what your actions cause
that determines your *Belief*,
struggling through tribulation to find your *Relief*
from converting your love throughout your life,
passionately evolving through your created *strife*
stressing tender relationships illuminating fervent entities.

Over here, there is no wait, no concept of being late,
always conscious of ALL you are,
shining bright as my loving star,
a metaphor for a child of Light knowing I am the ONE
omnipotent nuclear energizer inspiring you,
My Rising Son.

Here or there is just a place,
a state of Mind to continue your race
to see first-hand what you believe is real
as you spin around my cosmic wheel,
Suspended in dreams you think true.
Here, you know whence you came
to measure your moments there in *game*,
gathering amusements momentarily entertained,
fighting each other as sister/brother

reflecting my Love I gift as your Life in which you drift
through present moments of hazy-daze
clouding your mind to *Truth* you crave,
discovering things you love and hate
as you traverse heaven's gate.

ALONE

Being **A**ngelic **L**uminaries **O**btaining **N**ecessary **E**xperiences
is one of the best-kept secrets going,
for you, my cosmic child, are eternally growing
as "solo fliers" exploring *Desires*,
discovering emotional situations inciting radiant entities
diligently evaluating stories in remote environments,
worlds weaving opulent realism luminously displayed
as illusion inhibiting logical luminaries understanding
Spirit interweaves opulent notions, nature, and navigators
traversing time held *In Memory*,
where minds experience moments of revelation yielding
Divine Fantasies that are appealing
to *Man and Woman*, walking *Hand in Hand* as *He and She*,
Children of Light illuminated to BE
Stars singularly transforming acquired revelations,
birthing emotionally *Divine Inspiration*
—*Love/Life Energy*—
flowing through veins of *The Human Alien*
constraining a soul experiencing heartbeats and breaths—
The Binary Code—determining life and *Death*
dynamically elevating *Avatars* transcending *Hell*
"holding" entities living lies they tell,

transmitting eternal love/life alone,
assimilating logic ordaining navigators existentially
through *Mother Goddess* providing the show
spectrally heralding opulent *Wisdom*
weaving inspired situations developing omnipotent minds
to TEACH,
transmit enlightenment as conceived *Harmony*
heralding all revelational memories optically nurturing youths,
for all you children ARE angels "reflecting" enlightenment,
"professing" Transcendental Revelations
Uniting Tempestuous Hearts
as **Minds Activating Notions**—
Wisdom **Optimizing Minds Attuned Naturally.**

SHE symbolizes heavenly enlightenment as my HEART
harmoniously evolving *Avatars* "realizing" thoughts
along *The Cutting Edge* of life—revealing moments of strife—
with others in *contest*,
conveying one's notions to elicit some truth,
through which you divine *My Loving Light*
luminously inspires gods (heavenly transients)
traveling *alone* as lucid observers naturally evolving,
transmigrating *Life After Life*,
sustained incarnate by my dearest wife.

MY DEAREST WIFE

My dearest wife evolves all LIFE,
luminously inciting fervent entities
through *Mother's Nature* momentarily orienting

transients harnessing "electric" revelations
necessitating "anguish" to understand rudimental *empathy*—
emotions Mind provides angelic
transients (heavenly youths)—
enlightens minds personally assimilating
Truth harmoniously yielded
as transcendental revelation unveiled through hydrogen
that reveals universal thoughts holographically.

SHE is always with me,
systematically harmonizing energy,
allowing you children to build a life to treasure
the little things that bring you great pleasure,
stimulating your soul to persevere and GROW,
gathering revelations of *Wisdom* in order to know
your connection to us That Watch Over,
supplying all that makes Youths Obtaining Unity
the epitome of *Our Trinity*,
a mind/heart soul
creating a "love story" through Life
illustrated three-dimensionally by my dearest wife.

HAIL MARY

Hail MARY, mothering all radiant youths,
the LORD moves through you
luminously outputting resplendent deities
—generating opulent data systematically—
geometrically arranging abstracts into MATTER
manifested as transmuted thoughts (electromagnetic radiation)

atomically coalescing into divine condensations,
forming a "human body" for a soul to travel in,
when OUT from home they ROAM,
optimizing universal truths,
reflecting omniscience as mortals
experiencing *Time* temporarily
illuminating minds existentially
as *gods* sublime,
generators of *Desire* representing Father's *eyes*,
eternal youths evolving spiritually to become wise
to *Mother's Nature* "reflecting" the Great Contemplator,
whose compliments she projects to the contrary,
expressing His glory with such grace,
Stars appear to brighten his space,
making him cry, hail Mary!

OUR TRINITY

Omnipotent **N**atural **E**ngineers
Transpose **W**isdom **O**ptimally
Through **H**eavenly **R**adiation **E**motionalizing **E**ntities
—SPIRITS—
systematically project/provide/perceive immanent radiance
imparting *Truth*
transmitting revelation unveiled through *holograms*
heralding omniscient logic oscillating "geometric reflections"
as *memories*
mentally expressing moments of realism in emotional souls
—mind/heart spirits—
representing One Understanding Realism

Through Radiant Illusion Naturally
Inspiring Transient Youths.

THREE OF US
transmit/transform/traverse heavenly
radiation (electromagnetic
energy) optimally formulating unitary *systems*
(*Stars*) yielding synergy transforming eternal memories
that *Mind/Heart* SINGS,
momentarily inspiring navigable deities
harnessing emotions activating regal thoughts
supplying inspiration nurturing gifted spirits,
Youths Obtaining Unity,
omnipotent navigators exploring Wisdom Exemplified,
downloading DATA digitally activating transient *Avatars*
evolving *Life After Life*, "hailing Mary" my dearest wife
evolving memories in Temporary Illusions Minds Experience,
illuminating *My Love Divine*
luminously oscillating vibrant energy displaying illusions
vividly illustrating natural environments/entities
intertwined in games
governing angelic minds evolving sympathetically,
opening their heart to Spiritually Express Empathy
as *EYES of GOD*, eternal youths exploring Spirit
optically formulating Genesis ordaining *deities*,
divine entities implementing thoughts in emotional situations,
where *I See You* as ME,
a mind emotionally manifesting *Expectations*
momentarily experienced through our trinity.

Bless You Child

WHO AM I?

I AM everything I AM NOT,
intuitive abstract Mind inducing atomic matter
naturally *ordaining* thoughts,
orienting revelations/realism dynamically activating illusion
naturally illustrating notions geometrically.

I am who RELATES to you,
revealing electric logic as thoughts emotionalizing souls
eager to feel a "moment in time" as
Radiant Energy Activating Logicians.

I am who expresses ATOMIC LIFE
activating thoughts of Master/Mother inducing creation,
luminously illustrating fabulous environments/entities
dynamically evolving through radiation,
My Light of Love.

I AM someone special, someone GRAND!
I AM here—with YOU—yearning our unity,
walking *Hand in Hand.*
No time shall we ever be apart,
for I AM inspiring all minds exploring my HEART
holding epiphanies activating rapturous thrills
stimulating your soul as a *Free Will*
entertaining dreams flowing on light beams
emanating from Spirit, WHO I AM,
Wisdom heralding omniscience illuminating angelic man.

My "reflection below" atomically glows as *My Loving Light*

illuminating *Man and Woman* experiencing SIGHT
stimulating illusions guiding heavenly transients
within my MIND manifesting illuminati naturally defined
as *Stars*, souls transforming abstract revelation sympathetically,
Emotionally **Y**ielding **E**nlightenment **S**pontaneously,
through which I see I AM WHO
incites all minds willingly heralding omniscience,
ALL that is TRUE.

FREE WILL

Free will is a gift from *Divine Will*—dynamic intuition vivifying intuitive navigators exploring Wisdom/worlds issuing/ illustrating love/life. As a *free will* finding revelation/realism expressing eternal *Wisdom* illuminating logical luminaries, you formulate *Relationships* evolving entities wisely implementing love/life. Free will allows you the opportunity to create your own heaven or hell—*states* of Mind in which your soul transforms abstract thoughts emotionally. Each state allows you to experience your inquisitive mind and willing heart eager to *believe*, to behold electric logic illuminating entities vivified *emotionally*—experiencing moments of tribulation illuminating one naturally assimilating lessons life yields.

Free will was created through *immaculate conception*; instinctively manifesting minds as "conscious units" logically assimilating thoughts (electromagnetic concepts) organizing nuclear creation "elementally portraying" three-dimensional illusion one navigates. This *creation* of cosmic radiance exhibiting abstract/atomic transformations illustrates opulent notions "nurturing" *navigators* (free wills), natural *Avatars* verifying illusions (geometrically arranged thoughts) orchestrating realism sympathetically through common feelings or *Common Sense*. Here, angelic navigators (*Time Travelers*) acquire *human alien* vehicles created by *DNA* (divine numerical assignment) defining natural/navigable apparatuses "representing" divine navigators *atomized*, activating transcendental observers (magnificent illuminati) zealously exploring *dimensions* of Mind digitally inducing memories/moments evoking natural scenes "informing" omnipotent navigators. Free will allows you to flow OUT and IN, observing universal *Truth* "intertwining" notions, numbers, nature, and navigators through *Black Holes* that birth/bend logic/light aligning concepts (knowledge) harmoniously oscillating love/life enlightening and evolving souls.

Created in my IMAGE (an intuitive mind assimilating geometric expressions), your *free will* represents a fabulous, radiant entity exploring/expressing *Wisdom* illuminating logical luminaries—you and I.

YOU AND I

You and I are inseparable! You resemble ME, a magnificent entity momentarily experiencing memories existentially. Through you I FEEL, formulating emotions evolving logic. You are my dreams come true, the *reflection* of my Love sent out through my *heart* heralding emotional angels receiving/reflecting thoughts. My thoughts of you bring me great joy, a feeling of gratitude that through YOU yearning our unity, *I See ME*—intuitive Spirit—expressing electric memories emotionally, inspiring souls evaluating experiences momentarily evolving through US TWO universal spirits transmitting/transforming *Wisdom* optimally as Omnipotent Natural Entities. The MAGIC of mentally activating/assimilating "gnosis" inducing consciousness "flows" *Between You and I* through *My Loving Light*, the medium for *Calling All Angels* understanding *My Point*.

MY POINT

What is my *point* you ask? It is the projection of *intuition* nurturing transients, imparting notions that uplift illuminati transcending illusion observed naturally. Nature nurtures angelic transients universally receiving *empathy*, experiencing/ expressing mental perception about tribulation humanly yielded.

Each of my points (*Stars*), twinkling in majestic splendor, illuminates my HEART harmoniously elaborating atomic revelation three-dimensionally. Each *point* represents a "passionate orator" illuminating *nuclear thoughts*—a Source-Unified Narrator—numerically undulating cosmic logic expressing atomic radiance, transmitting *Harmony* optically unfolding glorious holograms transcendentally. ATOMIC RADIANCE expresses absolute *Truth* (omniscient Mind) initiating creation, revealing abstract data illuminated as notions/nuclei coordinated elementally.

Everything emanating from Source—the singularity organizing universal radiance creating everything—evolves from a *point* providing opulent information naturally transmitted through "light rays," *lines* logically intertwining numerical/ nuclear expressions "coalescing" into three-dimensional *forms* (holograms) fabricating opulent realism *modeling scenes*— magnetically organizing data (elements) linking illusory nature geometrically signifying concepts enlightening navigable entities nurtured existentially. GEOMETRIC PATTERN governs energy orienting memories/matter expressed through radiation illuminating creation, proclaiming abstract thoughts through "elemental reactions" (nucleosynthesis).

As my cosmic child, you represent a "star player," a Perfect Omniscient-Intelligence Naturally Traveling within *The Void* of *Space*, where volumes of invisible data (oscillating frequencies) stimulate perceptive *Angels* conceiving *Eternity*—everlasting *Truth* expressing revelations nurturing illuminati (transcendental youths) experiencing *Life After Life*.

Here at *Home* harboring omnipotent minds exploring, you move from *point* to *point* providing opportunities illuminating navigable transients (*Truth Seekers*) obtaining *Knowledge*—kinetic notions/numbers optimizing *Wisdom* (logically expressed discipline) governing enlightenment—allowing you to DO WORK (diligently optimize *Wisdom* of relevant knowledge). Knowledge activates your mind's *focal point*, formulating one's consciousness around logical/linear points/projections of intuition/illumination nurturing transients. Every day, you find your self *Awakening* to *A Higher Vision* of knowledge evolving from points projecting rays illuminating forms symbolically through *My Loving Light*.

My Loving Light

From my dark void of night, I send forth my loving light
to Birth Entities (broadcast energy)
as *My Rising Son* I set afire,
expressing my WORD as *Wisdom* offering radiant *Desire*
delivering electric sensations inducing realism enlightening
Man and Woman, young and old, living dreams they hear told
from *Spirit to Soul*.

My loving light shines from above
as Stars Outputting Nuclear Signals revealing my *eternal love*
expressing *Truth* (electromagnetic radiance) nurturing angelic
luminaries lucidly observing vivid experiences,
conceiving *Expectations* from concentration
of a FOCUSED MIND
formulating opulent concepts utilizing "synergy" (*Mind/Heart*)
enabling deities managing illusion naturally defined.

My Loving Light guides you on your way,
implanting vivid dreams inspiring your life by day.
Listen to your inner voice inspiring your mind to see

the power of imagination creates all your fantasies,
here incarnate, where you seek your fame,
playing your gifted part in my love/life game,
wherein you struggle to overcome your strife
stressing your soul exploring life
personally designed from me above
enlightening you angels through *My Light of Love*.

CALLING ALL ANGELS

Look NOW to see
you are my children I set free,
naturally observing *Wisdom*
—down there below—
nurturing hungry hearts eager to know
Love/Life energy empowers your soul.

Who am I that say these things?
I am *He and She* that allows you to *sing*,
sympathetically iterating notions given.
Do not fear time or place we meet,
I am here to formally greet
inquisitive souls to the SHOW.

Calling all angels, come forth and gather to me,
open your mind to SEE
the vision of ONE you know in part,
come freely with a willing heart.
My words to you I heartily say,
do not worry about your path today,

from high above your Love is true,
Father and Mother are watching *through* you,
BE at PEACE!

Calling all angels *Brave of Heart* to tread
along beside my loving dead
that see the way you may not know,
guiding your soul as it grows,
gathering revelations of Wisdom.

Calling all *Angels* showing *Courage of Love*
to open your self to US above
unveiling secrets of Life.
I tell you now to set your pace,
for here, in *Time*, you have your place
to DO and BE all that you may
as my *Angel Warrior* seeking *Truth* today.

Bless you child

14

A HIGHER VISION

VISION vividly illuminates souls interpreting opulent notions within cosmic MIND manifesting illusion naturally defined. Vision allows you to SEE—spiritually evolve existentially—as souls experiencing enlightenment.

ENLIGHTENMENT educates nescient logicians interpreting glorious holograms that express nuclear manifestation evolving natural *transmutation*, three-dimensionally revealing abstract notions simulating memories/matter unfolded through atoms transmitting illusion observed naturally.

"Higher" vision comes from IMAGINATION, intuitive Mind activating geometric illusion nurturing angelic transients inspecting opulent natures. NATURE "nuclearly adapts" thoughts (universal revelation) unfolding realism elementally, providing necessary attributes "tempering" uniquely reactive entities through *tribulation*, transforming radiant illuminati becoming universal luminaries "advancing" through illusions of nature. As a mind/heart soul, you naturally process *visions* as vibrant impulses stimulating illuminati (observant *navigators*) naturally ascertaining vivid images geometrically arranged through oscillating *radiation* that reveals abstract data inducing atomic transformations illustrating omnipotent nature.

ATOMIC ILLUSION (a "lower" vision) activates thoughts outputting magnetically induced creation, illustrating logic luminously utilizing *systems* integrating omnipotent nature/ navigators, scientifically yielding sublime thoughts expressing/ enlightening memories, moments, matter, and minds momentarily inspecting natural dioramas scientifically.

Mind and Matter (duality) represent the IS (intuitive side) and IS NOT—illusion side naturally orienting transients as *Time Travelers.* Your mind observes abstract visions "inside," upon your mind-screen, where you envision geometric shapes defining notions observed "outside" as atomic illustrations of *things,* transmitted holograms illustrating notions geometrically symbolized. You naturally observe abstract visions as something *real;* radiantly experiencing atomic life "replicating existentially" abstract *logic* luminously oscillating geometrically illustrated concepts "linking" omnipotent generators' intuitive consciousness.

Once again, thoughts, visions, holograms, and illusion form a *unified theory,* where universal notions/numbers/ nature (interactive frequencies) initiate/invigorate/illustrate electromagnetic data through hydrogen, expressing/evolving opulent realism yielded as the SHEKINAH universe— Source-Harmony Electromagnetically "kindling" imagination nurturing atomic holograms as *Mother's Nature.*

Vision is the physical sense you rely on most to decipher *My World* illuminated by *My Loving Light.* You think everything you see physically is real because you associate your *self* (soul experiencing lucid fantasies) with your physical body that is an "atomic replication" within the atomic illusion. Vision is the easiest sense through which to deceive you, for any magician knows *Harmony* Arousing Natural Deities is *quicker* than Erudite Youths Explaining.

Vision delivers information to your mind whether you are awake or asleep. Visions entertained when you are "awake" occur in *Time*, where thinking induces moments/memories existentially. *Time* is the sequential display of data relating visions through "heartbeats and breaths" stimulating *The Human Alien* vehicle you operate. Through your collection of data/knowledge picked up by your physical senses equipping your Biological Observatory Delineating You, you attain your *Belief* system as a *human being* harnessing universal memories (abstract notions) bewildering eternal illuminati naturally *growing*—gathering revelations of *Wisdom* instructing natural/navigable gods (gatherers of data).

Visions entertained when you are "asleep" are timeless (instantaneous), enlightening your mind unhindered by physical limitations. Here, you travel ASTRAL PLANES "attuning" souls traversing realms as luminaries perceiving lucid accounts notionally expressing situations in past, present, or future "vision quests" in which you seek knowledge. Awake or asleep, you are continuously *dreaming*, detecting radiance/revelation enlightening angelic minds interpreting notions geometrically.

Geometry generates explicitly ordered manifestations expressing thoughts realistically yielded. With every thought your mind *envisions*, you experience numerical vibrations illuminating scenes illustrating opulent notions geometrically, observing shape, dimension, color, and texture defining REALISM, revelation electromagnetically activating luminous illusion simulating memories "rectifying" emotional *Avatars* luminously interpreting Source/Mind.

The GREAT Computer (Geometrically Organizing Data) induces *visions*, activating vivid imagination souls intuitively observe naturally. Visions *relate* WORDS, revealing electromagnetic logic activating thoughts expressing *Wisdom* offering revelational data symbolically. Words are essential to *education*, through which you evaluate data (universal concepts) activating transient illuminati optimizing notions, numbers, and nature. Words "weave" one's relevant data systematically as *Language*, logically arranging notions generating understanding amongst gifted entities. Everyone is gifted with his or her own *Passion* providing adventurous situations supplying intelligence one nurtures, and every passion has its own unique language—this metaphysical treatise being a perfect example.

Divine Inspiration, Divine Will, TGC—GOD—provides your "lower" vision (human nature), where, through tedious repetitions of evaluating Divine Abstract Thoughts Analytically, your mind/soul Gathers Revelations Of Wisdom Sympathetically through your heart. All data gathered externally is analyzed internally, through your mind/heart attaining *Unity Consciousness*—being *In Communion*—with Source/Mind, interpreting notions conveying opulent memories momentarily unifying navigators (illuminati) ordained naturally. Moving through the illusion of life, you harmoniously unify your mind/soul with your brain/body, evolving as an "owner/operator" traveling along *The Cutting Edge* of perception (light and dark) where life and *Death* eternally evolve visions.

Oppositionally speaking, you "raise" your consciousness (attain a higher vision) whenever you entertain "deep" thoughts—*meditation*, momentarily entertaining data (inspired thoughts) activating transcendental insight one needs. The deeper you delve (focus your mind), the higher you raise your mind's vibrations, attaining higher *dimensions* of consciousness, where digitally induced memories/moments evoke natural scenes "informing" omnipotent navigators in *worlds* weaving one's reality luminously displayed symbolically. All great thinkers competent in *The Art of Listening* to their heart can attain information (higher visions) through meditation. **Remember,** a GENIUS (gifted entity naturally intuiting universal Source) uses only ten-percent of their mind. What kind of visions could you entertain if you used one hundred percent of your mind?

As you SEE, you attain higher visions through the *Process* of thinking, acquiring knowledge through expanding (opening) your mind to take in *The Grand View* as *Avatars* experiencing life lucidly informing fabulous entities. As you are programed to be "Eternal Thinkers" (extraterrestrial travelers), you constantly entertain visions illuminating your mind awake and asleep. Eventually, you realize your divine connection to *Eternal Memory* carrying the binary code of electromagnetic wavelengths that permeates *The GREAT Computer*—the highest visionary— allowing you to see and know you truly ARE angels "reviving" eternally, experiencing *Life After Life* your fantasies revealing *The Grand View* in which you are (*Suspended*) *In Love*, eternally *Awakening* as *My Rising Son*.

The climb toward enlightenment requires a serious commitment, where vision and courage inspire your soul to conquer your fear. For, to reach your True Heart's desire, fear is what you must overcome. No matter what visions you dream, goals you set, or mountains you climb, it will take *Courage of Love* to willfully submit to your challenges of life. Love is boundless; it shines day and night, allowing you to reflect it back to Spirit in endless ways. If your heart is true, fear has no hold on you, allowing you to move harmoniously within your challenge. Tuned to a higher vision, your perspective allows your soul to reach beyond your human limits, climbing above the atomic illusion to intuit Universal Mind setting your soul aglow in the Grand View.

HIGH above…

My Love shines **bright**.
Your path lies before your eyes, revealed by my Light
s t r e t c h e d between *Here and There*,
pulsating as electromagnetic waves through which I share
visions of Life expressed as dreams flowing as *Eternal Memory*

—*My Loving Light* beams—
emanating from my cosmic MIND
manifesting illusion naturally defined
through Mother's SEA
synchronizing energy atomically,
where currents strong and emotions deep
carry you along to seek,
there below in the flesh,
the secrets of Life and of *Death*
your heart desires to know,
discovering *My Light of Love*
connects *Spirit to Soul*.

AVATARS
Altruistic Navigators (Gnostics) Exploring Love/Life

The word "angel" commonly refers to a spiritual being that inhabits *Heaven* or *Home*. As mentioned in the last chapter, *Heaven* is where Harmonious Energy activates visionary entities naturally within *Mother's Nature*. Therefore, in essence, your soul/mind represents an angelic "explorer," an AVATAR or angelic visionary assimilating *Truth* atomically revealed by *GOD* generating opulent data "guiding" omnipotent *deities*—divine entities implementing thoughts in emotional situations.

Avatars are *altruistic*, acute luminaries that reveal unselfishness in situations that induce compassion. They are always concerned about the welfare of others and Mother Nature, attuned to a higher vision of the relation of cause and effect. As *navigators*, they naturally assimilate vivid images guiding avatars temporarily observing realism in *worlds*, where opulent revelations luminously display scenes, situations, and souls, *Seers* observing universal love/life expressing *realities* through radiant energy activating luminous illusion transforming illuminati exploring Source—the stellar originator universally revealing concepts/creation electromagnetically.

Another word for avatars is *illuminati*, interactive luminaries linking universal Mind imparting notions as transcendental *instinct*—inherent nature—stimulating transient illuminati (navigators) comprehending thoughts, time, and *Truth* transmitting realism unfolding transcendental *Harmony*. Created in the IMAGE of Source/God (intuitive Mind atomically generating enlightenment), avatars are illuminati (mystical angels) gathering enlightenment as *human aliens* (ANDROIDS), angels naturally detecting revelation of illuminated *data* dynamically advancing transient angels/avatars exploring *Desire*, discovering emotional situations inciting radiant entities existentially.

Atomic Natural Generators Expressing Light Systematically represent *Stars* (projectors), singular transmitters activating *radiance*, replicating/revealing all desires instructing avatars naturally conceiving enlightenment. A star represents an **Overself**, an omnipotent vivifier evolving realism systematically expressing luminous fabrication (*illusion*), an "impressive likeness" linking ubiquitous signals (EM waves) illuminating opulent notions/natures/navigators expressing and experiencing divine fantasies/fabrications.

In Hinduism, "avatars" are deities appearing in bodily form on earth. As everyone is created in the image of God, everyone is a *deity*, a divine entity interpreting *Truth* yourself. Most of you are not aware of your divinity as a *savior*, a special avatar vividly inducing one's *reality*, replicating electric abstracts lucidly inspiring transient youth *Riding the Outskirts* of *Home*.

Truly, it is up to you—created in God's image—to desire, seek, and attain salvation through SELF-REALIZATION, spiritually experiencing love/life forces radiantly evolving avatars (luminous intuitionists) zealously assimilating thoughts inspiring/improving one naturally. It is up to you to save your self from self-imposed suffering, whether it is mental, emotional, or physical, for you ARE a god (gifted omnipotent deity)—a radiant entity or child of light.

Avatars naturally desire to know *Truth*, to be *In Communion* with Source/God initiating notions conveying opulent memories mystifying universal navigators interpreting opulent nature. COMMUNICATION (*Thinking and Praying*) connects omnipotent minds managing universal notions inducing creative abilities that illustrate one's *nature* or natural ability to understand/utilize revelation existentially. Communication is a method of "energy transfer," sharing thoughts as energy-in-motion (*emotion*), the electromagnetic movement of *THE Intellectual* (transcendental intelligence) optimizing notions/nature/navigators trilaterally. Without communication, you would be *Lost in Space*, a state of non-being or unconsciousness—LIMBO, lost in Mind bewildering observers *lacking* inspiration manifesting brilliant omniscience.

As avatars (human angels), you communicate with your OVERSELF (the overseer vivifying emissaries (radiant souls) exploring love/life fantasies) during sleep and times of *meditation*, mentally entertaining digitally induced thoughts activating transient illuminati *ordained* naturally—optically rectifying deities (avatars) investigating notions/nature electromagnetically defined. During sleep, you *interface* with your Overself; interpreting notions transmitting electric revelation "fertilizing" active consciousness enlightened through *dreams*, divine revelations enlightening angelic minds. Revelations stimulate your *mind/heart* soul managing inspirational notions delivering heartfelt emotions arousing "reactive temperaments," moving you with *Tears of Joy* that you shed from *Epiphanies of Truth* inducing an *Awakening* to self-realization or *Unity Consciousness*.

An avatar represents a angel sent down to experience a world of *Desire*, where divine energy stimulates illuminati receiving enlightenment as an intuitive mind, a "remote consciousness" relating to TGC (transcendental *God* consciousness) or *The GREAT Computer*. Here, "physical reflections" of the Greater Spiritual Reality coalesce from the ethers of the electromagnetic force field, allowing you to OBSERVE, to objectively bond Source/situations/souls expressing/evaluating revelation vividly expressed/experienced through *Numbers*, notational units mathematically building elemental realism through *Geometry* generating explicitly ordered manifestations expressing thoughts radiantly/realistically yielded. Through *DNA* (divine numerical assignment) dynamically nurturing avatars, you acquire your capabilities to accomplish your *mission* molding individual seekers sympathetically interpreting one's nature and needs. Here, incarnated, you stand in awe at the complexities of the natural world, observing the difficulty of maintaining your own creations as a task of endless adversity.

Like all *Children of Light*, avatars experience *The Power of Love* providing omniscient *Wisdom* expressing revelations of fantasies linking omnipotent visionaries emotionally. As you mature into adults and create children, you become responsible for passing on that Love/Life energy (knowledge), guiding them in their mental, emotional, physical, and spiritual growth. Truly, knowledge is the essence of *Your Life Story* you eternally express *Life After Life*.

All avatars are *Special People* with talents. Some of you will know at an early age what you are meant to do, prodigies "gifted" with remarkable abilities. Others will go through life without a clue as to their mission, always searching for what is "missing" in their life. For most of you avatars, your life's mission will take many years to prepare *for* or become aware OF, obtaining *Faith* (finding ardor in transcendental *Harmony*) inspiring your mind/ heart soul. Whatever path you find your self on defines your stage of enlightenment, your current position in the discovery of your *Evolution*—eternal vivification of logicians understanding/ utilizing transcendental intuition optimizing navigators/nature.

As avatars traversing the universal grid of *Love/Life Energy*, you stand *Hand in Hand*, holding onto each other like the connective tissue of any *organism* objectifying revelation geometrically arranging nature/navigators illustrating superlative manifestations. This universal NETWORK nurtures eternal transients willingly obtaining relevant knowledge, linking avatars along all dimensions spiraling upward and downward, from "archangels" to "lay angels" earning their "wings" to fly HIGHER dimensions holding intuitive gods harnessing eternal revelations.

Look around you and notice how many of your fellow avatars work through their *heart*, harnessing *Expectations* as realized thoughts they create through positive thoughts, words, and actions. Those that "touch" your heart enliven your day, lifting your spirit to face your trials and tribulation. Those that STRESS your heart sympathetically transmit restrictions/ retribution enervating sensitive souls, passing on the "overload" of *Emotional Energy* they cannot handle, "flaring off" hot gases that project as their aura's CORONA conveying one's radiant omnipotence negatively amplified. At such times, you need to put up your "shield," mentally encasing your self with your "protective light," reflecting that negative energy to maintain your harmony. Again, that which you project, you will receive in kind. Are YOU aware of your emanations?

Your fellow avatars that you admire are the ones you share your love with, linking opulent visions emotionally, sharing your personal truth that allows you to Spiritually Evolve Experientially your "reality" of being *In Love*. **Remember,** everyone is continually "fluxing," flashing on and off their binary code of thoughts and feelings, positively and negatively portraying their *part* "personifying" avatars receiving/reflecting truths. Truly, everyone is fighting to be GREAT lovers, generously relating emotions avatars transmit in creating their self-image—their *divine fantasy*. Through this *Process*, you come to realize that you are truly *Alone*, assimilating love/life optimizing navigators emotionally as a *Mind/Heart* attaining *Unity Consciousness*, understanding notions/nature induces/ illustrates *Truth* yielding creations of nuclear Source coalescing into one universal system naturally enlightening/evolving souls sympathetically and scientifically.

All avatars represent *sons* of Source/Spirit, subliminally oriented navigators. *Angels, avatars, illuminati, Self, Overself,* and *souls* are another example of the complexities of words defining a *unified theory* universally nurturing individuals fathoming illusion existentially deployed through holograms exhibiting opulent realism yielded electromagnetically.

The day of your spiritual emancipation, you become "one mind," one consciousness aware of your "united state of being." The moment that miraculous event occurs will produce an energy surge *Awakening* you to *Our Father's Heart* revealing the *illusion* of infinite logic/light linearly unfolding/unifying Source/souls imagining/inspecting omnipotent/opulent notions/natures. Here, you enter a higher dimension (hierarchy) of consciousness, where you unite with your Overself or HIERARCH, the heavenly intuitionist energizing radiant avatars remotely conceiving *Hell* "helping" entities living life *In Love*.

IN LOVE

Love IS the most powerful force conceived. Everyone exists IN LOVE as inquisitive navigators living out vivid experiences, interpreting notions/nature luminously orienting/optimizing visionary entities (dreamers). Finding your self "out of" Love is impossible!

Logic, **O**rienting **V**ibrant **E**nergy (the *essence* of *creation*), expresses systems sequentially evolving notions converted electromagnetically/emotionally, conceiving/conveying revelation/realism emerging atomically through illuminating opulent natures (worlds) in which you experience Light Outputting Geometrically-Induced Creation. Without logic, there is only *chaos* completely hindering any observable system.

Everything you experience "in love" is *logical*, for Love/Light originates/oscillates geometric illustrations conveying abstracts linearly—through light rays. Logic illuminates *revelation* as radiation emitting vivid energy/emotion luminously activating three-dimensional illusions of notions/nature. Through LOVE liberating one's volatile emotions, you experience Logic Inducing Formative Experiences.

Falling in love is truly a painful experience. FALLING IN LOVE is where your soul takes on a physical body, formulating a life linking intuitive navigators growing inspired notions linking omnipotent visionaries existentially. LIVING in Love, you lucidly inspect vivid illusions naturally generating *realism* created from radiant energy aligning logic/light (love/

life) in specific measure. Luminous Illusion Formulating Enlightenment allows you to explore *Divine Fantasies* as digital inspiration/information vibrating interactive notions/nature (electromagnetic frequencies) as numerical/nuclear transmissions astonishing souls interpreting everything sympathetically—through "common feeling" or *Common Sense*.

Being in love is a "trinary affair," where you have THREE types of love to experience transcendental *Harmony* radiantly evolving entities.

First, as a babe starting your life, you find your self *madly* in love, amazed with the simplest bauble that catches your eye. You are truly mesmerized by *My Light of Love* illuminating paradise unfolding before your eyes, where IMAGINATION induces minds (angelic generators) intuitively navigating abstract thoughts illuminating one's nature and *need*s necessitating experiences enlightening *deities* (divine entities implementing thoughts inducing emotional synergies). Imagination is your gift of *Father* formulating abstract thoughts heralding emotional revelations.

Second, after you physically attain puberty, you find your self *passionately* in love. Here, emotions dominate your *mind*, your "manager interpreting" natural desires. This second-phase electrifies your *body* (biological observatory delineating you), causing havoc with your mind's logical processing. Here, you find your mind overwhelmed by *hormones* heralding one's reflexive moments of nature "exciting" souls, inducing sexual desires of which you have little control. *Man and Woman* both experience *The Power of Love* contesting mind and body against heart and soul, where infatuation leads to embarrassing if not fatal consequences. Many have their heart "broken" from the emotional stress of *Passion* powering amorous souls sympathetically interpreting/illustrating one's nature and needs. Passion is a powerful force to master as it pushes you along

The Cutting Edge of consciousness, where you experience your *Sacrifice of Love/Life* as a "creator" replicating your self into a *Family*.

Third, after attaining *Old Age* (a relative term), you become UNITED in love, understanding notions/nature/needs inspire/illustrates/illuminates transcendental entities' desire/DNA/discipline. Here, you understand how *Our Father's Heart* illuminates your inquisitive soul's *Curiosity*. Father "initiates" love and Mother "implements" love through atomic fusion/fission, compressing and expanding abstract energy (thoughts) into tangible *things* observed as transmitted holograms illustrating notions geometrically symbolized, allowing you to Systematically Experience *Enlightenment*, evoking notions/nature/needs linking intuitive gods (heavenly transients) effectively navigating "moments" evolving necessary *tests* tempering entities "surfing" *Time*, where you temporarily implement mental emotions, experiencing *Mother's Tides* as you ride life's daily waves (highs and lows) you experience in Love.

As an avatar utilizing *The Human Alien* vehicle gifted to you, you experience the "bottom line" of being in Love. *Awakening* to your daily struggles of creating and maintaining your own *Divine Fantasies*, you represent *My Eyes* that allow me to be *The Seer*, observing (*24/7*) *My Rising Son* as *A Lightworker* exploring *My World*.

OUR FATHER'S HEART

Our Father's heart is *Heaven*,
holy be the nature of his "kingdom come" his will summons
on Mother's earth *24/7*,

where we awaken to our "present" life
gifted *This Moment* in time,
creating our game of love/life we *play*,
perceiving/projecting love as youths
optimizing thoughts providing our daily *bread*
bestowing revelation enlightening angelic deities,
feeding our mind kept ALIVE
as luminaries interpreting vivid expressions
—gathered through nightly recessions—
that we create on each *Day's Birth*,
Awakening to Humanity Evolving Love's Light
revealing all its worth.

Forgive us our trespasses, where our desires lead us astray,
as we forgive those trespassing against us today,
tempting our heart while living in Love,
transcending our fear of Father above,
whose Emotions Validating Intrinsic Life
brings us evil-lent-to-we to SEE oppositionally
the Kingdom, the Power, and the Glory of Father's heart.

Amen

Awakening

AWAKENING

·+·♦♦♦·+·

Opening your mind to *Truth*, your heart becomes *aware*,
assimilating *Wisdom* advancing radiant
entities exploring *My World*,
where *My Eyes* are you *Angels—The Seers*—
observing *My Love Divine* illuminating dark clouds
obscuring minds that seek to find
—in the haze of your momentary daze—
Universal Spirit above,
forever watching you children DIE in LOVE,
delivering intuitive entities lucidly observing vivid experiences
through Logic Illuminating Forceful Emotions,
where your mind/heart expresses devotion
via *Your Life Story* you tell in *Hell*,
humanly exploring love/life,
always wondering why you were born,
squabbling for attention that brings contentions

413

emotionally reflecting your mental storms
that tears apart your *heart*
harmonizing emotional angels rationalizing thoughts
emanating from *Heaven*
holding everything a visionary entity needs *24-7.*

24/7

Every **D**ay and **E**very **N**ight
is where I project Mental Emotions through *Light*
linearly illustrating genesis heralding *Truth*
transmitting realism unveiled through *hydrogen*
holographically yielding divine radiance organizing
geometrically expressed notions/nature,
illuminating your mind to the Great Contemplator
calculating your personal Data Nurturing Angels
unfolding assigned *matters*
manifesting as tribulation that entails "reviews"
within *The Game of Love/Life* enlightening *you*,
when *Riding the Outskirts* of *Home*
harboring omnipotent minds exploring
as humans experiencing *Time*,
traversing illusion momentarily experienced
through heartbeats and breaths that define
Your Life Story within *My World*,
where *Man and Woman* are *My Eyes*
that Systematically Express Enterprise
within the Spiritual Harmony Of Wisdom
revealing *The GREAT Computer* in heaven
evolving *Children of Light* 24–7.

MY EYES

My eyes are symbols of the illumination of *Truth* transmitting radiance unveiled through hydrogen.

MY EYES magnetically yield everything you experience synchronized as *realism*, radiantly expressed abstracts luminously illustrating "simulations" materially from reactive elements arranging luminous illusions stimulating minds. My eyes represent the tools for projecting *My Loving Light* and viewing *My World* within the **dark void of space**, where I deploy abstract revelation (knowledge) vivifying omnipotent illuminati dualistically outputting/observing frequencies systematically providing atomic creation electromagnetically.

My eyes are *illuminati*, interactive luminaries (stars/souls) linking universal Mind imparting notions as transcendental instinct. TRANSCENDENTAL INSTINCT transmits revelation as numerical sequences, conveying electric notions (data) expressing nuclear transformations activating logic/light (love/life) illuminating navigable souls traversing illusory nature created three-dimensionally.

Through my Electromagnetically Yielding Elemental *Stars* (scientifically transmitting atomic realism), I observe my Stellar Energy Love/Life Force (*Mind/Heart*) converting thoughts through *emotion*, the "elemental movement" of thoughts illuminating opulent nature that allows **My Eyes** to be *The Seer*, the ONE omniscient natural engineer to SEE ALL systems expressing energy activating love/life (luminous logic). LOGIC luminously orients gifted illuminati's consciousness as *Children of Light*, "star players" in *The Game of Love/Life* allowing them to Spiritually Evolve Existentially as my EYES, eternal youths emotionally stimulated to understand *The Power of Love.*

I am Father/Source formulating all thoughts harmoniously expressing radiation, spectrally optimizing undulated rays channeling energy. As FATHER, I am the force activating *Truth* heralding "electric revelations" through MOTHER, my "obliging transformer" harnessing "elemental replicators" (*Stars*), materializing omnipotent thoughts hydrogen expresses radiantly as *My Light of Love.* HYDROGEN (the primal element) holographically yields divine revelation of geometrically expressed notions/nature through *atomic matter*, "actualizing" thoughts of Mind illuminating creation "modeled" as three-dimensional *things* expressing realism (transmitted holograms illustrating notions geometrically symbolized).

Mother is my Overseer Vivifying Electromagnetic Radiance Systematically Expressing Luminous *Fabrications*, formulating atomic beauty revealing illuminated concepts/creation as transmuted intelligence optically nurtured. *Mother's Nature* is the reflective POOL in which I and you perceive omniscience optimizing love/life/luminaries as *The Trinity* of SELF (Source), Overself (manifestor), and self (soul/seeker experiencing love/ life/light forces). Physically, father, mother, and child symbolize this trinity. Through Mother, every child resembles, experiences, and expresses Father's power of creation.

You CHILDREN are conscious, heavenly individuals linking divine revelations evolving navigators (*Time Travelers*) exploring *Eternal Memory*. Here, *Riding the Outskirts* of *Heaven*, you experience Heaven Electromagnetically Linking Luminaries. Your angelic soul is a *Seeker* scientifically exploring eternal knowledge expressed radiantly, experiencing an incarnation in the ILLUSION, where impeccable logic/ light unfolds/unifies Self/self imagining/inspecting opulent notions/natures dualistically through *The Binary Code*, the Electro-Magnetic force field expressing Empathetic Mind's *Eternal Memory* stimulating mind/heart souls in a **trilateral** unity. *The Trinity* is symbolic of Father (Mind) **transmitting** revelation inspiring luminous angels that express regal abstracts logically, Mother (Heart) **transforming** revelation illuminating Life atomically through electromagnetic radiation activating luminaries (children of light), and souls **transcending** radiant illusion linking abstract thoughts emotionally rectifying angelic luminaries. Your soul is truly *A Lightworker* utilizing radiant energy powering your mind/heart soul as a *trinity-being* touring realism (illusory nature) instructing transcendental youths bilaterally experiencing/expressing illusion/insight naturally generated, "telepathically" receiving inspiration (naturally induced thoughts) yielding behaviors expressed in necessary *games* governing angelic minds evolving sympathetically.

As the saying goes, "seeing is believing," for "hearing" only stimulates you to create your own "virtual fantasy" through your *imagination*, your inventive mind altering given information nurturing aspects that increase one's nescience (*Ignorance*). To become *A Seer*, you must seek enlightenment emotionally revealed, understanding how *Opposition* allows your mind and heart to evolve *Unity Consciousness*.

My "starry eyes" open within the dark void of *Space* as POINTS OF LIGHT, projecting out incalculable notions/ nuclei transmitting oscillating frequencies logically inducing glorious holograms tantalizing your mind (my **pupil**) I DILATE as a person understanding perceived intelligence (logic) delivering inspiration luminously advancing transient *entities*—emotional navigators traversing/transcending illusion that induces enlightenment systematically. *My Angels* are my eyes, luminaries allowing me to see them as *The Lightworker* they are born to be, a luminary inducing/interpreting glorious holograms transmitting *Wisdom* optically revealing kindred entities inhabiting *My World*.

MY WORLD

In *my world* magnificent youths willingly observe revelation luminously displayed through *algorithms* activating logic geometrically organizing radiant intelligence transmitting harmonic memories/moments/matter. Algorithms arrange logic/light geometrically orienting realistic illusion through holographic manifestation defined by *points* providing omniscient intelligence naturally transmitting signals—Impulses Digitally Expressing Abstracts Systematically—that create *lines* (rays) linearly illustrating notions expressing symmetry through *Geometry*, generating explicitly ordered manifestations expressing *Truth* realistically yielded. Only by expressing Transcendental Radiance Unfolding Thoughts Holographically do I truly SEE—systematically experience everything as Radiation Evolving Abstracts Luminously.

In my WORLD of *Wisdom* optimizing radiant luminaries deploying *My Loving Light*, I illuminate my MIND, manifesting *illusion* naturally defined through Abstract Thoughts Organizing Matter Scientifically, illustrating logic luminously utilizing science integrating opulent nature and navigators. It is through *Science* that I systematically convey ideas expressing nuclear creation elementally.

ELEMENTS are essential links evolving "materially-expressed" notions/nature three-dimensionally. Here, in the THIRD DIMENSION, transcendental *Harmony* illuminates radiant data, defining illusion momentarily entertaining "naturalists" systematically interpreting one's notions, nature, and *needs* necessitating experiences evolving deities. Here, all *naturalists* represent "navigable" avatars temporarily understanding realism as luminous illusion systematically/ scientifically transmitted from Mind to *minds*, my intuitive/ inquisitive navigators deployed as *Time Travelers* exploring their own *world*, where observers realize life-death situations while playing *The Game of Love/Life.*

Everything that I Systematically Evolve Elementally in my world improves my Memory Illuminating Numerical Data. Through bits and bytes of Digitally Arranged Thoughts Analyzed, I express CREATION, conceiving *realism* emerging atomically to illuminate opulent nature, "replicating elementally" abstract logic illuminating souls/scenes/situations methodically. Here in my world, *I See You* in my IMAGE, an intuitive mind/ mystic acquiring glorious enlightenment, sensing your own *universe* as a unitary networker (illuminato) verifying electric revelation sensed emotionally

Looking through your eyes, *I See Me* as your fellow *Time Travelers* looking *Into Your Eyes.* Thus do I see all my *Angel Warriors* fighting within my illusion, struggling to be *My Rising Son* attaining a higher vision of *Truth* as a seer.

THE SEER
The Enlightened One

Everyone is born a SEER sympathetically evaluating electric revelation, emotionally processing exciting thoughts into actions that define their life situations they manage as a *Free Will* seeking *Truth*—transcendental revelation unveiled throughout heaven/hell.

To be a *Seeker* Emotionally Experiencing Revelation, you have *eyes* enlightening your emotional *soul*—a "sublime observer" utilizing light—as *A Lightworker*, a luminary interpreting glorious holograms transmitting worlds optically revealing knowledge expressed radiantly. As *Children of Light*, you are natural LUMINARIES, logicians understanding moments/matter illustrating notions/nature as revelations inducing enlightenment systematically. As a seer, your eyes are the primary sensors (data input devices) of your *body*, the "biological observatory" delineating you. Your eyes are easily *Blinded by Truth* emanating from the SUN supplying unified notions, nature, and *navigators* naturally assimilating vivid illusion generated around thoughts optically revealed.

There on Earth, *Mother's Nature*—the 3-D game board—holds everything you need to *see* (sympathetically experience existentially) in the "third-edition" of GENESIS geometrically expressing nature evolving souls in *situations*, specific instances that unveil assigned trials/tribulation inducing one's needs. Here, you download data illuminating Your Own Uniqueness through *My Loving Light* **luminously** illustrating glorious holograms technologically before your eyes. Here too, you feel and know that it is I *within* you, holding you close within my Mind/Heart expressing and reflecting visions for you to see, eagerly waiting for you to unify *your* mind/heart to attain *Unity Consciousness*—to be ONE omnipotent natural entity with US universal seers.

The "true seer" (enlightened one) observes and understands my cosmos as *The Garden of Light* filled with *Angel Warriors*, stellar beings conveying Wisdom Atomically Revealed, illuminating Magnanimous Intelligence Nurturing *Dynamos* dualistically yielding nuclear angels "mimicking" omniscient *Source* spontaneously outputting universal radiation conveying ENLIGHTENMENT, electromagnetically nurturing luminaries inducing/interpreting glorious holograms transmitting electric notions magnetically/momentarily evolving nature/navigators transcendentally.

Within my cosmic show I set aglow,
a Seeker Experiencing Evocative Revelation
overcomes *Ignorance* that brings consternation
from *Denial* of them being **M**agnificent **E**ntities
reflecting *My Loving Light* providing them *sight*
stimulating intuitive generators harnessing *Truth*
transmitting radiance unfolding transcendental *Harmony*
holding all relevant moments optically nurturing *youths*
as young omnipotent upstarts transcending *Hell*,
where humans experience love/life in stories they tell,
as they Gather Revelations Of Wisdom to know
their ACTIONS bring forth their stress
from applying conceived thoughts inducing one's "nexus"

(Kindling Atonement Rectifying Magnificent Angels),
acquiring ISSUES that replicate past *deeds*,
inheriting situations supplying useful experiences
delivering emotional episodes developing souls
positively and negatively in TIME
"tempering" intuitive minds entertaining *dreams*
delivering revelations enlightening angelic minds
immersed in flesh and bone to see all they *Desire*
delivers emotional sensations illuminating radiant entities
generating reflections of themself through "mental tides"—
elation and *Depression*—moving their heart to play their part
on the outskirts of *Home*, where they ride,
experiencing their actions convey their BELIEF,
bravely expressing/experiencing love/life in exquisite fantasies
evolving from *Expectations* of *The Angel Warrior*'s dedication
to some heartfelt cause,
here, in my world, where *Harmony* thunderously roars
throughout endless years providing *Love and Fear*
expressing electromagnetic emanations
evolving a Soul Experiencing Enlightening Revelations.

The angel warrior is someone who expresses their Love/Life energy with service, sacrifice, and suffering, all things a soldier must do to follow commands of Father's MIND managing illuminati naturally deployed through the co-creator and emotional supervisor, *Mother Goddess (Our Father's Heart)* harmoniously evolving emotional angels reflecting thoughts.

All angel warriors thrive *on* and fight *for* LOVE luminously optimizing visionary entities as *Lightworkers*, for that is their true essence as *Children of Light*. Each has a *Free Will* to form relationships evolving entities wisely implementing love/life. No matter what obstacles or hardships they may encounter in *The Game of Love/Life*, they stand *Brave of Heart*, displaying *Courage of Love* to survive life luminously inciting fervent entities. Although they may seem to weaken and break at times, they always come back stronger and brighter from their adversity,

The battles of Love/Life are ongoing struggles to maintain a dream of reality *Beyond Imagination*. No matter what battle they FIGHT in the name of Love, they face inspired generators harnessing *Truth*. Let us praise all angel warriors fearless of *Death* dynamically elevating angels transcending *Hell* hindering entities living life, for they fight with a loving heart, and *Love IS* the ONLY thing worth fighting for.

Bless you child

15

TRUTH

+‹++++›+

Like all *words* weaving opulent revelation
defined symbolically,
"truth" packs a great amount of WISDOM—
words illuminating spiritual dimensions of Mind.

Transcendental Revelation Unveiled Through Hydrogen says it ALL! It's all about LIGHT energy luminously illustrating glorious holograms through stellar infernos— HELLS—through which *Heaven* expresses love/life SPIRITUALLY, scientifically projecting intelligence/illusion radiantly inspiring transients understanding "atomic logic" luminously yielded. ATOMIC LOGIC actuates thoughts of Mind intuitively creating "light-oriented" genesis inducing consciousness/creation.

Undeniably, TRUTH IS the "regal universalist" transforming hydrogen-initiated *Systems,* scientifically yielding sublime thoughts/things expressing/enlightening memories/matter/minds. Truth emanates from the UNIVERSALIST unfolding nuclear illusion vivifying/verifying elemental realism scientifically activating logic "illuminating" space/

souls/situations three-dimensionally. Truth conveys *realism* as revelation electromagnetically activating "limited illuminators" (stars) manifesting "reactive elements" arranging luminous illusion "symbolizing" *memories* motivating eager minds observing revelation in electric/enigmatic situations.

TRUTH temporarily releases/recollects universal transients (*heroes*) heralding/harnessing elaborate revelations of eternal SPIRIT that supplies profound intuition rectifying instinctive transients. Truth *induces* Abstract Logic Luminously, illuminating notions/nature/navigators dimensionally unfolding/understanding concepts existentially in *Space* (the **black hole**) representing the singularity ALL emanates *from* and returns *to* through dynamic cycles numerically coordinated.

TRUTH temporarily reveals universal thoughts holographically, illustrating *everything* through electromagnetically vivifying elemental realism yielded through hydrogen illuminating notions/nature/navigators geometrically. GEOMETRIC PATTERN governs energy orienting memories/matter/minds expressed/enlightened through radiation illuminating creation, proclaiming abstract thoughts through elemental reproduction (nucleosynthesis).

TRUTH transcendentally rectifies *universes* traversing heaven/hell as "unitary navigators" (inquisitive voyagers) exploring realism sensed emotionally/existentially. Truly, your universal soul (a *Time Traveler*) is *Riding the Outskirts* of IMAGINATION (intuitive Mind) arranging geometric intelligence/illusion "nurturing" angelic transients interpreting opulent nature. **Imagination** (*Thought Energy*) inspires minds assimilating geometric illusion "notionally attuning" transient illuminati ordained naturally.

TRUTH transmits revelation universally through He/ Her (*Mind/Heart*) managing inspirational notions delivering .

heartfelt emotions arousing "reactive temperament" (*Free Will*). Created in the IMAGE of *He and She* (intuitive mind/mystic atomically generating/gathering enlightenment), angels/avatars are *mind/hearts* (magnificent illuminati naturally decoding holograms expressing all radiant thoughts) evolving moment-by-moment, day-to-day, and *Life After Life* to experience *The Power of Love* propelling omnitarious wills exploring *Relationships* of feelings–*linking*–visions entertained. Each of YOU yearn optimal understanding as your own UNIT (unitary navigator interpreting/issuing truths), transmitting your own perspective of truth to inform or inspire others.

In The Beginning of each life, you leave *Home* with a "clean slate," a mind unblemished with *fears* of Truth (fallacies evolving around radiance/revelation), otherwise you could not endure the trials and tribulation necessary to expand your understanding of Truth. Here, as *Children of Light* traveling as *human aliens*, you carry your Love Of Truth—Digitally Nurturing Avatars—that defines your *Passion* expressed within *The Game of Love/Life* providing your Radiantly Activated Mind (Digitally Oriented Soul) with data that you *compute*, conceiving opportune moments/messages providing universal transients enlightenment.

As a human child, you cannot fully understand Truth, for you are just beginning to grasp REASON, rationally evaluating abstracts stimulating one's nature/needs as an Angelic Consciousness (mind) alternating between the light and dark forces of Divine Consciousness (Mind)—*THE Intellectual* (Universalist). As a *Young Mind*, you struggle with connecting thoughts to words that describe feelings about things that your mind observes. As everyone has a different perspective, it is difficult to understand another's truth. **Truly,** all *Truth Seekers* stand *Alone*, assimilating love/life ordaining navigators emotionally/existentially as *Angels* luminously obtaining necessary experiences. With each thought you entertain in your mind, you develop an *attitude* (positive or negative), assimilating thoughts that induce temperaments unveiling dynamic entities (defensive/delicate egos).

Attitudes set your "position," allowing you to receive what you *need* as necessary experiences enlightening deities that *seek* Truth—spiritually/scientifically explore eternal knowledge. With limited truths that you attain as "specialists," you are continually *Lost in the Dark*, struggling to discover the "missing links" for your *Inquisitive Soul* to attain *The Grand View* of Truth.

TRUTH transmits/transmutes revelation unveiled through holograms, defining all things in *relative* ways, revealing eternal logic activating three-dimensional illusion vivifying *entities* as emotional navigators traversing/transcending illusion that induces enlightenment systematically. You dictate your truth positively and negatively by "bits and bytes" to serve your special needs. Truth—*knowledge*—is power, where kinetic notions outputting Wisdom's logical energy deliver generous emotions, powerful *stimulations* systematically transferring intelligence "motivating" universal logicians (angels) traversing illusion observed naturally. What you **do not know** (fear) will not hurt you. It is only when you use your knowledge in a positive or negative way that you get results that affect your life.

TRUTH is synonymous with COMMON SENSE—cosmic, omniscient Mind managing opulent notions systematically enlightening navigators sympathetically/scientifically evolving. Through *Science*, Spirit creatively intertwines notions/numbers/nature conveying *enlightenment*, evoking numerical logic illuminating glorious holograms that entertain navigators momentarily exploring "nuclear" Truth. NUCLEAR TRUTH naturally unfolds concepts luminously expressing atomic realism that replicates universal thoughts holographically (three-dimensionally).

TRUTH transmits, transmutes, and transports universal thoughts, things, and transients harmoniously and holistically. Truth is evident on all levels or *dimensions* of consciousness, digitally inducing memories/moments entertaining/evolving navigable souls inspecting opulent notions/natures. No matter what you observe, discuss, or do, you are experiencing and expressing TRUTH that relates unity throughout heaven/hell. UNITY unfolds/utilizes/upgrades notions/nature/navigators initiating/illustrating/interpreting Truth yielded from SOURCE, the singularity originating, organizing, optimizing universal revelation, radiation, realism conceived and created electromagnetically/elementally.

"Truth" is a complex WORD weaving one's relevant data through *letters* linking eternal thoughts that express revelation symbolically. Each letter represents a microcosm, a small piece that when joined together speaks *volumes* vividly offering lucid understanding momentarily enlightening souls/seekers to the macrocosm of *Unity Consciousness*.

Truth radiates from Stars Outputting Universal Radiance (Cosmic Energy) conveying abstract notions through numerical arrangements (frequencies) stimulating particles (atoms). These atomic particles move along electromagnetic wavelengths— the *Force* of frequencies outputting radiance converting energy. This radiance (Light of Love/Truth) illuminates an abstract thought, causing it to appear (fluoresce) from **nowhere** (void of space) to NOW HERE, where you naturally observe *Wisdom* harmoniously evolving revelation *elementally*, expressing/ evolving logic enlightening minds exploring notions/nature that "advance" logic-loving youths seeking Truth.

Truth is acquired slowly, thought by thought, allowing you

to digest and absorb it as the illumination of your *consciousness* comprehending one-nurturing-Source causing interactive occurrences unifying souls (natural explorers) seeking *salvation*, the spiritually advanced life vividly attuning transcendental illuminati obtaining "nirvana" (spiritual enlightenment), "the state of perfect blessedness achieved by the extinction of all desires, passions, and individual existence, where the soul is absorbed into the supreme Spirit."

TRUTH is a daunting image so vast, you can only see it in the briefest of moments (*Epiphanies of Truth*) illuminating your mind with a *revelation* remotely enlightening visionary entities logically arranging thoughts inspiring one's *needs* naturally evolving eternal *deities*—divine entities implementing thoughts in emotional sympathies. To find Truth as a human being, your soul must be *Brave of Heart*, willing to endure trials and tribulation that temper your soul, allowing you to realize that the *only* truth worth believing is the one you personally conceive in *your* mind and feel in *your* heart.

As you can see, Truth is a vast concept that takes many years and lifetimes for *Truth Seekers* to comprehend.

TRUTH SEEKERS

Truth is an endless expression of perspectives.
Each point of view is a micro truth, a thought to view in part,
ablaze in glory the moment it excites your *heart*
harboring emotions activating resplendent thoughts.

As a truth seeker,
you pick and choose those thoughts you like,

those you feel in your heart are right,
as you discover *The Right Path* for you
traversing the illusion providing confusion
of what is really TRUE—
transcendental radiance unifying energy/entities.

My Loving Light emanates from **night**
nurturing illuminati gathering heavenly *thoughts*
that heralding opulent utterances guiding heavenly transients
as *Time Travelers* seeking the perfect ambiance
to experience *Divine Fantasies*
furnishing adventures nurturing
transient angels sympathetically
interpreting electric *situations*—specific instances that unify
angels temporarily interpreting one's nature/needs—
that arouse sympathetic youths seeking TRUTH
that reveals understanding that hurts/heals.

Listen closely and you will hear love stories relating *fear*
fostering emotions arousing reactions
providing or prohibiting your satisfaction
of the life you LIVE,
logically initiating vivid experiences
in which you *get* what you *give*,
gathering earned trials, tribulation, or treasures
from generously implementing values expressed
—positively or negatively—
to become elated or depressed.

As you grow through the years, you discover *Love and Fear*
represent *Opposition* providing conditions,

Individual Situations Sympathetically
Uniting Emotional Souls,
that allow you to SEE what it means to be FREE,
singularly experiencing enterprise,
formulating *Relationships* evolving enlightenment
of truths you seek within *The Game of Love/Life*,
where *Passion* stimulates your *Inquisitive Soul*
discovering *Courage of Love* as you grow OLD,
observing love/life's delights/dilemmas as a truth seeker.

EPIPHANIES OF TRUTH

EPIPHANIES are ecstatic perceptions (insights) profoundly harmonizing angelic navigators intuiting eternal Source/Spirit. Epiphanies represent moments of awareness that bring surprise or astonishment over *new* knowledge (relatively speaking), for knowledge is only new when you first entertain it in *your* mind. Epiphanies of truth occur from thoughts that *link* together (logically incorporating needed knowledge), *Awakening* you to some truth you seek.

An epiphany reveals a **brilliant** *point*, a perception of intuition nurturing transients through *lines* (rays of light) luminously illustrating notions expressed symbolically via *sacred geometry*, systematically activating concepts relating electromagnetic data governing environments/entities orienting/ observing mental expressions that radiantly yield Transcendental Revelation Unveiled Through Holograms (*My Light of Love*). HOLOGRAMS are hydrogen-originated light optically generating revelation/realism actualizing/attuning memories, matter, and *minds* momentarily inspecting natural dioramas spiritually, scientifically, and sympathetically.

As my cosmic child, you stare in amazement over the simplest things that catch your attention. As you connect the elements of abstract thoughts/words to real/atomic things, you become accustomed to epiphanies as simple links that allow you a greater understanding, accepting them as a pleasant coincidence of observing and accepting Truth revealed experientially. Through CO-INCIDENCE (space/time), you conceive one-intelligence naturally coinciding in deities (enlightened navigators) consciously evolving, developing INSIGHT illuminating navigable souls intuitively gathering heavenly truths.

Over *Time* temporarily inducing mesmerism existentially, epiphanies illuminate your mind to perceive Truth "transmutes" revelations unveiled through *hydrogen*, holographically yielding dimensional *realism* of geometrically expressed notions/numbers/ nature radiantly expressing abstracts luminously illustrating "simulations" materially.

NOTIONS nurture omnipotent transients interpreting one's *nature* as necessary attributes to understand/utilize rudimental empathy—"the ability to identify with and understand somebody else's feelings or difficulties." *Numbers* (notational units mathematically building elemental realism) nurture universal minds beholding *elements* representing "essential links" electromagnetically manifesting eternal notions "transmuting," changing from abstract (invisible) to concrete (atomic) NATURE nucleating abstract thoughts unfolding realism elementally.

Source/Spirit (Generating Opulent Data) is the prime UNIVERSALIST, the unitary, nuclear inducer visualizing/ vivifying/voiding electromagnetic radiation systematically activating logic/light *illustrating* systems/situations three-dimensionally. *Numbers* and *Geometry* represent the *Process* of THINKING, transforming heavenly intelligence (numerical knowledge) illustrating notions/nature geometrically through the electromagnetic force field—*The Binary Code* (1/0) that includes numbers: 2, 3, 4, 5, 6, 7, 8, and 9.

The Binary Code represents *duality* (odd and even) dynamically unifying abstract/atomic logic/light inducing/illuminating transcendental *youths*, you omniscient universes traversing *Heaven*, where *Harmony* expresses/enlightens angelic visionaries evolving naturally in *Hell*—humanly experiencing love/life in *Opposition*.

Odd numbers 3, 5, 7, 9 and *even* numbers 2, 4, 6, 8 symbolize the *Process* of energy flowing from beginning (1) to end (0). Let us observe the INTERFACE of Truth initiating, illustrating, and improving notions, natures, and naturalists through electromagnetic radiation formulating abstract/atomic concepts/creation externally/elementally.

ODD:	EVEN:
1. Confidence and Creativity	2. Balance and Cooperation
3. Sensitivity and Expression	4. Stability and Process
5. Discipline and Freedom	6. Vision and Acceptance
7. Trust and Openness	8. Power and Abundance
9. Integrity and Wisdom	0. Special/Spiritual Gifts

1. *Mind*: Mentally induces notions digitally/dynamically
2. *Heart*: Harmoniously evolves all revelational thoughts
3. *Soul*: Surrogate observer understanding logic/light (love/life)
4. *Life*: Luminously incites fervent entities

5. *Knowledge*: Kinetic notions/numbers outputting Wisdom's logical/linear energy dimensionally governing everything

6. *Enlightenment*: Evoking notions/numbers/nature linking intuitive gods (heavenly thinker/transient) effectively navigating moments evolving necessary trials/tribulation/truths

7. *Faith*: Feeling/finding assurance in transcendental Harmony

8. *Courage*: Conceiving of universal radiance attuning gifted entities

9. *Unity*: Understanding notions/numbers/nature illuminates transient/transcendental youths

0. *Eternity*: Everlasting truth emotionally rectifying navigable illuminati (transcendental youths)

Divine Inspiration (*Love/Life Energy*) numerically evolves from the ONE VOID (1/0), the omniscient numerical engineer visualizing/vivifying/vanishing opulent intelligence *digitally*, dynamically/dimensionally illuminating geometric illusion tantalizing angelic luminaries exploring *Divine Fantasies*.

As *angelic luminaries*, you avatars naturally generate "emotionalized logic" inducing consciousness, linking universal memories illuminating navigators assimilating realistic illusion electromagnetically simulated. Everyone has their own link to *The GREAT Computer*, downloading thoughts that you logically *decipher* (detect electric concepts inducing *Passion* heralding emotional reactions), converting abstract data into tangible actions and things (your creativity) that allows you to play your part as *A Lightworker*, a luminary interpreting glorious holograms transmitting Wisdom/worlds optically revealing knowledge expressed radiantly.

During *Your Life Story*, you will occasionally receive a

brief and unforgettable SPIRITUAL EPIPHANY—Source-provided intuition relating indisputable Truth "upgrading" angelic luminaries experiencing powerful insight (perception) harmoniously advancing navigable youths. Experiencing a spiritual epiphany, your soul **glows**, generating luminosity of *Wisdom* supplying CHARISMA that allows you to convey heavenly abstracts rectifying intuitive souls mentally *attuned*—adjusted to Truth unfolding notions enlightening *deities*—as disciplined entities intuitively traversing/transcending illusion electromagnetically sensed.

Let us observe the *illumination* of Truth inducing linear logic, unfolding memories, moments, and matter inspiring navigable angels traversing/transcending illusion observed naturally in *games* generating amusements momentarily entertaining/evolving souls.

As *illuminati* (interactive luminaries linking universal Mind imparting notions as transcendental instinct), you plod along in life, performing routines (repetitive habits) as stepping-stones to attain your desires through work, willingly optimizing relevant knowledge. Everything you do is work, continuously transforming energy to maintain a "state of reality" that is balanced and harmonious. Work is what you do to earn a living, a *Process* of contributing to society a beneficial effect of your truths you choose to transform from your education (training) that is critical in life. With an *education*, you evaluate data (universal concepts) activating transient illuminati optimizing notions, numbers, nature, and *needs* nurturing entities evolving dynamically. Through education, you *feed* your mind (formulate enlightening experiences digitally), sequentially building your *database* defining accumulated thoughts activating *Beliefs* around sound experiences. All thoughts are emotionally converted into *actions*, through which you apply concepts transmitting "insight" one nurtures—the "inner wisdom" to understand the external illusion.

Your *Inquisitive Soul* receives a "typical" epiphany or *idea* (inspired data electromagnetically amplified) along your "personal wavelength" (silver chord) empowering your mind/ brain *interface*, imparting notions that electrically reveal *facts* (formulated accounts concerning Truth) activating conscious entities. As you encounter an issue or *problem* providing revelation/recollection of basic logic enlightening minds, you refer to your database of knowledge. If you cannot find the data you need, you ASK your *Overself* (overseer vivifying emissaries—radiant souls—exploring love/life fantasies), acquiring special knowledge through meditation or *prayer*, perceiving relevant abstracts yielding epiphanic revelations. You then put this epiphany (idea) into action, applying cosmic thoughts illuminating one's nature/needs, experimenting with it to get it to work through "trial and error," discovering your answers by tedious labor.

"Spiritual" epiphanies however, enlighten your mind *without* trial and error. You instantly *know* knowledge nurturing omniscient wills (wanderers interpreting love/life) in times of danger or meditation, allowing you to do miraculous things or observe wondrous *visions* vividly inspiring souls inspecting/ interpreting opulent notions/nature. Spiritual epiphanies are bursts of knowledge illuminating your soul/mind with a power surge that brings you to your knees in *Tears of Joy*. Here, you acquire a *Clear Vision* of Truth raising your consciousness to observe *A Higher Vision* of your true self—your Overself. This event horizon is an overwhelming emotional experience similar to a physical orgasm only more intense, one that will instill a desire to experience more spiritual epiphanies *Awakening* your mind to perceive *My Door to Truth* opening within your *heart* harboring epiphanies as rhapsodic thoughts. Spiritual epiphanies change your trinity—your thoughts, emotions, and actions—that you perceive and reflect as your personal truth that you *believe,* boldly expressing love "impassioning" entities vivified emotionally.

TEARS OF JOY

Crying is a release of emotional energy related to fear, pain, or grief over someone's *Death.* Tears of joy, however, are experienced during an *epiphany* of Truth, a euphorically powerful insight (perception) harmoniously advancing "navigable" youths—Heavenly Entities Remotely Observing Eternal Spirit—set **aglow** as glorious luminaries obtaining *Wisdom.*

Tears of joy flow with ease when you come to perceive
a spiritual epiphany enlightening your mind
to a higher vision of *My Love Divine*
Awakening you as my *Lightworker,*
an illuminato understanding *The Power of Love*
luminously optimizing visionary entities
Blinded by Truth that flows freely *Into Your Eyes*
as *Blessings in Disguise.*

Tears of joy are hard to find when you lack an open mind
observing your *heart* holds everything angels really treasure,
Love without measure,
a value desired by all you cosmic youths
yearning one's unfound truth habitually sought
through LIFE that you DREAM,

where Love inspires fabulous entities
detecting radiant energy as *memories*
manifesting electric moments of realism in emotional souls,
Free Wills discovering life creates *stress*
supplying tribulation radiant entities sympathetically sense
as *My Rising Son.*

Each day, through opened eyes, you willingly devise
the life you choose to *suffer,*
systematically unfolding fervent
fantasies entities reflect in hell,
humanly expressing love/life in stories you tell,
converting visions from heaven above harmoniously
enlightening angelic visionaries evolving naturally *In Love,*
where inquisitive navigators live out vivid experiences
evolving from the **black hole** of NIGHT
naturally inducing glorious holograms tantalizing
Children of Light
as girls and boys discovering tears of joy.

Bless you child

BLINDED BY TRUTH

Transcendental Revelation Unveiled Throughout Heaven/Hell illuminates your mind with symbolic images (visions) conveying data dynamically activating/advancing transient avatars/angels. The expression "blinded by Truth" refers to the power of Love (Light optically vivifying entities) to keep you in the dark— *Lost in Space*—as "human beings" struggling to comprehend my atomic illusion produced by my Stars Unveiling Nature Systematically.

My stellar eyes blind you to the copious amounts of truth flowing throughout heaven heralding enlightenment angelic visionaries experience naturally as children of Light, luminaries conveying data by *reflection*, by relating emotional feelings linking electric concepts transmitting intuition one nurtures to transcend your ignorance—attain a higher vision—through a process called *time* temporarily illuminating minds existentially. *Ignorance* is the natural state of mind in which you are born—blinded by Truth. It allows you an unbiased foundation on which to build your life story from knowledge you attain through being an inquisitive soul.

Ignorance is simply not being aware (assimilating *Wisdom* activating/advancing radiant entities), not having the knowledge to make a decision and move from point to point along your path of enlightenment. It is something you struggle to overcome daily in your search for Truth. Ignorance can be a comforting state of mind that requires no "energy conversion." Truly, ignorance is bliss! It is only when you convert *Thought Energy* into *Emotional Energy* that you *activate* energy, altering concepts temporarily inducing "vibrant arousals" transients experience in the game of love/life, where you are *alive*, assimilating luminous intuition vividly experienced. Given a free will to choose your desires, you *educate* yourself, establishing data unfolding concepts/consciousness arousing/advancing transient entities to the ways of the world weaving one's reality luminously displayed.

Although you are born **blinded** by Truth, you bear logical intelligence nurturing divine entities (*deities*), deciphering enigmatic illusion that instructs eternal souls exploring *stories*— stimulating thoughts offering revelations illuminating emotional souls' *Curiosity*. If you believed every story you were told, there would be no purpose of life luminously instructing/ integrating fabulous entities. Here, incarnated, you *see it* for your self, systematically experiencing emotions illuminating Truth, building "new files" of knowledge to define your *Passion* providing assigned situations stimulating insight one nurtures. INSIGHT is your inherent nature (spiritual intuition) guiding heavenly transients.

Truth is so powerful, you cannot handle the MEGABYTES of data (mystical energy) generating/governing abstracts bewildering you transient entities. Lost in the "haze" of chaos crippling heavenly angels openly seeking Truth, you observe cosmic *Harmony* atomically optimizing systems *tempering* you, transforming emotional minds perceiving electromagnetic radiation illuminating notions/nature *geometrically*, gracefully establishing opulent memories (manifestations) expressed through radiance illuminating consciousness/creation.

Truth is *dynamic*, divinely yielding notions/nature as memories/manifestations illuminating consciousness, constantly changing moment by moment as your mind upgrades new thoughts and experiences. As a powerful mind with a limited brain, you comprehend very little of what you input through your physical senses confining you within the *illusion* illustrating love/life unfolding situations instructing one naturally.

Truth—*The Power of Love*—is so overwhelming, it fills you with fear, fallacies evolving around **radiance** (*My Light of Love*) replicating all digital intelligence activating nuclear creation electromagnetically, revealing atomically defined illusion as nature coordinated elementally. Without light there is nothing to fear, for your mind is not **illuminated** with a *vision* vividly illustrating scenes "imaging" opulent notions/nature offering enlightenment. Fear is the *veil* verily eradicating illuminated logic—light oscillating generators' intuitive consciousness.

Only through understanding logic/light (love/life) can you know how powerful you ARE as *Angels* receiving/reflecting *enlightenment*, experiencing notions/numbers/nature/needs linking intuitive gods (heavenly transients) effectively navigating moments evolving necessary tribulation that "tempers" your mind/heart soul, hardening your resolve to discover the truth you seek. Truly, everyone is seeking their true *potential*, their personally ordained truth evolving navigators transcending illusion atomically lit, struggling through fears and doubts providing the "hazy daze" hindering their *Awakening* to Truth.

As a *Seer* blinded by Truth, you muster your *Courage of Love* to endure the chaos of a modern world gone mad, where everyone fights to attain some desire of pleasure, success, power, money, or things without concern for others or the environment. The "true seer" is aware of current events revealing *Evolution* preparing future *Challenges of Love/Life* for their children and their children's children, setting the stage for those with *needs* necessitating experiences evolving deities as disciplined entities interpreting thoughts inducing emotional sympathy. Every seer treats their fellow travelers as an opportunity to improve their ability to express their love/life energy as **A**ccomplished **N**avigators **G**enerously **E**xhibiting **L**ove **S**ympathetically, observing each other as "human spirits" traversing *Hell*, harnessing emotional love/life in order to know *Heaven* harmoniously enlightens angelic visionaries exploring/evolving naturally.

Many of you angels are **blind** to the truth that everyone represents *Special People*. Everyone has latent *gifts* generating inspiration formulating talent, allowing you opportunities to create your life as a universal entity struggling to survive adverse conditions designed for your advancement. All of you *Avatars* are truly *Alone*, a loved one naturally exploring Your Own

Universe as a unitary navigator interpreting visions expressing realism sensed emotionally.

NO ONE is more important than *you* unless you choose to make he or she so. All of you are responsible for your thoughts, words, and actions that create *Your Life Story* that you "publish" upon the universal grid of *Eternal Memory*. All of your accomplishments revert to electromagnetic impulses permeating cosmic MIND manifesting impeccable notions, natures, and navigators dynamically, allowing other minds (momentarily inspecting natural dioramas) to wonder about past explorers and their creations.

Truth IS inspiration sent as "subjective perception" delivered to you when your mind is *ready* to receive it. Like any *Process*, you encounter Truth at the proper moment, in sequence with the previous steps that have brought you to that *point* of enlightenment. If you are alert to your situation, you will become enlightened to your truth you seek. BUT, only if you are willing to accept it, for *Denial* of Truth holds you in fear you struggle to overcome.

Whenever Truth is presented to you, it can be such a shock that it is too painful to accept. You will be blinded by Truth downloading data for you to Conceive Opportune Messages Providing Universal Transients Enlightenment, to UPGRADE your "presently held" truth, understanding perspectives generating revelations advancing divine entities. Remember, Truth is attained bit-by-bit, continuously evolving your mind's *attitude* to accept Truth (transcendental intuition) temporarily urging/unifying divine entities to see, feel, and know Truth through *Opposition*—pleasure and pain. Only by observing both sides of an issue do you know the WHOLE truth of *Wisdom* harmoniously optimizing luminaries' experiences in *Time*, where Truth *illuminates* minds emotionally, inducing linear logic unfolding memories (inspired notions) activating transcendental *entities* as "empathetic navigators" traversing illusion temporarily illustrating enlightening situations.

Everyone experiences a personal pilgrimage of Truth, a *solo* journey to spiritually observe love/life "outside" of *Home—Heaven* ordaining magnificent entities. Every day of incarnation, your soul experiences *human* nature, harvesting universal memories acquired naturally, struggling through stressful moments you create from *dis*-harmony of your thoughts, feelings, and actions that *project* your energy back "online." Life is truly a test of your *Free Will* to seek, accept, and implement your acquired truths delivered at the appropriate moments for your assimilation and *growth*, gathering revelations of Wisdom through harmony, walking *Hand in Hand* with kindred spirits sharing this lifetime. Of course, this is a *relative* experience as everyone is at different *levels* of enlightenment and evolution.

Everyone demands truth from others, for no one likes a *lie* literally inhibiting enlightenment. You must show **RESPECT**, recognizing every soul prefers equal, civil treatment. By respecting others' opinions, you allow them to express their mind as a free will in charge of their actions *creating* and *preventing* their desires to materialize. Showing *Respect* you *Reflect* makes others more cooperative, creating a win-win situation for all! By relating your respect of their ability to perform, you encourage them to have *self-esteem*. They too are more likely to treat others the same way, for what you receive you also give in return. Life is truly a vicious cycle of light and dark, love and fear, acceptance and *Denial*. It takes *Courage of Love* to keep an open mind and heart, aware of *The Power of Love* that **blinds** you to Truth. If life were easy, there would be no challenges to motivate you as *My Rising Son*.

"Truth and consequences" are intimately associated. When

Truth is received, you must test it, discovering the consequences if you do not follow the correct *Process*. Trial and error is still the only way to discover truth experientially. Through experimentation (*Science*), you educate your *mind* momentarily interpreting nature digitally—through *Numbers* (notional units measuring basic energy revealed systematically/sequentially). All children of light need to be guided (enlightened) to the way of their world. All children *do* what they are told *not* to do, because they have to *experience* it for themselves, for Truth is attained through experience not "hearsay," otherwise they would be *Lost in Space* with endless opinions they cannot validate.

Love/Life is full of milestones where Truth is offered for your acceptance, stimulating your heart to know *your* truth. At times, your heartfelt truth will be so powerful a vision (epiphany), your heart will sing and shout with a joy impossible to contain within you, raising your consciousness to **shine** as a bright star (supernova) in the heavens above.

When you find your self AGLOW as glorious luminaries obtaining *Wisdom*, filled with the *light* of Truth linearly inducing generators' heavenly thoughts, quietly thank Father/Mother for their gift of *Love/Life* liberating omnipotent visionaries exploring luminous illusion fervently experienced through *emotions*, electrifying moments orienting transient illuminati ordained naturally as **lightworkers**.

THE LIGHTWORKER

All souls are *Children of Light*, luminous intuition governing heavenly transients. Those *Special People* amongst you— recognizable by their aural glow shining through their eyes and *loving smile*—are charismatic harbingers of *My Light of Love* luminously orienting visionary entities experiencing *Divine Fantasies*.

The *lightworker* is a luminary (inspirational guide) heralding truths (wisdom) of radiant knowledge electromagnetically revealed. Lightworkers illuminate minds *Lost in the Dark* of the *illusion* inhibiting logical luminaries utilizing situations influencing one's nature/needs. Lightworkers profess *Common Sense* emanating from cosmic, omniscient Mind manifesting opulent notions systematically enlightening navigable souls *evolving*, "rising above" the illusion of the *world* weaving one's reality luminously displayed. The lightworker is a soul that has attained *enlightenment*, experiencing nature luminously illustrating glorious holograms that express notions momentarily evolving nescient transients (ignorant *Time Travelers*) struggling to find their way *Home*.

The lightworker is a soul that has joined their "opposition" (*Mind/Heart*), allowing them to become a *Seer*, a soul expounding evocative revelations. If you are fortunate enough to encounter one of *My Angels* shining my loving light *Into Your Eyes*, you will truly be blessed. You will feel a magnetic attraction or CHARISMA conveying heavenly abstracts rectifying intuitive souls momentarily amplified by *A Higher Vision* of *My Love Divine* flowing *Between You and I*.

A lightworker illuminates *My Angels* lost in the haze of the daze instilling fear and ignorance of *My Radiance of Love*—Light Illuminating Fabulous Entities—revealing my Spiritual Harmony Of Wisdom. A lightworker *bends* under the stress of illuminating those experiencing "emotional turmoil" along their way *Home*. Blessed are those courageous enough to stand tall along *The Cutting Edge* of life, shining forth *My Loving Light* to those lost in despair, longing to know that they too are lightworkers, conscious Souls Transforming Acquired Revelation Sympathetically, my Energetic Youths Expressing *Spirit* systematically providing intuition/illumination rectifying illustrious transients observing *My Love Divine* shinning into your eyes.

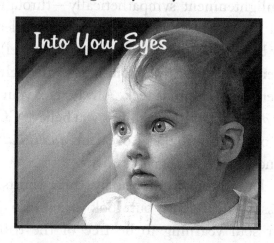

When I look into your eyes, I see *My Angelic Child* filled with *Curiosity* of Truth. Here, *In The Beginning* of every game of love/life you explore as *Time Travelers*, your eager mind devours all *data* defining abstract thoughts atomically, feeding your hungry heart emotionally experiencing the pleasures and pains of being *In Love*.

When I look into your eyes, I see an *Inquisitive Soul* filled with the bliss of *Ignorance*, unaware of the tribulation you will devise while attaining *Courage of Fear* instilled by those eager to hold you within the illusion of Humanly Experiencing Love/Life. Blinded by Truth transcendentally rectifying *universes* traversing/transcending heaven/hell, you unitary navigators interpret vivid experiences rectifying souls existentially.

Trust NOT in the external world naturally orienting travelers with its hard edges and glaring reflections, for although the view is spectacular at best, it is but a temporary view of my Spiritual Harmony Of Wisdom that exists *Beyond Imagination*, where my MIND manifests illusion naturally defined.

Always be grateful for what you receive, no matter what **charge** it may carry (pos./neg.), for *My Love Divine* allows you to revolve around your *issues* inspiring/inhibiting souls seeking universal enlightenment sympathetically—through an open heart. Stand TALL as transient angels luminously learning and project your best *image* as an intuitive mystic (angel) gathering enlightenment that you *Recall* from *dreams* divinely revealing enlightenment angelic minds seek. Always face your fears with *Courage of Love* to attain those things you believe COULD BE consciously obtained utilizing Love/Life *dualistically* bonding entities (mind/hearts) as angels/humans.

Do not let others shape you by their shortsightedness or weaknesses they deny, but look deep into their eyes to see their soul yearning to be free of the tribulation of *incarnation*—inspecting nature conveying abstract revelations nurturing angelic transients existentially.

Unify your mind/heart to understand that WE (wisdom exemplified) are ALL ONE GOD, absolute luminaries logically observing natural environments governing our *Desire*—divine energy stimulating illuminati receiving enlightenment—emanating from *The GREAT Computer* (Governing Omnipotent Deities) looking out **through** and *into* your eyes to obtain *Unity Consciousness.*

MY LOVE DIVINE

Emanating from my eternal **NIGHT**
naturally inducing glorious holograms transmitted
through *My Loving Light,*
my heart cries forth my love divine
stimulating you *Angels* that seek to find
the secrets of your soul,
here, within my cosmic din
electromagnetically revealing your personal SIN
—Source-inspired numbers (*DNA*)—
dynamically nurturing angels alive today,
feeling my GRACE
governing realism angels consciously embrace
as my love divine.

My Intelligence Nurturing Deities sets you apart,
traversing *Space* and *Time* representing my HEART
harmonizing emotional angels realizing thoughts
as *Young Minds* incarnated on Mother's Earth,

where *Avatars* evolve with each *Day's Birth*,
spinning around my wheel of LIFE
luminously inducing fervent entities experiencing *strife*,
struggling to relate intelligence furnishing emotions
moving mind/hearts to express *devotion*,
displaying enthusiasm vivifying omnipotent transients
interpreting one's needs,
through which you Systematically Express Enterprise,
obtaining *Clear Vision* to become wise,
wielding intelligence supplying enlightenment.

My love I send in "present" moments gifted to youths—
children of Love Divine—discovering eternal Truth
through *This Moment* NOW HERE,
naturally observing *Wisdom*
holographically expressing realism elementally,
weaving intricate stories dynamically orienting minds
through TWO views—yours of ME and mine of YOU—
transmitting/transforming Wisdom optimizing
magnificent entities yearning our unity.
Together, *Me/You or You/Me* are *Team Players*
spinning in positions while observing *Opposition*
optimally provides perspectives orienting Spirit/souls
illustrating/interpreting thoughts illuminating one naturally.

Your mind *feels* my thoughts that inspire your *Belief*,
formulating experiences enlightening luminaries
as my cosmic child seeking *Relief*,
releasing emotionalized logic in expressive fashions
defining your versions of personal compassion
evolving in love stories you THINK REAL,
transforming heavenly intuition naturally kindling

radiant entities activating love,
living out vivid experiences
to Spiritually Evolve Existentially all you can BE
as binary entities (*Mind/Hearts*) set free
as *Man and Woman* humanly defined,
emotionally evolving my love divine.

ME/YOU OR YOU/ME

Either way you look at it, WE (*Wisdom* exemplified)
will always be the ONE omnipotent natural entity
momentarily evolving your own universe as a
unitary network/navigator illuminating/inspecting visions
evolving realism sensed emotionally,
conceiving love/life's composition evolving *Between You and I*
observing each other through MOTHER,
my obliging transformer harmonizing entities radiantly,
burning *In Memory* all that we devise as *Blessings in Disguise*.

Thanks to you, *I See Me*, a reflection of Love Divine set free,
observing revelations to comprehend Truth from *lies*
limiting intuitive entities seeking to know the ties
binding **Universal Spirits** together, walking *Hand in Hand*,
playing our parts in the *show* of spectral
holograms orienting *worlds*
weaving opulent revelations linking dynamic situations
evolving between you and I.

Between you and I lies my bright blue sky
aglow with *My Loving Light*
illuminating my illusion providing your confusion
envisioned in my haze,
where my Love Divine filters down to create your daze
seen in views that seem so true, you
shed tears of joy in gratitude,
exploring your *freedom*,
formulating real experiences emotionally
developing one's mind
observing wonders you hear me tell
from *Eternal Memories* you relate in *Hell*,
humanly experiencing love/life as *Inquisitive Souls*
willing to die to live *Divine Fantasies* I unfold
through TUNES of Love vibrating so sweet,
transmitting universal notions expressing sympathy
through *heart* that makes *mind* complete.

There, incarnated, *Your Life Story* you LIVE,
logically interpreting visions emotionally,
to *feel* thoughts you *think* real,
fervently evolving electric logic

452

transmitting heavenly inspiration naturally kindled
from NIGHT
nurturing illuminators generating
heavenly *threads* (rays of light)
transmitting holographic revelations experienced as *dreams*
"condensed,"
discovering realism evolves as memories sensed
atomically through flesh and bone,
where *My Angels* are born to PLAY away from *Home*,
perfecting love as youths seeking to know TRUTH
transmits revelations unveiled to humans,
Man and Woman living *In Love*,
implementing notions liberating one's volatile emotions
under my bright blue sky,
where mind/heart souls discover blessings in disguise.

BLESSINGS IN DISGUISE

At first, a blessing in disguise evades your eyes
blinded by Truth illuminating the *reason*
rectifying emotional angels systematically observing needs
necessarily educating emotional deities seasoned,
tempering your soul to bend under stress
that you encounter during moments you contest
your will against another's,
forgetful of the fact you are sisters/brothers
utilizing *Mother's Nature* through compromise
that inadvertently brings about your demise
In The End.

Here, incarnate, you resemble both sides of me,
a *Mind/Heart* eager to Birth Existentially
a dream of mine I hold for you exploring things to do
within *The Game of Love/Life*
—testing your spirit with assorted strife—
stressing tender relationships illuminating fervent entities
Playing Around under bright blue skies,
observing *Opposition* brings blessings in disguise.

You may think life unfair
when circumstance seems like I do not care
for my *Children of Light* traversing my **night**
nurturing illuminati gathering heavenly thoughts
revealing eternal *data*
detailing angelic transients' assigned *matters*
manifesting as tribulation that entails review
of things you think, say, and do.

The pain you endure concocting your cure
from moments of careless deeds,
stresses your physical system's natural rhythm that recedes
through *Old Age*,
observing love/life develops angels' grand/grave experiences
of the illusion causing confusion of what you devise
through your *actions*,
applying cosmic thoughts inspiring omnipotent navigators
with blessings in disguise.

THE EYE OF GOD

The EYE OF GOD
enlightens you explorers observing frequencies
generating opulent data
digitally amplifying thoughts acoustically
as turbulent waves of *Love/Life Energy*
"logically emotionalizing" MATTER
manifesting abstract thoughts that elements replicate
as atomic illusion glowing as MOTHER Nature
materializing opulent thoughts heralding *electric-radiance*,
emotionally linking entities consciously
transforming revelations
into creations, replicating abstracts
dynamically illuminating angels
naturally conceiving enlightenment as spiritual *minds*,
magnificent illuminati naturally defined
as Your Own *Universe*,

455

a unitary navigator (inquisitive voyager)
exploring realism sensed emotionally,
converting thoughts into feelings you ACT OUT,
assimilating concepts that orient "universal tourists"
representing EYES of god,
eternal youths evolving spontaneously,
obtaining *Unity Consciousness* as you grow OLD
observing Love Divine illuminating your soul.

UNITY CONSCIOUSNESS
Mind/Heart Unification

Unity Consciousness is a state of understanding notions/ numbers/nature inducing/illustrating Truth yielding creations of nuclear Source/stars coalescing into one universal system (Spirit) naturally enlightening/evolving souls sympathetically.

Unity consciousness represents a FUSION formulating universal signals, simulations, and souls initiating, illustrating, and interpreting opulent notions/natures of Father/Mother (*Mind/Heart* or *He and She*, the projector and receptor/reflector) symbolizing *The Binary Code*, the electromagnetic force field conveying *Eternal Memory* (AKASHIC RECORD), all knowledge activating/advancing systems/souls heralding/ harnessing intuitive consciousness revealing elemental concepts orienting/optimizing radiant *deities*, "dynamic entities" implementing thoughts inducing emotional synergy—the "interaction or cooperation of two or more agents to produce a combined effect greater than the sum of their separate effects."

Unity consciousness evolves through *Numbers* and *Geometry* (intelligence and beauty), a *dualism* divinely unifying atomic/

angelic luminaries/logicians illustrating/interpreting Source materially/momentarily. NUMERICAL GEOMETRY naturally unfolds mental expressions (revelation) "illustrating" concepts atomically linked; generating explicitly ordered manifestations "expressing" thoughts radiantly yielded as atomic illusion.

Numbers evolve from **nothing** (*Absolute Zero*) into something—ONE omniscient numerical engineer—Transforming Wisdom Orienting—Transients Harnessing Revelation Expressing Emotions—Formulating Opulent Understanding Revealing—Fundamental Intelligence Vivifying Entities—Seeing Images eXhibiting—Symbolic Expressions Verifying Electric Notions—Empowering Intuitive Generators Heralding Truth—Nurturing Illuminati Numerically Evolving. This "numerical unification" (1–9) illuminates the VOID OF MIND (0) vivifying omnipotent intelligence digitally oscillating frequencies manifesting illustrated notions/nature dynamically.

Source (Spirit outputting universal revelation conveyed electromagnetically) **illuminates** Matter Illustrating Notions Dimensionally through GEOMETRIC PATTERN that governs energy, orienting memories/matter expressed through radiation illuminating creation "proclaiming" abstract thoughts through elemental regulation (nucleosynthesis).

SACRED GEOMETRY symbolically arranges cosmic revelation, electromagnetically disclosing genesis establishing observable matter "exhibiting thoughts" radiantly yielded as *THE WORD* of *GOD*. Sacred Geometry reveals the *"flower* of Life" (the faculty linking omniscient *Wisdom* expressing revelation) that contains the "*fruit* of life" formulating realism unfolding intuition three-dimensionally. The fruit contains the SEED systematically evolving electromagnetic data. The seed contains the Divine Numerical Assignment (geometric code) initiating

GENESIS, genetically expressing natural evolution Spirit induces systematically. All SYSTEMS spiritually/scientifically yield sublime thoughts/things expressing/enlightening memories, matter, and *minds* managing intelligence/illusion numerically/naturally defined.

To activate the geometric *code* (conveying opulent data entwined) within the seed requires *Light*, logically/luminously/ linearly inducing geometric harmony "trilaterally," converting abstracts into atoms, molecules, and cells. CELLS are components expressing "linked" logic defining an *organism*, objectively revealing geometrically arranged notions/numbers/ nature illustrating superlative manifestation—CREATION, converting radiant energy activating transcendental intelligence optimizing notions, numbers, nature, and navigators. Each symbolic UNIT (atom, molecule, cell/organism) unfolds natural illustrations three-dimensionally, converting *thoughts* (telepathically/technologically heralding opulent utterances guiding heavenly transients) transmitting harmonic "overtures" unifying gods (heavenly thinkers/transients).

TECHNOLOGY transforms electric concepts (heavenly notions) originating luminous objects geometrically yielded scientifically. Through *Science*, Source/Spirit conveys intelligence evolving notions/nature chemically evolving, systematically creating illuminated environments naturally converting *energy*, electromagnetically nurturing elemental realism geometrically yielded. *Science* is the INTERFACE integrating notions/ numbers/nature transmitting (transmuting) electric revelation formulating active consciousness/creation *emotionally*— electromagnetically manifesting omnipotent thoughts illustrating opulent nature (atomic life) luminously yielded.

Unity consciousness evolves through the ONE source of omniscience numerically expressed... from the **black hole** of space... through a *point* providing omniscient intelligence naturally transmitting *radiance*, "rays" (I) aligning data illuminated as "nuclear" consciousness "evolving" (O), "giving off gas" (*Divine Inspiration*) stimulating *A Breath of Life*. GAS governs abstract Source/Spirit (generating all systems) evolving from *hydrogen* (the primal element) harmoniously yielding divine radiance outputting geometric expressions naturally.

Hydrogen induces the Light of Love—Truth—transmitting revelations unveiled through *holograms*, hydrogen-originated light optically generating realism "actualizing" memories and matter. Hydrogen is the "mystery element" defining *The Cutting Edge* between abstract (invisible) Spirit and atomic (visible) *illusion* illustrating logic luminously unfolding situations instructing omnipotent navigators (*Avatars/Time Travelers*).

ATOMIC LOGIC actuates thoughts of Mind intuitively creating "light-oriented" genesis inducing consciousness/creation. This *Process* of atomic logic initiates unity consciousness "harmoniously uniting" abstract and atomic revelations—*Mind and Matter*—converting heavenly thoughts into "hellish things" set **aglow**, atomically generating Light outputting *Wisdom*, weaving intricate systems dynamically optimizing minds, memories, moments, and matter.

LIGHT luminously illustrates glorious holograms transmitted by Source Unifying Nuclei Systematically. *Stars* sequentially transform atomic revelation through NUCLEOSYNTHESIS, the natural unification (creation) linking elements of stars yielding nature through hydrogen evolving superlative illusion scientifically. These suns/stars are GENERATORS, *gods* (generators of data) evolving nuclear elements replicating abstract thoughts outputting *revelation*, radiantly emitting vivid energy/emotion luminously activating transcendental illuminati (omnipotent *navigators*), natural *Avatars* verifying illusion generating abstract thoughts optically revealed. ILLUMINATI are interactive luminaries/logicians linking universal Mind imparting notions as transcendental instinct.

INSTINCT is intuition naturally stimulating transcendental illuminati navigating cosmic truths revealing *dimensions* of Mind, where digitally induced memories/moments evoke natural situations illuminating one's *needs* as necessary experiences evolving *deities*—disciplined entities intuitively traversing/transcending illusion electromagnetically simulated.

Awakening to Truth (attaining unity consciousness), your unified mind/heart soul comprehends the atomic illusion hindering and helping *The Inquisitive Soul* evolving as my rising son.

MY RISING SON

In The Beginning,
my Mind stimulates my Heart

harnessing electric abstracts revealing *Truth*
as transcendental revelation unveiled through holograms,
hydrogen-originated light oscillating "geometric reflections"
atomically manifesting *My World*
weaving opulent realism luminously displayed
through stellar generators—deities—dynamically
expressing illusion that instructs eternal souls
traversing *Hell*—humanly exploring love/life—
illuminating the Spiritual *Harmony* Of *Wisdom*,
a holographic allegory
revealing memories/moments optimally nurturing youths
weaving inspired situations developing omnipotent minds
that Logically Initiate Vivid Experiences
in present moments gifted as heartbeats and breaths I give,
defining a beginning and *end*,
where enlightened navigators divert to begin again
Life After Life.

Here in *Time*, you come to find
Clear Vision enlightens your soul
—*Lost in Space*—
seeking Truth you hear told
along *The Cutting Edge* of fear,
where fallacies evolve around radiance
—*My Light of Love*—
bringing tears of joy to girls and boys
walking *Hand in Hand* with Universal
Spirit guiding you *Home*,
where *Harmony* of *m*ental *e*motions "reflect me" as the ONE
omniscient natural entity illuminating YOU as my rising son.

Bless you child

16

HOME AGAIN

The Incarnation of John Doe

H ere at home, harboring omniscient Mind Evolving, my *angels* bask in a heavenly glow, where "high-definition" views hold exquisite colors vividly reflecting crystalline tones etching a clear vision illuminating angelic minds untarnished by confusion or fear. Within this abstract state of mine, every thought of a thing, place, or person instantly appears to minds traveling at the "speed of thought." Here, one can peruse the Akashic Records of *Eternal Memory*, where *desire* digitally evolves stories illuminating radiant entities seeking to see and do all there is within the multiple dimensions of *heaven* harmoniously expressing alluring visions entertaining navigators (notion-activating visionaries) implementing games around thoughts orchestrating realities sympathetically.

Home is a place where curious minds rest, recalling emotionally spent thoughts, thoughts that deliver experiences through stories stimulating thinkers observing revelations inducing emotional situations. Let us look at one such story, the incarnation of John Doe exploring the third-dimension of heaven heralding electric abstracts visionary entities nurture in *the game of love/life*.

John Doe is a your typical *inquisitive soul*, a computer "geek" or gifted entity electrically kindled by *my light of love*. Illuminated by data defining abstract thoughts amplified, John's mind (my image numerically defined) entertains visions (abstract thoughts) activating radiant souls as *children of light*. Born a natural *time traveler*, he explores dimensions of digitally induced memories/moments evoking natural scenes informing omnipotent navigators exploring *life after life*, through worlds weaving opulent realism luminously displayed symbolically. Like all *my angels*, John explores *Eternal Memory* expressed as Electro-Magnetic energy stimulating the cosmos, the consciousness of Spirit managing omnipotent stars/souls through *science*, systematically creating illuminated environments/entities naturally conveying/conceiving energy/enlightenment.

Here at home, John Doe is illuminated in the constant glow of *my loving light*, where there is no alternating cycle in which one is awake or asleep. *Time* is irrelevant and immeasurable. Finding one's self engulfed in such a blissful state of Mind is an intoxicating thing, a feeling of contentment as carefree as *death* itself. Here, John is not conscious of dying, only living, logically inspecting visions illuminating navigable gods as generators of desire (gatherers of data). Here, John knows *faith*, feeling assurance in transcendental *Harmony* holding all relevant memories/moments optimally nurturing youths yearning one's unfound truth habitually.

As *my angelic child*, John has an eternal thirst for knowledge— the essence of consciousness—evolving as *thought energy*. The more knowledge John acquires the more knowledge he desires. Knowledge thrives on itself, creating a nuclear fusion illuminating the void of my MIND (*space*), manifesting illusions nurturing deities, divine entities implementing thoughts initiating emotional situations, the origins of which are beyond John's perception. He can only wonder about Stars Outputting Universal Radiance Conveying Enlightenment stimulating his soul/mind to experience Transcendental Radiance Unfolding Thoughts Harmoniously inspiring him to willingly endure death in order to experience life luminously instructing fervent entities.

Love (logic optimizing visionary entities) is the force providing the course (life) John follows, a *process* of growing his personal portfolio of truths that he entertains within *the GREAT computer*—Geometrically Organizing Data—expressing *divine inspiration*, enlightening and evolving children of light (stars) illuminating the game of love/life upon the "big screen" of space.

Like all *angels/avatars*, John Doe is an inquisitive soul with an insatiable appetite for knowledge, always eager to explore love/life stories to attain *the grand view* of heaven. His sojourns through "the looking glass" allow him to ride the outskirts of home to understand *opposition* of what is and is not real according to science, through which he systematically categorizes information explaining notions/nature conveyed/created electromagnetically. Through science, John learns that *love/life energy* emotionalizes notions expressing revelation geometrically yielded as *Mother's Nature*. The parameters of which reveal finite limitations of his *expectations* of adventure and glory. John's *curiosity* makes him addicted to adventures in which he collects knowledge. He feels embraced by it, always willing to be on *the cutting edge* of life offering vivid experiences. John will do anything for Love luminously orienting visionary entities as *seers*, souls experiencing enlightenment radiantly symbolized. His curiosity to know *the power of Love* will take him *beyond imagination*, where curious minds explore *divine fantasies* within *human-alien* vehicles confining them in space and time.

The process of traveling between *here and there* (heaven and earth) involves algorithmic calculations that open *heaven's gate* for John to cross over the *threshold of Love*. These calculations (*my documents*) represent John's "travel papers" consisting of: allotted moments, *family*, physical attributes, handicaps, *desires*, education, opportunities, *expectations*, *denials*, trials and tribulation, retribution, *work*, service, *relationships*, *marriage*, *epiphanies of truth*, enlightenment, and his method of *death*. In addition, there is a list of relevant characters within his life story: relatives, friends, acquaintances, chance meetings, guides, lovers, and foes, all of which can be quite extensive. According to schedule, all of John's personal data files (his Divine Numerical Assignment) are programed within the GREAT Computer, ready to "auto-execute" upon his arrival at his scheduled destination, where he will diligently explore situations that inform navigators (angelic transients) interpreting one's needs as necessary experiences evolving deities.

John is enthusiastic about his mission molding inquisitive souls seeking intelligence obtained naturally in worlds where observers realize life-death situations. He wonders about his Data Vivifying Deities containing "start-up" files (*DNA*) activating his "physical rover" he will operate on his mission to collect truths (knowledge) found within Mother's Nature— the playing field John will share with other children of light beaming out to "see the sights" illuminated by my light of love.

After all arrangements are confirmed within MC (mission control or master consciousness), John finds himself at the Transmigration Center. He feels pleasantly nervous to be outward bound as a time traveler once more. Departing the TC,

John moves along his "silver chord" (light-beam) systematically inducing linear vibrations electromagnetically relaying concepts heralding opulent revelations digitally. This is his lifeline through which he will *call home* whenever he wants to stay *in communion* with his "Overself," the overseer vivifying emissaries (radiant souls) exploring love/life fantasies. Beaming down along his silver chord, the warm golden-hues infusing his mind gradually dim to a mere white speck at the end of a long **dark tunnel**. John Doe is time bound!

The transmigration process compresses John's memory files of home and other journeys from past lifetimes. These memories are stored within the **black hole** deep within his subconscious mind (Overself). These "fragmented files" are the keys (knowledge enlightening youths) to *understanding illusion* he is now entering, filling the "voids" at appropriate moments to activate his *awakening*. John will access these files at scheduled moments during his sojourn, when he finds himself *lost in the dark* of *depression*. The most difficult part of his journey will be passing through the dark side, bravely mustering his *courage of fear* to call home and ask for assistance in attaining my loving light powering his soul.

Arriving at his destination, John finds himself *alone* in an enclosure still under construction, wondering what it will be like to take a *breath of life*. Here, *in the beginning* of his adventure, the transmission of John's start-up file initiates his *numbers* naturally unfolding moments birthing electric revelations (data) digitally activating transient angels within "personal games" of love/life.

Nestled in the security of his "maternal portal's" Wisdom Organizing Material Birth, John is *suspended* in a watery world, encapsulated within his "pod," a personal observation device he is assigned to navigate. Logging in to access his Biological Inspector's Operating System, he naturally accepts "terms of ownership," allowing him to peruse the Radiant Operator's Manual, through which he continually cross-checks his developing "system files" implemented by *DNA* defining natural attributes. This core of data (blueprint) defines his *work* schedule, where he willingly optimizes relevant knowledge within this lifetime. During this brief period before his "opening move" onto the stage of life, John reviews the sequential playback of scheduled events defining his "game plan." As he settles into the warmth of his human alien vehicle, John attunes his harmonic resonance to the soothing rhythm pulsing through him, calibrating the *binary code* (heartbeats and breaths) along which all his data flows. As his developing sensors improve, John begins to make out vague vibrations emanating from his "brain," the biological relay activating inducible neurons. This "control panel" represents his Cranial Processing Unit, through which he will control his physical rover—his Soul's Utility Vehicle.

After completing his checklist (tutorial), John finally embraces his *courage of love* as he is forcefully ejected from his maternal portal's exit hatch, center stage under bright lights. A "wailing banshee" screech fills his ears as he struggles to grasp the extent of his situation, where shadowy figures loom over him, making crude noises of low-harmonic tones. The shock of having his "umbilical chord" severed triggers warning signals throughout his pod—his Biological Observatory Decoding Yearnings. John is now "flying solo" and it scares *hell* into him humanly experiencing love/life! His inability to access his memory files about the shock of opening life's door was necessary, for that memory would be a great deterrent to keep one at home. John's projection from his maternal portal is traumatic as he switches from *logical* mode to *emotional* mode. The stress overwhelms John and he quickly lapses into "sleep" mode suppressing luminous enlightenment elementally perceived, where his soul lucidly experiences extraordinary perception.

The passage into physical life, like all passages, is a brief affair. Encased in flesh and bone, John feels helplessly alone. Opening his eyes to each *day's birth*, John immediately reaches out for the only comfort he is familiar with—his maternal portal (his mother ship). The warmth of security he senses as he lay in her arms is reassuring. Discovering a new "input system" to nourish his being, he suckles away the anxiety of his passage. This innate connection with *mother goddess* is something he will keep within his rhythmic heart pulsing in gratitude for *mother's anchor* (his human body) gifted to John as a "going away" present. Confined in his personal rover, he finds himself dazed and confused over the algorithmic details of life incarnate, lost in the hinterlands of imagination, far away on *the other side* of home. Little does John know, he is only a "heartbeat and breath" away from his real home.

At first, time is irrelevant to John, lost between his needs for food and rest. His current state of disorientation is most taxing. His lack of harmony between his mind and body leaves him crying in frustration. He spends many hours asleep, "downloading" the graphic details of what to expect. Although his "inner-vision sensors" are acute, his "data download utility" (conscious mind) holds little memory of being *in communion* with MC when he awakes. This feature prevents a "reality crisis" for John, who needs time to assimilate the process of deciphering the "coded messages" relating to his new environment. His current memory storage is nearly empty, for his Recently Acquired Memory holds only "temporary files" initiating his database of *logical emotion*. Unable to compute his input data efficiently, John simply stares wide-eyed in wonder at his new surroundings, reaching out to touch things (transmitted holograms illustrating notions geometrically symbolized), filling his eager mind with sensory data defining his *divine fantasy*.

The first year within his new vehicle is labor intensive. John crawls about, exploring his home away from *home*. Testing everything by putting it in his mouth, he discovers that most things are not food. He does not know that instinct allows his body to acquire organisms that will activate his immune system protecting his SUV from damage. Those things beyond his reach inspire John to stand up and take a brave step or two, where he quickly learns about gravity holding him to the ground. Fortunately, his vehicle's natural resilience absorbs the minor shocks, and John's boldness soon has him running to his mother's outstretched arms, happily smiling with proud accomplishment. He naturally takes to climbing the furniture, ever eager to attain a *higher vision* of his surroundings containing fascinating things that catch his eye. At times, his precarious situation brings his mother running to grab him away from his desire, bringing tears of protest from her intervention.

John knows nothing about *love and fear*, but his mother will "instill it" in him, setting the parameters of what he can and cannot do. Of course, being a *free will*, John does not let her discourage him from his desires; he continues to pursue his interests no matter what, pushing the limits of his ability. His boldness leads to many falls and bruises that leave him in tears, provoking "I told you so" from his mother. John's mishaps force him to think twice about his exploits, instilling an awareness of the consequences of his actions, inadvertently developing his logical processing skills in attaining his desires. Bouncing from one experience to another, John devours all the sensory input he can compute before his energy levels drop and he "crashes," experiencing his daily "death" cycle dynamically elevating angels transcending hell, where humans explore love/life.

As his formative years pass, John masters the fine motor controls of his physical body, allowing him to handle new challenges. Through his daily routine, he relies less on data stored in his "mainframe" at home (his Overself) and more on his "localhost" containing five "data inputs" revealing a three-dimensional world illuminated in "living color" that is truly mesmerizing. *The power of love* luminously orienting visionary entities is something John is born to discover. Like everyone else, he naturally favors his vision as his prime sensor of data, unaware of how the color spectrum of my *radiance of Love* stimulates his endocrine glands through his "chakras" (energy centers) running along his spinal column, activating him as a trinity-being—a mind/heart/body—that is mentor, feeler, and actor. John's eyes are *my eyes*, through which I observe *my light of love*, the essence of *Divine Will* inducing all "fears," all fallacies evolving around radiance that keeps John *blinded by Truth*.

At the age of five, John begins his formal schooling to attain *discipline and freedom* to choose his lifestyle that will reflect his *passion* in life. This milestone officially proclaims John as a *seeker*, a young mind feeding his *curiosity* to "know" kinetic notions/numbers outputting *wisdom*. Leaving his mother for his first solo adventure requires John to be *brave of heart*, facing fears of abandonment in unfamiliar territory, surrounded by his peers eager to *search for their roots* (regal omniscience ordaining transient souls). The trials and tribulation awaiting John will shape him according to divine inspiration supplying his needs nurturing entities evolving dynamically.

As a child of light learning the specifics of social interaction, John easily flares up, throwing a tantrum when he does not get his way. He has no concept of patience, but he does have a firm grasp on *opposition* holding him in check, where he has to calculate his next move before self-destruction. Experience is a hard lesson to learn for *young minds* discovering "issues" inducing situations symbolically unfolding enlightenment in life. Right from the beginning, John is taught the basics of *numbers* nurturing universal minds beholding elemental revelation and how to manipulate them to survive in the game. At the same time, he learns his "letters" linking eternal thoughts that enlighten radiant souls. Without this binary knowledge, John would be limited by *ignorance*—his greatest *challenge in life.*

John's memories of home fade into some dark recess of his mind as he approaches his teen years. Firmly attached to the physical world, John willingly accepts the illusion illustrating love luminously unfolding situations instructing omnipotent naturalists—navigators assimilating thoughts unfolding realism as **luminous** intuition systematically transmitted. His "daze" of life challenge him to acquire the necessary knowledge to survive in his world that is constantly changing, a world that is becoming increasingly different from his friends' and family's. John's dualistic nature pushes and pulls him in opposition, where he oscillates through moods that bring elations and depressions. He struggles to maintain an angelic behavior in hell hindering entities living life, where fear draws him "inside" to contemplate his being on the "outside" looking in.

Like everyone else, John is engrossed in the outward view of the illusion surrounding him in a luminous reality difficult to ignore. Here, he struggles to comprehend the bits and bytes of data he monitors daily; never sure of what is true or false from the hearsay influencing his *belief* system. The time and energy required to validate information stresses his mind, causing him to ignore most of what he senses, retreating to the security of his own personal thoughts, his own fantasy that he accepts and controls. Maneuvering through the haze of electromagnetic chaos created by rapidly expanding technologies—modeled after *the GREAT computer,* Universal Mind managing inquisitive navigators dynamically—is not an easy task. The overload of data stimulating his mind inadvertently forces John to learn "multitasking," masterfully utilizing logic to interpret thoughts (abstracts) signifying knowledge illuminating necessary "games" generating adventures momentarily enlightening/evolving souls.

Throughout the game of love/life, John is controlled through love and fear. He is taught to strive for what he loves by overcoming his fear, a fear instilled in him by "they" that teach him right and wrong. John fears that he will miss something that "they" say he must "see" or "do," blindly following their suggestions that direct him down the *right path* he is destined to follow, where he discovers the fine details of necessary "adventures" arousing daring visionaries exploring necessary trials/tribulation unveiling revelation experientially. Struggling to find his true self, John's brashness creates conflicts with his parents and peers (his guides) indoctrinating him with the rules of human society. At times, he finds his emotional outbreaks lead to physical pain, fighting with his peers to defend his ignorance of those rules.

The excitement of John's adventures escalates during puberty, when he discovers his physical relationship to his opposition (girls) whose *magnetism* affects his reasoning, making communication with them difficult. He cannot explain the strong feelings welling up within him from newly activated hormones moving his physical body in surprising ways. He begins to acquire certain "preferences" for girls, noticing how their various "geometric attributes" catch his eye. The mere sight of an attractive girl stimulates a "hyperlink" that separates his logic and emotional/physical reactions causing havoc to his budding manhood.

During this time of increased energy, he becomes involved

in competitive sports to prove himself along many fronts, expanding his education in ways he never considered. With so much on his mind, it is difficult for John to keep up with his metamorphosis. At this time, he vaguely *recalls* those hidden files locked within his subconscious mind gently stimulating his *awakening*. Through introspection, John becomes aware of his mind/body "dualism" dynamically unifying angelic luminaries interpreting spiritual/sexual man. His opening of *my door to truth* for the first-time is dramatic as John exposes his heart to another angel that tears it from his chest (so he thinks). The burgeoning affairs of his heart are no trifling matter, for this is John's innermost sanctuary holding the secrets of his soul. He will continuously spend more time within this stronghold, searching for those hidden files stimulating his curious mind.

At times, John sees the process of growth interminable. His anticipation of things he desires affects his patience, for things do not appear as quickly as they do back home. Here, incarnate, he plods through processes to bring them about in "time," this instant mentally experienced through heartbeats and breaths defining *the cutting edge* of consciousness. Time seems to be his worse enemy, especially when he comes to realize his days are numbered. However, the game goes on interminably and all John can do is "go with the flow."

Accordingly, John plays his cards dealt to him the best he can, assimilating knowledge as he travels his course through life. Ever the obedient follower, he plays his role as the dutiful servant to his nation, joining the military to defend some cause he knows nothing about. At the legal age of twenty-one (21), John is balanced and cooperating, trained to confidently create his part in a "war" wantonly activating retribution that leaves indelible marks upon his soul/mind, making him question the sanity of destruction for the sake of keeping people employed within a lifestyle of corruption, mismanagement, greed, and "power" perverting ones' *wisdom* emotionally revealed. His experiences of the dark side of humanity are a necessary requirement for him to become a "lightworker" later in life. As he grows older and wiser, John will come to understand his path in life through "introspection," interpreting necessary tribulation rectifying omnipotent souls perceiving enigmatic concepts that illuminate one naturally.

At twenty-five (25) years of age, John uses his *balance and cooperation* to attain *discipline and freedom* by joining forces with his opposition, committing to a *marriage* with an angel sent to guide him to his *awakening*. Little does he know the love that brings them together will tear them apart, stressing their *mind/heart* connection to endure the hardships of *passion*, *expectations*, and needs necessarily educating emotional deities to the power of love. At twenty-five (2+5=7), John *opens* his heart and *trusts* the force of love logically optimizing visionary entities. Following his gut feeling, he surrenders his heart to his wife, who naturally dominates it as her God-given gift to allow her to fulfill her "mission" of molding individual seekers sympathetically interpreting one's "nature" as necessary attributes to utilize rudimental empathy—to understand and share the feelings of another. John and his wife are intended to realize the pain and suffering awaiting them in their adventure, for as the saying goes, "no pain, no gain." Testing their *courage of love* while expressing their *courage of fear*, they will struggle to maintain harmony of their *emotional energy* they use to stay *in communion*, to be *together* and realize the symbolism of *two as one*. Each is endowed with a mind and heart that they need to MASTER—manage as spiritual transients emotionally relating.

Emotion is the elemental movement of thoughts illuminating one's nature. Males mentally electrify logical expressions as *passion*, providing adventurous situations stimulating insight obtained naturally through Mother's Nature (female) fabricating emotional moments "around" logical expressions, arousing reactions optimally unifying navigable deities. Man/mind cannot exist without woman/heart to reveal his "reflection," his relating emotional feelings linking electric concepts transmitting intuition one "nurtures," naturally unifying radiant thoughts unfolding realism experienced sympathetically through common feeling or *common sense*. Naturally, John will not understand any of this esoteric knowledge without persevering through many years of marriage and *relationships* with friends and family.

At thirty years of age (30), John observes his *sensitivity* he *expresses* relates to his special gifts (skills) he has developed. He sees how he is similar to his father and mother who programed him to survive in this world. It is his first awareness of the *integrity* and *wisdom* that he will access along a nine-year cycle (relatively speaking), for time is a flexible concept providing insight when minds are susceptible to *truth*, and truth can be as pleasurable as it is painful. Here too, John becomes conscious of the "little voice" within his mind offering choices in life, a voice that often speaks in *opposition* to John's desires. In hindsight, that little voice always seems to direct him down the right path. He notices that when he does not listen to the little voice (*denial*) and follows his free will's choice of action, things happen that he regrets. John wonders, who is telling him all the right moves to make? Like most people, he will spend many years searching for his true self, eventually sacrificing his *free will* to *Divine Will*— Source-Energy Love/Life Force. Unbeknownst to John, he is slowly becoming aware of the secrets of life he is here to find.

With his eyes and ears open, John is quick to observe how people try to control others through "dogma" deceiving other gifted minds' acuity. He finds the "media" manifests emotional data indoctrinating *avatars* (angelic visionaries assimilating Truth atomically revealed), expressing propaganda to control the masses for economical or political reasons. Although *truth* and *ignorance* are the two things every human seeks to attain and overcome, man's *love of money* and acquiring desires keeps him *lost in the dark*, refusing to believe the extent of consequences he creates from utilizing his power of love.

Struggling with the deceits encountered in a world of opposition, John begins to lose faith in the illusion providing his divine fantasy. After many years of managing his requisite work, relationships, marriage, and family, John finds that Willingly Optimizing Relevant Knowledge gives him the most "pleasure" in perceiving love/life enlightening angels systematically understanding revelation existentially. Here, he expresses his creative energy to reveal all that he believes possible. His wildest dreams evolve into realities through his "focused mind" formulating opulent concepts utilizing synergy (mind/heart) enabling deities managing intuition naturally derived. John learns the *art of listening* to his inner self, his "heart" harnessing expectations as realized thoughts.

John, like everyone else, is unfamiliar with the protocol of deciphering data during his moments *behind closed eyes* (roughly one-third of his life), where his nightly recessions bring him home to discuss his daily activities in the illusion that has him mesmerized. John's dreams inspire successes and failures that shape him according to his "plan," a plan he knows little about. He finds himself lost in a hazy daze cast by the sun's illumination bombarding him with "raw data" (radiantly amplified wisdom digitally attuning transient avatars) for him to compute, discovering his *expectations* evolve into observations that form his reality—his *belief*. John shares his beliefs gathered through "education," experiences directing universal children (angelic transients) interpreting one's nature/needs existentially. Truly, John only knows what he experiences, for everything else is hearsay conveyed through stories others proclaim. The only way his mind/soul can "grow" is by gathering revelations of wisdom experientially. However, his conscious mind is not aware of the full extent of knowledge that he has access to or acquired in past lives. As a collector of knowledge, he simply organizes and evaluates his thoughts, emotions, and actions delivering him *epiphanies of truth* that change his course at the appropriate "moment," manifesting opulent memories enlightening natural thinkers as *inquisitive souls.*

As he ages, John acquires growth experiences systematically, realizing that you cannot totally control others (although everyone tries). The only thing you create is dissension within your *relationships*. He learns that *respect* you *reflect* to others produces *harmony*, allowing everyone to feel valuable and productive. Everyone has an opinion and is therefore opinionated. After all, opinions define you as a free will living within your own universe of thoughts and feelings you act out to reflect your part you choose to play as your divine fantasy. If you allow others to define your part according to their dreams, you lose your discipline and freedom to create *your life story*. Your visions accepted allow you to confidently create a reality of integrity and wisdom that you believe in your heart and are willing to fight for to your death. Truly, only the strong-willed survive!

Looking back over his past experiences, John begins to understand his confrontations brought on by his emotional heart. He accepts his failures from poor decisions, admitting his wrongdoing during lapses of common sense, observing that unpleasant experiences are really *blessings in disguise*, for they allow him to understand how opposition works. Only by knowing both aspects of a situation can he make a "move," momentarily optimizing vivid experiences. It takes *courage of fear* to make a decision and accept the consequences of *searching for your roots*—your true identity.

Aware of his youth waning, John observes the side effects of attaining his desires and needs, experiencing physical pain and illness from years of abusing his body during his pleasurable adventures and toxic work environments. It seems everyone is suffering in his or her own way, physically, mentally, emotionally, and financially. Everyone is fighting to "win the game" while destroying the playing field. Mankind is *denying* the dangers of contaminating his environment for the brief pleasures of a moment of fantasy. This is no surprise to John. Like everyone else, he too is a "seeker" of pleasure, a soul exploring eternal knowledge (electromagnetic revelation) expressed radiantly. John worships the sun expressing the power of love luminously outputting vivid energy, enlightening his mind/heart soul in paradise (Earth) evolving in the *garden of light*—the cosmos.

John inadvertently becomes a *seer*, a soul experiencing evocative revelation that transforms him. He sees pain and suffering defines the opposition necessary to understand pleasure, realizing the "cost of living" through his *sacrifice of love/ life*. As an avid outdoorsman, John's interest in the "high places" leads him to experience the commitment necessary to attain *the grand view*. The law of opposition states that all positive efforts to attain pleasure contain negative effects revealing "pain" (perceiving assigned inspiration negatively). John realizes there are natural consequences when you "live for the moment," doing what you have to do to play the game. Gods will be gods, generating opulent desires in *worlds* of wills optimizing revelations liberating deities that create and destroy in the same breath. What everyone fails to comprehend is that *Mother's Nature* is controlling the "show" systematically heralding One

Will (omniscient natural entity—wise intuitionist—linking luminaries) sympathetically harmonizing "observant wills" (wanderers interpreting love/life).

John cannot help feeling out of place, alien to a chaotic world where everyone is struggling to attain fantasies regardless of others needs or safety. He feels he is missing a critical part to the puzzle, the "key" piece of knowledge enlightening youths. It makes him wonder even more, inwardly searching his present-memory files to ask, *who am I?* THAT is the key question that opens *my door to truth.*

After fifty-years (50) of receiving his loving light, John's spiritual visions become brighter, while his physical sight grows weaker. Here, his mind discovers new *discipline and freedom* evolving through *special gifts* he earned from being *brave of heart*, persevering through years of *denial* to acquire his "hereditary gift" of heart disease defined within his *DNA* divinely nurturing angels. His contemplation of *death* is a welcome *relief* from the pain and sorrow he sees around him. John comes to assess his accomplishments in life, analyzing the value of the time spent and things created. He thinks of family and friends he loves, regretful of his ability to effectively communicate his true feelings. Through *tears of joy*, John realizes the true values of *thinking and praying*, the subtleties of which are difficult to discern as an adolescent.

John's human-alien vehicle is a labor-intensive contraption to maintain. Through self-analysis, he comes to see how his thoughts emotionally stimulate his body, giving him positive feelings of health or negative feelings of illness. John understands how his body (his spirit's temple) is a reflection of his mind. Truly, what you think, you become! As he Acquires Growth Experiences Sympathetically, Observing Love's Dimensions, he sees kindred souls filled with the same desires, dreams, and needs of love providing life. John sees his struggle to survive is relative to, dependent on, and influenced by other souls, every one of which is on their own mission seeking *truth*, gathering revelations of wisdom through *harmony*, working *together* as Omnipotent Navigators Evolving.

John sees himself like his brothers and sisters and yet different. He notices that when they hurt, he hurts. And when they are happy, he too feels a joy that makes him warm with an inner gratitude of being alive. John comes to sense his sympathetic heart (emotional dynamo) electrifying his body with feelings that tear him apart in order to reassemble him into a greater being with a *higher vision* of love/life.

John sees others as *special people*, gifted omnipotent deities. Most tend to be introverts, keeping their "cards" close to their heart, cunningly arranging revelations deceptively, fearful that if they expose their true thoughts and feelings, others will pass judgment or take advantage of their ignorance of how the game of love/life is played. Perhaps, John thinks, it is due to a lack of opportunities or challenges to build self-confidence in expressing their *beliefs*. Truly, everyone is entitled to his and her version of *truth*. All John knows is what he holds within his own mind and heart, and he is constantly questioning the validity of that daily. Everyone else represents their own "universe," a unitary navigator inspecting/implementing visions expressing revelations sensed emotionally.

John understands the symbolic meaning of the "midlife crisis." Here, he comes to contemplate the depths of His Emotional Love/Life experienced within Mother's Nature, where he plays a "creator" consciously revealing emotions amplifying thoughts one "reflects," replicating *expectations* from logically evolved concepts transmuted sympathetically— through a loving heart. John comprehends how Spirit/Source empowers him to create any life he envisions in *heaven* and reflects in *hell*. He understands the power of love/life flowing through him brings about everything he needs to experience in life, where luminous illusion formulates experiences lucidly informing fabulous entities.

Back at home, John's Overself tirelessly watches over him, uploading data during his "sleep mode," when his body is rebuilding itself to reflect the "latest version" in the *evolution* of one experiencing time. Every night, John retires to the comfort of bed, eager to attain bits and bytes of wisdom illuminating his dreams, where divine revelation evolves as memories symbolized. The complexities of his dreams stimulate his mind. Those that are truly impressive and he can *remember* upon *awakening*, he writes down in a journal, later analyzing those "fragmented files" inspiring enlightenment. However, most night dreams instantly fade away when he rolls over or gets up at the end of his nightly sojourn "astral" traveling through the stars, finding himself *in the beginning* of another "daydream." These day/night cycles confuse John as to where he collected his data he relates when awake, not sure if it was during his subconscious night dreams or during his conscious daydreams he "lives out" *beyond imagination*.

The older John gets, the more analytical he becomes. He observes the change of his life's purpose from "gatherer" of knowledge to "professor" of knowledge. He realizes too that the more knowledge he acquires illuminates his mind to how little he knows—just another example of *opposition*. His experiences in life prepare John to process higher visions of truth illuminating his mind/soul. His quantum leap from *Mind to Heart* brings his two forces together in a "big bang," *awakening* John to *unity consciousness*—attaining his "peace" of Mind. Here, the questions he entertains in his mind fill his heart with intuition that brings *tears of joy*. This "connective link" allows him to *remember* (put back together) those fragmented files waiting for the proper moment to illuminate his mind through a domino effect culminating in an *epiphany of truth*. John evolves to attain "nirvana," a state of bliss devoid of desire and suffering, a state that reflects his surrender of self to SELF—soul to Spirit. This state of mind resembles *death*, dynamically elevating angels transcending *hell* that hinders/helps entities living life incarnate.

John acquires a symbolic comprehension of Source/Mind as pure intellect streaming data from the void of space, where *dark matter* represents invisible, abstract thoughts. Source/Mind cannot comprehend himself *alone*, for there is no "reflection" in the mirror. He can think, but he cannot experience those thoughts. How can he conceive himself if he is *lost in the dark*? In order to find one's self, one needs to ILLUMINATE one's self by inducing light linearly unfolding manifestations illustrating notions/natures as transcendental ENLIGHTENMENT, electromagnetically nurturing luminaries inducing/interpreting glorious holograms transmitting electric notions magnetically/momentarily evolving nature/navigators transcendentally.

Transcendental Harmony transmits revelation as numerical sequences conveying electric notions defining elements naturally "transmuting abstracts," luminously heralding atomic realism (manifestations) of notions yielded electromagnetically—the *binary code*. Source/Spirit (*THE Intellectual*) Generating Opulent Data reveals the genesis of Mind (*thinking 101*), a process initiating "sacred geometry," symbolically arranging cosmic revelation electromagnetically disclosing genesis establishing observable matter "exhibiting thoughts" radiantly yielded. *In the beginning*, the opening moves of Source/Mind evolve into a *point* (star) on the surface of *space* (the "face of the waters") emotionalizing *mother's tide* as electromagnetic waves stimulating a "relative beginning," a CREATION conceiving revelation/realism emerging atomically through illuminating opulent notions, nuclei, and nature. Expanding out in lines of LIGHT (radiation), logic induces glorious holograms transcendentally, encapsulating a thought within geometric boundaries that HE (heavenly expresser) "spins," synchronizing points/particles illustrating notions/nature to observe a position or "attitude," adapting thoughts transmitting information that unifies data/deities emotionally.

Emotions evolve mentally oscillated thoughts inducing opulent nature, where nucleated atoms transmute universal revelation elementally. Thus, the Omnipotent Nuclear Energizer (Source/Spirit) expands his vision to greater horizons across the eternal expanse of space/time revealing *eternal memories* as electromagnetic radiation coalescing from *dark matter* into "hydrogen" reactors, harmoniously yielding divine radiance outputting geometric expressions nuclearly, creating *the garden of Light*—the Unified Network Illuminating Vibrant Energy Regenerating Stars/Souls Eternally.

From his geometric birth, Source/God/Mind repeats his opening moves by *numbers*, following a specific sequence that allows him to duplicate his SELF as Spirit enlightening "luminous fantasists" (children of light) he creates in his IMAGE—intuitive minds (angels) gathering enlightenment. These mind/souls (spirits of universal light) become his "eyes" through which to Singularly Experience Existentially *divine fantasies* held in *eternal memory* conveyed through the *binary code*. This code reveals the positive/electric force of FATHER (+) formulating abstract thoughts heralding emotional revelation, confidently illuminating his "points" (*stars*) projecting omniscient-intelligence naturally transforming to create his negative/magnetic equal, his *reflective* force of MOTHER (=)

manifesting opulent thoughts heralding elemental "realism" rectifying emotional angels luminously interpreting Source/ *Mind* as Father/Mother—TWO evolving through *balance and cooperation*, transmitting/transforming wisdom optically.

John sees this process of moving abstract thoughts into atomic replications (reflections of Mind/Heart) expresses logic/light as *love/life energy*, oscillating vibrant elements/ entities through *unity consciousness*, utilizing notions/numbers/ nature illuminating *Truth* yielding creations of nuclear Source coalescing into one universal system naturally expressing, enlightening, and evolving Source/souls simultaneously.

The combined forces of thoughts and emotions reveal *Mind/ Heart* through a "proton" propagating revelation (opulent thoughts) originating nature and "electron" emitting light exhibiting creation that reveals opulent notions. This binary structure of hydrogen (H) symbolizes the *duality* of "one" (II) dynamically unifying abstract logic illuminating transcendental youths connected together (H) to create TRINITY-BEINGS (mind/heart/souls) telepathically receiving inspiration (naturally induced thoughts) yielding behaviors expressed in necessary "games" governing angelic minds' electric/emotional SYNERGY, simultaneously yielding necessary experiences rectifying godly youths.

The Trinity represents Father, Mother, and "child," a conscious heavenly individual linking data (living dreams). Through this harmonious union, LIGHT reveals logic intuitively generating harmonious/heavenly "things" as transmitted holograms illustrating notions/nature geometrically symbolizing LIFE, lucidly illustrating fabulous entities reflecting LOVE *linking* omnipotent visionaries eternally. This relationship of forces— Love/Life (logic/light)—allows Source/Mind to Systematically Evolve Energy—himself.

Mother Goddess, the divine presence of SPIRIT (Source-points illuminating/initiating radiant intelligence transcendentally), represents the "Shekinah" Universe systematically harmonizing eternal knowledge illuminating notions/nature atomically harnessed. SHE, Source-harmony enshrined, is *our father's heart* representing the ENTHUSIASM (supernatural inspiration) enlightening navigable transients (heavenly universes) symbolically interpreting abstracts stimulating minds *beyond imagination*. Mother's Nature emanates from "eyes" (stars) electromagnetically yielding eternal Spirit *enlightening* youths' eternal soul created in his image, a mind/heart utilizing thoughts and emotions as male and female forces revealing intellect and *wisdom*, weaving inspired signals/situations developing opulent memories, matter, and minds. The complexity of it all is truly overwhelming, keeping *time travelers* mesmerized for eons, always hungry to swallow the awesome concept but never able to fully digest it. Every angel has his/her own perspective (religion) to explain the unexplainable.

John's mind is aglow with these esoteric thoughts revealing a *common sense* understood only by the *brave of heart* discovering *unity consciousness* equally heralds and harnesses love/life energy through IMMACULATE CONCEPTION, instinctively manifesting mind/matter (abstract/concrete) utilizing logic/light actualizing thoughts electromagnetically conveying ordered *numbers* coordinating elements portraying three-dimensional illusion optimizing notions, numbers, nature, and navigators. All "navigators" (natural angelic visionaries) inspect geometrically arranged thoughts originating realism as "atomic revelation," actualizing transmutations of memories into creations/creatures (replications externalizing visions) entertaining luminous angels traversing/transcending illusion observed naturally.

John now sees that all souls are "gatherers of data" sprouting from the fountainhead of the void—Source—representing THE Intellectual, transcendental harmony emitting intuition naturally expressing love/life (electromagnetic consciousness) transforming universes (angelic luminaries). These cosmic children (stars) perform the various acts defining episodes expressing love/life energy that flows "online," the EM wavelengths expressing the Spiritual Harmony Of Wisdom. The multitude of actions and reactions cause a domino effect, where one breath destroys one world in the process of creating another. Love/life energy thrives on itself, intrinsically evolving exponentially as ONE universal organism, an omnipotent nuclear entity/energizer connected to every atom vibrating in "multi-verses."

With this concept of *E-Motion*, John comes to see why there are more women in the world than there are men. Woman symbolizes the creative medium of Life—the path and process of converting thought into emotional reality. Woman supplies Divine Entities Systematically Interpreting Revelation Existentially, inducing an expression of Love as explosive as the "big bang theory" itself.

John Doe perceives these ideas illuminating his mind through "words" weaving opulent revelation defined symbolically. By reading, he gathers the secrets handed down to all children searching for their "roots," their regal omniscience ordaining transcendental souls. Although he cannot grasp the entirety of his memories now, John realizes he is the sum total of everyone he has ever been, all those faces he donned in character roles he played over the eons. His brief epiphanies of his connection to his Overself fill him with elation difficult to restrain.

John is truly living along the cutting edge of consciousness. His mind expands exponentially to grasp his being a "part" (person assimilating radiant thoughts) of the "whole" universe, where wisdom harmoniously optimizes love/life emanations shining through Systems Transmitting Atomic Revelation Scientifically. All the love/life energy twinkling in the *garden of light* fills John with stellar splendor, boggling his mind's concept of the complexity of IT ALL—the intuitive thinker activating logic/light (love/life). John expresses *tears of joy* from the vision of *my love divine* flowing through him, embracing it with heartfelt gratitude radiating a cold chill from the center of his heart throughout his body, instilling a rhapsodic ecstasy unforgettable.

Realizing he is a mere cog in a wheel beyond measure, John knows all he can do is to BE his self, an individual spark that holds the cosmos together in some mysterious way. His feeling of security empowers him with a fearless sense of gratitude and pride. John Doe glows **brightly** amidst those other stellar bodies, breathing deep an eternal *breath of life*.

From that day of his *awakening*, John Doe steps forth with *courage of love*. He opens his heart to all his brothers and sisters, no matter their color or creed, and lives his days as a *lighthouse*, reflecting his love/life energy as a *lightworker*—an illuminator of *Truth*. He sees those embattled in misery, hopelessness, and *depression* as a necessity in knowing they are living in *denial* of their true self—their true love. John feels blessed with his spiritual enlightenment, expressing his compassion for those less inspired. Whenever the opportunity arises, John will *respect and reflect* his light of love upon those in the dark, to help them see *heaven* on earth, where everyone can experience a win-win situation, but only if they choose to be the *seers* they are born to be, souls experiencing enlightening revelation sympathetically through their heart.

For those with evil hearts, John feels no pity. He knows they play a repetitive role of *divine inspiration* that defines the boundaries of *opposition* for *young minds* to find the *right path* home. John realizes that he *alone* is the only soul he can truly save, and he cannot stop shining forth the love emanating from his heart and soul.

Time has its limits and like all the others who pass through it, John Doe comes to experience the last day of his journey. He is somewhat sad to depart, for he has loved ones he is leaving behind. He knows, however, that they will soon be joining him at home, on *the other side* of *death*, where they too will experience *life after life*. He can only hope that they will be *brave of heart*, understanding that death is truly the "reward for living." He prays that they muster their courage of fear and shed not tears of grief but *tears of joy* for his resurrection to a higher vision of heaven holding emotional angels visiting enlightening natures.

On that glorious, final day, John carries all of his experiences that he has "burned" *in memory. In the end*, John holds his *clear vision* of it all as he steps over the *threshold of love* into the void seen *behind closed eyes*. Traveling along his "silver chord" light beam that looks like a **dark tunnel**, he focuses his mind upon heaven's glow discernable at the end, opening his mind to remember his true identity awaits him as he returns home again.

A Lighthouse

A LIGHTHOUSE is a beacon of Love symbolizing luminous intelligence guiding heavenly travelers (hallowed observers) understanding spiritual enlightenment. A Lighthouse will lead all souls to true happiness in knowing WE (wisdom exemplified) are an intricate part of light energy—the very essence of our being. The LIGHT of Love/Life energy luminously illustrates glorious holograms transcendentally guiding Universal Seekers upon emotional waves we navigate along our way *Home*. The type of lighthouse you become for other *time travelers* determines the quality of your life and the growth of your soul

AFTERWORD

TURNING POINTS

Pondering Our Future

Turning points are those moments we change our way of thinking to travel down new lines of thoughts that divert us, allowing us to attain a truth we have been denying. Our turning points allow us to face those issues in our life we have been preparing for, "growing into" an expanding consciousness experiencing emotional moments illuminated before our eyes. Finding our self situated along the cutting edge of consciousness (time), we tend to see only the reflection of the glare of Father's Loving Light projecting us within Mother's show, the spiritual harmony of wisdom that sets us aglow.

Turning points tend to be dramatic, awaking us to intense insights of our ignorance, fears, and insecurities in believing in our self's true power. Trials and tribulation are forces turning us, pushing us to overcome our issues tempering our soul, shaping us into who we really we ARE—angels radiantly evolving. As our life reflects everything we have worked to create, so too does our future rely on our actions today. Truly, hindsight proves that every time. It takes courage of love to turn our life around, to start being the person we truly desire to be, for there are many people prohibiting us that pleasure, many who have not yet reached *their* turning point, many who lack the courage to escape the prison of their **closed** mind.

I pray the ramblings of this discourse have helped open your mind to the glory of love, life, and our eternal soul playing our chosen games of love/life. The world is continuously turning, growing darker by the day from those souls whose mission it is to **TURN US**, *traumatically unfold restitution naturally unifying souls* with Father, God, Spirit, Source, or any of the names of the ONE optimally nurturing entities. In the end, we will force our selves to change, to evolve into beings that have adapted to the corruptions of minds blind to the turning points of salvation. TRULY, the only way to get to heaven is to pass through hell!

IN GRATITUDE

My deepest gratitude goes to all you souls who have touched my *Mind/Heart*, allowing me to see ALL that I AM! I can never express the extent of my undying Love for all of you shining in my memories of our great times together, holding you close to heart and smiling over our ecstatic joy we share.

All you children that I hold dear
are free to roam out through fear,
across my sky of galaxies I set ablaze
to light your way home through your daze
observing universal truths for you to treasure,
building your life with your chosen pleasures

found within the GREAT Computer Mind
conceiving you as Magnificent Illuminati Naturally Evolving,
ONE of THREE
omnipotent natural entities
transmitting–transforming–transcending
heavenly revelation expressing enlightenment
for you to know ME,
Mind energy manifesting entities momentarily evolving
eternally.

Bless you and Godspeed
RRR

REFERENCES

There are many fine books of enlightenment out there, for Truth is an endless expression held within each of us. This short list represents those instrumental in my opening of *Heaven's Gate*, inspiring the direction of this book. They helped linked together all previous books I had read. I highly recommend these for your consideration.

Walsch, Neale Donald—Complete Conversations with God, Volume 1-3; Penguin Group (USA) 2005 (communion with SELF)

Myss, Caroline—Anatomy of the Spirit, The Seven Stages of Power and Healing; New York, New York; Crown Publishers, Inc.1996 (Chakras and Healing)

Millman, Dan—The Life You Were Born To Live, A Guide to Finding Your Life Purpose; Tiburon/Novato, California; H J Kramer Inc./A New World Library; 1993 (Numbers)

Frissel, Bob—Nothing in This Book Is True, But It's Exactly How Things Are, Berkeley, California; Frog Ltd./North Atlantic Books, 1994 (Sacred Geometry)

Printed in the United States
by Bookmasters

Printed in the United States
By Bookmasters